Paul A. Tucci is a writer/researcher and author of *Traveling Everywhere* (2001), *The Handy Geography Answer Book* (2008), *The Handy Personal Finance Answer Book* (2011), and numerous articles on the information industry. He has guest lectured in international management, marketing, and strategy at various universities, including New York University, Northwestern University, the University of Michigan, and Oakland University. An amateur investor for over 30 years, and a former global information and publishing manager, he is also a business owner and partner of an innovative IT services and software development firm, a consultant to and investor in small private equity funded businesses, and a member of the board of directors of the Rislov Foundation, a charitable foundation dedicated to providing funding for classical music education, instruction, and programming, and iwerk. He resides in Michigan.

Also from Visible Ink Press

The Handy African American History Answer Book
by Jessie Carnie Smith
ISBN: 978-1-57859-452-8

The Handy American History Answer Book
by David Hudson
ISBN: 978-1-57859-471-9

The Handy Anatomy Answer Book
by James Bobick and Naomi Balaban
ISBN: 978-1-57859-190-9

The Handy Answer Book for Kids (and Parents), 2nd edition
by Gina Misiroglu
ISBN: 978-1-57859-219-7

The Handy Art History Answer Book
by Madelynn Dickerson
ISBN: 978-1-57859-417-7

The Handy Astronomy Answer Book, 3rd edition
by Charles Liu
ISBN: 978-1-57859-190-9

The Handy Bible Answer Book
by Jennifer Rebecca Prince
ISBN: 978-1-57859-478-8

The Handy Biology Answer Book, 2nd edition
by Patricia Barnes Svarney and Thomas E. Svarney
ISBN: 978-1-57859-490-0

The Handy Civil War Answer Book
by Samuel Willard Crompton
ISBN: 978-1-57859-476-4

The Handy Dinosaur Answer Book, 2nd edition
by Patricia Barnes-Svarney and Thomas E. Svarney
ISBN: 978-1-57859-218-0

The Handy Geography Answer Book, 2nd edition
by Paul A. Tucci
ISBN: 978-1-57859-215-9

The Handy Geology Answer Book
by Patricia Barnes-Svarney and Thomas E. Svarney
ISBN: 978-1-57859-156-5

The Handy History Answer Book, 3rd edition
by David L. Hudson, Jr.
ISBN: 978-1-57859-372-9

The Handy Law Answer Book
by David L. Hudson Jr.
ISBN: 978-1-57859-217-3

The Handy Math Answer Book, 2nd edition
by Patricia Barnes-Svarney and Thomas E. Svarney
ISBN: 978-1-57859-373-6

The Handy Mythology Answer Book
by David A. Leeming, Ph.D.
ISBN: 978-1-57859-475-7

The Handy Ocean Answer Book
by Patricia Barnes-Svarney and Thomas E. Svarney
ISBN: 978-1-57859-063-6

The Handy Personal Finance Answer Book
by Paul A. Tucci
ISBN: 978-1-57859-322-4

The Handy Philosophy Answer Book
by Naomi Zack
ISBN: 978-1-57859-226-5

The Handy Physics Answer Book, 2nd edition
By Paul W. Zitzewitz, Ph.D.
ISBN: 978-1-57859-305-7

The Handy Politics Answer Book
by Gina Misiroglu
ISBN: 978-1-57859-139-8

The Handy Presidents Answer Book, 2nd edition
by David L. Hudson
ISB N: 978-1-57859-317-0

The Handy Psychology Answer Book
by Lisa J. Cohen
ISBN: 978-1-57859-223-4

The Handy Religion Answer Book, 2nd edition
by John Renard
ISBN: 978-1-57859-379-8

The Handy Science Answer Book®, 4th edition
by The Science and Technology Department, Carnegie Library of Pittsburgh
ISBN: 978-1-57859-321-7

The Handy Supreme Court Answer Book
by David L Hudson, Jr.
ISBN: 978-1-57859-196-1

The Handy Weather Answer Book, 2nd edition
by Kevin S. Hile
ISBN: 978-1-57859-221-0

Please visit the "Handy" series website at www.handyanswers.com.

THE
HANDY
INVESTING
ANSWER
BOOK

THE HANDY INVESTING ANSWER BOOK

Visible Ink Press®
43311 Joy Rd., #414
Canton, MI 48187–2075

Visible Ink Press is a registered trademark of Visible Ink Press LLC.

Most Visible Ink Press books are available at special quantity discounts when purchased in bulk by corporations, organizations, or groups. Customized printings, special imprints, messages, and excerpts can be produced to meet your needs. For more information, contact Special Markets Director, Visible Ink Press, www.visibleink.com, or 734–667–3211.

Managing Editor: Kevin S. Hile
Art Director: Mary Claire Krzewinski
Typesetting: Marco Di Vita
Proofreaders: Paul Cain and Barbara Lyon
Indexer: Shoshana Hurwitz
Cover images: Shutterstock

ISBN: 978–1–57859–486–3 (paperback)
ISBN: 978–1–57859–527–3 (pdf ebook)
ISBN: 978–1–57859–529–7 (Kindle ebook)
ISBN: 978–1–57859–528–0 (ePub ebook)

Library of Congress Cataloging–in–Publication Data
Tucci, Paul A., 1962–
The handy investing answer book / by Paul A Tucci.
    pages cm. – (The handy answer book series)
  ISBN 978–1–57859–486–3 (paperback)
  1. Investments. 2. Finance, Personal. I. Title.
  HG4521.T777 2015
  332.67'8–dc23   2014017821

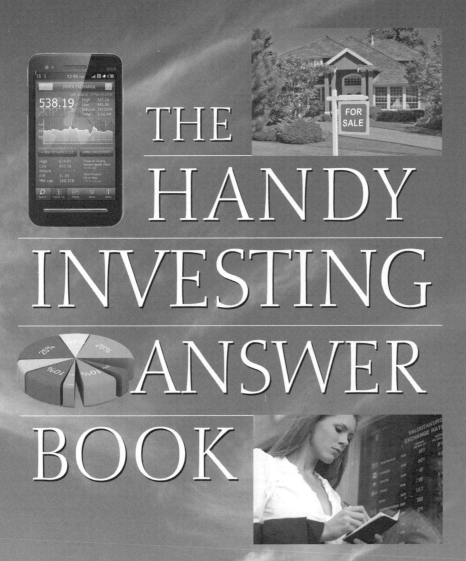

THE
HANDY
INVESTING
ANSWER
BOOK

Paul A. Tucci

VISIBLE
INK
PRESS

Detroit

Disciaimer

The material in this book or its affiliated websites have no regard to the specific investment objectives, financial situation, or particular needs of any reader, user, or visitor. This book, and any ancillary electronic content so derived, is published solely for informational purposes, and the information contained within is not to be construed as a solicitation or an offer to buy or sell any securities or related financial instruments. Your access and use of this book or affiliated websites is subject to the following terms and conditions and all applicable laws. By accessing and browsing this book or its affiliated websites that may use this content, you accept these terms and conditions without limitation or qualification. This information is provided "as is" without warranty of any kind, and Visible Ink Press and its licensees, if any, make no representation, expressed or implied, as to the accuracy, reliability, or completeness of this information, or the timeliness of any information in this book or its affiliated websites that may use this content.

References made to third parties are based on information obtained from sources believed to be reliable, but are not guaranteed as being accurate. Readers, users, or site visitors should not regard it as a substitute for the exercise of their own judgment and research. Any opinions expressed in this book are subject to change without notice, and Visible Ink Press or its licensees are not under any obligation to update or keep current the information contained herein.

Under no circumstances shall Visible Ink Press or its authors and editors have any liability to any person or entity for (1) any loss or damage in whole or part caused by, resulting from, or relating to any error (neglect or otherwise) or other circumstances involved in procuring, collecting, compiling, interpreting, analyzing, editing, transcribing, communicating, or delivering any information in this book or its affiliated websites, or (2) any direct, indirect, special, consequential or incidental damages whatsoever, resulting from the use of, or inability to use, any such information.

Visible Ink Press accepts no liability whatsoever for any loss or damage of any kind arising out of the use of all or any part of this material. Our comments are an expression of opinion. While we believe our statements to be true, they always depend on the reliability of our own credible sources. We recommend that you consult with a licensed, qualified professional before making any investment decisions.

Contents

ACKNOWLEDGMENTS *ix*

PHOTO CREDITS *xi*

INTRODUCTION *xiii*

INTRODUCTION TO PERSONAL INVESTING ... 1

History (1) ... The Basics (6) ... The Investor Mindset (21) ... Investing Risks (25)

SAVING, MANAGING DEBT, AND BUDGETING ... 27

Managing Debt (29) ... Credit Card Debt (33) ... Mortgages (36) ... Home Equity (43) ... Credit Problems (46) ... Budgeting (48) ... Setting Your Investment Goals (50) ... Investing versus Speculation (54) ... Risk/Reward (55) ... Beta (60) ... Creating Wealth (61)

INDIVIDUAL STOCKS ... 65

The Basics (65) ... Selecting Individual Stocks (71) ... Understanding Financial Markets (87) ... Interest Rates (92) ... Inflation and the Consumer Price Index (95) ... Price/Earnings Rations and Other Calculations (97) ... Online Trading (101)

BONDS ... 105

The Basics (105) ... Corporate Bonds (110) ... Treasury Bonds and Treasury Bills (112) ... Municipal Bonds (114) ... Assessing Default Risk on Bonds (116)

MUTUAL FUNDS ... 119

The Basics (119) ... Differences between Types of Mutual Funds (125) ... No-Load and Loaded Mutual Funds (127) ... Index Funds (129) ... Closed-Ended Mutual Funds (138) ... Exchange Traded Funds (140) ... Unit Investment Funds (141) ... Ratings Companies (142) ... Hedge Funds (144) ... Socially Responsible Investments (SRI) (145) ... Expense Ratios (149)

INVESTING IN CASH ... 151

Banks and Credit Unions (152) ... Money Market Funds (158) ... Certificates of Deposit (CDs) (159) ... Online Banking (161)

REAL ESTATE ... 165

The Basics (165) ... Home Ownership as an Investment (170) ... Owning versus Renting (176) ... Commercial Real Estate (179) ... Second Homes (184) ... Rental Properties (186) ... Return on Investment (ROI) (189) ... Real Estate Investment Trusts (REITs) (192)

SMALL BUSINESS INVESTING ... 195

The Basics (195) ... Financing Small Businesses (197) ... Starting a Business (200) ... Investing in a Small Business (206) ... Managing a Small Business (212) ... ROIs and Small Businesses (217) ... Private Equity (220)

OTHER INVESTING OPPORTUNITIES ... 223

Gold and Other Precious Metals (223) ... Futures and Options (226) ... Investing in Art (231)

TAXES ... 235

Investing and Taxes (235) ... Long-/Short-Term Capital Gains/Losses (238) ... Small Business Taxes (241) ... Retirement Taxes (242) ... Federal Taxes (245) ... State Taxes (247) ... Local Taxes (249)

INSURANCE ... 253

The Basics (253) ... Insuring Your Home (254) ... Renters' Insurance (257) ... Insurance as an Investment (258) ... Business Insurance (260)

THE FUTURE ... 263

Saving for Retirement (263) ... Investing for Retirement (265) ... IRAs (269) ... 401(k)s (272) ... Life State Investing (277) ... Saving for Education (281) ... Teaching Children about Investing (289) ... The Future of Investing (302)

INVESTING RESOURCES ... 307

Investment Experts (307) ... Financial Planners (310) ... Avoiding Scams (317)

FURTHER READING   *321*

GLOSSARY   *323*

AN INTERVIEW WITH THE EXPERTS   *343*

INDEX   *359*

Acknowledgments

I would like to thank the following people for their assistance and support in this project: Nick Demopoulos, Kevin Hile, Roger Jänecke, Evelyn Katz, Jim Quimby, and Zach Savas.

Photo Credits

Introduction

The investing system is among the most highly complex systems that exist because there are so many variables and strange constants. It seems easy to understand the simplicity of it all, as buyers and sellers meet in a market. And based upon this, prices are created and money is exchanged. But the numerous variables that play a large part, as well as the unknown or unexpected events and happenings that can occur, can in seconds devastate a position or lead to wealth.

Combine this with the crowdlike movement of the participants, the information flows that influence variables, and government action or lack of action, and it can get pretty confusing. There are even unpredictable natural events thrown in.

But it can all be understood by any ordinary person. *The Handy Investing Answer Book* question-and-answer format helps readers break down the investing tree into its essential branches, twigs, and leaves. Most likely, one can garner some tiny piece of information that may greatly help with financial decision making.

Fear, and the movement of investors as a result of their perceptions of the markets, news, or variables that may impact a stock, category, or economy, plays a big role in determining how successful an investment will be, both in the short and long term. Your time horizon—whether you are investing for the long term or you are interested in making a rather short-term gain—may determine what the best strategy is, the approach to take, and the risk you are willing to bear. Depending on how you look at an investment, your overall performance may be greatly different.

This book does not go into a great deal of depth into a few areas of investing that are quite complex and outside its scope: technical analysis, options and futures trading, day trading, hedge funds, currency trading, and derivatives can even be tough for professionals to excel in. Instead, I try here to cover the most essential areas of investing and give mention to other areas with the hope that you will learn more about other investing subjects separately if you wish to explore them in greater depth. *The Handy Investing Answer Book* will take you through a logical progression of questions and answers to provide you context, definitions, and explanations so that you may make better-informed investment decisions.

I hope you enjoy it.

—Paul A. Tucci

INTRODUCTION TO PERSONAL INVESTING

HISTORY

How long have people been investing?

In approximately 1700 B.C.E., the Code of Hammurabi, discovered in 1902, laid out a set of rules for investing. Babylon, an ancient city in what is now Iraq, was ruled by various kings; the sixth king, Hammurabi, ruled for nearly 43 years. Under Hammurabi, a set of codes were enacted that helped the king rule his people. Although many of the codes described basic laws and governance, some codes described rules involving investing, loans, and financial transactions. Some copies of the original codes predate the main codes, which were etched upon a large stone, by several decades.

What do the Hammurabi Codes describe?

Some of the codes or laws describe what happens if commercial deals are not paid, the transfer of property, loan repayment, rent/lease arrangements, interest on property, and contract laws, among many other subjects.

What other city-states helped contribute to modern-day investing?

There are many other places around the world and in different periods of time that shaped and formed modern-day investing. In the 1300s, the city-state of Venice was a major center for the clearing or exchanging of obligations held by one owner, and exchanging them with another owner. Venetians began to do what today's modern brokers do: bringing buyers and sellers together in order to transact a financial obligation. These same Venetian traders even engaged in international finance by buying and selling obligations owned by various European governments.

1

Stock tickers like this one, invented by Edward Calahan in 1863, reported changes in stock prices by printing out long strips of paper. They were not replaced until computers came into more common use in the 1970s.

When was the stock ticker invented?

Although it was invented by Edward Calahan in 1863, it was unveiled in New York City in 1867. The stock ticker machine was later improved by Thomas Edison in 1869 and was widely used until the 1970s, when it was gradually replaced by computer terminals. The machines were able to communicate current prices of stocks, which previously had been handwritten, or expressed verbally, and could transmit and ultimately print the quotes at one character per second. The great significance of the invention of the ticker machine is that it enabled the dissemination of prices across a large audience. Stock prices could be known by buyers near real time, allowing the markets to become more efficient and competitive.

What is a "ticker symbol"?

A ticker symbol is a unique series of characters, as many as five characters long, that identifies the name of the investment actively traded on an exchange. For example, Google is known as GOOG on the National Association of Securities Dealers Automated Quotations (NASDAQ) exchange, and Ford is known as F on the New York Stock Exchange (NYSE).

Why were these machines called Stock Ticker Machines?

The machines were called ticker machines because of the distinctive ticking noise the machines made while printing the ticker symbol and brief information about the stock price, on thin paper called ticker tape.

Specifically, what do ticker symbols indicate?

When you see ticker symbols moving across a screen, they usually tell us several things. The abbreviated letters, of one to five characters in length, indicate on what exchange the stock is listed. Symbols that are from one to three characters represent companies listed on the New York Stock Exchange, while symbols that are four or five characters represent companies listed on the NASDAQ Exchange. What you often see after the stock symbol is a recent price, change in price, and, in some instances, the volume of shares traded. You still see ticker symbols today, and the above information floating across a television screen or monitor as you watch financial programming or peruse financial websites.

What are "dividends"?

Dividends are the distributions of profits or earnings of a company to shareholders of record. It is generally defined as a distribution of some of the company's profit to a specific class of shareholders as determined by that company's board of directors, and is usually issued on a per share basis. If you have more shares, you are paid more of the company's earnings during the period set forth by the board of directors.

What is a "blue chip stock"?

A blue chip stock is a publicly traded company that is usually very large, may be distributing profits in the form of dividends for many years, is a leader in the sector in which it competes, has notable stability and growth, and has the ability to adapt to changing market conditions successfully.

Where did the term "blue chip stock" originate?

It is thought by many to be derived from gambling, specifically the card game "poker," where in betting, the use of the blue-colored chips represents the most expensive chip at the table.

When did *The Wall Street Journal* begin to publish a Dow Jones Industrial Average?

The Wall Street Journal began publishing an average of the prices of stocks listed on the New York Stock Exchange in 1896.

What is the Dow Jones Industrial Average (the "Dow" or "DJIA")?

The DJIA is a price-weighted average of thirty blue chip stocks traded on the New York Stock Exchange. It is often seen as a barometer of the health of the stock markets.

How important is the DJIA to the investment community?

The DJIA is widely regarded as the most important index to follow in the world. It broadly indicates stock prices and investor confidence.

Who picks which stocks are components of the Dow?

The editors of *The Wall Street Journal* decide which companies should be included in the Dow. They search for a balance of companies reflective of the U.S. economy as a whole.

Who created the DJIA?

Charles Dow created the Dow, picking 11 stocks, then increasing this number to 12 stocks before publishing the average in 1896 that made up the Dow.

How else do I use the Dow in order to analyze my portfolio?

You may use the Dow in order to compare the performance of your stocks, bonds, and mutual funds, and ask yourself whether you are outperforming or underperforming the Dow. It helps to see this comparison over different periods of time in order to assess the success of your investment choices.

What is the oldest company in the Dow?

Of all the companies that composed the original Dow, only one—General Electric—remains today. General Electric has been a component of the Dow since 1907.

This is the General Electric Building in Rockefeller Center in New York City. GE is the only original DOW company, first listed in 1907, still in existence.

What are some of the newest entries in the Dow?

Cisco Systems and Travelers were added to the Dow in 2009. Nike, Visa, and Goldman Sachs were added to the Dow in 2013.

How many times has the list of Dow companies changed since its inception?

The Dow components have changed 99 times, including increasing the number of components from 12 to 20 in 1916 and increasing them again from 20 to 30 in 1928.

Why are companies removed from the list of companies on the Dow?

Individual companies that compose the DJIA are removed because of economic and managerial trouble. Others no longer offer a good representation of index components reflective of the American economy at large, and must be replaced by healthier, more representative companies.

> ## What are some of the largest percentage moves of the Dow?
> **O**n March 15, 1933, the DJIA gained 15.34%. On October 19, 1987, the DJIA declined by 22.61%.

Still other companies tracked by the Dow are removed because their stock price is very low, and not as relevant as other firms in the average.

Why are some stocks with low prices specifically removed from the Dow?

Since the companies tracked by the Dow represent an average of the prices of shares in the securities that compose the index, stocks with lower prices tend to pull the average down, making the index less effective as a barometer of the market at large.

Which companies have been recently removed from the Index?

General Motors, Citigroup, AIG, Altria Group, Honeywell, Hewlett-Packard, Kraft Foods, Bank of America, and Alcoa.

How much did the Dow fall at the onset of the Great Depression?

On October 29, 1929, at the onset of the Great Depression, the Dow Jones Industrial Average plunged more than 11%, to 230.07 points. The average had hit a peak of 381.17 the month before, but would not reach this number again until 1954.

What are some other notable dates in NYSE history?

In 1987, the DJIA plummeted more than 22% in one day, yet the next day, the volume of shares traded (600 million) created a new volume high record. By 1997, daily trading volume of shares exchanging hands reached one billion. In 2001, in the wake of the World Trade Center attack, the NYSE was closed for four sessions, the longest period of time the exchange was closed since 1933. Yet when the exchange reopened on September 17, 2001, the NYSE hit another record, with over 2.37 billion shares traded. In November 2013, the Intercontinental Exchange Group (ICE) acquired NYSE Euronext, creating the leading global network of regulated exchanges and clearing houses for financial and commodity markets.

How is the Dow important to our understanding of the activity and performance of blue chip stocks?

The Dow has been tracking the performance of a price-weighted basket of 30 blue chip stocks since late 1928, and is seen by many as a barometer of the overall health of the economy and markets.

How well has the Dow performed since it began?

Through 2009, the Dow has risen in 64% of years, and declined in 36% of years.

Why is ICE so important to the investing community around the world?

ICE is so important to the investing community around the world because now, one-third of the world's global cash trading flows through its systems; it trades more than 50% of the world's crude and refined oil futures contracts; it lists 90% of the Dow Jones Industrial 1000 and 78% of S&P 500 listed companies; it introduced 120 Initial Public Offering (IPO) transactions, raising $36.9 billion in 2012; and it currently captures 53% market share of all technology IPOs through the third quarter of 2013.

How important is the NYSE to global equities trading?

The NYSE is very important. With its membership greater than 8,000 listed companies, approximately 40% of all global equities are traded on the NYSE.

THE BASICS

How do I begin investing?

Investing begins with an understanding of asset allocations, or how you divide your investment capital into different categories or classes, such as stocks (and mutual funds, foreign stocks, or global stocks), fixed income securities, real estate, commodities (including gold, silver, petroleum, etc.), and cash. It may also include private equity investments in small companies or businesses and foreign currencies, among many other types of investments.

What is a very important consideration when thinking about investing?

One of the most important concepts in investing is to limit your risk through diversification of your investments. The thinking is, if your portfolio is sufficiently diverse, your exposure to the declines in any class of investments is mitigated, as other classes of investments may increase in value, thus protecting your total portfolio.

Why is diversification necessary?

When you invest, it is generally thought that if you spread your investments in a variety of classes, and their values do not move up or down in the same way, this diverse portfolio will have less risk than if you invest all of your money in just one class or type of investment. A diversified portfolio may also have a weighted average risk less than the average risk of each of the investments in the portfolio. It is also accepted that, over time, a diverse portfo-

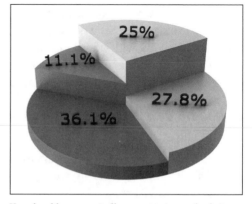

You should never put all your eggs in one basket, so to speak. Instead, diversify your portfolio with a mix of low- and higher-risk investments to get the best return over time.

lio will yield higher returns than one that is relatively less diverse and more concentrated, and will yield a higher overall return than any one individual investment in the portfolio. The main thinking is that positive results of these diverse investments should help reduce the effects of other investments that may decline, as long as your investment choices are not correlated or synchronous. If you have investments in U.S. stocks and Brazilian stocks, and a problem arises in the U.S. economy that may not affect the Brazilian markets, perhaps the investments that are exposed to the U.S. economy may decline, while the Brazilian stocks may not decline, or may even increase.

What are some other reasons why I should diversify my investment portfolio?

Diversification will not guarantee that you won't lose money or make big gains with your investments. But it will help you to have a portfolio that matches your appetite for risk, especially if your investment choices are less relatively tied or correlated. The most important point about investment portfolio diversity is that in a perfect world, while the value of your total portfolio will increase less than your best-performing investment, it will never do worse than your worst-performing investment.

What are some important questions to ask myself when managing the diversity of my portfolio?

Some of the more important questions to ask yourself include:

- What capital have I committed to investing in various investments? Am I reinvesting the proceeds? If so, into what investments?
- Is my portfolio out of balance because of this, and into what areas of concentration?
- What is the value of each category of investments in my portfolio, and what would I like it to be today, and in the near- and long- term future?
- What investments have I made lately, and in what categories?
- How have my investment choices and the values created today changed over the past one, five, and ten years?
- Have I kept the losers?
- Have I created more winning investments?
- What investments am I thinking of acquiring next, when, how much, and why?
- Will I sell something to do this, or will I invest new capital into this idea?

What is "correlation"?

Using historical returns on individual investment choices, you can see if two investments move in the same way, using various statistical analysis methods. If two stocks are 100% correlated over some time period, this means they move exactly the same way, given some event or market condition. If they are 50% correlated, then approximately half the time, over some period of time that is analyzed, the two stocks move in the same way, either up or down or even flat, with no change. If the correlation is –50% between the pair of investments, it means that they are moving in opposite directions, so as one goes up, the other goes down. As you build a diverse portfolio of investments, it is generally accepted that good investors, over time, find and invest in different classes whose returns do not move in the same or similar fashion.

What is "concentration"?

Concentration occurs when you invest your capital in a few investment classes or one class. The thinking behind this approach for certain investors is if one investment or investing idea is outperforming other investments, perhaps it is a good idea to focus or concentrate your investment in this idea, in hopes of making relatively higher returns. Of course, your acceptance of this concept certainly depends on how much risk to your portfolio you are willing to accept, as a more concentrated investment choice may carry more risk than one that is relatively more diverse. Some investors even believe it is better to decide to invest their money based upon fewer choices or less diversity, as the returns are thought to be higher.

How often should I check or analyze my portfolio to make sure it is properly allocated?

You should check your investment portfolio to make certain it is properly balanced at least quarterly—if not monthly—in order to ensure that your investments are not too synchronous or correlated. Of course, this allocation depends on such factors as how much you have to invest, what your financial goals are, how much time you have before you need access to the capital (your time horizon), your tolerance to risk, and whether you are undertaking some sort of big financial challenge (losing a job, changing a job, health issues, etc.).

What is a "cyclical investment"?

A cyclical investment could be any investment that is highly correlated to some chronic economic event, condition, or pattern. People buy fewer cars and travel less if they are not employed. So investments dependent upon demand created by the level of employment of these cohorts may perform less than desirably, as the unemployment rate increases.

What are the two major stock exchanges?

Although there are many different stock exchanges in the United States, the two

Financial challenges, such as whether you are looking for work, are something you should consider when evaluating your stock portfolio for risky versus safer investments.

most important ones are the NYSE and the NASDAQ. The NASDAQ is the second largest stock market in the world, behind only the NYSE in terms of market capitalizations.

How old is the New York Stock Exchange?

The New York Stock Exchange is the oldest stock market in the United States. It was founded in 1792 by 24 stockbrokers who met at 68 Wall Street, but it was not officially founded until a constitution was signed in 1817.

What is the first step to accumulate wealth and savings?

Most experts agree that you must first understand your financial picture, to see what areas need to be altered or changed, by identifying your net worth. Others believe you must first change your basic attitudes and beliefs about money and wealth in order to reach your financial goals. And still other experts believe you must first establish financial goals—without them, you have no way to attain success. Perhaps combining the above ideas is a prudent course of action.

What is my "net worth"?

Your net worth is one of the most important measurements of how much you are "worth" financially. Your net worth is the value of all your assets, including cash, stocks and bonds, mutual funds, retirement accounts, including your IRAs and 401(k)s, and equity in your homes, any metals (such as gold or silver), minus all of your liabilities, that may include car loans, mortgages, credit card debts, student loans, significant health-related expenses, and any other obligations you may incur.

What is a "high net worth individual"?

A high net worth individual is someone who has a net worth, excluding the value of his principal residence, in excess of $1 million.

Why is knowing my net worth important to attain my financial goals?

Understanding and computing your net worth provides instant feedback as to your ability to save money, shows you how indebtedness may drain your savings, and fund the costs of your borrowing to cover expenses. Knowing your net worth also provides you with a way to visualize how you, in certain conditions, create wealth through borrowing, especially if you borrow money at interest rates that are low enough, and invest this cash in, for example, a real estate market that has increasing values over time.

What is the midpoint, or median net worth, of families in America?

According to a 2007 report by the U.S. Census Bureau, the median or midpoint of all families reporting shows that their net worth is $221,500, of which nearly 90.3% is in the form of equity in their houses. Of course, since the crash of the real estate markets in the United States in 2008, this number has decreased in some markets rather significantly. But it does demonstrate that many families derive a great percentage of their net worth from home ownership.

What kinds of information can help me understand and learn more about investing?

There are many sources of information available to help you understand the financial world and the world of personal investing, including online blogs, newsletter feeds, thousands of websites, government websites, non-profit websites, weekly magazines, newspapers, books, and TV and radio programming.

Isn't it easier for me to just have a financial adviser, so that I don't have to spend time learning about personal finance?

No. In order to make the best use of anyone's advice, you must take the time to be well informed so you can understand different options or strategies. Millions of people feel a financial adviser can make decisions for them, or that they can pay someone to "manage" their finances, so they need not learn about it. People often fail to learn enough about personal finance, and cannot tell the difference between bad advice and good advice. If you are not well informed about the myriad choices available to you and your advisers, it is very difficult to know what option is best for you.

What are some good personal finance blogs?

According to experts at the website www.technorati.com, some of the top personal finance blogs include: Free from Broke (http://freefrombroke.com/), Digerati Life (http://www.thedigeratilife.com/blog/), Oblivious Investor (http://www.obliviousinvestor.com/), Cash Money Life (http://cashmoneylife.com/), and Get Rich Slowly (http://www.getrichslowly.org/blog/).

There is so much information online. How do I choose what to read?

It is important to use the Internet to search for broad topics, beginning first with various financial sites, and then digging deeper into the subject before moving on to the next subject. If you study this information in small increments, over time you will learn a considerable amount about each of the areas of personal finance of interest to you. When you feel the subject matter is getting too technical for you, stop and move on until you are ready for more details. Websites are developed and produced in the same manner as newspapers and magazines. Editors and writers cover many topics, from basics on personal finance to very advanced technical analysis of individual stocks and trading strategies. Find websites that are at your level, and just dive in. If the story or topic is too deep, try Googling that word or phrase, and read a definition of it before continuing. After you do this daily or weekly, you begin to see similar stories covered many times, and you will be able to develop an opinion on that idea after reading so many different perspectives. This is how you begin to build your knowledge on personal finance and keep current about what is happening with your money.

How many people use the Internet to find economic or financial information?

Of the approximately 220 million online users in the United States, according to the Pew Research Center, nearly 70%—or 154 million people—seek some form of economic information while surfing the Internet.

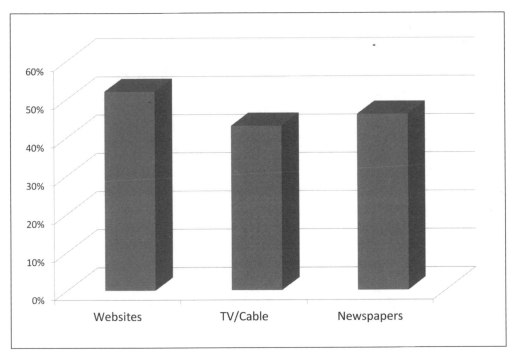

Where Americans get their financial and economic news.

What are the most popular sources of financial information?

Among Americans who use broadband to connect to the Internet, 52% get their financial and economic information from the Web, compared with 43% for TV/cable, and 46% for newspapers.

How do Americans find economic information?

Americans use a variety of sources: talking to people; using the Internet; hearing about some financial information while watching TV; listening to financial programming on the radio; and reading a newspaper.

How active are Americans in using the Web to find financial and economic information?

Only 18% of Americans actively use the Internet every day to find financial and economic information. About half of all Internet users get this information every few days.

What percentage of online economic users receive alerts or feeds about news and information pertaining to their investments?

About 13% of these users utilize Really Simple Syndication feeds ("RSS feeds") and other alerting tools that allow them automatically to receive information from a website, blog, financial company, or news source that is relevant to their investments or investing ideas.

What percentage of economic users online use the Internet to find information to protect their personal finances?

Twenty-seven percent of all users use the Internet in some form to seek information to protect and grow their investments. Seventeen percent use the Web to compare financial companies and professionals who work in financial services.

Does access to so much information come at another hidden price?

According to the Pew Research Center, 37% of all economic Internet users feel more worried about our nation's economic future, compared with 10% who feel more confident about it. The access to so much information, both good and bad, shapes how we feel about our investments and future financial picture.

What percentage of all online economic users feel they have learned something about our financial crisis?

Thirty-nine percent of these users feel they have increased their own understanding of the situation by using the Web.

What percentage of all Americans have contributed to content about the recession online?

About 23% of all adult Americans have contributed something online about the recession, through blogs, social media sites, comments on news sites, and discussion boards.

Who are the financial information seekers online?

The majority of Internet users seeking financial information are older than 30. In fact, 14% are age 30–49, 13% are 50–64, and 15% are 65 and older. Only 6% of these users are age 18–29.

What is "investing"?

Investing is the act of using money to buy a financial product with the expectation of making more money over a period of time than what you used to buy the financial product.

How long should I hold an investment?

Some people who trade stocks can make a return on their investment in a few seconds, while others take a few months or even years. If you keep your money invested in cash in a bank, you might make anywhere from 0% interest to a few percent return on the investment over a few years.

What must I consider before investing?

You must decide what type of investment to buy, how much money to put into the investment, how long you will hold it, how much of a return you wish to make, how much risk there is of losing money on the investment over time, how much could you potentially make, and how much you can afford to lose.

What is "total return"?

Total return means how much your investment grew over a period of time, including all interest, dividends, and capital appreciation, less fees and/or commissions.

How do I compute the total return?

Your total return is computed by taking the amount your initial investment increased (your gain) plus all dividends or interest you received while you owned it. To calculate your percentage of total return, take the number you calculated above and divide by the amount of your initial investment. In order to compute your total return on an annual basis, take your percentage of total return and divide by the number of years you held the investment. Of course, these calculations are not adjusted for any taxes due on the investment gains. Please consult your tax adviser for further information.

What is a simple example of return on investment?

If you bought a stock for $5,000 on January 1, and sold it one year later for $5,500, your return would be 10%. You can compute this by subtracting $5,000 from $5,500, dividing this number ($500) by $5,000, and multiply by 100. This means your investment earned a one-year return of 10%.

What is "return on investment"?

Return on investment, expressed as a percentage, means how much more money you will make or earn over a period of time as a result of buying the investment.

How do I compute my return on investment?

You can figure your return on investment by taking how much money you originally put in when you purchased it, and subtracting it from the value of your investment when you sell it, less any fees/commissions or taxes, and then dividing this number by the amount you originally invested. Multiply this number by 100 to reveal your return on the investment, expressed as a percentage.

Why is patience important to successful investing?

Patience is important to successful investing because you may have to ride out what may be temporary short-term storms or declines in the market and keep a long-term view.

Why are people afraid to invest?

Most people fear investing because they lack knowledge about investing, don't know how to manage the risks, and hear and read about various crashes in the markets that happen periodically, which can cause people to lose a lot of money.

What are some of the biggest mistakes individual investors make?

People investing in the markets typically sell when the price is low, during or at the end of a notable decline, out of panic. And they may buy at the highest price, once they discover a new investment they hear of from their friends, who heard it from their friends, and so on. Or they buy when the markets are reported by various media outlets to be at their all-time high. By the time the news reaches you, it is probably long past the time to have invested.

What are some other mistakes that investors make?

Investors often make emotional decisions about owning investments, perhaps by refusing to sell the stock of a company because a relative worked there, or being afraid to sell a stock because of losing a certain amount. If the investor had sold it, he may lose less than if he had kept it, but because of emotions, the investor holds on to it, hoping the price will go back up.

What types of investment or financial products exist?

There are many different financial products, mostly divided into one of these broad categories: stocks, bonds, and cash. In addition, there may also be real estate, insurance policies, private equity ownership, currency trading, and hybrid investment products that combine the benefits of a mixture of these and other investments.

What are some of the most important investment types?

Some of the most important investment types include: emerging market stocks; foreign stocks; U.S. stocks; precious metals; commodities; high yield corporate bonds; municipal bonds; cash; treasury bills; money market funds; U.S. high quality bonds; European bonds; global bonds; and long-term U.S. government bonds.

What is a "portfolio"?

A portfolio is a mixture of investments of different types and risks that an individual or institution may own in hopes of making more money over time. It is generally defined as the collection of investments held by an individual, investment company, or mutual fund.

What is "diversification"?

Diversification is the act of making investments in different categories with the hope and expectation that the risk of losing money is spread out or diversified within the portfolio, thus reducing the overall risk of losing money on the whole portfolio.

How does diversification reduce my risk?

Diversification reduces your risk because when you have a variety of investments in a portfolio, the fluctuations in the value of any one investment have less of an effect. If you have several uncorrelated investments, you may minimize the risk of losing money.

What does the saying "Don't put all your eggs in one basket" mean?

It demonstrates the need for diversification. If you put all your investments in one stock, and the stock price falls, you lose a major amount of money. If you had put your money in three different stocks, and two of the three go up, and only one goes down, you could still have made money, or perhaps lose less money than if your investment was concentrated in one stock.

What is an "individual investor"?

An individual investor is a person who directly or indirectly purchases stocks or bonds, and invests in the market on his own account.

How many individual investors exist in the United States?

It is very difficult to estimate the precise number of individual investors in the United States because so many people invest in the markets in some way: by having retirement funds; buying individual shares of stock in a company; keeping money in a money market fund, which, in turn, invests the money; owning mutual funds; and payment of insurance premiums. All told, there are most likely more than 200 million Americans with some exposure to the financial markets.

What is an "institutional investor"?

An institutional investor is a large organization that pools money together with other large organizations, as well as individuals, and invests this money in private and public companies.

Who are these institutional investors?

Institutional investors can be commercial banks, investment banks, mutual funds, pension companies, retirement fund companies, and hedge fund companies.

Why is it good to be an institutional investor?

Because of their size, institutional investors can obtain a better price for the shares they buy. They trade in huge volumes of stock, both buying and selling, and their effect can swing stock prices at any moment during the day. Institutional investors also can command the best price when they are interested in selling their positions because they hold so much of a particular stock.

What other benefits do institutional investors have?

Because of the magnitude of the number of shares they own, institutional investors' positions can allow them to have management say in the direction of a company, and they are occasionally given a seat on the boards of both private and public companies they may own.

INDU	−325.76	VOLU	5,803,831,690
INDP	8498.22	UVOL	383,496,458
NY*	−386.48	DVOL	751,509,641
NYA	5109.17	TRIN	1.90
UTIL	−5.21	TRAN	−75.38

What is a "bear market"?

A bear market occurs when there has been a decline in a stock market average of 20%

Bear markets are protracted periods of time in which stock prices go down.

from a high, and is often characterized as a period of time when stock prices are in a state of decline, reported profits of listed companies are less than expected, inflation is increasing, interest rates are relatively high and increasing, and money is flowing out of the stock markets.

Why do bear markets happen?

Bear markets happen for many reasons. According to many experts, bear markets occur because investors are pessimistic about where the economy is headed, causing the declines to sustain themselves over a long period of time. Investors sell their shares, anticipating losses, and other investors see more losses in their portfolios, so they sell also. During bear markets, capital may be sidelined, or may be directed toward other investments such as bonds or cash in expectation of a signal to return to the equity markets.

What duration of time defines a bear market?

A bear market is a period of time in which the prevailing stock prices trend downward by more than 20% for at least two months.

What is a "correction"?

A correction occurs in the stock market when the trends of indexes show a decline in prices of 10–20% over a short period of time, from one day to less than two months.

Are corrections good for some investors?

Some investors look at corrections as buying opportunities, as often overvalued stock prices are reset to a lower level, representing their true value, and giving investors an opportunity to buy at a lower price. These same investors will typically have ready access to liquid assets, such as cash, in order to take advantage of the perceived bargain during a correction.

What are some of the greatest declines of the Dow during a bear market?

In October 2007, the Dow entered a bear market that lasted 517 days, and saw the DJIA decline by 53.9%. By contrast, the initial 1929 Dow crash, that heralded the Great Depression, saw a decline of "only" 47.9%, and lasted 71 days.

What is a "bull market"?

A bull market is a period of time during which there are more buyers than sellers of stocks, causing overall stock prices to rise, and when investor confidence trends higher in anticipation of rising prices, increasing their investments over time.

Periods of stock market prosperity are called bull markets.

How long does a bull market last?

Through the year 2009, and for the 113 years since the inception of the Dow, the average length of a bull market has been 2.7 years.

How much personal wealth was lost during the Crash of 2008?

Eleven trillion dollars of Americans' personal wealth, whether in the form of stocks, bonds, cash, or real estate, was wiped out in a very short period of time.

What percentage of Americans saw their portfolios decline during the period of economic decline 2008–2010?

Thirty-five percent of all Americans saw a decline in their personal investments.

What are seven factors to consider before investing?

According to the U.S. Securities and Exchange Commission (SEC), investors should evaluate their current financial plans; evaluate how much risk they are comfortable taking; diversify their investments; create and maintain an emergency fund; consider using dollar cost averaging when making an investment; rebalance their portfolios when necessary; and avoid circumstances that may lead to fraudulent investments.

What is "timing the market"?

Timing the market is the act of using economic, fundamental, and technical indicators to predict future performance and time one's decisions to enter or exit a stock position based upon this information.

Why is timing the market controversial?

Timing the market is controversial because some experts believe the markets are random yet efficient; there are exactly the right number of buyers and sellers at any given point during the day, so the most efficient price is always realized. Because of the randomness of market movements, it cannot be accurately timed. Other experts who trade every day rely on technical and fundamental analysis to determine their trading positions, and believe that—given certain clues—the markets can be timed, allowing an investor to make profit as a result.

When should I rebalance my portfolio?

When you rebalance your portfolio, you make a personal decision based upon many factors, including your aversion to risk, your return goal, what period of time you are willing to wait for the return you expect, what industries or sectors make up the portfolio, and how they are weighted. A professional portfolio manager may choose to rebalance a portfolio when a single holding reaches a higher percentage than a certain percentage of the total portfolio, determined well in advance.

Why should I invest my money?

People invest their money for a number of important reasons. They wish to have some level of financial security now and in the future. They understand the concept of saving compared with spending, and wish to earn some return on their money over a period of time. They also wish to have someone pay them either interest or a share of the profits of a company, or to realize gains in the share prices or value of their investment choices. If you were to invest your money in a bank savings account, the money earns interest in exchange for the bank's use of the money. If you buy shares in a company, you have the potential to earn income through distributions of profits of the company, and if you sell the shares, you have the potential to sell the shares at a higher price than what you paid for them initially when you invested. If you buy anything of value, and hold it until it increases in value relative to what you paid for it, you are investing.

What is the most important consideration before deciding to invest?

One of the most important considerations before deciding to invest is knowing that you can lose some or all of your money when you invest, and that you must know beforehand how much risk you are willing to tolerate. On the other hand, you are also aware that you can make a great return on your investments, and that the benefits of investing may outweigh the risks you perceive with the investment you undertake.

Depending on your age and how long you have until retirement, you will want to invest in either safer, income-generating investments or, if you are young, gamble on more high-risk, high-interest stocks. The later you start investing, the more you'll have to save per month to retire comfortably.

Why is time so important in investing?

Because of the compounding of our returns, your money can potentially be more valuable over a long period of time. A simple example might be a person who starts to invest at age 18 at five dollars per week. If his overall investments earn 8% per year, he might have $134,000 in his portfolio by the time he reaches the age of 65. If he were to delay for just one year, and begin at age 19, the portfolio will be valued at $10,000 less than if he started at age 18. And if he waits until he is 40 years old to start investing, he would have to put away approximately $32 per week just to have the same amount by the time he reaches age 65. So time does matter when it comes to investing.

How can I protect my investments before I begin to invest?

The SEC believes you should ask certain basic questions, whether you are a beginning investor or have invested for many years. Consider if the seller of the investment is licensed to sell the investment, as most financial fraud is perpetrated by unlicensed dealers who are trying to separate you from your money. You should also look into the accreditations of your adviser. Thousands of people have been given poor advice from unlicensed financial advisers, who may try to steer their clients into the wrong investment choice in order to make a bonus or commission on the sale of that investment choice. The SEC also recommends that you check if it has registered and approved the investment sale.

How do I know if a potential investment is fraudulent?

If the marketed investment shows that it is too good to be true, it may be fraudulent. Generally, you should compare various attributes of the investment to some benchmark, such as the annual returns, expenses, earnings, or debt. If these comparisons are not in line with the normal returns for this type of investment, you should probably avoid it.

Do higher rates of returns generally mean that my money may be more at risk?

Certain more exotic investment vehicles, such as collateralized mortgage obligations, promise higher rates, but are quite risky, as they may be derived from more at-risk loans and mortgage products in order to attract investors. So it is very important to know fully what investments you are making and their inherent risks before you commit.

What is "dollar cost averaging"?

Dollar cost averaging is a simple timing strategy of investing, whereby an investor buys the same dollar amount of a stock at regular intervals (say $100 per month of a certain stock). If the price of an investment increases over time, we acquire fewer of these shares. Conversely, if the price of the investment drops, we acquire more of these shares. This lowers the total average price per share of an investment, meaning the investor is able to invest more profitably than if he were to "time the market." Dollar cost averaging is a worthwhile investment strategy employed by many investors in order to fix the amount invested each period for the purchase of shares, or for the purchase of an investment.

Why is dollar cost averaging a beneficial strategy for investing?

When it comes to investing in such investments as mutual funds, the prices may fluctuate as the value of the underlying portfolio may increase or decrease. This fact, coupled with dividends from shares held within the portfolio as well as changes to fees that are charged to account holders, may change the price you pay to acquire shares. Through dollar cost averaging, you are able to acquire more shares if the price drops and fewer shares if the price increases. This means you reduce the risk of acquiring many shares just before a major decrease in the price of the shares, which helps mitigate your overall risk in these investments. Although it is relatively easy to employ dollar cost averaging when it comes to investing in mutual funds, some individual stocks also allow for the regular acquisition of shares. You should consult your investment adviser for specific information on using dollar cost averaging to acquire individual shares.

What is another popular approach to investing?

Another popular investment strategy for long-term investors is an approach called buy and hold in which the investor selects an investment, buys it, and holds it for a defined period of time, or until the return goal is met.

What is an "asset allocation strategy"?

Many investors adopt an asset allocation strategy in which you buy and invest in a mix of investments believed to achieve the highest return for whatever level of risk with which you are most comfortable. The main logic behind asset allocation strategy is that each category of investment, if properly selected, may perform differently than the others, given different economic conditions. Typically, as stocks or equity investments rise, bond investments may not perform as well. When institutional investors begin to load up on bonds, equity markets may not do as well. With asset allocation, you try to balance your portfolio in an attempt to take advantage of the ebb and flow of various economic and market conditions.

THE INVESTOR MINDSET

Why does investing require a specific mindset, so that I may be prepared for the long road ahead of me?

According to experts at Morningstar, the mutual fund analytical research company, investing requires a certain mindset in order for you to reach your long-term goals. It suggests that you try not to overreact to the various ups and downs of market cycles. According to Morningstar, when the news is spreading about a possible increase or decline in various markets with which our investments may be correlated, when the talk on the street is all about the financial markets, this is precisely the wrong time to sell or buy equity investments. Morningstar further suggests that you stay on track to hit your long-term goals, and try to develop the discipline to keep to your long-term financial investing performance goals.

Why am I so important when it comes to investing success?

Morningstar further reports that we tend to give an inordinate amount of attention to our investments themselves: what they are, what their returns have been, how well the company is doing. We seem to forget that the buying and selling of these investments depends strictly on our own behavior and emotional state at the time we buy and sell. If you extrapolate this sentiment to millions of investors, you can begin to see how each investor's individual attitudes and behaviors may shape and form the markets in which you invest, as well as your own performance within these markets.

What did experts at BlackRock—the world's largest global asset management company, serving both large institutional investors and individual investors—find in their landmark 2013 study of investor attitudes?

BlackRock, along with the private research firm Cicero, surveyed approximately 17,600 investors from 12 countries to try to gauge the pulse of the investment community. From this initial survey, BlackRock polled 4,000 investors and 500 financial professionals to analyze the U.S. investment community. Their survey concluded several themes, including: investors' concern about their financial futures; more reluctance to invest and wish to preserve cash; a knowledge gap when it comes to evaluating opportunities to generate income; tightness on household income; and widespread fears about meeting retirement goals.

After the stock market turmoil of 2008 to 2009, what did one of the largest mutual fund companies in the world, Vanguard, find in its survey of over 3,000 U.S investors, age 21 to 79?

In a short period of time, from May-June 2009, experts at Vanguard surveyed U.S. investors, finding that three-quarters of all American households with $5,000 or more to invest, invest a portion in equities. Overall wealth and educational level attainment are related to a household's participation in investing, as is the age of the investor. Investors who are at or near retirement age have less exposure and are therefore less likely to hold equities than

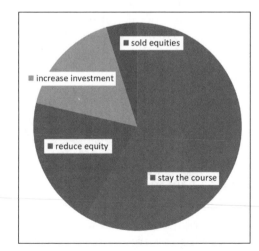

Of Americans who had money in equities during the stock market correction of 2008–09, 60% kept their money where it was, 21% reduced their exposure to equities, 17% increased their investment, and 5% sold all their equities.

are younger investors. The survey also found that even during the correction in 2008 to 2009, 60% of investors stayed the course without making major changes to their investments; 21% of investors reduced their exposure to equities; 5% sold all their equity holdings; and 17% saw the correction as an opportunity to increase their investments in equities. Some reasons for this dynamic may include how near investors were to reaching retirement age during this period of turmoil, their individual mortgage financial position at the time, and whether their jobs were secure.

What other insights does the Vanguard study show about investor attitudes?

The Vanguard study makes some interesting conclusions from the results of its survey, including that investors who are more dependent on the work of financial advisers and those who invest only in tax-deferred retirement plans are less likely to panic. Fully three-quarters of survey respondents were strongly or somewhat aware that large market declines are possible. Half of all respondents felt the risks inherent to investing were worth taking in order to realize long-term gains. Another 50% of respondents felt that during this period of time the stock markets were riskier than in past years. Many respondents also felt their retirement was somewhat impaired by the "crash", and their responses were tied to similar factors, including how near they were to retirement, how secure they felt in their current job or career path, and their housing/mortgage situation.

After a market correction, what attitudes of individual investors seem to be apparent?

The Vanguard survey found that individual investors, when faced with a notable market correction, seem to be confused about what to do next. If your savings decline, your logical and natural impulse is to reduce your spending so that you can build up your savings. At the same time, you may also see the correction as an opportunity to buy by adding money to your long-term investing accounts. But experts at Vanguard saw that, psychologically, many individual investors have a difficult time doing this, since the emotions and sentiment associated with a significant decline may cause many investors to leave the market. Many respondents felt they would merely work more or delay retirement, if they were several years from actually retiring.

What mindset helps me become financially successful?

You should begin to think that you live in an abundant world, a place where earning money is unlimited, smart work is rewarded, and financial goals are always attained. Think of how you feel, for example, when you do not have to worry about making a mortgage or rent payment, or what it feels like to create a budget and stick to it each month. It is very important to believe that you can control your finances and create wealth. No matter your background, whether you have struggled to make ends meet or came from a relatively more affluent family, or somewhere in between, you should have a clear picture in your mind of where you want to be in terms of your personal finances.

How do I know if I am not in control of my finances?

Everyone is in control of his finances, to a certain degree. We all choose every day whether or not to purchase something. If you were to rent an apartment, or buy a car, you decide based upon how much income you have, and whether it is affordable or not. A person who cannot tell the difference between an apartment that is too expensive, compared with one that is within his budget, would be more out of control with regard to spending. Someone who spends more of his income than he makes would be less in control. A person who has learned to consistently make the right spending decisions over time—someone who manages to have a large net worth on a relatively meager income, but understands and practices personal finance each day—is very much in control of his finances.

If I just make more money, would I still have to worry about my personal finances?

Yes. Just having a high income does not ensure your financial security. Millions of Americans make much more than average, and yet are still one paycheck away from disaster, because they spend nearly all they make, and have no short-term or long-term financial plan. Many experts suggest evidence of this phenomenon by looking at the number of foreclosures of very expensive houses, condominiums, and vacation properties that came on the market after 2008. Many of these people made well over $100,000 per year, yet did not have emergency funds available to ride through a job change or other life change because they spent everything they made and more.

How much does my ability to delay present gratification in favor of future gratification play in personal financial success?

The belief that it is acceptable to do without something now, and save for something in the future, is the core to your financial success. You have to make the decision every day—that it is acceptable to delay your rewards today, in favor of future rewards. This is something you can learn to do each day, so that you may become comfortable getting rewarded for your work many years later.

What do average investors do that decreases their returns?

Many investors buy investments when markets are at their highs, and panic and sell their investments when prices are at their lows. This happens because these investors do not understand that they "are" the markets, or at least participants in a rather large way in the markets. As more stories fill the airwaves and Internet saying

Too many investors panic when the market takes a downturn, forgetting the wisdom of always buying low and selling high because they fear losing money in the short term.

the market is at an all-time high (meaning prices of investments and demands are high), these investors buy stocks, mutual funds, and other investments. And when the opposite happens—when prices fall, demand decreases, and stories fill the airwaves and Internet saying a crash is happening—these same investors sell at precisely the wrong time. The markets may be depressed compared with an over-inflated price before. So some investors see crashes as great opportunities during which to invest. These same investors see market highs as when prices are peaking, and sell when everyone else is buying.

INVESTING RISKS

What is "risk"?

In investing, risk is a quantifiable number that compares an investment's actual return against what was expected. This number is probabilistic, and gives an investor an indication as to how the investment might perform against some benchmark.

What are some examples of risks?

Some examples of risks that may affect the prices of investments include: a natural disaster that causes Wall Street to shut down; a disruption in the pumping and transportation of oil; an abrupt change in the exchange rate between two currencies; an abrupt change in interest rates; corporate expenses that never made the expected return for the company; and use or misuse of technology in a company. All may have an adverse effect on an investment's price at that moment in time. Some of these events may have extremely short-term effects on the prices of target investments, while others may affect the long-term prices of potential investments. Short-term and long-term risks need to be considered when making investing decisions.

How can potential investors evaluate risks?

It is important for you to understand the concept that you must balance risk with reward, and evaluate investments that reward more highly than riskier investments. At the same time, you must be quite clear in evaluating your own personal tolerance for risk.

How do I determine my tolerance to risk?

To determine your tolerance to risk, you can simply ask: If I were to lose a sum of money that I am thinking of investing, how much of this portfolio am I willing to lose? According to CNN/Money, investors tend to underestimate risk when financial markets are doing well, and overestimate risk when markets are in a tailspin.

What tools may investors use to evaluate risks of default?

If a company is having serious financial difficulties, this usually is reported to a third-party company, that in turn measures the health of many companies, especially their ability to repay obligations. Many companies, such as Standard & Poor's, Moody's, Dun & Bradstreet, and Fitch Ratings track how well companies are meeting their obligations. Companies with little debt and lots of cash, and that always pay off debts and obligations, are relatively safer investments than those that cannot.

Are questionnaires available that may help people evaluate their tolerance for risk?

There are hundreds, perhaps thousands, of online tools—many for free—that allow users to evaluate their own personal feelings toward risk.

SAVING, MANAGING DEBT, AND BUDGETING

What is "saving"?

Saving, or savings, has many definitions in the English-speaking world. But most definitions describe saving as the act of putting aside money, after all consumption expenditures, for future use. Some experts add to the definition that savings may be more liquid and accessible than investments, which may not be immediately accessible.

What influences my ability to save?

Among many variables, the most basic influence is your preference, belief, and ultimately your decision to do without or abstain from present expenditures in order to have the ability to use this money at some time in the future. You should understand or have a goal in mind, and then make adjustments in current expenditures in order to meet your goals.

Why should I save my money?

Many people save money in order to attain certain goals. Some of the most widely accepted reasons to save money include: having extra money in order to invest regularly; accumulating money in case of an emergency (usually three to six months of living expenses in the form of cash); deferring on paying taxes by using before-tax income and employer matching funds (in an IRA, 401(k) or other retirement account); putting away money in order to purchase a principal residence; saving for vacations, to purchase cars, or unexpected medical expenses; and to fund your current or future educational expenses. Before you begin investing, you should have your emergency funds set aside, and should exclude these sums from what you will ultimately use for your investments.

What are some strategies to help me save money?

It is important to understand that the act of setting aside just a tiny amount of money on a regular basis quickly multiplies. If you save only one dollar per day over the course of a year, with even a fraction paid in interest to you, it will result in helping you achieve some of your financial goals. But it is not necessarily the amount that you ultimately save. It is having the financial discipline to stick to your plan of accumulating money that guarantees your success over time.

What are some other strategies to assist us in saving money?

Some of the best strategies employed to assist us in saving money include: knowing where you are in terms of our income/expenses and net worth today, and creating a goal with a time frame of where you wish to be. Caring about saving even small amounts gives you the practice and trains you to have the discipline to save and care about larger amounts. The very act of keeping track of our spending will cause many people to begin to see how they can cut their expenses, by not purchasing on impulse, comparison shopping for lower prices, decreasing the usage of credit/debit cards, and creating and sticking to a monthly or weekly expense budget.

Why should I get in the habit of paying myself first?

In light of everything written above, it is important to create the behavior of paying yourself first. This means setting aside money from your normal weekly or monthly expenses that you use only for your savings and investments. Even if it is a small amount, it is important to set this money aside first so that it is not redirected to meet other expenses.

What is a "cash cushion"?

A cash cushion is a special savings that you may cover three months to one year of your expenses. The amount you need to accumulate depends on knowing your current expenses. The amount you need to save is also dependent on your ability to find another job should you abruptly change employers, which may be several months, or even years. So it is good to plan accordingly.

Why else should I have a portion of my portfolio in cash?

Many experts believe that holding a certain percentage of your portfolio in cash has many benefits for investors. Although it is important always to have a certain amount of cash on hand for emergencies or unplanned expenses, you should also have cash on hand to acquire investments when the opportunity arrives, so you do not have to sell other successful, longer-term positions—and pay the capital gains taxes—in order to purchase more investments. You

Don't have all your money tied up in bonds and stocks; keep some in cash for emergencies so that you have it available for unexpected investment opportunities.

can simply use cash. Other experts believe in holding a certain percentage of your portfolio in cash as a way to preserve your capital in a down market. Cash also increases value over time during periods of deflation. When purchasing a house or other real estate investment property, using cash to increase your down payment may enable you to obtain better terms on your loan and to make a more attractive offer for the property.

Why else is cash important to my portfolio as an individual investor?

According to experts at *The Wall Street Journal*, cash plays a very important role for all of our portfolios at different stages in our financial lives. First and foremost, by preserving capital and insulating it from the downward trend of a market, you have more money available to invest later. There is also a big opportunity cost that must be considered when you think of selling off investments—instead of using cash—in order to acquire new investments. By selling prematurely, you may not realize the gains you wished to make, and may actually incur losses. Many experts believe that if you need cash to make big-ticket purchases such as cars or houses, it is better to hold this money in the form of cash than to invest the money and have to sell the investment after poor performance, or at a loss, after a relatively short period of time. One expert cited the fact that many central banks have priced cash at levels approaching zero (percent interest), creating volatility in the prices of other investment vehicles. So it is best to have a strategy for the proper allocation of cash within your portfolio.

MANAGING DEBT

How can I get out of debt?

The most important step to getting out of debt is to understand what behaviors or circumstances caused the debt to begin with, and then focus first on changing those behaviors. This means that if you have incurred a lot of credit card debt because of undisciplined spending habits, you must immediately attack the root cause of the debt in order to reduce it. If you incurred a debt because you obtained a mortgage for more house than you can afford, you must find a way to sell the house without incurring a loss, and purchase a smaller, more affordable house.

What is the second most important step to getting out of debt?

The second step is to save this money you used to pay off loans and credit cards, and to pay special attention not to take on any more debt going forward. In other words, take the money you used to pay for your monthly credit card bill or car loan, and put it directly into a savings account, spending nothing on your credit card going forward. And remember to pay yourself first.

What is the average percentage of a typical American's gross income that is used for mortgage and consumer debt payments each month?

According to the Federal Reserve, Americans spend about 11.89% of their monthly gross income on mortgage and consumer debt payments. Homeowners (those who specifically purchased homes with mortgages) spend about 15.27% of their monthly gross income.

Why is debt management important to an investor?

There are many reasons why managing your debt is an important component of investing. All debts carry some sort of obligation and fee associated with the use of the money. In addition to the principal that needs to be repaid by a certain date, so do all fees and interest on the debt. In order to repay this debt, money that would normally be invested from your current earnings must be redirected to pay off this debt. So you lose both the current earnings and the potential to earn more on this money if it were to be invested.

What is the hidden cost of debt to an individual investor?

The hidden cost of debt to the individual investor is the opportunity cost or lost opportunity of using money that could have been invested earning some return, in order to pay off debt and interest charges.

What are some warning signs that my debt may be a problem?

According to the U.S. Department of the Treasury, many signs that help evaluate the health of a financial institution are relevant to individuals as well. Among these warning signs are failure to file taxes and other financial statements in a timely fashion; slowing or decrease in one's income over time; deterioration of our available cash; decline in our assets as percentage of our total assets (e.g., the value of our principal residence and its equity declines); our debt increases; and keeping poor financial records (not knowing our current financial situation).

What is a front-end ratio?

A front-end ratio is calculated by dividing your total monthly housing cost by your gross monthly income.

What is a back-end ratio?

A back-end ratio is calculated by dividing your total monthly housing cost plus all other debts by your monthly gross income.

Why are front- and back-end ratios important?

Front- and back-end ratios are important because they indicate to lenders and creditors how much debt you can afford.

Why use a debt-to-income ratio?

In order to prevent people from buying a house they may not be able to afford, lenders will establish how much debt you can handle, and use this as one factor to determine your loan amount.

How much debt can I afford?

The amount of debt you can afford depends roughly on your front-end and back-end ratios, or debt-to-income ratio. Although the use of the ratios differs from lender to lender, on average your front-end ratio should never exceed 28%, and your back-end ratio should never exceed 36%.

What if my debt-to-income ratios are higher than average, and a lender still will give me a loan?

Just because a lender qualifies you for a loan, that does not mean you should take it. The lender may not care about your long-term financial success. Having a worse than average debt-to-income ratio means trouble on the horizon if not corrected, and should signal action on your part to reduce the debt.

What is "debt consolidation"?

Debt consolidation is the act of taking out a loan in order to pay off several others. Assume that you have credit card debt carrying interest rates as high as 20%, and you have a home mortgage (with some equity in your house) with an interest rate of 5% for 30 years. In a consolidation, you take out a home equity loan (which charges a smaller interest rate) for the value of your high-interest credit card debt, and then make payments on your equity loan until the debt is repaid.

What is a "debt consolidator"?

A debt consolidator provides a service wherein he looks at a client's debt situation and creates a strategy designed to pay off the debt, in exchange for a fee.

What is the trouble with debt consolidators?

According to many experts, the main trouble with the debt consolidation industry is that it is a largely unregulated business, and many companies that promise unsuspecting families assistance end up taking fees and leaving town. They may promise to work with banks to arrange for your loans, and in the end may take what little money you have.

How do I check the credibility of a debt consolidation company?

It is important to check with your state's attorney general's office, as well as the Better Business Bureau, before seeking the assistance of a debt consolidator. You may also search online to see if there have been

Be careful whom you choose to assist you with debt consolidation. The industry is barely regulated by the government, and you might get an unscrupulous "debt consolidator" who will leave you high and dry.

any negative comments or stories written about the company. Check with the company's references to see if the company is legitimate. Also, contact the local chamber of commerce in the city in which the company is located to see if there are any complaints about it. If you sense any time pressure from a pushy debt consolidation representative, find another company. This is a sign that the business may not be legitimate.

How might I locate the name of a legitimate debt consolidator?

To find the name of a legitimate debt consolidation company, many experts suggest you visit the National Foundation for Credit Counseling website to identify registered members. After selecting a credit counselor, you may then meet to identify a reputable debt consolidator, if it is recommended as a strategy.

If I have a much lower interest rate for my old credit card debt, by using the equity I have in my home, what else could be wrong with debt consolidation?

After you consolidate all of your debts into one loan, it may be amortized over many years. Because the debt is now spread out over a long period of time, if you make the minimum payments each month, you may pay much more in interest to retire the debt.

CREDIT CARD DEBT

What steps can I take to minimize my credit card and other debts?

According to experts at the Federal Trade Commission (FTC), the first step to liberating yourself from credit card debt is to get a realistic picture of your income and your expenses. You may divide your expenses into two categories: fixed expenses, meaning those expenses that don't really change from month to month, such as rent or mortgages; and variable expenses, items that may change from time to time, such as utilities, food, and entertainment. If you have received notices from creditors, you should contact them directly and ask to arrange for a way to reduce your monthly payment to a reasonable level. Stop using your credit cards so that you may begin to improve your financial picture. The FTC notes that your debt can be secured or unsecured. When debt is secured, ownership is not conveyed until all payments are made, such as your house or car. If you stop making payments, you may lose that asset. When debt is unsecured, it is granted with no ties to any particular asset, such as credit cards, signature loans, and medical bills. But most lenders are willing to work with you to create a more reasonable payment plan, so you should speak with your creditor when you have a problem. Creditors—especially credit card companies—may change the terms of your agreement and reduce your annual percentage rate to a more reasonable level.

How does credit card debt affect older Americans?

According to a recent report by the AARP (formerly American Association of Retired Persons), older Americans (those over age 50) carry more credit card debt than younger Americans. Half of these older Americans carry some medical-related bills on their credit cards, especially prescription bills and dental expenses. Forty-nine percent of older Americans reported that car repairs also contributed to their credit card debt; 38% stated that home repairs contributed to their overall credit card debt; 34% rely on using credit cards to pay for basic living expenses such as rent/mortgage payments, food, and utilities, because they lack the cash in their checking and savings accounts to pay for them; 25% of older Americans say that a loss of employment contributed to their credit card debt; 18% drew upon retirement funds to pay down debt; and 23% got into debt in order to help other family members.

How much total debt should I have?

To be safe financially, the monthly payments on all your debt should be less than 36% of your monthly gross income.

What steps can I take to increase my available funds so that I may invest?

The most important step to increasing your funds available for investing is to understand your true financial picture by taking into account your income from all sources, your complete debt picture (including all loans, credit cards, and other obligations), understanding your daily or monthly expenses, paying special attention to areas where you can eliminate or reduce these expenses, and directing this money to investments that earn a return.

What are the next steps to increase my available funds so that I may invest?

You should pay off all higher-interest rate debts first, since those debts use so much of your income. You should stop using credit cards in favor of cash, and be sure to pay off the balance of what you used on a credit card in full each month, so that you do not take on any more debt. And never pay only the minimum amount that credit cards request, as this will keep you in the debt cycle for a very long time.

How can I calculate how much credit card debt I can afford?

The easiest answer to this is zero. Credit cards should not be used as a way to finance purchasing anything, because the interest rate and finance charges are too high ever to justify it. If you were to use a card to buy an expensive TV, it will end up costing you twice the original price if you use a credit card and pay the monthly minimum payment and "finance" the purchase. Credit cards should only be used to make purchases for an amount you can pay off entirely each month.

How long does it take to resolve a credit card issue?

According to a survey by Javelin Strategy & Research, the average time to resolve a credit card fraud issue dropped 30% to 21 hours.

What are the best credit cards?

According to a 2010 J.D. Power survey of card holders, the best cards in terms of overall customer satisfaction are: American Express, Discover, U.S. Bank, Wells Fargo, Chase, Barclaycard, Bank of America, Capital One, Citi, and HSBC.

If I have a balance of only $1,000 on my credit card, with a 15% interest rate, and I only make the minimum payment of $15 each month, how long will it take me to pay off the balance, and how much will it really cost me in the end?

By paying only the minimum due on a credit card balance in the example above, it would take about 12 years to pay it off, and end up costing you more than $2,000.

What are the first steps to eliminate credit card debt?

The first step to eliminate credit card debt is to destroy your card. This will prevent you from adding further debt onto the card.

What are additional steps that I can take?.

The next step is to analyze how much you can afford to pay each month, and make it a priority to pay both the monthly payment and a part of the balance each month so that you may reduce the balance that is accruing interest and fees as fast as possible. Never believe that you can get out of debt by paying the minimum monthly payment on your credit card.

What is the average amount of credit card debt for a typical American family?

Approximately $15,788.

How many credit cards exist in the United States?

There are 609.8 million cards being used in the United States.

What is the average number of cards owned by each person?

The average number of cards that people carry is 3.5.

How many credit cards should I have?

You probably should have not more than two cards, in case you absolutely need to use one, and have one as a backup in case your primary card does not work.

Why use credit cards?

Credit cards give you access to cash immediately so that you may pay for many different expenses, from food to utility bills, without having to carry large amounts of cash. Consumers only have to write one

When in deep credit card debt, the first step to take is to cut your cards so you won't use them anymore.

check each month to cover many monthly expenses. Some credit cards allow consumers to earn points for using the card, which are later redeemable for products or services.

What is the first rule of using credit cards?

Do not use a credit card unless you can pay off the balance in full each month.

Why pay off the balance each month?

You want to pay off your balance each month to avoid paying interest on your balance, which can be exorbitant, depending on your credit history and interest rate calculation.

What does my credit history have to do with my credit card interest rate?

Card issuers look at your credit history to see what kind of risk you might be to them, what chance you will default, and how much debt you can handle. Depending on this, the card issuers decide on an interest rate that will cover the costs of defaulting accounts, fraud, and profit, and this number is the rate that they then charge the consumer.

So if I have a great credit rating, I might get a card with better terms?

Yes, if you are less of a credit risk, have a higher steady income, and own other assets, you will likely be approved for a lower-interest-rate credit card.

MORTGAGES

What is a "mortgage"?

A mortgage is the amount of money loaned from a bank for the agreed-upon price of a house that is financed by the bank in the form of a loan to the buyer, less down payment and closing costs at the closing of the transaction.

What about interest rates and their effect on housing prices?

The higher the interest rate for a mortgage, the more the demand for mortgages is suppressed, since buying a house becomes more unaffordable to many potential buyers. As interest rates or the price of money decreases, the more demand there is from buyers, and this makes prices more buoyant over time.

How low are today's mortgage interest rates?

Interest rates on loans for houses are lower than nearly any time in the past 50 years. They may go even lower before we see a bottom in the interest rates for mortgage loans.

Why are there fewer potential buyers for houses today?

There are fewer potential buyers for houses because many fear employment loss, an inability to obtain a loan, an inability to manage current expenses, and expectations that

While mortgage rates have risen slightly in 2014, they are still around 4.5% for a 30-year fixed mortgage, which is a great deal for investors and home buyers.

prices will further decline. Potential buyers would rather wait out a decline in price than jump in now. Sellers are holding out for the best price because they need to pay off their mortgages, and pull as much value from their house as possible in order to buy another house.

What does the term "underwater on a mortgage" mean?

When you are "underwater on a mortgage," you cannot sell your current home because you owe more on the balance of your home mortgage than you can make when you sell the house today.

How does increasing my down payment help protect me from going "underwater"?

Increasing your down payment provides some protection to you because if you put more money down to purchase the house, you owe less money on the mortgage in the future, and when it is time to sell, you will be able to sell at the market price with less risk of owing more than the house is worth.

What tax advantages does home ownership provide?

One of the great benefits of home ownership is the tax-shielding aspect of having a mortgage. Essentially, the government allows you to deduct, or not count, the amount of mortgage interest against your income that you pay in one year. Another sizable advantage—and one of the principal benefits of home ownership—is that up to a certain capital gain ($500,000 for a married couple), you do not have to pay taxes on the gain in the value of your house. If you itemize deductions, you may also deduct your property taxes when you file your income tax returns.

What is the general rule for obtaining a home loan?

The general rule is that a good borrower can afford monthly payments—including principal, interest, insurance, and taxes—equal to 25% of his gross income. Some experts believe that you can have a debt income ratio as high as 28% to cover your mortgage, insurance, and taxes. You should also have a total debt income ratio (of all of your debts plus the mortgage payment) of less than 36% if you wish to qualify for a mortgage.

What is "mortgage fraud"?

Mortgage fraud involves a crime committed in order to secure or grant a mortgage, falling into two categories: misrepresenting information on a mortgage application (59% of all cases), and appraisal-related misrepresentation (33% of all cases).

Which states lead the nation in mortgage-related fraud?

According to a report issued by the Mortgage Asset Research Institute, Florida, New York, California, Arizona, and Michigan lead the nation in mortgage fraud.

What percentage of buyers ultimately pay cash to purchase an existing house?

In 2010, more than 25% of all existing houses sold were purchased by cash buyers, who didn't need or want to obtain a mortgage.

Why do mortgage companies, banks, and finance companies require homeowner's insurance?

Mortgage companies, banks, and finance companies require homeowner's insurance because they technically own your home, and want to be sure they get paid for the mortgage loan plus interest, even in the event the house burns down. The insurance will cover the costs to replace the house, and ultimately the homeowner will be able to continue to pay the mortgage or sell the house.

What types of mortgages are available to consumers for a home purchase?

There are many types of mortgages available to consumers to purchase a home, depending on your financial situation, including fixed-rate mortgages, FHA loans, interest-only loans, and adjustable-rate mortgages.

What is a fixed-rate mortgage?

A fixed-rate mortgage has a fixed interest rate for the period of the loan, and allows you to pay off the loan over a period of time. Such amortization periods can be 10 years, 15 years, 20 years, 30 years, and even 40 to 50 years.

What is the distinction between the different loan periods?

The shorter the period of the loan, the higher the monthly payments, and the less interest you have to pay over time, since you are borrowing and using the money over a shorter period of time.

What is an "FHA mortgage"?

The Federal Housing Administration, which provides mortgage insurance through FHA-approved lenders, is the largest insurer of residential mortgages in the world. Depending on the state in which you live, the amount you can borrow for a mortgage may differ.

Who uses FHA mortgages?

FHA mortgages are used by first-time homeowners because they require a smaller down payment than conventional mortgages.

How long must I pay for mortgage insurance with an FHA loan?

FHA loans require the borrower to pay for the insurance for five years, or until the loan-to-value ratio reaches 78%, whichever is longer.

What is a loan-to-value ratio?

A loan-to-value ratio is the loan amount divided by the house's selling price.

What is "mortgage insurance"?

Mortgage insurance protects lenders from losses if a mortgage is not paid in full. Depending on the amount of your down payment to purchase a home, you may be required to obtain mortgage insurance until you have paid off enough of the loan, minimizing the risk of defaulting on the loan.

What is an interest-only loan?

It is a loan that allows a person to pay, for a period of time, only the interest on a loan. At the end of this period, the borrower must make a balloon payment of the value of the entire loan, or refinance the loan into a conventional loan.

The Federal Housing Administration (FHA) is the largest insurer of mortgages in the world and a great resource for first-time home buyers.

What is an adjustable-rate mortgage (ARM)?

An ARM offers a fixed-rate of interest for a short period of time, usually three, five, or seven years. At that point, the interest rate may change up or down, depending upon the index to which the interest rate is tied. These loans also have limits as to how high the rate can change in a year, and in the life of the loan. The borrower may continue paying the loan at this variable or adjustable-rate, or may refinance the loan to a fixed-rate conventional mortgage.

What are the steps involved to get a mortgage?

The first step is to order your credit report, to discover if it contains any errors and/or inaccuracies. The bank will also order its own copy of the credit report to initiate your loan. The credit report will be used by the loan officers to determine whether you are a good candidate for a loan, as well as how large a loan you can obtain. Next, it is important to have a clear picture of all your debts—the amounts of the balances, and the monthly payments. You should also have your most recent pay stub, showing your current income, and the last two to three years of your IRS W-2 forms, because as your income will be used to determine your eligibility. You should also have your most recent bank statements and investment account statements, showing your most recent balances. At this point, you should also know how much money you will use in cash toward a down payment on the loan.

Does it matter to lenders how large a down payment I will require?

The larger your down payment for a house, the more favorably your lender will consider your mortgage application, and the better your terms will be. You will also benefit from paying less interest over the life of the loan.

Should I pay down my debts before I apply for a mortgage?

If at all possible, in order to reduce your normal monthly expenses, it is a good idea to try to reduce your debt load, as it will help you secure a mortgage. You also benefit by eliminating high-interest rate debts before taking on a relatively lower-interest rate mortgage.

How should I choose a lender?

You should choose a lender by comparing the interest rates, the amount of money required for a down payment, and any fees or points associated with the loan. You may also

---

What are "points", or loan origination fees?

Lenders charge points for mortgages, including fixed-fee mortgages. One point represents 1% of the loan amount. Not all lenders charge points for loans, so shop around to find the lowest fees.

Getting preapproved for a home loan will give you extra bargaining power when bidding on a house. Sellers are more inclined to agree to an offer if they know a lender has thoroughly checked your credit and financial stability.

want to inquire how long it will take to process your loan. Always speak with several different lenders, and beware of lenders offering comparatively low interest rates, as they may just be "teaser rates" designed to get you to come in and speak with them. You should meet with lenders after you have learned as much as possible about their current rates and practices, as well as fees, so that you will know who is giving you the best deal.

Should I sell my house before getting a loan for my next home purchase?

Your chances of obtaining a mortgage will be far better if you sell your current house, because your income may not support the payment of two mortgages. Also, sellers look more favorably on offers without house sale contingencies.

What does it mean to be "preapproved" for a loan?

When someone is preapproved, the lender has already investigated his creditworthiness, and has established that he can borrow up to a certain amount from the lender. A home-buyer often receives preapproval before making an offer on a house, in order to make his offer more attractive to a seller.

Why is it important to be preapproved for a loan?

When comparing offers to buy a home, a house seller would prefer to consider an offer from someone who has a letter from a lender stating that he is already approved to borrow the amount of the sale price of the house over someone who makes the purchase contingent upon getting a mortgage or financing.

What does it mean to be "prequalified" for a loan?

Prequalification for a loan means the bank or mortgage company has looked at the borrower's income and debt to determine the approximate amount of the loan. It does not mean the borrower has been approved for a loan.

Can adding just a few hundred dollars to my mortgage payment help to reduce my debt?

Yes. You can choose to add an additional sum to your normal monthly mortgage payment to pay down your loan principal. The effect can shave several years off your mortgage, and save you thousands of dollars in interest payments, depending on your loan size, your interest rate, and how many months you have remaining on your mortgage.

How many homes are in foreclosure in the United States?

According to experts at Realtytrac.com, as of March 2014 there are 483,224 bank-owned homes in the United States, with 51% still occupied by the former owner or tenant. This is down from a peak of about one million homes in 2010.

The real estate bubble that precipitated the U.S. recession of 2007–2009 resulted in widespread home foreclosures. Even today, home ownership in the United States is at a low not matched since 1960.

How many people risk home foreclosure?

in 2010, 1.7 million homeowners were notified that they were at risk of defaulting on their loan because of missed payments. This means one in 78 homeowners was at risk.

How many U.S. homes received foreclosure filings in 2010?

According to RealtyTrac, more than 3.8 million foreclosure filings—including default notices, scheduled auctions, and bank repossessions—were reported on a record 2.87 million U.S. properties in 2010.

How long does it take for a home to be foreclosed?

Within 15 months after you stop paying your mortgage, your home reverts to the lender.

What states have the highest rate of foreclosure?

Nevada, Arizona, Florida, California, Utah, Georgia, Michigan, Idaho, Illinois, and Colorado have the highest rates of foreclosure.

What does the foreclosure rate mean for American home ownership?

The foreclosure rate means that home ownership most likely will fall to its lowest level since 1960, when 61.9% of American families owned their own homes, and perhaps even lower over the next few years.

HOME EQUITY

What is a "home equity loan"?

A home equity loan, or second mortgage, is a loan financed by a bank that allows a homeowner to receive a lump sum cash payment for the value of the equity he has accrued in his house, or leverage the accrued equity of his principal residence. After you have been living in your house for some time, assuming that real estate prices have been increasing, you begin to build equity in your house. Banks allow you to borrow from them this value, or equity, in the form of a line of credit that can be paid off over time at the prevailing interest rate when you secure the loan. Many people use this loan to make necessary improvements on their home, which may increase the home's value. As the house appreciates in value from the time of purchase, and the value of this asset changes over time, the house's equity is the value of the house (according to the lender) minus the value of any previous loans or mortgages on the property. This value can be loaned back to the owner, to make improvements to the property, consolidate debt, or pay other expenses. You may borrow a certain percentage of this equity. You must pay fees and closing costs, and must pay off this loan, including interest, according to the terms set forth by the lender. Typical terms to pay off home equity loans range from five to 15 years. The full amount of the loan must be repaid if the house is sold before this term expires. The AARP reports that 16% of Americans age 50+ used their home equity to pay down credit card debt.

How does a lender know the value of a house, if it is not for sale?

In order to compute the house's worth, lenders use a variety of data points, including recent sales of nearby property, property records, deeds, mortgage records, and current appraisals.

What is a "home equity line of credit" (HELOC)?

A home equity line of credit is similar to a home equity loan, except the lender gives you the opportunity to use all or part of the credit over a certain period of time. Lenders may offer initial low interest rates, and may attach conditions as to when the credit line is to be paid back or closed, so it is important to understand the fine print on a HELOC. The interest rate may also be fixed or variable, depending on the terms established by the lender, allowing a homeowner to access as much of the credit as he requires.

Why are home equity loans desirable to homeowners?

Home equity loans are desirable because they allow a homeowner the chance to access the equity that he has accrued in his house, rather than waiting until he sells it to realize these gains. Typically these loans carry a much lower interest rate than other types of loans or lines of credit, such as credit cards. If the loan is used to make capital improvements to the secured property, it may actually improve the value of the property. A home equity loan is sometimes used by someone who wishes to consolidate his credit card debt in favor of obtaining a lower-interest-rate home equity loan, and pay off expensive credit card balances without incurring exceptionally high credit card interest rates and other associated fees. The interest on home equity loans may also be deductible against your adjusted gross income, so please check with your tax adviser for the most current rules when filing your tax return. Many lenders offer online calculators to help a user understand how large a loan he can obtain. If you have a steady income, and control over your living expenses, a home equity line may be a good option to help solve a financial need.

Why can a home equity loan be dangerous for homeowners?

There are many reasons why obtaining a home equity loan can be troublesome for homeowners. The equity that a homeowner gains as the value of his house increases over time can be loaned back to the homeowner, and paid back over time with interest. Most experts agree that it is inadvisable to obtain a home equity loan, especially when house prices are falling. If the value of your local real estate market plummets after you obtain a loan, you could be "underwater" on the mortgage, a very dangerous financial situation in which to find yourself. Obtaining a home equity loan may not solve the initial financial problem that led you to obtain the loan in the first place. You need to control expenses and improve income. A home equity loan may also artificially create a sense of higher income, which is dangerous if you cannot control expenses. And obtaining such loans or lines of credit may help perpetuate poor spending patterns, especially if you use the credit unwisely.

What is the downside of using a home equity loan?

Some people use home equity loans to buy cars and clothes, fund vacations, or purchase second homes. This may lead to major financial problems in the future, if not correctly managed. Often home equity loans are given to people with terms that allow them to pay only the interest on their line of credit each month. This means the borrower never pays off the principal of the loan, and could end up paying a notable amount of money in interest payments. This is often written in the fine print of the loan documents, and is concealed from borrowers to make the loans appear more attractive.

Is it easy to get a home equity loan?

It is easy to get a home equity loan if you have owned your home for many years, and have a good credit history. An equity line may be obtained as soon as the bank can schedule an appraisal of your home to determine its present value. Assuming you have no other loans on the property, you can usually obtain a home equity loan in a matter of days or weeks.

What are other considerations or requirements to obtain a home equity loan?

The borrower should have a good debt-to-income ratio, and is normally required to make minimum monthly payments on the loan.

How do I determine the market price of a house?

The market price of a house is derived from the recent sale price of comparable houses (comparables or "comps") found within a specific radius of the house, the quality of the house, the neighborhood, and the market demand for the house at that price.

What is a "home equity conversion mortgage"?

A home equity conversion mortgage is another name for a reverse mortgage.

What is a "reverse mortgage"?

A reverse mortgage is a financial product for people aged 62 and older with significant home equity. The homeowner may be able to pull out this equity in the form of a mortgage, whereby the bank actually pays the homeowner a lump sum, monthly checks, or a line of credit for the amount of equity the homeowner wishes to receive. There are significant fees in order to do this, usually 10% of the home's value. It al-

If you have owned your home for a number of years and have a good credit rating, it can be fairly simple to get a home equity loan.

lows a retiree to pull out equity in his home without having to incur a home equity loan, allowing him to receive additional income. The reverse mortgage is then paid off when the home is finally sold. The reverse mortgage also incurs interest fees, which are paid back when the home is sold.

What are the requirements to obtain a reverse mortgage?

To obtain a reverse mortgage, you must be at least 62 years old, must own your home (meaning you have either no mortgage on your home or a very small balance due), and must live in the home.

How much equity may a homeowner pull out in a reverse mortgage?

The amount a homeowner may pull out in equity in a reverse mortgage depends on the age of the youngest borrower/owner of the home, the current interest rate, the current appraised value of the home, and any mortgage insurance the lender may be required to purchase.

Why are reverse mortgages controversial?

Reverse mortgages are controversial because many lenders target an older, less informed market of potential clients who may not be aware of the many risks of removing equity from their homes. The fees are very large, compared with other forms of loans, and there is a risk that home prices may not increase, therefore making it very difficult for the loans to be repaid. There are no strict income requirements to obtain this type of loan.

When must the homeowner pay back a reverse mortgage?

The homeowner must pay back a reverse mortgage when an owner sells the home, moves out of the home for 12 consecutive months, or fails to pay the property taxes or property insurance on the home.

What is an alternative strategy to using or obtaining a reverse mortgage?

Many retirees choose to downsize their lives and sell their principal residence in order to monetize their home equity, and subsequently pay cash using this equity to purchase a smaller home. This strategy contributes more to sustaining your wealth than pulling equity from the house in the form of a home equity or reverse mortgage.

CREDIT PROBLEMS

How do I rebuild my credit history after filing for bankruptcy?

In order to rebuild your credit history after a bankruptcy, try to establish a line of credit in small amounts, and pay off these amounts every month. Decide never to spend more on your credit cards than you can afford to pay off entirely each month. If your issue was overspending, learn how to create and live within a budget. If your issue was large medical expenses for you and/or your family, consider getting a job that offers more affordable or subsidized medical insurance at better rates. If your issue is not having adequate savings to survive economic downturns, work hard to save six months to one year of expenses, and do not touch these savings, no matter what happens.

What is the best order of priority to pay off credit card debt?

You should make a list of all your credit card debts, and determine the interest rate on each of these obligations and each monthly payment. Give highest priority to the credit card debt that carries the highest interest rate and highest monthly payment. Give higher priority to debts with no tax advantages, such as credit cards, than to debts such as mortgages, as there are tax advantages to having the mortgage.

How many U.S. households have credit cards?

There are 54 million households with credit cards in the United States today.

How much credit card debt exists in the United States?

Roughly $866 billion in credit card debt in the United States exists today.

What is the average amount of credit card debt for U.S. card holders?

The average card holder has $15,788 in credit card debt. This could be debt related to anything from everyday purchases of food and gas to clothes, large household items such as TVs or washing machines, to monthly utility bills.

What percentage of card holders are more than 60 days delinquent on their credit cards?

Nearly 4.27% of all card holders are more than 60 days past due on their credit card payments.

What is the difference between a debit card and a credit card?

A credit card allows you to borrow money from a card issuer in exchange for paying the provider of the goods or service in full. You must pay off the balance of the purchase in full, plus any interest or fees charged during the statement balance period. A debit card deducts money immediately from an account (usually a checking or savings account at a bank), and there-

About 54 million households in the United States have credit cards, and the average person has 3 to 4 cards.

fore incurs no interest payments. The bank then sends you a monthly statement that shows all transactions cleared for the month on the debit card.

BUDGETING

What does "living within your means" mean?

Living within your means is defined as the amount of income you take in, less your taxes, is the same as the amount of money you need in order to live.

What does the phrase "living beneath your means" mean?

Living beneath your means is defined as the amount of income that you take in, less your taxes, is less than the amount of money you need to live.

Why is budgeting so important to create wealth and financial success?

If you are good at managing your expenses—spending less than what you bring in—you will find money left over each month, which can be directed to savings or investing. Living beneath your means is one of the most important keys to financial success.

What must I do in order to live beneath my means?

The answer to this is found within your attitudes about money and material goods, and your ability to postpone or do without certain items now, in expectation of getting some future payback as a result of your frugality. For example, you must decide that having a stress-free financial life—by driving a paid-for, ten-year-old car—actually feels better than the stress created by having to pay off a $20,000 loan to finance a brand new car.

Why create an expense budget?

You can create an expense budget so you may attain or reach some financial goal in the future, whether to save a certain amount of money for a future purchase, such as a house down payment, educational expense, a vacation, or a large appliance, or to pay down debt.

How important is it to have a goal in mind when I decide to create an expense budget?

It is very important to have a goal in mind when you create an expense budget. Visualizing the goal makes it much easier to check your progress toward that goal, and measure your progress, whether positive or negative. Having the end prize in mind—whether an amount, or an actual physical item you would like to purchase—makes the goal more tangible and, in the end, more easily attainable.

What is a "budget"?

A budget is the established limit of the amount of expected expenses during a defined future period.

Setting up a family budget is an important step in keeping expenses under control and staying out of debt.

What is "zero-based" budgeting?

Zero-based budgeting is a method by which one accounts for the spending of every dollar of income from all sources. If any one category must be revised upward, another must be revised downward so the effect is zero on the total amount that is spent during the budgeting period. This way, your expenses can never exceed your income, if you stick to your budget.

What are some steps in using a budget?

The steps in using a budget are Goal Setting, Budgeting, Analysis, Monitoring Actual Expenses, Improving the Budget, and Adjusting Behavior.

What are some typical family budget categories?

Food (groceries, restaurants); Housing (mortgage/rent, property taxes, insurance, utilities, repairs); Clothing; Transportation (public, fuel, insurance, lease payments, car loan, rental); Health Care (including insurance premiums, co-pays, deductibles, prescriptions); Entertainment; Personal Care; Education; Communications (land line, cell phone, Internet, cable); Computers/Technology; Income Taxes; Pensions/401(k); After-Tax Investments/Savings; Charity; Life Insurance; Lawn Care; Credit Card Debt; Other Loan Payments; Hair/Salon; and Travel.

SETTING YOUR INVESTING GOALS

What are some steps to establishing the right goals for investing?

At the onset, you should be able to articulate the reason why you are investing in the first place. The reason for this is that by illuminating each reason, you can see why you are investing, and each activity's time horizon. Perhaps your goal is retirement savings, so that you accumulate enough capital to fund your living expenses during your retirement years. Depending on your age at the time you invest, this goal could be long term. Perhaps you wish to invest your money to fund educational expenses that you may need in a few years. This reason to invest may have a short- or medium-term time horizon, and would require different strategies and risks. It is good to have a clear expectation in terms of what returns you would like to see, perhaps on an annual basis. You must decide what percent return you wish to obtain, and what you are willing to lose during this term. As in all complex projects, it is good to divide your goals into attainable subgoals. You should begin investing in choices that you understand, and that match your competency. You also need to have a clear understanding as to how much time you should spend managing your investing activity, as some investment choices may require you to spend more time researching, reading, and deciding than others.

What is another important step in setting my financial goals?

You should understand that to be successful at investing, you must have a clear picture of where you are today, a snapshot of your financial picture. This analysis is not difficult to perform, but it does require some time. If you know where you are today, then you have a value with which to compare your investing strategies and to measure how they contribute or detract from your goals and objectives.

Why should I invest regularly?

Investing regularly teaches you the discipline and commitment necessary to achieve your financial goals. It also directs money that may have been used for unnecessary expenses into investments that help you achieve your long-term financial goals.

How do I create a goal?

You may create a goal around nearly anything that you can imagine. It is very important that you focus on attainable goals that are easily manageable.

Must I have personal financial software in order to be successful at managing my financial goals?

No. Your money can easily be managed on anything from the back of a napkin to an Excel spreadsheet. What you must focus on is to adopting behaviors that will allow you to begin to accumulate wealth, keep your spending in check, and be sensitive to your financial goals. Software merely helps you keep track of most of your sources of spend-

> ### What do I do if my investing goals conflict?
>
> Sometimes investing goals conflict. You may want to save to purchase a house, and simultaneously save to help fund your children's education. You will always have choices, and it is a personal decision to fund one choice over another. But one thing is certain: If you cut expenses and increase your income, you will be better able to fund more goals than if you do not.

ing and saving in one place, and imports data automatically from your banks and investment accounts, saving you time that would be spent doing everything on paper.

Why should my goals be easily manageable?

As you make these life changes, you will want to see results and reward yourself many times, in order to reinforce the changes in behavior and attitudes that financial success requires.

What are some examples of financial goals?

Some financial goals might be: reduce debt by 20%; save 10% of what I earn; save $20,000 to pay for a house down payment, reduce my credit card debt to $1,000.00, save $10,000 per year for my children's education; and reduce my heating expenses by 25%.

What are some basic steps that I can design in order to attain my personal financial goals?

There are several steps we all should take in order to be successful at creating and reaching our financial goals. We should begin by thinking of and assessing our attitudes toward money, and focus on what thoughts or attitudes seem to be blocking our ability to attain our financial goals. Many of these concepts started at an early age, by observing how our parents and other significant players in our lives dealt with financial issues. All the beliefs and attitudes about money that are blocking us can easily be changed. We should begin to read and learn about personal finance by using information that is available to us, such as by searching the Internet, reading magazines on personal finance, paying attention to the business and financial section of the newspaper, and watching personal financial shows on TV and online.

It may seem a bit intimidating at first, but after a while, the information begins to make sense. You begin to see how small economic changes affect variables such as today's stock price, but not next year's stock price. You begin to see which economic variables affect each other, why the price of oil is so critical to the economy, or the effect of the interest rate in a capital such as Tokyo or London. You should assess your financial picture and have a truthful and open view of where you are in terms of your income and expenses. You should seize every opportunity to improve your income. You should look at your expenses and discover the overages. You should see if you have at least six months

51

of emergency funds set aside—in case of a job change or other life event—so that you can easily ride through it. And you must consider paying yourself a certain percentage of your income each pay period first, never touching these funds unless they are to support some financial goal, such as education, retirement, etc. You should design attainable short- and long-term goals. This allows you to build confidence that you can attain a goal before moving on to the next. It allows you to visualize a long-term goal, and not let your current desire to buy some new thing get in the way of attaining that goal.

Once you have your goals in mind, it is time to execute your strategies to attain your goals. By this point, you have some ideas or strategies in place that help you reach your short-term and long-term goals. You may decide to begin taking money from your paycheck and direct it to a retirement fund. You may decide to sell the leased car, buy a cheaper used car, and begin saving the monthly payment. Suddenly, after 12 months, you find you have an additional $2,400 available to invest. Your personal finance journey also involves learning how to analyze your performance, and how well you meet your short- and long-term goals. Should you sell the investments that are doing poorly in the short term? Do you have too much money tied up in real estate? Should you now move from keeping cash to investing in mutual funds?

It is important to look at the performance of our portfolio in order to make sure it is helping you meet your goals, or make the necessary changes. Finally, personal finance teaches you to have the flexibility to occasionally readjust your goals and strategies, and to make adjustments in both your spending habits and savings habits, depending on what events life throws at you. You learn how to make the right choices at the right times, and see opportunity to improve your methods and strategies as you reach different stages in your life.

How does having and maintaining an expense budget help attain my financial goals?

Having and maintaining an expense budget provides you with a map of your current and future expenses, and is a great guide that describes in detail where you are headed financially. An expense budget allows you to make changes in each item or category within your budget, in order for you to redirect that money to attain a goal.

How do I begin to set my investment goals?

Many experts agree that you must first establish how much risk you are willing to

Make your plans as far in advance as possible, and take small, incremental steps to reach larger, long-range financial goals.

take, since different portions of your total investment will have different risks and different potential returns. If you are averse to risk, you cannot expect to have investments that earn double-digit returns, since those types of investments tend to have more risk associated with them.

Why is attaining great financial goals easier than we think?

Great financial goals are actually a series of small financial goals. If you make saving and investing and the general management of your money a priority over a long period of time, each of your financial goals is attained. If you do anything in small incremental steps, larger goals are attained over time. And because the changes can be small steps, it is actually very easy to attain large financial goals.

What are some further steps we must take in order to establish investment goals?

Expert investment managers assert that we need to decide several important subgoals in order to establish our investment goals. These subgoals may include the ultimate use for the money, the time horizon for when the money will be needed, the amount of money needed, how much money we have already saved, what types of investments might help us achieve our goals, and the current performance of all types of our investments.

How much time is considered to be short-term, near-term, and long-term?

It is generally accepted that short-term goals may require one to two years, near-term goals may require five to seven years, and long-term goals may require 10 or more years.

What types of goals should I consider before I begin to invest?

You should consider your goals for the use of your investments, in terms of short-term, near- or medium-term, and long-term. Within short-term goals, you might include such items as travel, large consumer purchases, marriage, or health care-related expenses, and perhaps even current income. Within the near- or medium-term category could be such goals as capital for a home purchase, repairs/renovations on a principal residence, creating a business, or acquiring a second home/rental property. Long-term goals could be such items as funding higher education, retirement income, or passing wealth to heirs. It is important to note that your goals may change, especially short-term goals, as your ideas and outlook changes, so you need to be flexible in establishing goals.

Even before I establish goals, what are some things that experts believe help prepare me financially for successful investing?

Experts believe that well before you begin to invest, it is prudent for you to reduce as much as you can any credit card or debt interest and finance charges you pay every month, as these payments ultimately will suppress your investment earnings. You should also have a cash emergency fund set aside that may cover three to six months of living expenses. To

53

establish this, all you must do is identify your expenses for the past few months, and begin to find ways to save this amount to be used in case of any emergencies.

What are some other keys that may assist me in establishing investment goals?

Investing editors at *U.S. News & World Report* assert that in order to properly establish investing goals, you need to decide what to expect in terms of returns on your investments, set achievable goals in terms of how much you are willing to invest, determine how frequently you are going to invest, and always purchase investments you know and understand.

Even if you only started with small, piggy-bank-type savings, that regular investment can grow surprisingly large if you begin saving when you're in your early 20s.

What is an important consideration when I think about investing for my retirement?

When you think about establishing goals in order to fund your retirement years, it is important to consider when to begin investing. You may obtain a completely different result if you begin investing for retirement in your twenties rather than beginning to invest in your forties or fifties.

How does creating specific investment goals help me achieve my overall goals?

When you have a specific goal in mind, the goal provides you needed direction, so that you may focus your attention and behaviors toward attaining this goal. A goal may help motivate you to make necessary changes so that you may attain it. Goal-setting forces you to take responsibility for your ultimate financial situation, and with this stronger feeling of ownership of your goal, you will feel successful when you achieve it.

INVESTING VERSUS SPECULATION

What is the difference between "investing" and "speculating"?

The difference between investing and speculating can be a complex topic. Its origins go back many years, perhaps to the 1920s, when economists and writers tried to illuminate the distinctions between the two concepts. At this time, the only vehicle considered by many to be an investment was bonds, because they provided a steady return, and you could retrieve your principal. When an asset or a share in an asset is acquired with the hope that the investor will receive a profit from the revenue generated by that investment, in addition to retrieving one's principal, this is characterized by many as investing. Speculation is defined by many as when someone buys a share of an asset (believing its market value may rise), holds it for some period of time, and sells it to someone else at a higher value.

How do I make decisions to buy or sell if I am investing or speculating?

When you are investing, according to author Ben Graham, you decide to enter or exit a position based upon the underlying economics or analysis of that asset. When you are speculating, you decide to enter or exit a position based in large part on your belief regarding the near-term movement of the value of the asset.

How does *Forbes* characterize the difference between investing and speculation?

In a 2012 article summarizing a book by Jack Bogle, the founder of Vanguard Mutual Funds, the author states there is "harm done when a culture of short-term speculation focused on the price of a stock overwhelms a culture of long-term investment focused on the intrinsic value of a corporation."

What is the problem with speculating?

When you speculate, you make an investment or buy a stock strictly because you think its price will increase over a relatively short period of time, because of an observed trend or widely held belief. When you invest, you use your fundamental analysis of the inherent value of the asset, believing it will appreciate over time, providing you with a return and the ability to get your principal back at a later date.

RISK/REWARD

What is a "risk/reward ratio"?

A risk/reward ratio is defined by many as a comparison of the expected returns of an investment versus the amount that an investor could lose with the same investment. It is generally thought that the more return one expects to make, the higher the investment's risk.

How do I calculate a risk/reward ratio?

You may calculate a risk/reward ratio by first deciding the highest price at which you are willing to sell, as well as the lowest price at which you are willing to tolerate, and then deciding how much of your investment you are willing to lose. You divide your net profit, which is the reward (after fees and commissions) by the price of your maximum risk. Through the use of stop-loss orders, you can sell at or near your target prices.

What are some limiting factors in using risk/reward ratios?

Most experts agree that use of risk/reward ratios is limited, as they do not take into consideration the probability of attaining a certain target or goal, or the probability of a certain downside risk. But through careful research, you may see the potential high and low. The model also does not take into consideration time or the occurrence of a macro-economic event that may, in the short term, radically change the price of your investment, thus affecting our reward. So use risk/reward ratios as only one tool when making investment selections.

What is the progression of risk, from low to high, among different classes of investments?

Normally, each type or class of investment carries its own reward and risk associated with the investment that may be plotted on a graph. Moving from low potential return/low risk to high potential return/high risk, there are short-term government debts (from financially secure sovereign nations); mid- to long-term government debts, short-term loans to the highest rated blue chip corporations; real property that is purchased and then rented or leased; high-yield debt to less stable governments and lower-rated corporations (junk bonds); equities (including small, medium and large capitalized corporate equities); and options and futures contracts (wherein you leverage or borrow funds in order to purchase an investment).

What is the theoretical risk-free investment, and why is it so important?

The theoretical risk-free investment is the return that an investment may bring from an investment that carries no risk. The problem with this definition is that there are no truly "risk–free" investments. Even keeping cash under your bed is risky, as it could be lost or stolen. Also, inflation of prices over time—coupled with government monetary and fiscal policies that may change with different political regimes—may reduce the value of that cash under your bed. So risk-free investments exist only in theory, but are still highly important because they allow you to compare the risks of other investment choices.

Younger people can tolerate more risk in their investments because they are in it for the long haul.

Does my tolerance to risk depend on my age or stage in life?

It is commonly thought that younger people should be more tolerant of risk, for a few good reasons. When you are younger, you may have the opportunity to earn and keep earning money to replenish any losses you may incur. You also have a much longer time horizon in which to offset your losses with gains, should you make an improper investment decision. People nearing retirement may need access to their portfolios in order to provide daily income—and therefore would likely have less tolerance for risk—than someone in his twenties who has many decades of earnings and returns ahead of him.

What is "systematic risk"?

Systematic risk is the risk associated with broad events that affect the entire market or market sector that cannot be mitigated through diversification.

What is "unsystematic risk"?

Unsystematic risk is the risk associated with a particular industry or market sector that can be mitigated through having a diversified portfolio of stocks.

What is a "risk/return trade-off?"

A risk/return trade-off is the principle that the higher the level of uncertainty as to a potential return, the higher the reward. An investment with a relatively predictable low

57

level of uncertainty will have a lower return. This is why individual investors must clearly understand their personal tolerance for risk in order to make the right choices when investing in individual stocks.

How many individual stocks must I own to have enough diversification against unsystematic risk?

Although many experts disagree with assigning an exact number, a diversified portfolio of individual stocks should fall within a range of between 12 and 25 stocks. The answer may be quite complex, as it based upon your tolerance for risk. Investors who are quite risk-averse will seek more diversification, and hold more individual positions. In contrast, an investor with a high tolerance for risk may hold fewer individual positions.

How do professional investors feel about risk?

Many professional investors believe the mitigation of risk is probably as important as analyzing and making specific investments. Over time, investors are rewarded with higher returns in exchange for putting their money at higher risk. But many professional managers believe you can mitigate risk by buying and holding various assets over time, and selecting assets with minimal correlation, so that if any one asset decreases in value, others may increase in value or be unperturbed by the cause of the decline. By diversifying your portfolio with uncorrelated assets, you may be able to experience increases in the values of your portfolio without having to deal with sharp declines.

Why is risk a standard deviation?

As we compare how a potential investment performs against a benchmark, and how far this performance deviates from a norm, the risk can be expressed mathematically, indicating how precarious the investment may be. In other words, the further from the norm, the riskier the investment.

What types of risk exist?

Risks to our investments may be categorized as market risk, default risk, inflation risk, and mortality risk.

What is "market risk"?

Market risk is an investor's risk in incurring losses due to price movements. There are many types of market risks, as there are many different markets in which we can invest. Some of the most common risks include: Equity Risk (the risk that an individual stock, index, or mutual fund price or the volatility of that investment may change); Interest Rate Risk (the risk that interest rates, the price of money, or the volatility of these categories may change); Currency Risk (the risk that the price of a foreign currency relative to another currency, or the volatility of this price, may change); Commodity Risk (the risk that the price of a particular commodity a company uses, or the volatility of the price of this commodity, may change).

What is "default risk"?

Default risk, or credit risk, is the risk associated with investments in which the company cannot pay its debt obligation. Lenders and investors are always exposed to default risks. Our financial system is built in part on mitigating the effects of these risks by having lenders pay a higher return on a relatively riskier investment, and lower returns on a relatively safer investment. Risks to lenders include loss of principal and interest, disruption in expected cash flows for these payments, and costs borne by the lender in his attempt to collect the amount owed.

Why is "inflation risk" bad for my portfolio?

Inflation, the increase in prices over time, gradually erodes the value of your money. Since 1926, the gradual increase in prices has increased, on average, by approximately 3% per year. In some outlying years, the increase has been very high—approximately 13.5% in 1980, and averaging approximately 6% during the 1980s. This means that if you are planning for retirement soon, you may need much more saved and invested in order to have adequate income later on, as the value of your money may be less because of this inflationary price tendency.

What is "mortality risk"?

You will certainly die. It could happen during the next hour, day, or year, and insurance companies price their products accordingly, using actuarial calculations to factor the probability of the timing of your mortality. Regarding your pension or other post-retirement benefits, your mortality risk is generally accepted to be the risk of dying earlier than expected while you earn such benefits.

What is the opposite of mortality risk?

The opposite of mortality risk—and another important consideration when it comes to considering our retirement planning—is our longevity risk, the risk that we live longer, and therefore have more need for income, than expected.

Why is longevity risk sometimes considered a "silent" risk?

Most other risks have short- and medium-term consequences. With longevity risk, the risk that we may require much more income because our lives will last longer than planned, has a very long-term consequence, and is not very often considered by profes-

Americans are living to unprecedented ages in the 21st century, and that means it is best to plan for living into one's 90s or even 100s.

sional investors or individual investors trying adequately to plan for their retirement. Unexpected expenses—such as medical expenses and home care expenses—may also occur later in life, and may greatly decrease your available resources during retirement.

BETA

What is the "beta" of a stock or mutual fund?

The beta of a stock/mutual fund is the result of a mathematical equation that measures the volatility of that stock/mutual fund when compared against some benchmark, such as other stocks of similar qualities or, in the case of a mutual fund, a benchmark index. Beta measures how the price of a stock or mutual fund might react to changes in price of the benchmark. The benchmark and the investment vehicle may be highly correlated; if the benchmark price increases, so does the investment vehicle, and vice versa. Accordingly, an investment such as a mutual fund with a beta of 1.0 will have a price that will, more likely than not, move with the market. It is closely matched with its benchmark, but a mutual fund with a beta less than 1.0 will not move with the market. A mutual fund or stock with a beta of 1.2 will be about 20% more volatile than its benchmark.

Why do stocks and mutual funds have different betas?

Investments with betas less than zero will move in the opposite direction of the market. Investments with betas of 1.0 will move in the same direction as the market. Investments with betas of 1.0 may also be a major contributor to the benchmark itself. And investments with betas above 1.0 will be more volatile, and may be more affected by minute-by-minute news and market trading activity.

How is beta calculated?

Beta is calculated by analysts using statistical analysis techniques, and is often provided for you when you are analyzing different investment choices, such as individual stocks or mutual funds. Typically, beta is derived by analyzing how an investment choice's volatility compares to some broad index—in many cases, the S&P 500.

What is the relationship between beta and risk/rewards?

Beta relates to the risk and rewards that might be attained through entering into an investment because a specific investment that has a high beta (more volatility compared with some index) would imply a higher reward or return for the investment. That makes it rather easy to determine if the betas of various investment choices are worthy of further study if their rewards match the implicit volatility.

How do I use beta to analyze an investment choice?

You use beta calculations by first looking at the beta of a benchmark and the expected return of this market index. If the beta of the market as a whole is 1.0, and this broad index returns to investors 8% per year, an investment choice with a beta 50% greater (1.5), should provide a return of approximately 12% (since 12% is 50% greater than the 8% return of the broader index). If, through careful analysis, you do not see this investment choice providing this level of return, it is typically filtered from the list of possible investment choices.

How is beta analysis misused or misinterpreted?

The use of betas in analyzing possible investment choices may be misused or misinterpreted in a number of ways. Typically, high-tech investments may have high betas, yet may be good long-term investments. Utilities typically have lower betas by comparison, but offer very good returns in many investor portfolios. Beta also reviews the past, and past performance is not always an accurate indicator of future performance. Beta may not take into account current or upcoming changes to the company, or broader market shifts that may positively or negatively affect the earnings of a typical investment vehicle. Beta also does not necessarily take into consideration what happens when markets advance forward, whereby a company with a beta greater than 1.0 may outperform the market as a whole.

How can I use beta analysis to help in my investment selection?

Many experts assert that it is good to use beta analysis when you are engaged in short-term analysis, such as when you are planning to acquire/sell an investment vehicle within a short period of time. However, for longer-term investing, it is more prudent to use a variety of analytical tools to assist in filtering various investment choices.

CREATING WEALTH

What is "wealth"?

Wealth is the state of your abundance of assets in terms of marketable or saleable value, minus any liabilities owed, and is often examined in comparison to others in some reference group. Assets of value include cash, investments, home equity, and other valuables such as jewelry, art, and precious metals. The term "net worth" is also used in place of the term "wealth" when it comes to personal finance and investing.

How much must I accumulate in order to be considered wealthy?

According to experts at CNBC, citing a 2013 study by UBS Investor Watch wherein individual investors were asked "Are you wealthy?", the survey revealed that 60% of respondents who had more than $5 million in net worth described themselves as wealthy, while 28% of respondents with a net worth between $1 million and $5 million described themselves as wealthy.

How do respondents describe the state of being wealthy?

Fifty percent of the UBS survey respondents believed that being wealthy meant "having no financial constraints on activities," 16% believe it constituted "surpassing a certain asset threshold," and 10% believed it meant "not having to work again."

What percentage of American households lack an emergency fund with enough cash to cover three months of living expenses?

Financial experts at Time Inc. assert that roughly half of all American households do not have such an emergency fund.

You don't have to be worth $76 billion dollars like computer business magnate Bill Gates to be wealthy; a million or more should suffice.

How do I attract wealth in my life?

You have to look first at your attitudes toward money, and understand how these attitudes contribute to your financial situation today. By recognizing these attitudes, you can see which are helping you, and which are blocking your goals. You may have to change some of your beliefs about money and finances in order to begin to attract wealth. Your imagination is very important. In fact, your imagination drives your desire to buy items, since you have a mental picture of the new car or cell phone that you want, you see images of it in commercials, your friends talk about it, and then you buy it. It is a little more difficult to imagine a pile of money 20 years from now that you will use to pay for your kids' tuition. So you have to teach yourself how to envision personal financial goals, and actually visualize them. You have to give yourself permission to be wealthy, that it is not something reserved only for other people. By having a vision of how it feels to have wealth, it makes you more able to use behaviors and see opportunities that create wealth. Some people think of wealth like water, something that flows to you. If you begin to act as if you already have financial security and have the discipline to meet your goals, financial security and wealth will occur.

How important is the place where you live influencing your perception of wealth?

According to researchers at *The Wall Street Journal*, attitudes about being wealthy in a rural part of America may be far different from attitudes about being wealthy in Manhattan, perhaps because it requires much more income to live in Manhattan than in rural America.

Why do people spend down their savings?

People are comfortable with predictability, and have a hard time getting used to new situations. If they grew up in an environment where there was never enough, and suddenly have a lot, no matter how painful, people will spend their money down to the level with which they are most familiar and comfortable. If you never had more than $500 in your checking account, and suddenly receive a $1,000 bonus, people without financial goals will find a way to spend that $1,000 down to $500, because they are more familiar with having no more than $500 in their checking account. A person committed to attaining a financial goal will get the money, put it away safely, pretend it doesn't exist, and maintain his customary spending behavior. A goal-oriented person will change the way he views his checking account, and decide that having $1,500 is his new minimum balance. While the spender is spending the excess, the saver has changed his view of what should be in his checking account to a minimum of $10,000, and is setting aside this extra income to reach that new goal.

So wealth creation is really about my thoughts?

Yes, it doesn't really matter what your background is, if you decide that it actually feels better to be independent and living debt free, you will begin to take the proper steps to make this happen. You will resist the urges to spend, in favor of a longer-term goal. If you tell yourself that it is OK to have $500 in your account, you will take steps to make this happen. If you tell yourself that it is OK to have $100,000 in your account, you will also take steps to make that happen as well.

Where do the highest and lowest number of high net worth individuals live?

According to the IRS, the states where the highest number of people with a net worth greater than $2 million live are California, New York, and Florida. The states with the lowest number of people with a net worth greater than $2 million live are Alaska, North Dakota, and Vermont.

INDIVIDUAL STOCKS

INDIVIDUAL STOCKS: THE BASICS

What are "stocks"?

Stocks are a way to own the assets and earnings of a company. Companies that offer the opportunity for investors to own their stock place a value on the shares or pieces of the company based upon the value of all the assets of the company and the value of its past, current, and future earnings. A stock can be traded (purchased or sold).

How do companies use the proceeds of a stock issue?

A stock may also be created, and then marketed and sold, when a company wishes to raise capital or cash to help fuel its business development, to pay off loans and other debt, and perhaps to buy back shares from other investors at attractive prices. A company's stock is originally valued when the company first begins, based upon its capital or cash and other initial assets.

What is a "stock market"?

It is a place—whether a physical building or an online virtual environment—where stocks are bought and sold. Stock markets or exchanges, as they are also known, can trade stocks, bonds, and derivatives of stocks and bonds, along with many other financial instruments.

Which stock market opens first?

As the day begins in each part of the world, there is a flow of stock trading. The first of the major markets in the world to open are those in the countries nearest the International Date Line. New Zealand's market opens first, followed by Sydney (Australia),

Tokyo, Hong Kong, Singapore, China, Mumbai (India), and Moscow. Europe then follows, with Switzerland, France, Germany's Frankfurt Exchange, and London, England. Then the North American markets open, in Toronto, New York, and finally Chicago.

Does the stock market ever close?

Because there are stock markets in many parts of the world, investors may trade 24 hours a day.

What are the largest stock markets in the world?

By far the largest stock market is the New York Stock Exchange, which trades $30 trillion worth of stock, followed by National Association of Securities Dealers Automated Quotations (NASDAQ) in New York ($15 trillion); London, England ($10 trillion); the Tokyo [Japan] Stock Exchange ($6.4 trillion); Euronext [Belgium, France, Holland, and Portugal] ($5.6 trillion); Frankfurt, Germany ($4.3 trillion); and Shanghai, China ($4.1 trillion).

How many countries have stock markets?

Stock markets are found in 77 countries around the world.

The New York Stock Exchange building in New York was constructed in 1903.

What are some of the pitfalls of buying individual stocks?

Although buying individual stocks can be economically rewarding, many experts believe that for the individual investor there can be many factors that detract from whatever benefit we might enjoy. Acquiring individual stocks requires a great deal of time to do research to decide the safety of the stock. To have a diverse portfolio, you must have many individual stocks, and each needs to be researched and followed. It may take more time to do so than you have.

What types of risks could I see if I own individual stocks?

Inherent to individual stock ownership is the concept of various types of risks that must be understood prior to acquiring individual stocks. Broad economic risk may occur and temporarily or permanently depress a stock's price after you purchase it. Economic risk could be the effects on the economy and the stock investing community's perception from such events as high unemployment, lower than expected exports, a drop in consumer purchases or confidence, an abrupt devaluation of a currency, or an unexpected increase in interest rates, among many others. Industry- or market-specific risks may also negatively affect the price of an individual stock, as perhaps a game-changing introduction of a new technology, or availability of cash for consumer credit, may negatively affect a stock's price.

A change in government policies (political risk) may also cause a stock's price to be depressed (for example, if the government decides to levy a tax or duty on the sale of a particular product). This may have both short- and long-term consequences. Materials and other input risks may influence the price of a stock, if the materials represent a rather notable component to the underlying product the company creates and sells. (Inputs are things used to make products, especially commodities like steel, copper, and petroleum.)

As prices for such inputs increase, profits of the company may fall. If profits fall, influencing the stock price, the value of the shares may fall. Technology risks may occur, and may have an immediate or delayed effect on the stock price. An example could well be the effect of the usage and proliferation of the Internet, and the effect this has had on industries such as the video rental market, music industry, and book publishing industry. How the target stock's competitors develop and innovate may also affect the price of a stock, as a competitor may develop and apply a manufacturing or logistical methodology that makes it far more competitive, and therefore relatively more valuable to the market, perhaps affecting the price of stock.

Giant lawsuits may present legal risks, especially in such industries as finance, health, pharmaceuticals, and chemicals. An unforeseen lawsuit settlement may cause a company to file for bankruptcy protection, which would have an immediate effect on its share price. If a competitor to the target company attracts more competent management, or if the management of the target company is engaged in illegitimate activities, and less than competent management practices, these factors may also greatly influence the value of a stock.

What other risks are inherent to individual stock or mutual fund investing?

Many experts believe the most apparent risk of investing in an individual stock or mutual fund is market risk. Market risk occurs when the market in general does not move in the "right" direction. When this happens, there is a tendency for the majority of stocks—regardless how good—to follow in the same direction. This means that whether or not the investment is sound, with great potential, a short or long market dip will tend to move even the best of stocks down. Sector risk is similar; even if you invest in a winning sector, if the market in general declines, it may affect this sector as well. Some sectors may move less or more, given a variety of variables that influence that particular sector. Even if you pick the right stock and sector, an unexpected event that affects the stock price, value, or demand for the stock may occur, and this may negatively affect your returns.

Why is information overload a huge risk factor when I invest in individual stocks?

In hopes of generating more viewers and readers, media companies must create stories to keep their consumers interested. With the proliferation of Internet usage by the individual investor, the once secretive investment community may in fact use and have access to much of the same information that individuals use. Financial stories abound in today's world, and the less-than-savvy investor may become overwhelmed or panic upon the release of any news story. Many people in the investment community believe the global financial news has a degree of homogeneity, in which all media sources report on approximately the same stories, making individual investors who follow such news outlets and networks unnecessarily anxious, even when the story may have little impact on the stock's long-term price . The unprofessional investor may be unable to distinguish the difference between a meaningless piece of information and one that may affect a stock's price.

What are some common mistakes investors make when thinking of buying stocks?

Some common mistakes may include buying at a high price and being averse to suffering a loss, therefore holding the stock too long; putting too much weight in past historical information to guide him in making an investment decision; an inability to distinguish between many investment choices; and insensitivity to brokerage and management fees associated with trading individual stocks. Some experts also note the failure on the part of the individual investor to understand how difficult it is to "beat the market," to do better than the returns of an underlying stock exchange, or to outperform a broad array of stocks such as an index.

Why do some experts believe the individual investor should avoid investing in individual stocks and mutual funds, and should rather invest in indexes such as the S&P 500?

In a recent article, *Forbes* cited a few studies that support the argument that we should avoid investing in individual stocks. In a study published by Dalbar, Inc. in 2003, researchers found that in looking at average annual returns from 1984 to 2002, the annual average return of the S&P 500 was 12.2%, while mutual fund managers achieved a 9.3% return during the same period. The article also cited an annual report issued by Standard & Poor's, the S&P Indices Versus Active Funds Scorecard, finding that by mid-2012, 89.8% of all managed domestic (U.S.) funds failed to beat the performance of the benchmark S&P 500 Index. Furthermore, the scorecard reported that in 2009–2012, 73.2% of managers underperformed the Index, and in 2007–2012, 67.7% underperformed the Index.

What about the success of high-performing stocks?

The experts at *Forbes* also cite a study by Longboard Asset Management that analyzed 3,000 individual stocks from 1983 to 2007. Their findings showed that 39% of these stocks were unprofitable, that 19% lost 75% or more of their value, 64% underperformed the market, and that just 25% of the stocks were responsible for the great gains in the stock market during the period analyzed.

What are some important points to know when I invest in stocks?

According to experts at *CNN/Money*, you need to understand several important points when you begin to invest in stocks. A stock represents your ownership in a company, and also represents your ownership of assets, liabilities, and current and future earnings or profits of the company (and the perception of the possibilities of hitting these earnings targets). The stock market is a very diverse marketplace consisting of many entities that can be arranged and understood by several attributes, including the size of the com-

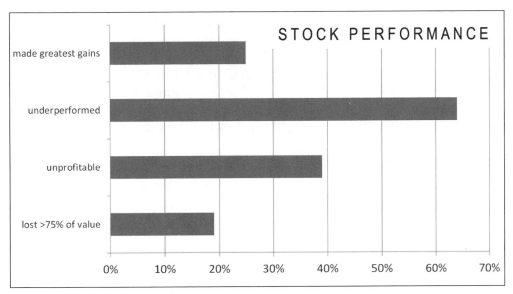

From 1983 to 2007 only 25% of stocks were responsible for most of the growth in the market, while the majority either underperformed or were unprofitable.

pany (measured by market capitalization), the sector in which it competes, and its type of growth pattern based upon historical performance, among many others.

The price of a stock at any given moment depends on a wide variety of factors, including earnings, especially for the long-term investor. It may also be influenced by the sentiment of its buyers and sellers, fear created by information about the company and its competitors, and macroeconomic news that may have an effect on the company's performance. According to the same experts, since the 1940s, stocks (as compared against bonds, cash, real estate, and other savings choices) provide for nearly a 10% return over the long term, better than most other investment choices. It is important to note that the performance of any one individual stock does not represent the overall performance of the market. A great individual stock may beat an index over time, but may also decline even when the market in general is booming.

Because of the dynamic nature of businesses and the marketplace, it is difficult to use a stock's historical performance to gauge whether or not its value will continue to grow; even great companies run into unexpected problems. These unexpected occurrences may influence a stock's price and value. Diversification of a portfolio seems to mitigate many risks. Furthermore, you should not judge a stock simply by looking at its price or the relative price in its sector or industry, because there are many fundamental factors that may contribute to a stock's underlying price. For the long-term investor, it is better to buy and hold great stocks than to generate many short-term trades for a variety of expense-related reasons, such as short-term capital gains taxes, commissions on trades, and exposure to many market risks.

Can I pay too much for stocks?

Yes. Like anything you buy, if you are first in line to buy a stock, you may get a very good deal, because the company may have anticipated less demand for the stock than there really is. So if there is great demand for a stock, the price of the stock may increase quickly—in a few minutes, or even seconds, from the initial offering price, until all the stock's buyers and sellers have been satisfied during the trading day. If you arrive at the sale late, the price could be many percentage points higher than in the morning, and you may end up paying more than the person who bought the stock first thing in the morning.

What is an "initial public offering" (IPO)?

An initial public offering occurs when a company wishes to offer its stock shares to the public, hoping to raise capital for the first time.

Why should I care about IPOs?

An IPO can give you the opportunity to invest in a company at an early stage in its development. Individual investors may be able to purchase those shares that large institutional investors haven't purchased, giving you the opportunity to profit from the sale of the shares.

How many initial public offerings occur in a year?

In the 1990s, because of the onset of the Internet era, an average of 193 IPOs occurred per year. After the economic crashes in the 2000s, IPO activity fell to an average of 48 per year.

How large is the IPO market at the NYSE?

The NYSE/Euronext raised more proceeds for the initial public offerings of stock than any other exchange in the world. In 2008 alone, the NYSE raised $45 billion in IPO proceeds, approximately 21% of the total IPO capital raised throughout the world. The next largest market for IPOs, Hong Kong, raised $12 billion.

On average, how long has a company been in business before it issues shares for the first time to the public?

On average, most companies have been around seven to eight years before they "go public." At this time, after the IPO is made, the original investors in the company may be paid back money for their initial investment.

SELECTING INDIVIDUAL STOCKS

What are some decisions an individual investor must make before investing in a particular stock?

Many experts believe you need to make certain decisions before you begin to invest in a particular stock. Some of these decisions may include: the point or price at which you will buy and sell the equity, how long you plan to hold the equity, and at what price increase or decrease you are willing to sell the equity.

How do I begin to select individual stocks?

Many experts agree there is no perfect method for individual stock selection; the choice of what procedure to follow depends upon each individual investor. Most experts agree that at the very beginning of developing your stock portfolio, you should engage in intensive research. In the research phase, you may identify themes, markets, segments, industries, or brands on which to focus. This may be followed by an analysis of such fundamental variables as the potential target's size, debt load, P/E ratio, competitive threats, and earnings potential. Some experts will even test to see how the stock price moves upon the release of news, or how the stock price reacts to certain events that may occur during the course of a year or other historical period. Other investors who seek growth in a stock's price from the date of purchase may look at the company's asset value to see if there is hidden value the market seems to have missed. Many experts assert the importance of knowing at what price to acquire a stock, since if you acquire the equity at a relatively high price, it may take a much longer time to realize your goal for the expected rate of return on the investment.

What are some other considerations when I try to identify individual equity target companies?

There are many different considerations when investors try to distinguish winning stocks from potential problem stocks. Some experts who seek undervalued companies understand that the value of a company may be quite different in the future than it is today. A company may have a short-term management problem that may be solved next month. Meanwhile, the broad investor market may have already abandoned the company, thereby depressing its price. Value investors look very specifically at companies that appear undervalued to try to see if they have the ability to correct themselves over time. Other experts look closely at companies' and their competitors' debt to measure the strength of the target company's financial position. A company that is ready and able to clear away debt may be viewed more favorably than a company that cannot seem to get out of debt. Debt can depress a company's earnings, and can also cause a company eventually to fold and declare bankruptcy.

Why do some people prefer to buy individual stocks, instead of purchasing an index fund or a mutual fund?

There are several reasons why some individual investors prefer to choose and invest in individual stocks, rather than invest their money into index funds or mutual funds.

Some people might want to invest in companies that they consider to be socially or environmentally responsible, such as a clean energy business.

Some experts believe that when you buy an index or mutual fund, you may get many lower-performing stocks along with many top-performing stocks. Even if the top performers do very well, their performance is pulled down by the poorer-performing stocks. Although diversifying one's portfolio may be a great strategy over the long term, some individual investors believe in specializing in a sector, as they can become more familiar with and learn the dynamics of the sector, and earn a profit. The investor who researches and acquires individual stocks also has a strong interest in the stock market, and is willing to spend the time to do so. Individual investors who cannot be bothered with spending the time to identify, analyze, and invest in individual stocks would probably be better served by buying index or mutual funds. Other experts assert that some individual investors perceive an investment in an index or mutual fund is in some way "safer" than owning a portfolio of individual stocks. If you own an index fund, and the underlying index or market falls—no matter how diversified the index may be—the value of the portfolio will decline, in the same way it would if there were a broad decline in some of your individual stocks. Many experts believe that simply owning an index or mutual fund is no guarantee against losses.

How do I buy individual stocks?

You can buy individual stocks through a stockbroker, a stock brokerage firm, certain banks that offer stock investments, online brokerage firms, and directly from some companies that offer stocks directly to consumers.

What are some general factors that might be interesting to use while I evaluate a stock?

Some general factors might be interesting to use while you evaluate a stock, including: whether it is a company you know and understand; is in an industry that you understand; has a stable management team; is diverse geographically (not concentrated in any region or country); and is a great place to work.

What are some macroeconomic factors that might influence the growth of a stock's price?

Many macroeconomic factors might influence the growth of a stock's price. Economic trends that might affect a stock's price help place the stock in the context of aspects of the economy that may suppress or grow the company's earnings. The company could be dependent on oil prices, employment rates, currency values, prices of commodities, etc.

What types of financial signs should I investigate?

Investors need to look for various financial signs that signify a buying opportunity. Many experts believe that investors should 1) find companies with strong quarterly earnings growth over a long time period; 2) consider the size of the company's debt load (especially relative to other competitors); 3) consider the diversity or concentration of the company's income streams; 4) consider the company's annual sales growth over time; 5) identify the company's ability to make great products year-in and year-out; 6) determine the company's ability to control expenses; and 7) determine whether the company uses capital wisely. You may also want to investigate if the company spends money appropriately on other cash-intensive items, such as people, equipment, marketing, research and development, etc.

What about the analysis of the stock itself?

It is good to see if the company's stock price is outperforming its peers, whether the price of the stock is too high or too low, and the reasons why. You may also want to know if any single individual or entity owns a large percentage of the stock, which could influence its price. It is also good to know if the company regularly pays a dividend to its shareholders.

What is "preferred stock"?

Preferred stock is stock or equities issued by a company that combines some qualities of common stock with some qualities of a bond. When you own preferred stock in a company, it is considered preferred because under normal circumstances, the shareholder is paid a dividend on the shares before all other classes of stock issued by the company. In the event of the company's bankruptcy or liquidation, preferred shareholders receive their share of assets before common stockholders (but behind bondholders). The terms of the preferred shares in which you may invest are found in the prospectus of the investment offering, and in the company's articles of association. Preferred stock is also rated by many ratings agencies (e.g., Moody's). Preferred stock may be either cumulative (the company must pay a stated dividend in arrears, if it misses that payment) or non-cumulative (the company does not have to pay a missed stated dividend payment in arrears). Each class of preferred stock in a company confers upon the owner certain rights, as each class or issuance of preferred stock may have different terms. Convertible preferred stock allows you to convert the preferred stock to shares of common stock. Investors in preferred stock generally do not experience the great variations in price that common stockholders experience, so long as the company is paying its stated dividends to the preferred shareholders regularly.

What is "behavioral economics"?

Behavioral economics, or behavioral finance, is a relatively new science that tries to help you understand why people make often irrational financial decisions, based upon their own perceptions and biases. For example, if the consumers of a product or stock investment perceive the supply is somehow diminishing, they may be more prone to purchase it now, rather than waiting for a better, more rational time during which to purchase.

Using principles of behavioral economics, how do men and women differ when it comes to investing?

After concluding a study of the investing behavior of men compared with women, experts from the University of California found that single women investors outperformed single men investors by a 2.3% average return. When it comes to investment groups, female-based investment groups outperformed male-based investment groups by 4.6%. The experts assert that the reasons behind this are that men traded 45% more often than women, generally making poor decisions, and holding on to a position too long because of ego and a constant comparison to other investor friends, as opposed to rationally selling laggards and retaining winners.

How do I purchase a company's shares directly from the company, rather than using a broker?

In order to avoid paying transaction fees, many individual investors purchase stocks directly from companies, rather than going through a broker and paying commissions on

Studies have shown that female investors have outperformed their male counterparts because they tend to trade less often and make better, less ego-driven decisions.

the purchase and sale of the stock, which may amount to several percent of the value of the trade. In this case, individual investors may buy shares directly from some companies by identifying the target company's stock transfer agent, discovering if the company offers shares directly to individual investors, and opening an account on the transfer agent's website. The company may require a minimum investment.

What are some important stock market indexes that I should consider when I am investing, and why?

There are many key markets and indexes upon which investors may focus when measuring investing success. Each composite market and its underlying index has its own character, created in part by the types of stocks that are listed, as well as historical factors. Companies that are listed on various exchanges may change, and the market on which they are traded may also change. Some important indexes are the NASDAQ Composite Index (many key technology-based stocks), Standard and Poor's 500 Index (includes blue chip stocks and key stocks on different exchanges), and the Russell 2000 Index (small capitalization company stocks often valued below $1 billion).

What are the New York Stock Exchange's "circuit breaker" rules?

Circuit breaker rules limit steep, unexpected declines in stock prices, as they are being traded, to prevent market price collapse, and to offer some protections to both buyers and sellers. The circuit breakers comprise three levels: Level 1 (a 7% decline between 9:30 A.M. and 3:25 P.M.), Level 2 (a 13% decline between 9:30 A.M. and 3:25 P.M.), and Level 3 (a 20% decline at any time during the trading day). When the NYSE reaches the Level 1 or Level 2 threshold, the NYSE pauses trading for 15 minutes. When the NYSE reaches its Level 3 threshold, all trading activity is halted for the remainder of the trading day. The circuit breaker rules also mandate that each level can only be reached once per day. So if the markets decline by 7%, and after a 15-minute pause, decline by another 7%, trading continues until the next level is reached, and that rule will be used once. If prices slide and the 20% decline level is reached, then trading is suspended until the next trading day. The rules are meant to prevent bottomless declines in stock market prices or severe crashes.

What are "growth stocks"?

Growth stocks have had—and may continue to have—good track records for growing revenues, profits, and market share, even as larger economic forces may depress the performance of other similar companies. For example, many experts believe these types of stocks may include great companies in industries such as health care and food as people need to eat and receive medical care despite any current economic conditions.

What are "cyclical stocks"?

Cyclical stocks typically signal the recovery of a period of economic decline, as they tend to begin to grow early as a recovery is under way. Experts like to include companies

> ## How much change must occur in a stock market in order to call it a correction?
>
> **A** stock market correction occurs upon a 10% decline from a high observed on a major exchange or composite stock average.

within certain industries such as automotive, steel, heavy machinery, and mining, as indicative of an impending recovery as they may recover sooner from a decline, and play a pivotal role in the general economy.

How much of an increase in the average price of stocks must occur in order to declare a bull market?

In order to better understand broad movements in the market—and whether today's conditions represent buying or selling opportunities—investors characterize increases in the price of stocks in an average by more than 20% from a low as a bull market. It characteristically is a period in which stock prices are rising, profits are increasing, inflation is low, interest rates are relatively low, and money is flowing into the stock market.

How do companies use an initial public offering to help support their continued growth?

An IPO is a way in which a private company raises capital in order to fuel further expansion and investment. Typically, a private company may need more capital than what its current business generates in order to expand its market imprint, product offering, innovation, manufacturing, information systems, or a combination of all of these. Company founders may desire a liquidity event in order to cash out of the company. By making an offer for the sale of equity (shares), the company can quickly raise capital needed and continue to generate or improve its profitability over time.

What kinds of information can I find by using the U.S. Securities and Exchange Commission (SEC) website?

The SEC website makes available to the public all information concerning publicly traded companies' filings that are required by law. This library of business information may provide the details necessary to make informed decisions regarding purchasing or selling stocks in publicly traded companies. It includes such information sources as the EDGAR Company Database (Electronic Data Gathering, Analysis, and Retrieval System), and publishes all corporate filings and forms necessary for publicly traded companies, as well as earnings reports, annual reports, and IPO forms. The site also includes tutorials and information for individual investors, including tips and information regarding stockbrokers and firms to see if they are properly licensed, or have complaints or actions against them.

According to the SEC, what types of questions should I ask when trying to decide which broker to choose?

The SEC recommends that investors ask potential brokers the following questions, in order to determine if the broker is legitimate, properly licensed, and trained. Questions may include:

- What experience do you have, especially with people in my circumstances?
- Where did you go to school?
- What is your recent employment history?
- What licenses do you hold?
- Are you registered with the SEC, a state, and/or the Financial Industry Regulatory Authority (FINRA)?
- Are the firm, the clearing firm, and any other related companies that will do business with me members of the Securities Investor Protection Corporation (SIPC)?
- What products and services do you offer?
- Can you recommend only a limited number of products or services to me? If so, why?
- How are you paid for your services?
- What is your usual hourly rate, flat fee, or commission?
- Have you ever been disciplined by any government regulator for unethical or improper conduct, or have you been sued by a client who was not happy with your work?
- For registered investment advisers, will you send me a copy of both parts of your SEC Form ADV?

What is a "stock split"?

A stock split happens when a publicly traded company decides to divide its outstanding stocks in half, or split (doubling the number of shares outstanding), while cutting the price of the shares in half. Investors usually view this as a favorable indicator for the company's stock, and normally will wish to acquire more shares at a more favorable price. It also indicates the company's belief in its own future prospects. Some experts discount the perception that stock splits are generally beneficial for the company or investor, as a company has inherent value no matter how many shares are available.

What is a "reverse stock split"?

A reverse stock split occurs when a company decides to consolidate its outstanding shares. If a company has two million shares outstanding, it may wish to consolidate these shares down to one million by doubling the price of each share. So instead of having two million shares trading at $50, the company now has one million shares trading at $100. Companies normally decide to engage in reverse splits when they have a depressed stock price, and that decision generally is not seen by the investment community favorably.

What are stock or share "buybacks"?

Yet another strategy that companies may employ is share "buybacks," or the purchasing back of shares from the open market. Since the earnings of a company are often calculated on a per share basis, a company can make its earnings per share radically improve if there are fewer shares on the market. An important way to tell if a company is in fact buying back its shares is to scrutinize its quarterly reports, and find the line item "shares outstanding." From here, you may compare past quarters or years to see if any buybacks have occurred.

What is another strategy that a company might employ to make its stock attractive to potential investors and current shareholders?

Another strategy that companies might use to distinguish their stock from all others is by paying dividends or distributing the earnings of the company either on a regular quarterly basis or, in some cases, as a one-time event. Normally, a company announces the record date, which is the date that any shareholder must own stock prior to the payment of dividends, and distributes the dividend, usually shortly thereafter. When a company has amassed a lot of cash, it may pay out a special dividend to shareholders of record. Companies that regularly pay dividends tend to be large, predictable, and profitable companies, such as many companies listed in the Dow Jones Industrial Average.

What is a "market order"?

When you purchase a stock, you may request your broker or online brokerage interface to enter a market order. A market order is an order to purchase or sell a stock at the best available price. Even if the order is executed immediately, it does not necessarily mean that you will get the last traded price, as prices change every second, and the price you receive may be quite different from the price you originally wanted.

Why is there a difference in price from the time that I want to buy or sell a stock and the time that I actually buy or sell that stock?

When you call a broker or click the "execute" button on an online interface, your trade ultimately goes to an intermediary, who must determine to which market to send the order. The stock orders may or may not be packaged together with many other orders to be fulfilled at the most favorable price. According to the SEC, there

A lot of people still picture stockbrokers shouting out orders to buy or sell stock, but these days computer transactions make the process a lot more quiet.

are no current regulations making brokerage firms execute trades within a certain time, only that the firm cannot deceptively advertise its ability to trade, and must meet its promises to its clients.

What is a "limit order"?

A limit order allows an investor to buy or sell a stock at a specific price. If the limit order is a "buy" limit order, it may be executed at the stipulated price or better. If the limit order is a "sell" limit order, the brokerage firm or site must execute this trade at the limit price or higher, so that the client receives the most money in exchange for his shares at the time of order execution.

Why are limit orders good to use?

For investors who are buying or selling positions, limit orders help ensure that the investor is getting the best price for his transaction, and does not pay more or sell for less than a predetermined amount. Limit orders provide investors with some protection against volatile price movements of securities while trades are moving through various electronic systems. Limit orders may be more expensive to execute than market orders, so experts generally assert to check with your brokerage firm regarding its fees.

What other types of special orders may help investors when executing trades?

In addition to market and limit orders, there are a few other special orders that may be available to the investor, either at a brick-and-mortar brokerage firm or an online brokerage site. A stop order or stop-loss order is used when you want to buy or sell a stock at a specific price, also called the stop price. A buy-stop order is executed at a stop price somewhere above the recent market price. A sell-stop order is executed at a stop price below the current market price. Investors like to use buy-stop and sell-stop orders to limit losses and to protect profits when executing trades. You should check the specific rules at your brokerage firm (whether full service or online) regarding at what price your order will be executed. Some firms use current quoted prices, while other firms use the last-sale price to determine the stop or buy limit price to be executed.

What other special orders can investors use to help secure a certain price or limit a potential loss?

Investors may use other order instructions to help protect their profits or limit potential losses. "Day orders" mean the order is to be fulfilled during the trading day. "Good-til cancelled" means the order is in the system for whatever time it takes for the order to be fulfilled and transacted. "Immediate or cancelled order" means an order must be transacted immediately, or it must be cancelled. Check with your firm to discover how it defines the word "immediate." Other special orders may include a "fill-or-kill" order, when an order for stocks must be filled in its entirety, and an "all-or-none" order, in which the trading order to either buy or sell must be executed in its entirety immediately. If it is not executed immediately, an "all-or-none" order will remain active unless it is executed or cancelled by the investor.

What if I want to buy or sell a stock after regular market hours?

Normally, if you wish to buy or sell a stock after regular trading hours, the transaction is settled at the next opening price. However, the timing of these trades depends upon the brokerage firm, so check with your firm for additional information.

What types of factors affect my ability to execute a trade when I want?

There are many different situations that may cause a trade not to execute at the exact price, or the precise time we want. Some situations that influence your order execution may be the volume of Internet traffic at the very moment you are making a buying or selling order, the volume of orders for the security that may be taking place simultaneously, and limits to the technology of the individual trading platform the firm is using. Even when you are given notice that an order was received by your broker, it does not necessarily mean your order was executed. It may just be an order confirmation, so please check with your brokerage firm about its notification procedures.

What are some common myths or beliefs that limit what I may earn as an investor?

Experts at both Investopedia and NASDAQ believe potential investors may have certain inaccurate beliefs about investing that may cause problems when you first invest. One belief is that stocks that plummet in price eventually will bounce back, which is not necessarily true. The reasons why a stock drops in value may be complex in origin, and good research on the investor's part may help limit losses in this environment. Another belief may be that people who actively trade stocks and manage their personal portfolios are part of some sort of exclusive club. This is simply untrue, as many millions of individuals actively engage in learning and managing personal stock portfolios, either indirectly through brokers and advisers, or directly through their retirement plans and personal investments. Another widely held belief may compare the investment in stocks to gambling in Las Vegas. This is also an erroneous belief, as with proper research, risk analysis, long-term strategies, discipline, and diversification, an investor can actively obtain his results without ever having luck involved in the equation. Yet another widely held belief is that stocks that rise in price over time must always come down. Many experts assert this is simply incorrect, as some companies are so well managed that their stock price may continue to rise even when purchased at a high point. Over a longer period of time, the stock's price may continue to rise. And finally, that only a bit of knowledge about the complexities of investing in the market is enough for all of us to invest in the market. This belief may also cause many problems with new investors, as it takes a considerable amount of learning, training, and understanding of this complex system in order to do well as an investor.

Another widely believed myth is that investing in stocks is about as safe as gambling in Las Vegas. With proper research and help from a professional, it is actually considerably safer.

How do I begin setting up a brokerage account?

You can easily set up a brokerage account by completing and submitting an online application or mailing a completed form that can be downloaded from most brokerage firms' websites. The form asks for basic information about yourself, and may also ask you to fill in some personal financial information, such as your annual income, net worth, investment goals, likely frequency of trading, etc. You may also be asked to associate your new account with another external bank account, or use the firm's banking products, if available. You may also be asked how you wish to keep your uninvested cash on hand. Many firms will give you different choices for how you wish to save or invest this cash, used to execute trades and invest proceeds. Many firms will require some sort of minimum deposit to begin trading, so you should check with each individual firm.

What is "insider trading"?

Insider trading occurs when corporate insiders (who may be officers, directors, and/or employees of a company) buy and sell stock of the company that employs them. When corporate insiders trade in their own securities, they must report those trades to the SEC, which makes this information available to the public. All publicly traded firms are required to monitor and control all trading by corporate insiders, and may even exclude certain employees from participating in the purchase of the company's stock or related investments altogether.

What does insider trading tell me as an investor?

Any reported activity of corporate insiders (buying or selling the company's stock) usually indicates that something is changing in the company's market, changing within the company itself, or changing within the company's products and services. It may also indicate whether the price of the shares is too high or low, depending on whether the management is buying or selling its own shares. You may also want to pay special attention to when corporate insiders buy their company's shares.

Are there any other factors to consider when investing in a company?

You may want to know if the company was recently in bankruptcy, merged with another company, or if the company is for sale, as all of these events could affect the share price, both in the short and long term.

Former Enron president Jeffrey Skilling was convicted of insider trading and other crimes in 2006. It is illegal for corporate employees and other insiders to trade in their own securities without reporting the activity to the SEC.

Where can I find information to analyze a potential target company?

Thousands of sources provide information that answers many questions about a company and its stock. Some notable sources include Google Finance and Yahoo! Finance, the EDGAR database, financial pages of such sites as *The Wall Street Journal*, *Investor's Business Daily*, MSNBC, *The Economist*, *The New York Times*, *Forbes*, *Fortune*, and local newspaper sites and financial blogs, among many other information sources.

What are the top financial websites that can help typical individual investors learn more about investing?

Some of the top websites that can help typical individual investors learn more about investing include Yahoo! Finance, MSN MoneyCentral, Google Finance, MarketWatch, CNBC, CNNMoney, Bloomberg, and The Motley Fool.

What are some great financial sites that investment insiders use?

Some of the best sites that investment insiders use include gurufocus (www.gurufocus.com), Mish's Global Economic Trend Analysis (http://globaleconomicanalysis.blogspot.com), King World News (www.kingworldnews.com), Mauldin Economics (www.mauldineconomics.com), The Street (www.thestreet.com), Minyanville (http://www.min

yanville.com/), Zero Hedge (http://www.zerohedge.com/), FT Alphaville (http://ftalpha ville.ft.com/), Business Insider (http://www.businessinsider.com/), Financial Times (www.ft.com/home/uk), The Wall Street Journal (http://online.wsj.com/home-page), and Bloomberg (http://www.bloomberg.com/).

Can I learn anything from visiting the websites of the stock exchanges themselves?

Yes, you can learn much about investing by going to the websites of the stock exchanges themselves. Each stock exchange website disseminates an incredible amount of information, including trading models, activity of share trading, data as to which stocks are increasing or decreasing in price the most, which stocks are hitting new highs and lows, etc.

How does the movement of prices in stocks that compose the Dow Jones Industrial Average indicate movement in the price of my stock?

The Dow is a broad indicator of share prices. It is based upon 30 stocks traded on the New York Stock Exchange, and is considered by many to represent the stock market as a whole. It is used to indicate whether broader market share prices are moving higher or lower, and may indicate if a very specific stock price may increase, decrease, or stay the same.

What else affects the price of a stock?

Because stocks are traded in a market (where buyers and sellers meet), market price is determined by how many shares are available to buy, how many buyers are willing to pay, and at what price. Because of the demand or lack of demand for a particular stock at a particular moment during the day, the price may change.

What are a company's "assets"?

Assets are any tangible or intangible economic resources that, when given a monetary value, have the potential to produce value for the company.

What are "tangible assets"?

Tangible assets might be physical buildings, property, factories, products in a warehouse, stocks, or cash in a bank.

What are "intangible assets"?

Intangible assets are non-physical, and could include registered patents, the company's brand identity, logos and trademarks, or the sum total of the experience of the firm's employees.

What is "volatility"?

Volatility is the relative rate that the price of a stock or market index moves both up and down. If a price moves up and down over short periods of time, it is described as highly volatile. If the price doesn't move very much, it has low volatility.

What are the two most important methods to analyze stocks?

The two most basic methods employed by many in order to discern in which stock to invest are fundamental analysis and technical analysis. With fundamental analysis, an investor tries to determine the real value of the company, to ultimately determine the "true" price of the stock, and to use many different data points, including data covering economic conditions and reported financial data. Based upon this analysis, an investor may determine the best time to buy or sell the stock, when its share price strikes the appropriate level, based upon this research. With technical analysis, securities are often analyzed strictly based upon market trading activity, using such indicators as the volume of trades, changes in prices of securities over time, and analysis of charts and graphs to help illuminate opportunities. In technical analysis, no attention is paid to the inherent value of an individual stock, nor necessarily to its financial performance last quarter or last year. Technical-based traders attend only to market trends, in order to identify optimal buying and selling opportunities, often on a second-by-second basis.

How does technical analysis work?

Technical analysis—the method of understanding the patterns and trends of stock prices—is used by investors in order to observe certain trends in the movement of a stock's price, as seen on a graph or chart that would indicate a buying or selling opportunity. The model doesn't necessarily consider how "good" a company is, the quality of its products, or whether the unemployment rate just increased. The primary focus is to analyze the mathematical variables that may influence the trend in the price of a stock, and to use this information to profit in the future from those trends.

What are some basic assumptions employed when using technical analysis?

When you use any technical method to analyze stocks, it is generally thought to be based upon a few assumptions. Some assumptions include: that the price moves of stocks are completely dependent upon supply and demand for that stock, or for any stock; that human trading behavior is observable and repeatable over time; that important technical indicators and rules of when to buy and sell have been tested over many market periods; and that the historical price movements have a similar shape and form, indicating what might happen in the future to a security's price.

Technical analysis is the method of understanding the patterns and trends of stock prices in order to make smarter investment decisions.

What is "fundamental analysis"?

Fundamental analysis is the analysis of the effects of various economic indicators and reported financial information that have influenced (and may influence) the prices of stocks in financial markets.

How does fundamental analysis work?

Investors employing fundamental analysis may look at a company's financial information and other economic data in order to gain an understanding of the company's ability to use capital wisely to create products and services, and to generate earnings in what is considered the most productive way.

What are some basic assumptions employed when using fundamental analysis?

When you use fundamental analysis, you must assume that the reported financial information is legitimate and correct. Experts also often assume that a company's past performance and metrics may continue into the future. You also assume certain factors about the economy and market conditions, and hope they will continue to be favorable from the time of your analysis into the future.

What information does a fundamental investor often review?

A fundamental investor may analyze a company's ability to generate profit and sales growth, and reduce expenses (cost-cutting measures), which can influence a company's profits. He may also analyze macroeconomic variables such as jobs reports, trade data, oil prices, and interest rates in order to predict a stock's future price. Fundamental investors also analyze a company's inherent value, and try to discern if the shares trade at a premium or discount to this valuation of the company.

UNDERSTANDING FINANCIAL MARKETS

Why is understanding financial markets so important to everyone?

Our understanding of financial markets is important to each of us because financial markets are fundamental to the way in which we all live our lives and contribute to our society through our work. In this complex world, financial markets impact nearly all aspects of our lives. Understanding how financial markets work may allow us to make choices that may help us grow our financial assets and provide income to us in the future, and allows us to have many more options as to how we wish to live our lives.

What are the main markets that make up our economic system?

The best way to begin to think about our economic system—and to understand ultimately how these systems interact with each other, and what information is relevant to our understanding of financial markets—is to divide our complex system into three main markets: Services, Products, and Financial. At its core, ultimately there are people (who create the demand that fuels the system), capital (used to clear the transactions), and buyers and sellers. The understanding of how these components work together and affect each other is the basis for understanding how to invest in these markets.

What is the basis of our financial markets?

The basis of our financial markets, a key component of our economic system, is needs-driven. For example, a financial institution may need capital, and must then find an intermediary to obtain this capital. At the same time, a corporation may need capital to retool an old factory, and seeks it from a financial institution. A corporation may also need to raise capital through the sale of its equity, using a price determined by the perceived value of the company's ability to be profitable, as well as the inherent value of the company's products or services, its assets and liabilities, the supply and demand for equity of similar companies, and the broad economic conditions when the company makes the offer, among many other variables.

What are some important economic concepts that may affect bonds and stock prices at the macroeconomic level?

It is generally accepted that great economic growth in an economic system is good for stocks. As the economy expands, in order to meet demand, companies produce and sell more of what they offer. As a result, more people or workers are needed, and incomes

87

begin to rise, fueling more demand and purchases, and so on. Consumers also will have more disposable income to save, invest, or direct toward purchasing more goods and services. But as this economic activity helps us all, it has some hidden consequences that may generally affect the prices we pay for stocks and bonds. Many practitioners believe this economic expansion may lead to inflationary movements, as material inputs and labor become scarcer. This begins the spiral of a gradual price increase. Higher wages and benefits within the labor pool of these producers must be recovered by slight price increases, which, when multiplied by millions of companies, helps to create a gradual inflationary chain of events.

Any indication of inflationary moves may adversely affect the prices of bonds, as available credit becomes more expensive. Bond prices must tick downward in order to create demand for the bonds. Higher interest rates eventually occur, and although it is considered good to maintain a large portfolio in cash, bond investors see a gradual decline in yields. When the economy begins to contract from this period of growth, interest rates commonly decline gradually. Bond prices tend to increase inversely to interest rates. Less economic activity means there is less demand for capital or credit from both end consumers and businesses because the price (or interest rate) of money becomes unaffordable.

The Federal Reserve, headquartered in Washington, D.C., was created by the U.S. government as a central bank to provide stability and flexibility to the nation's financial system.

What impact does the Federal Reserve (the "Fed") have on bonds and equity investments?

The Federal Reserve's policy has an enormous effect on what happens in financial markets. It is charged to maintain the overall stability of our economic system so that it does not expand or contract too quickly, which could devastate our financial markets. As economic expansions occur, and equity investments increase in value, the Fed may tighten the availability of credit and raise interest rates in order to avert high inflation. This action may abruptly affect some equity investments in the short term, as some investors may move money from equities to cash in order to take advantage of increasing interest rates. This may depress overall equity prices, as a greater supply and less demand for equities may occur. In times of economic contraction, the Fed may do the opposite—reducing interest rates and making credit more widely available, in order to stimulate a stagnant economy.

What is a "key" or "leading" economic indicator?

You can read many statistics that illuminate the overall health of the activity of an economic system. These statistics, often referred to as key economic indicators or leading economic indicators, are widely published by many sources, including government organizations, research centers, and companies engaged in actively tracking the progress of many economic systems, or specific sectors within an economy. Some of the more important ones include: indexes of various investment vehicles, profit/earnings reports of key companies, unemployment rate, rate of people quitting their jobs, housing starts, Consumer Price Index (CPI), Consumer Leverage Ratio, Producer Price Index, industrial production, bankruptcy reports (both individual and corporate), Internet penetration, retail sales, interest rates, and changes in the supply of money. Of the hundreds or perhaps thousands of data points released or known in an economic system, some data points may be important to understanding an economy's health. These data points may also indicate the changes that happen in an economy before the entire economy undergoes a change, especially in the short- to medium-term.

Why are these indicators so important to the general understanding of financial markets?

Indicators play a critical role in understanding what is happening in an economic system for a variety of reasons. If an economy is relatively transparent—if what is being reported actually did happen—at the most general level, we can observe what has just happened to the economy, and have more indications or proof as to what may happen next, an important factor when it comes to investing. But the assumption is that whatever investments we are tracking are in some way related or dependent on an economic indicator. Many money managers and investors react profoundly upon the release of some information, either by increasing positions in investments, selling positions in investments, or holding steady during the chaos created by the introduction of some indicative report.

How can I misinterpret an indicator?

When a report is released, it is naturally scrutinized and judged by all who read it. Some investment managers and individuals may review the same figures and draw completely different conclusions, based upon their own biases, trading rules, theories, or bets. A great example is the Quit Rate, or how many people voluntarily give up their jobs. On the surface, an increase in this rate—issued by the Bureau of Labor Statistics, and analyzed by dozens of other organizations—may appear bad, as more people may become unemployed. But it may also indicate some type of economic turnaround is occurring, as people may have more confidence in the economy to leave a job voluntarily in order to find another job. Although there is only one number released, it may be interpreted in many different ways.

What is the Conference Board, and why is it so important to the understanding of financial markets?

The Conference Board, a non-profit organization that releases authoritative research and reports on the state of our economy, began in 1916 as the National Industrial Conference Board. It is composed of members—often high-level managers of many of the largest corporations, as well as researchers, analysts, and writers—who regularly release statistics and analysis about the health of our economy. Often, Conference Board reports are indicative—and perhaps to many, predictive—as to where the economy is heading. It is thought to be one of the most important generators of economic reports and analysis, publishing such reports as the U.S. Consumer Confidence Index, Leading Economic Indexes, Employment Trends Index, Help Wanted OnLine, and the CEO Confidence Survey. It is widely followed by the investment community, and—depending on how the Conference Board report is interpreted—may have a profound effect on investing behavior in the short term.

What constitutes the Conference Board's Leading Economic Index?

The Conference Board creates and publishes its own economic index that comprises ten indicators: Average Weekly Hours (manufacturing), Average Weekly Jobless Claims, Manufacturers' New Orders for Consumer Goods/Materials, Vendor Performance (delivery time), Manufacturers' New Orders for Non-Defense Capital Goods, Building Permits, S&P 500 Stock Index, Money Supply (M2), Interest Rate Spread, and the Index of Consumer Expectations.

What are "lagging indicators"?

Lagging indicators are economic indicators that may capture what is or has been happening in an economy from a few months to a few quarters after a change occurred. For example, a corporation's profit reporting, although made on a regular basis by publicly traded companies, may indicate success or trouble with practices or decisions made many months before, since it takes so much time for such strategy and tactics to run their full course. Such lagging indicators are important to understand if a company, sector, or economy as a whole is on the right, wrong, or steady track. The Conference Board also publishes an Index of Lagging Indicators that helps thousands of people in their quest to illuminate what may happen in the future.

What are the components of the Conference Board's Index of Lagging Indicators?

These components include Average Duration of Unemployment, Value of Outstanding Loans (commercial and industrial), Change in CPI (services), Change in Labor Cost per Unit of Output, Ratio of Manufacturing and Trade Inventories to Sales, Ratio of Consumer Credit Outstanding to Personal Income, and Average Prime Rate (charged by banks).

What types of economic indicators help me understand and evaluate local investment opportunities?

Many reports and analyses published by organizations on a regular basis may assist us to understand what is happening locally. Some indicators could be local housing rentals, housing purchases, public transportation usage, utility usage, local employment rates, and passenger landings at local airports, among many other indicators.

What are some of the key organizations that generate influential economic research?

Some organizations that regularly report their analysis and findings include the Conference Board, U.S. Bureau of Labor Statistics, U.S. Federal Reserve (Federal Open Market Committee), the Organization of Economic Cooperation and Development, the American Institute for Economic Research, the World Bank, and the U.S. Department of Commerce-Economics and Statistics Administration, among hundreds of other organizations.

What is "full employment"?

Full employment is the economic condition in which no cyclical deficiency in the number of people required to sustain the economy with little acceleration in prices exists. Many economists believe a range of unemployment between 0% and 5.5% constitutes full employment, as a percentage of the working population is always moving and changing jobs.

American economist Harry Dexter White (left) and renowned economist Lord John Maynard Keynes of Great Britain founded the World Bank and the International Monetary Fund.

What effect did the 2013 government shutdown have on the U.S. economy?

The shutdown of the federal government—while the U.S. Congress tried to decide how much money to fund the federal government in October 2013, according to experts interviewed by National Public Radio—did unnecessary damage to both the U.S. economy and the country's reputation abroad. Standard & Poor's asserted that the disruption caused the loss of approximately $24 billion from the economy, representing more than half a percentage point of growth in the final three months of the year. And according to S&P's chief U.S. economist, since the agreement only kept the government funded until mid-January 2014, hundreds of thousands of federal workers had uncertainty, affecting non-government workers as well. Many businesses decided to delay hiring and investment. The bond market was affected as well, as interest rates on very short-term U.S. Treasuries went from near zero to almost half a percent when investors realized investments in short-term U.S. bonds were no longer risk-free. The U.S. government had to pay higher interest rates to service its debt. For every tenth of a percentage point increase in interest rates, the United States must pay $2 billion more per year in interest in order to service its debt.

INTEREST RATES

What is an "interest rate"?

An interest rate is the price of using some entity's money for a period of time, or the price of your money that you use to acquire goods and services. When you loan money to another entity, the price you charge for that money is the interest rate. When you use another entity's money to acquire something, as in the form of obtaining credit for a loan or to use a credit card, the price charged to you for using that money over some period of time is commonly referred to as the interest rate.

What is the "Federal Funds Interest Rate"?

The Federal Funds Interest Rate is the price the Federal Reserve charges member institutions to borrow money. Any change in this interest rate does not necessarily cause a short-term change in stock market prices, but it does affect the movement of various stock market prices. Because the Federal Reserve tries to manage inflationary or deflationary movements of prices by changing the amount of money circulating in the system (by changing the price of money or interest rates), it may have a slowing or accelerating effect on how much money is circulating in the system. For example, if we raise interest rates, the belief is that if the Fed slows down the amount of money available and circulating within the economic system, perhaps the prices of goods and services may begin to creep downward, reducing inflationary price pressures. Most of the world's central banks and governments try to use a similar strategy to manage inflation.

What happens when the Federal Reserve changes the interest rate it charges to member institutions?

When the Federal Reserve changes the interest rate it charges to member institutions, banks must immediately spend more to acquire capital, and therefore must increase the rate they charge individuals and corporate entities to use their funds. Because of this movement, individuals must pay more for their variable interest rate loans, mortgages, and perhaps even their credit cards, which may redirect money used to buy goods and services, and directs more of this money to pay for finance and interest charges. If people buy fewer goods and services as a result, a corporation's sales revenues and profits may begin to suffer. Corporations also feel the effects of these interest rate changes because they must now pay more to borrow money to finance short-term dips in their available cash, as well as money used to develop products, fix factories, and begin new ventures, among many other corporate uses of credit. These factors may affect a company's profitability, which ultimately may affect the stock's price.

What was the highest interest rate for U.S. Treasury Bills?

In 1981, the interest rate for three-month U.S. Treasuries hit an all-time high of 14.03%. Since this period, interest rates have fallen to their present-day rate of approximately 1%.

What is the relationship between the interest rate and the stock market?

The relationship between the prevailing interest rate and the stock market is not a simple correlation, but is rather complex when considering all the different types of investments. For example, experts believe that as interest rates increase, bond prices tend to decrease. This generally makes bonds a less attractive investment than stocks, because the previously higher-earning bond is now lower in value. And as interest rates increase, they may lead many in the investing community to believe they should invest in stocks, since many investors may believe they can earn more return if the same dollars are invested in stocks rather than bonds. In this scenario, since more buyers than sellers are now entering the equity market, it may increase stock prices, making the stock market climb.

What may happen to the stock market if interest rates decline?

As interest rates decline, the costs of borrowing and credit become cheaper for both individuals and corporations. Accordingly, consumers may finance more purchases with credit, and corporations can borrow necessary capital more cheaply. These factors may affect their bottom-line profits, further supporting the ever-increasing stock market.

Why might it be true that as interest rates rise, the stock market may not necessarily fall?

Experts cited in a recent *New York Times* article believe we must review the rationale behind increasing interest rates, yet not draw too many conclusions based simply on the fact that interest rates have increased, and their projected effect on the stock

The U.S. Treasury Department is headquartered in Washington, D.C. It is charged with managing the country's financial resources and protecting the integrity of the financial system.

market. Much of the reason for this has to do with perceptions as to why we are increasing interest rates. In May 2013, interest rates ticked up, yet the NYSE still managed to trend upward. Investors may perceive that improving interest rates may signal the end of an easing strategy by the Fed, and perhaps less risk of deflation, both thought to be good signs for equity investors. But it is important to note that if interest rates hit a certain threshold, the opposite scenario may in fact happen. If the interest rates increase beyond a certain point, and more expensive credit makes it more difficult to obtain mortgages or purchase larger-ticket consumer items, causing more softness in the economy, it would begin to have a deleterious effect on the stock market, and may cause it to trend downward. If the markets perceive climbing rates as indicative of the return of an inflationary period, it may also weaken stock prices and demand for stocks.

What is the threshold interest rate that seems to signal a decline in the broad stock market?

The New York Times experts—some of whom studied the correlations between equity prices and bond yields of U.S. Treasuries over many periods—found that the threshold interest rate that seems to signal a decline in the broad stock market is approximately 6%. One expert believes the reason for this is because equity investors would be quite nervous if the cost of long-term capital equals an economy's nominal long-term growth rate. Some would argue that if returns on less risky investments such as government bonds are sufficiently high, it would naturally pull investors from higher-risk equity investments.

> ## Looking back more recently, what effect has the increase in interest rates had on the stock market?
>
> For the period June 2004 to June 2006, the Fed raised interest rates 17 times, yet the stock markets did very well, rising 11.3% (S&P 500) and 22.5% (Russell 2000).

If interest rates increase, does this harm bank stocks and financial sector stocks?

Some experts agree that as interest rates rise, banks and some financial stocks may make more profits, as they are able to loan more expensive money and pass the increases in the price of borrowing to their clients. Other experts see rising interest rates as harmful, as they may stifle demand for credit and cause a slowing effect on profits. In the example of rising mortgage interest rates, increases may make many people refinance at a higher rate, which is better for the lender's profits, but may stifle demand for new mortgages. Higher interest rates may also be passed on to millions of consumers who use credit cards, effectively generating more profit for credit card issuers as well.

INFLATION AND THE CONSUMER PRICE INDEX

Why is price inflation so harmful to my retirement investments?

Inflation is harmful to your retirement investments for a variety of reasons. Since 1926, even with periodic market crashes and movements in the equity markets, the average return on one's investments have been approximately 11%. The inflation rate has increased by approximately 3.1% in the same time period. It is generally thought that we need to earn more on our investments than the inflation rate, since when we figure our real rate of return, we must subtract the rate of inflation from whatever return we are getting on our current investment portfolio. So if we are getting a 4% return on our investments, it is really a 0.9% return before taxes (after adjusting for inflation). This erosive effect is the main reason why we actively need to seek good investments that provide good returns on our principal.

What can I do to mitigate this inflationary risk?

The best way to mitigate the effects of inflation is to save during your high-earning years, and earn more on your investments than the average rate of inflation over a long period of time.

What is the Consumer Price Index (CPI)?

The Consumer Price Index (or Indexes, as it is officially called) is created and published monthly by the U.S. Bureau of Labor Statistics. It represents data collected on the prices paid by urban consumers for a representative sample of many goods and services, in order to gauge changes in prices over time.

How is the CPI created?

The CPI is created both by real shoppers, who acquire specific goods, and by detailed interviews and price diaries kept by thousands of contracted families across the United States, detailing what they have purchased, and at what price, during a certain period of time. The basket of real products that are analyzed includes more than 200 categories of goods and services divided into eight groups: food and beverages, housing, apparel, transportation,

The Consumer Price Index is calculated using data based on prices that actual shoppers pay at the register.

medical care, recreation, education and communication, and other goods and services. The Bureau of Labor Statistics also analyzes the prices of approximately 80,000 items in its market basket each month from thousands of retail stores, service establishments, rental units, and doctors' offices across the country.

How might the CPI be biased?

The CPI may be biased if the consumers who participate in the studies, in reaction to the changing price of one item, may substitute it for another item, or abruptly change their pattern of consumption. If this finding is extrapolated to millions of consumers, as more consumers move to purchase another substitute, it may increase the price of that substitute product in the short term.

How has the Bureau of Labor Statistics revised its calculations, given the changes in methodology, to arrive at the CPI figures we see today?

The Bureau of Labor Statistics revises its methodology of data collection and analysis in order to update old data using current methodology to create and compile the CPI.

How is CPI data used in our economy?

CPI data is used heavily in our economy, with the release of every monthly report, in order for the government to decide social security payments, to correctly compute federal tax rates, and as one of many variables that may be considered when organizations such as the Federal Reserve try to establish interest rates correctly.

Who uses the CPI?

The CPI is used by thousands of people, including investors, economic analysts, legislators, federal policy officials, and members of the media in order to understand the effects of inflation.

How does CPI affect the investing community?

The release of CPI data and subsequent reports are used by the investing community to ascertain the values of various fixed income securities in the pricing of bonds and the values of pension plans. The equity markets also take into consideration a rather steady or fairly predictable change in overall prices in an economy. But if prices rise too much—if the costs of goods and materials used by companies to make products ultimately increase—this can suppress profits for those companies, as products produced become more expensive. Also, products that are sensitive to price movements may see a decline in demand, as prices increase.

Are declines in prices also bad?

In the most basic example, during the period of the Great Depression, prices declined greatly, yet there were no buyers at any price, since millions of people were not earning income. So a drastic lowering of prices, or, indeed, any type of volatility, is normally viewed by investors as being relatively bad for an economy.

How does the employment rate contribute to inflationary pressure?

As the economy expands, and as we move near rates of full employment, in which there remains only a fraction of the available workforce unemployed, this expansion is often accompanied by rising prices, since there are more people working and spending income on goods and services. As shortages of workers are realized in an economy at or near full employment, many economists argue that stimulating demand for goods and services by actions of the federal government, in addition to the high employment rate, may eventually lead to rising inflation rates.

PRICE/EARNINGS RATIOS
AND OTHER CALCULATIONS

What are some of the most important metrics that measure the health or performance of a company, and ultimately its stock price?

When we look at different companies, there are certain performance measures, or metrics, that help us understand the relative health of the company in order for us to gauge

97

the risk of such an investment. Many experts look at several important metrics, including: Price/Earnings (PE) Ratio, Price-to-Book (P/B) Ratio, Debt-to-Equity (D/E) Ratio, Free Cash Flow (FCF), and Price/Earnings-to-Growth (PEG) Ratio.

What is a "Price/Earnings" Ratio?

A price/earnings ratio, or P/E ratio, is the current price of a stock divided by the amount of earnings per share. The earnings number used could be several past quarters of reported earnings, or even include a forecast of future quarterly earnings. Different industries have different growth prospects, and companies with high P/E ratios are expected to grow very quickly. In order for you to compute a price/earnings ratio, merely take the share price of the stock and divide it by the earnings or profit per share. But it is important to note that comparisons of P/E ratios work best when comparing similar target companies in similar lines of business. You cannot have a good comparison when you compare the P/E of an old yet highly profitable industrial company against a new startup Internet company, as their P/Es would be quite different.

What might affect future growth rates in a company's earnings?

Many factors may affect the future earnings of a company, including changes in market conditions and demand; problems or delays in product introductions and manufacturing; disillusionment on the part of the investing community; management changes; and game-changing product or industry movements.

What is "EBIT"?

Earnings Before Interest and Taxes, or EBIT, is used as a metric to understand a company's financial position. When you try to understand the financial health of a company, you can look at cash flows and net income or profits, principally the way in which companies may perform in managing their tax payments in order to improve their financial performance. Some companies excel at managing their tax liabilities, which may make their financial performance appear better than it is. Many experts generally recommend looking at a company's earnings before it accounts for items such as taxes and interest expense payments to finance various aspects of an operation. Do not consider interest, because a company's management can select many different and creative ways to finance loans. Do not consider taxes; many times taxes may spill over to the following

Earnings Before Interest and Taxes, or EBIT, is a metric used to understand a company's financial position.

year, or the company may be very aggressive in managing its tax payments in order to change its ultimate profitability.

How do I compute a company's EBIT?

You may compute EBIT by taking the revenue of a company, subtracting its expenses, and adding back its interest and taxes paid, in order to get a clearer picture of the company's earnings.

What is "EBITDA"?

EBITDA, or Earnings Before Interest, Taxes, Depreciation and Amortization, is similar to EBIT. But it also takes into consideration two important tools that companies use to improve their tax liability and, therefore, their profitability. It is a company's net income, with the interest charges, depreciation, and amortization added back into the equation.

Why is EBITDA sometimes perceived as an unreliable metric to evaluate a company?

It may be unreliable because it does not give a clear picture of a company's cash flows, and also does not take into consideration the capital required to run the business, or capital required to replace large capital items that companies often need to upgrade their operations. The public disclosure of EBITDA by a publicly listed company is not required by the SEC.

Why do some investors like EBITDA measurements and comparisons?

Many investors like to use EBITDA measurements because they allow for more transparency in understanding a company's true profitability, without consideration as to its tax efficiency. Some experts would argue that it is important to consider a company's tax efficiency; based upon this, a company may outperform its competitors.

Where can I find information to help me compute EBITDA?

The information that can help you compute EBITDA may be found in a company's various financial statements. The earnings, taxes, and interest figures may be found in the company's income statement. Information pertaining to depreciation and amortization may be found in the company's cash flow statement.

What is a "Price-to-Book Ratio"?

The P/B ratio describes what the investment community is spending to own a share of the stated value of a company's hard assets, less such intangibles as goodwill.

What is a "Debt–to-Equity Ratio"?

A D/E ratio measures a company's leverage, and how wisely the company is using debt to finance its operations. It is derived by taking the company's total liabilities (both

What is "goodwill"?

The term goodwill is often referred to as the value of a company's intangible assets. These intangible assets may include such items as brand equity, outstanding customer relations, good employee relations, patents, and any proprietary technology. The term can be found on a company's balance sheet because it is not a physical asset such as product stock, buildings, or equipment.

short- and long-term) and dividing this number by the value of shareholders' equity. A company with higher debt equity ratios over time means the company is using debt and available credit to finance its growth, rather than using its own current cash flows from generating revenues through sales of its goods and services. A company may likely incur major interest charges to service this debt, which may affect the company's profitability over time. On the other hand, companies that wisely use debt to generate earnings may generate them by incurring debt rather than relying only upon their own available cash to fuel growth and expansion. If the costs of the debt are higher (especially in an increasingly high-interest-rate environment) than the amount of profit the organization can generate, it could mean an investment in such a company would incur higher risk.

What are "cash flows"?

A corporation's cash flow tells how much money is flowing into (on the revenue side) and flowing out of (on the expense side) a corporation. Its analysis is often a key metric to understand if a company is doing well. It also may indicate the overall financial stability of a company's goods or services, and ultimately the legitimacy of the value of the company's shares. Free cash flow analysis may show an investor how well a company can pay its debts and obligations, distribute profits generated in the form of dividends, affect the price of his shares by buying back stock, and make investments in the company for marketing, product development, innovation, etc. According to many experts, superficial cash flow analysis often may not reveal a true picture as to what is happening in a company, as companies may conceal problems and hide successes, and strategically release information when it is most beneficial.

Why are cash flow-based metrics important to analyze equities?

When deciding to invest in a stock or equity, many analysts believe that any increases in available cash could positively affect a company's earnings or profits. The opposite is also often true. Companies that report declining cash may have some profit problems in the near term, as earnings then begin declining. When a company has plentiful and growing available cash, and its share price is relatively low, value investors see acquiring this company's stock as a great move; over time the company may be more capable of creating profits in the future than what the market believes today, as reflected in the current share price.

How do I compute a company's free cash flow?

You can compute a company's free cash flow by looking closely at its financial statements, specifically the cash flow statement and balance sheet. In these sections, you can see a line item called Cash Flow from Operations (or operating cash flow). Subtract from this amount any capital expenditures made during the reporting year, and you will see the company's free cash flow.

What is a "price/earnings to growth ratio"?

We use the PEG ratio to delve deeper into understanding the potential growth hidden within a company's price/earnings ratio of a company. Since it is generally thought that an analysis of a P/E ratio alone would make fast-growing companies appear overvalued or overpriced when compared with others, the PEG ratio is a slightly better measure, especially when comparing companies with different rates of growth. Companies with lower PEG ratios tend to be more undervalued. If a stock has a PEG ratio of 1, it is thought to be fairly priced. We are paying the right price for the stock and the growth in the company's earnings. Some experts believe that in extreme cases, when comparisons are being made by extremely fast-growing companies, the PEG ratio becomes less valid. Also, many experts are unclear about what numbers are being used to compute the PEG (whether or not the analysts are using trailing 12-month earnings reports, or near-term future expected earnings to compute the growth rate), so it may be difficult to rely upon a company's published PEG ratio alone. Some experts believe it is often preferable to use expected (future) earnings growth rates, but not too far into the future, as it makes the underlying data less reliable. To compute the PEG ratio, divide a stock's P/E by its annual earnings per share growth rate. The lower the ratio, the cheaper the stock, and vice versa.

What is a "multiple"?

In the example of a company with a P/E ratio of 15, also called "trading at a multiple of 15," someone who buys stock is willing to pay $15 for every dollar of earnings, or a multiple of earnings. The P/E ratio may be used to see how a company compares to its peers, and whether a stock price is too expensive or trading at a discount relative to its peers. Stocks with very high P/E ratios are very highly in demand, as investors have bid up the current price of a stock in order to profit on expected earnings in the future.

ONLINE TRADING

What is "online trading," and how does it differ from "day trading"?

When we buy and sell securities using the Internet or some other electronic method, we engage in online trading. We may be using a proprietary trading interface specific to the online firm with which we have an account. We use online trading instead of speaking directly with a broker, either in person or by phone, to execute a trade. Day trading, on the other hand, is the action or strategy of buying and selling securities of all types, and holding them for seconds, minutes, or hours, in order to profit from minuscule price movements during the session, often trading into and out of a security within a day.

The advent of the Internet has made trade of stocks and bonds without the use of a broker possible. It also makes day trading possible in which you can buy and sell stocks extremely fast.

What are some top online stock trading sites?

While an individual investor may use many sites, some sites seem to be favored by many investors because of the cost of executing trades, cost of regular maintenance fees, ease of use of the interface, trading tools available, investment choices offered, ease to initially establish the account, low/no minimum investment requirements, speed of trade execution, availability of mobile applications, face-to-face support, and customer service. Some of the top sites include optionsXpress (Charles Schwab), OptionsHouse, TradeKing, Scottrade, Fidelity, E*trade, Charles Schwab, TD Ameritrade, ShareBuilder, and Firstrade.

Why do experts suggest using online investing brokers?

There are quite a few reasons why some experts prefer online brokerages to traditional brick-and-mortar brokerage firms. Some reasons for using online brokerage sites include: Ability for an investor to buy and sell an investment vehicle online (as opposed to speaking with a physical broker, who then enters a trade into a system); discounted commissions to be paid when trades are executed; sometimes free or heavily discounted investment services; instant updating of account activity and investment performance information; online education and information services available to account holders and/or users; ease of use of the interface; and ease of setting up/managing an account.

Even given the many choices of online brokerages, how do we decide which firm is best to use?

Experts cited in a recent *Money* article suggest that fees charged to execute trades are a very important factor, since these fees depress an investor's returns over time. *Money* cites a study by the popular online site NerdWallet that found investors are overpaying certain very large and reputable online brokerage firms $1.8 billion per year in fees. The article also concludes that the fees are not necessarily justifiable, as investors are not necessarily receiving additional services in exchange for paying higher fees.

The trades are not executed any faster, and research and investing resources are no better at some online firms that require a higher fee compared with other online discount brokerage firms that charge clients a lower fee. Moreover, although many firms charge a fee to switch accounts, the fee normally pays for itself within months of paying reduced fees at a new firm. The author of the *Money* article finishes by stating that investors should shop around and compare the details of fees of each online brokerage firm before deciding to set up an account.

What do the rankings of online brokerage firms really mean?

When you see various rankings of online brokerage firms, most of what you see are rankings related to the satisfaction of the firms' users. Many rankings seem to focus on the price of trades, and our media seems to pay more attention to the cost side, rather than the ease of use of the interface, additional services provided by the firm, speed of trade execution, or human customer service availability. So it is best to be diligent when choosing an online brokerage firm.

Why use a human broker instead of an online broker?

When you use a brick-and-mortar brokerage firm, where you actually interact with a human broker, you pay a fee for your transactions. You pay this fee to the firm to obtain additional services that you may not receive using an online brokerage firm to engage in your investing activities. Bricks-and-mortar investment firms may consult you in order to better understand your investment objectives, risk profile, and life stage, and may make recommendations as to your investment choices and timing, among many other helpful recommendations. This would be difficult to achieve using a strictly online brokerage firm. Other traditional firms may provide guidance to investors such as asset allocation strategies, estate planning, and tax guidance, if they are licensed and trained to do so.

Why else should I use a human broker instead of an online broker?

Some experts maintain that if you are uncomfortable creating a portfolio and selecting different investment vehicles, and occasionally require proper investment guidance, you should seriously consider using a brick–and-mortar type institution instead of an online brokerage firm. But some experts caution that if your broker calls you to sell you a product (i.e., "Buy this hot stock now"), it is best to steer clear and identify another broker.

Many people are better off contacting a broker and meeting him or her in an office rather than online.

What are some of the principal features of online brokerage accounts?

Principal features of many online brokerage accounts include: online trades (with an associated fee, and sometimes including a certain number of free trades), over-the-phone trades, broker-assisted trades, automatic investments, various types of accounts with either no or low minimum investment (including brokerage cash accounts, brokerage margin accounts, and retirement accounts), online trading and banking, mobile trading, access to foreign exchange trading, options trading, mutual funds trading, dividend reinvestment plans, local offices to assist you, and many tools/research and information at your disposal.

How do I open an online investment account?

Although most online brokerage firms offer online account applications, most firms require a physical, signed authorization before your account is activated and trading may begin. Some firms may also require a savings or checking account to be associated with the primary account holder's investment account, and it may take several days for electronic verification. Please check with your online brokerage firm to see what it requires to set up an account.

What is a "cash account"?

Cash accounts are used by investors to pay for the full cost of acquiring or selling securities properly. The account may be used to buy the security and pay any fees due at the time of buying or selling.

What is a "margin account"?

Margin accounts are generally used by investors who, after being authorized to do so, are able to borrow a percentage of money against the value of their account to acquire securities. The brokerage firm loans the money to the investor who, in turn, tries to earn profit from the transaction, and pay back the loan with the proceeds from the trading activity. But investors who do so are taking a relatively larger risk should the investment idea falter and losses be incurred. If the value of the securities backing up the loan from the brokerage firm declines, the brokerage firm may call the entire loan, and require immediate payment for the transaction by selling off the securities. Please check with your brokerage firm about its rules of engaging in margin-based trades.

BONDS

THE BASICS

What is a "bond"?

Generally, a bond is an investment vehicle that is in many ways quite similar to a loan, debt security, or IOU. When you purchase a bond, you lend money to an issuer, which could be a government, local municipality/entity, corporation, or federal agency. As part of the deal between the bond issuer and the bond buyer, the issuer promises to pay the buyer a specific and stated interest rate during the life of the bond, and to repay the face value of the bond when it becomes due or reaches maturity.

What types of bonds exist?

Bonds are generally divided into different classes, including U.S. government securities, municipal bonds, corporate bonds, mortgage- and asset-backed securities, federal agency securities, and foreign government bonds. There are also the same categories of foreign bonds, denominated in local and other currencies, although the way in which you acquire these bonds may differ depending on the country. Please check with a foreign bond specialist for further information.

Which performs better, stocks or bonds?

For many years between 1870 to 1940, bonds performed better than stocks. Since then, stocks have performed better during most economic cycles.

What affects bond prices?

Many factors influence the prices of bonds, including interest rate movements and investor demand. Bond prices move in the opposite direction of interest rates; when interest rates rise, bond prices fall, and vice versa. If you buy a bond at a discount and hold the bond for its full term, you will get all your money back plus interest. If there is not much investor demand for a particular bond, the issuer may have to lower the price of the bond in order to create more demand for it.

Is your money safe in bonds?

As long as the issuer is financially sound, there is little risk of default on bonds. But if the company or government that issues the bonds has a major economic catastrophe, there is a risk—as in all other forms of investments—of losing your money.

What is a "prospectus"?

A prospectus is a document, sometimes known as an offering document or official statement, that provides an explanation as to the bond's terms, features, and risks all investors should know before entering into an investment. It may help an investor to decide if the bond issuer can reliably make stated interest payments. The prospectus is used as a small information component that may include credit ratings agencies' reports, market reports, and professional analyses published by sector specialists at investment organizations and banks. Please see your financial adviser for further information.

Is owning a bond like owning a stock?

No. When you own a stock, you actually own a piece of the company, its assets and profits. When you own a bond, you are giving the issuer a loan, for which it pays you interest on the loan, and refunds your principal when it is due.

Is a bond like an IOU?

Yes. A bond is an IOU, with the added advantage that you receive interest on the IOU, as well as the original amount you loaned.

Can you invest in bonds through mutual funds?

Yes, you may invest in all types of bonds through the use of mutual funds. Investors may even invest in mixtures of different types of bonds by buying bond mutual funds.

If you buy bonds through a broker, is there a commission?

Bond brokers and dealers may not use the term "commission," but they nearly always

You can think of a bond as being like an I.O.U., except that bonds also earn interest.

charge some sort of transaction fee. Check with your broker to discuss all fees, whether buying or selling to make sure you are aware of any fees.

What are tax-free or tax-exempt bonds?

Tax-free or tax-exempt bonds are issued by a municipal, county, or state government, with interest payments that are not subject to any state, local, or sometimes federal taxes. These rules depend on what bonds you buy, and in what state or municipality you reside.

Why do we invest in bonds?

We invest in bonds as part of our overall goal or strategy to achieve some modicum of diversification within our investment portfolios. And because bonds typically pay out interest semi-annually (twice per year), they may provide a source of cash and income or liquidity that investors may prefer, because the income is relatively predictable and reliable.

What are some important variables I may use when comparing the quality of different bond investments?

Some of the most important variables to compare different bond choices may include: the price of the bond; the interest rate to be paid; the yield of the bond; the term or time to maturity of the bond; rules guiding redemption of the bond; the past performance and history of default of the bond; the credit worthiness or rating of the bond; and the bond's tax status (whether it is taxable or tax-free).

What is a yield curve?

When you compare the yields of different bonds over different periods of time, you use a graph called a yield curve. On the horizontal axis is the time to maturity. On the vertical axis is the yield of the bonds you are comparing. The yield curve graphically demonstrates that in a typical fashion, as bonds rise in maturity, so do their expected yields. Generally, when you compare bonds that are nearer in terms, such as short-term versus intermediate-term bonds, the expected yields will be higher for the intermediate-term bonds.

What is "principal"?

Principal is the face value of a loan or bond, the original loan amount that is used to calculate interest payments. The principal and interest is what an investor receives when a bond comes due, or matures.

How do I buy bonds?

You can buy bonds through a full-service broker or discount broker. Some large banks also can provide their clients access to bonds. You may also buy bonds directly from the U.S. government at www.treasurydirect.gov.

How are bond prices determined?

Bond price determination can be a very complex subject that extends beyond the scope of this publication. But in general, bond prices are determined by many variables, including: prevailing and expected interest rates; current interest rate policy; supply and demand for bonds; particular classes or types of bonds; liquidity; the quality of the credit; date of maturity; and tax status. It is important to note that newly issued bonds usually sell at or near their nominal face value, or principal value. But it is equally important to note that any bonds selling in the secondary markets may trade at different prices, given the demand for the particular bond, and may actually be sold at a premium (priced above its face value), or sold at a discount (priced below its face value).

What about bond interest rates?

Bonds have a stated interest rate that may be dispersed and paid to a bondholder in a few different ways. Bonds may pay interest to investors at a fixed-rate or a floating rate, whereby the rate is adjusted periodically and tied to bond benchmark interest rate indexes such as the London Interbank Offered Rate (LIBOR), U.S. Treasury Bills, or other benchmarks. Please consult your bond expert for further information on the interest rates of bonds you may be considering.

What is a "coupon payment"?

When a bond issuer pays the bond buyer interest periodically on a bond investment during its term, it is called a coupon payment. For example, the issuer of a $10,000 bond paying 8% would send a coupon payment of $400 twice a year to the bond investor. When the bond matures, in addition to these semi-annual payments, the bond investor will receive the full face value of the bond.

What are the different categories of the term or maturity of bonds?

Bond maturity terms usually fall anywhere from one to thirty years. Short-term bonds typically mature in less than five years. Medium-term bonds reach maturity in five to twelve years. Long-term bonds mature in periods greater than twelve years.

What is a "zero coupon bond"?

Some bonds that do not make regular coupon payments, but instead pay all interest compounded when the bond matures, are called zero coupon bonds. These types of bonds are typically sold at a substantial discount to their face value, and all accrued interest and the principal are paid to the investor when the bond reaches maturity. It is important to note that the prices of zero coupon bonds tend to fluctuate more than their coupon-paying counterparts.

Why does the term of a bond matter when I think about risk?

The term of a bond matters greatly when you invest because of the length of time you must wait before the bond's principal is paid back. Typically, short-term bonds are less risky, since the principal is paid back sooner than higher-risk, medium- and long-term bonds. But to compensate investors, in exchange for accepting these risks, medium- and long-term bonds tend to offer higher returns and interest rates to bondholders.

What is the connection between prevailing interest rates and a bond's maturity?

Changes in prevailing interest rates may change a bond's returns, but not in the same way for all bonds. If a bond is relatively long term regarding the date when it matures, its price may be more affected when compared with a bond with a relatively shorter maturity. Generally, bonds of longer duration and maturities will offer yields that help to compensate investors for this extra interest-rate risk.

What happens when bond yields for short-term maturities are higher than their long- or intermediate-term counterparts?

When yields in a yield curve move in the opposite direction than expected, it is likely that investors see a recession looming, and that interest rates may decline in the future.

What is the connection between bond prices generally and the health of the economic system in which I may invest?

It is important to understand that the price of debt or bonds is related to the general economic cycle of an economy, and the perceptions by the market at large of the prevalence of inflation or a period of falling prices (deflation). It is generally thought that in order to fuel an economy, we must make just the right amount of credit available, and price loans and bond instruments at the appropriate level. If we make credit too cheap, or price our money and debt instruments too cheaply, it may exacerbate inflationary tendencies in an economy. Conversely, if we make the price and availability of our credit too expensive, it may also have a deleterious effect, and cause an economy to slow down. So the pricing of our debt and the availability of credit has great bearing on, and influence upon, economies.

What is "laddering"?

Laddering is a strategy of staging the maturity dates of bonds in order to maintain your portfolio's fluidity, so that you may not have to purchase many bonds when interest rates are low and favorable. As each bond reaches maturity, you can reinvest the principal into a new bond, with a new maturity date. Many people use laddered investments as sources of income, as each bond may generate income to the investor at different times. When the bond comes due, many investors move the money into more liquid, easily accessible investments.

Why do advisers like to use laddering techniques?

Investment advisers like to employ laddering techniques because they allow clients to preserve their portfolios without having to liquidate positions in other investments, such as equities or other longer-term investments such as mutual funds, since they may still produce income.

How much money flowed out of U.S.-listed bond mutual funds and bond exchange-traded funds in 2013?

According to experts at TrimTabs Investment Research, as reported in *Bloomberg*, investors in U.S.-listed bond mutual funds and exchange-traded funds (ETFs) withdrew a record $86 billion in 2013, topping the previous record outflow of $62 billion set in 1994.

CORPORATE BONDS

What are "corporate bonds"?

Corporations may issue bonds to raise capital to fund projects (instead of issuing new stock). The bonds are usually denominated in amounts of $1,000 and $5,000 with interest normally paid semi-annually. Corporate bonds come in several forms, depending on the maturity: short-term (less than five years), intermediate-term (five to twelve years), and long-term (over twelve years).

What do companies do with the money they make from selling bonds?

The proceeds from the sale of the bonds may help fund new plants and factories, purchase new equipment, upgrade old facilities, or retire more expensive debt, that ultimately may make the company able to compete and thrive in the future.

Are corporate bonds risky?

Corporate bonds are the riskiest forms of bond investing because of the risk that the company can default and fail.

Why are yields higher for corporate bonds than for government or municipal bonds?

Yields for corporate bonds tend to be higher than government or municipal bonds because of the risk. The higher the risk, the higher the return must be in order to make the investment attractive to investors.

What are some risks associated with corporate bond investments?

Although returns generated by corporate bond investments may be relatively high, they do come to investors with some risks. Both investment grade and high-yield non-in-

Corporations have board meetings to decide on issuing bonds to raise money for such things as plant construction or upgrading equipment.

vestment grade corporate bonds may be exposed to event risks, as when, for instance, the corporation experiences an event such as a severe change in the price of a material or commodity the company uses to manufacture its products, an unexpected takeover or some form of corporate merger, or the company's restructuring. Corporate bonds may also be exposed to risks in factors that affect the equity value of the company, such as a difficulty in meeting cash or profit targets, or a general economic decline.

What are some of the main reasons why investors include corporate bonds within their portfolio?

Aside from the diversification strategy many investors employ, corporate bonds make up a portion of many investors' portfolios because they offer good yields when compared with same-maturity government bonds, and because of their predictable income while preserving capital. Additionally, since you can see the ratings of various corporate bonds, you may find the bonds with the best ratings that are likelier to repay principal and interest, allowing you to compare your various choices and risks. Additionally, corporate bonds can be sold before maturity to help an investor have more liquidity.

Where do corporate bonds trade?

Most corporate bond transactions trade "over the counter," meaning they are traded by bond dealers, brokers, and traders in many different locations. Some corporate bonds trade on established exchanges such as the NYSE/Euronext Exchange.

What types of companies issue corporate bonds?

The types of companies that issue corporate bonds are typically public utilities, transportation companies, large industrial companies, financial companies, and large conglomerate companies that may be involved in many industries and services, among many others.

How does the IRS treat the interest I receive on a corporate bond?

The interest you receive while you hold a corporate bond sold before it matures is subject to federal income taxes. As long as the bond is held up to a year from the time of purchase, it is taxed at your ordinary income tax rate. If it is held for longer than one year, it is taxed at the current long-term capital gains rate. If you sell a bond at a loss, you may use this loss to offset gains made by other investments. Depending on the size of the loss, you may deduct the loss during that reporting year, or carry over the loss to subsequent reporting years. For additional information, please consult a tax professional.

TREASURY BONDS AND TREASURY BILLS

What are "government bonds"?

A government bond is an interest-generating security, issued by a government, that promises to pay an investor a specified sum of money on a specific date. Government bonds fall into three categories: treasury bills, which mature in less than one year; treasury notes, which mature in one to ten years; and treasury bonds, which mature in more than ten years.

Are U.S. government bonds safe?

Because they are backed by the U.S. government (meaning that all principal and interest will be paid on time), they are considered extremely safe, as there is very little risk that the U.S. government will default on the loans. In 2013, while the U.S. Congress was deciding how to raise the debt ceiling, there were fears that the U.S. debt ceiling would not be raised, making many holders of U.S. backed securities fearful of default, but America did not default. Since there is a very large global market for U.S. Treasury securities, they can easily be purchased and sold.

Are all government bonds safe?

U.S. Treasury securities are a safe way to invest, as the U.S. government guarantees the investment. Foreign government bonds may be riskier as the debt of those countries—and possibly a potential inability to pay back the loan—may cause both economic collapse within the issuing country and potential losses for investors. So one must consider the region and the country before investing in foreign government bonds.

What countries are having major debt problems, making investments there relatively riskier?

Besides the United States, some notable European countries that have been having economic problems lately include Greece, Ireland, Portugal, Spain, and Italy.

What are "Treasury Bills"?

U.S. Treasury bills, or "T-bills," are short-term debt obligations backed by the U.S. government that mature in one year or less, and are purchased for a price less than or equal to their face or par value. When they mature, the government pays the face value plus any interest that may have accrued. The interest is the difference between the original purchase price of the bill and what ultimately is paid at the time the bill matures. As an example, if you purchase a $10,000 treasury bill for $9,750, and hold it to maturity, you would be paid $9,750 plus interest of $250.

Can I automatically invest in U.S. Savings Bonds using my IRS tax refund?

Yes. Beginning in 2011, a taxpayer may use a tax refund to purchase up to $5,000 of U.S. Treasury Series I Savings Bonds, low-risk bonds that grow in value for up to thirty years.

How are Series EE Savings Bonds different from Series I Savings Bonds?

You cannot purchase paper EE bonds, but you can purchase paper I bonds. Interest paid on a Series EE Savings Bond depends on when it was purchased. If an EE Savings Bond

U.S. Treasury bonds are a safe and secure way to invest your money, though they do not earn interest rates as high as some stocks. You trade some income growth for security.

was purchased after May 2005, it earns a fixed-rate of return. Any Series EE Savings Bond issued from May 1997 through April 2005 earns variable rates of interest, based upon 90% of the six-month average rate of five-year treasury security yields. Series I Savings Bonds earn a combined interest rate, a fixed-rate disclosed when you buy, and a semi-annual inflation adjustment.

How are Series EE Savings Bonds similar to Series I Savings Bonds?

Both bonds may be purchased electronically through www.treasurydirect.gov, and can be purchased for any amount to the penny, beginning with a minimum investment of $25. You may cash in the bonds after 12 months. Both bonds earn interest monthly, and are compounded semi-annually.

What are the minimum investment requirements if I am interested in investing in U.S. Treasury securities?

If you are buying U.S. Treasury securities directly from the U.S. Treasury, the minimum amount that you can purchase is $1,000. Savings bonds have a very low minimum purchase amount, and may be purchased for $25.

What is the maximum amount I am allowed to invest in Series EE or Series I Savings Bonds?

Each investor (with a discrete social security number) is allowed to invest $10,000 each calendar year. Investors may also buy up to $10,000 in Series EE Savings Bonds and up to $5,000 in Series I Savings Bonds with an IRS tax refund each filing year.

How do I open a treasurydirect.gov account?

It is very easy to open a Treasury Direct account to purchase treasury securities. Go to www.treasurydirect.gov, and click on the link to open an account. In three steps, you may begin to invest.

MUNICIPAL BONDS

What are "municipal bonds"?

When city governments need capital to fund the building of a water system, improve roads, build new schools, or desire funding for other large infrastructure projects, they often fund these activities through issuing a bond. Many state and local governments issue debt-based securities to raise needed capital for capital-intensive projects.

What are the two different categories of municipal securities in which I may invest?

Municipal bonds or "munis," as they are often referred to, are divided into two categories: general obligation bonds and revenue bonds. They distinguish themselves pri-

Municipal bonds are used to pay for improvements like road construction and new schools.

marily from the source of their interest payments once the debt is sold. General obligation bonds may raise taxes on a municipality in order to pay for its obligations of interest and principal payments. Revenue bonds, on the other hand, are often tied to specific capital-intensive projects that may be required by the municipal authority, and may be transportation- or utility-related. They are backed financially by the revenue that may be generated as a result of the project. Since the cash they may generate is quite variable, revenue bonds tend to be riskier than general obligation bonds.

What is the length of time to maturity of typical municipal bonds?

Municipal bonds have a wide range of yields and maturities, but many mature in a relatively short period or term, and tend to have lower yields. For projects of longer duration that require a longer term in order to repay all the principal and interest to bond investors, these longer-term bonds will have higher yields.

Are municipal bonds a safe form of investing?

Yes; the chances of an entire city going bankrupt is pretty remote. But there are interest rate risks and risks of default, and you must consider the economic prospects for the city before you invest in its bonds.

What if the municipal bond issuer defaults on the bond?

If you invest in bonds for a city that goes under, you may lose all of your investment, plus any interest payments due to you.

What percentage of municipal bondholders are individual people and mutual fund investors?

About 80% of all municipal bonds are held by individual household investors, either directly or through mutual funds that invest in those bonds.

What is the average five-year cumulative default rate for investment-grade municipal bonds?

According to Moody's, the average five-year cumulative default rate for investment-grade municipal bonds is less than half a percent, making municipal bonds a very safe investment.

Are municipal bond defaults rising?

Yes. In 2009, more than 183 borrowers defaulted on their loans, many in Florida. By contrast, in 2007 only 31 defaults occurred, according to *Fortune*.

Why would a municipality default on its loans?

A variety of reasons affect a municipality's ability to repay its bonds, including: high unemployment, which affects tax receipts; low consumer spending; underfunded municipal pensions; labor costs; loss of people; and gross mismanagement of the municipal government's finances.

ASSESSING DEFAULT RISK ON BONDS

What happens when a bond issuer defaults on the bond?

When a bond issuer defaults on a bond, it fails in some way to meet certain obligations, such as the regular payment of interest and principal due to the bondholders. Sometimes bond issuers may be in default if they fail to report or file information properly, or if they enter into bankruptcy.

If the bonds I hold are in default because of the issuer's bankruptcy, might I still be able to retrieve my principal?

It depends on what type of bond you purchased. It is very important to understand that, in general, the higher the interest rate and return you are promised, the higher the risk of something adversely happening to your principal, even if you buy a bond that is highly discounted from its face value. You must read the fine print and consult an expert financial adviser before you enter into a bond-based investment. Since bondholders or owners are creditors to the bond issuer, they are treated with a higher priority than stockholders or equity owners of the same company or corporate entity when it comes to getting paid after a bankruptcy/restructuring event/liquidation, when all assets of the entity are sold to pay off creditors. When a bond issuer defaults during a bankruptcy, the priority of who is to be paid is determined by the type of bond held or owned.

What is the order of priority of payment during a bankruptcy or liquidation of a company or corporate entity?

In order to determine the order of priority of paying creditors during a bankruptcy or liquidation of a company or corporate entity, we start by looking at the company's assets. Those investors who are entitled to a piece of the value of a company's assets, in order of priority, include investors who hold senior debt/bonds, investors who hold subordinated debt/bonds, and shareholders. When a company is given credit, it is often stipulated that some sort of collateral be offered in order to secure the credit. Secured bonds are generally first to receive any proceeds from the sale of collateral of the company or corporate entity should it enter into bankruptcy or liquidation.

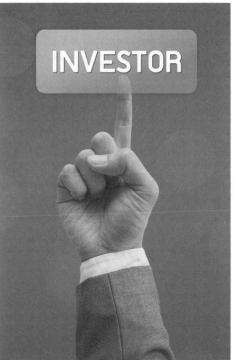

What is a "secured bond"?

A secured bond is backed by some form of collateral. If the bond issuer is in material default, secured bondholders are highest in priority to be paid, even though they may not receive all of their principal. So it

When paying off creditors during a liquidation process, money goes first to those investors who own a piece of the company's assets.

is very important to understand the potential risks of default even when buying corporate secured bonds.

What is an "unsecured bond"?

Unsecured bonds typically have no collateral to provide investors protection against default, and therefore offer a higher interest rate and return in exchange for this risk.

How do I know which bond investments are riskier than others?

The risk of bonds can be seen with U.S. Treasury Bonds as the least risky bond investments on one end, and perhaps bonds that are not of investment grade, such as small start-up companies or companies nearing a bankruptcy filing as perhaps the riskiest of bond investments.

If bonds can be so speculative, how can bond markets and bond buyers know the worthiness of their investment?

Since bonds are just another form of credit, financial information reporting gives potential bond buyers a glimpse into the bond issuer's overall financial health, and allows comparisons to be made, conclusions to be drawn, and prices to be offered for these bonds. A bond issuer must provide enough information regarding its financial health before going to the market to find credit. Much (but not all) of this financial information can be found by carefully reading the bond's prospectus, and consulting an adviser. The prospectus covers many aspects of the bond and corporate entity's financial picture, and may provide information to help an investor decide whether to purchase the bond.

What are some of the top bond ratings organizations?

To a large degree, the bond market relies on the analytical work of several important ratings organizations, including Moody's Investors Service, Standard & Poor's, and Fitch Ratings. Each ratings organization may report on such important details as the financial health of the bond issuer, the management team of the issuer, economic conditions that may affect the issuer, the various characteristics of the debt, and sources of revenue that may secure the bond over time. Typically the best bonds are given ratings of AAA (by Standard & Poor's and Fitch), or Aaa (by Moody's). Many consider bonds rated below BBB/Baa quite speculative and highly risky.

THE BASICS

What is a "mutual fund"?

A mutual fund is a professionally managed investment vehicle that pools funds from many investors and collectively invests them in stocks, bonds, cash instruments, commodities, other mutual funds, real estate, and many other types of investment instruments. A mutual fund enables its investors to gain (or lose) from the fund's performance.

How much money flowed into U.S. equity mutual funds and exchange traded funds in 2013?

According to experts at TrimTabs Investment Research in a report published in January 2014, a record $352 billion flowed into U.S.-listed equity mutual funds and ETFs in 2013, breaking the previous record inflow of $324 billion set in 2000.

What about the success of high-performing mutual funds?

Experts at *Forbes* magazine cite a 2003 study by mutual fund analysis company Morningstar that looked at a 20-year period beginning in 1976, analyzed the returns in five four-year periods, and compared the returns of the best 30 funds in each of those periods against the performance of those same funds over the next period. They found that the star funds did very well during the first period, averaging a return of 28.3%, but in the next period, not only did many of these same funds drop out entirely, but those that remained had returns of only 1.8%. This data is relatively easy to find.

When did mutual funds start?

Many believe the first mutual funds were organized in Northern Europe, specifically in the Netherlands, by King William I in 1822. Others cite 1774, when a Dutch merchant   **119** named Adriaan van Ketwich created *Eendragt Maakt Magt*, which means "unity creates strength." He may have influenced King William I to create his fund some years later. According to academic researchers at Yale University, Ketwich sought investors and invested primarily in bonds (debt) of such countries as Austria, Denmark, "German States", Spain, Sweden, Russia, and colonial plantations of Central and South America. Since very few "equities" existed on the Amsterdam Stock Exchange at the time, investors could only invest in bonds. The fund also held no Dutch bonds; in today's jargon, it would be called a "foreign bond mutual fund" or a "closed-ended trust." By 1775, most of the shares of this fund were freely traded on the Amsterdam exchange. Ketwich was not personally involved in the daily investment decisions of the fund, and only administratively managed the fund. The fund also guaranteed a 4% dividend to all shareholders, slightly lower than the nominal interest rate of the bonds in the portfolio. The fund lasted until 1782, when it was officially dissolved.

When were the first mutual funds started in the United States?

Some experts believe that the first mutual funds in the United States began in 1893 with the advent of the Boston Personal Property Trust. The Alexander Fund in Philadelphia, founded in 1907, was one of the first funds that allowed its investors to make withdrawals or redeem shares on demand. The first mutual fund appeared in Boston in 1924 under the name Massachusetts Investors Trust, and would be characterized as an open-ended fund, allowing for issuing, buying, and selling shares on the open market. The fund started with $50,000 and finished its first year with $392,000. The fund went public in 1928, and the name was changed to MFS Investment Management. It thrives today as one of the oldest continuously

Mutual funds are a great way to quickly diversify your portfolio without investing a lot of money up front, if you don't wish to.

operating mutual funds in the United States, employing more than 1,700 people worldwide, and, as of 2012, managing more than $338 billion and operating 75 funds.

Why should I read a mutual fund's prospectus?

By reading a mutual fund's prospectus, you see how the fund is managed, its portfolio, its sectors, percentage of portfolio for each holding, the fees and expenses associated with the fund's management, and past performance history. You can begin to understand how a mutual fund manages risk in order to receive high returns on invested capital.

How is a mutual fund priced?

The price of a mutual fund is its net asset value. The individual share price of an open-ended mutual fund is determined by the value of the net assets of the fund minus any liabilities held by the fund, divided by the number of shares outstanding. If a mutual fund has assets of $100 million, and liabilities of $10 million, its net assets are $90 million. If there are nine million shares of the stock outstanding, then the net asset value is $10.

How does a mutual fund work?

A management team of the fund seeks to invest in specific industries or ideas that they think will grow over the short-, medium-, or long-term time horizons. They create a portfolio of investments in individual shares of many companies, and intensely follow every nuance of the financial, marketing, product development, and competitive threats of the companies within the portfolio in order to provide strong returns to investors.

How does a mutual fund make money?

The collective investments of the mutual fund may earn dividends on the shares they own and capital gains on shares they purchased and sold (as well as capital losses if they have sold shares at less than the purchase price). The fund also charges a management fee to all shareholders. After subtracting the expenses from the gains, the earnings of the fund are distributed to each investor in proportion to the amount of shares invested. Investors believe that although any one stock or group of stocks in the fund's portfolio may go up or down, the total gains of the portfolio will be positive over time.

Why buy mutual funds?

You buy into a mutual fund in order to have instant diversification of your money. Since buying one share of a mutual fund gives an individual investor access to a large, diverse portfolio of other shares, exposure to the risk that the investment will decrease is diminished.

Is there such a thing as a risk-free mutual fund?

No. There is no such thing as a truly "risk-free" mutual fund. The risk of loss never entirely goes away, no matter how diverse a portfolio is, but it may be less risky than investing in any single share of a company directly.

What are two of the oldest mutual funds?

In 1924, a private investment fund was started in Boston, calling itself the Massachusetts Investors Trust. It later offered its shares to the public in 1928, and today it still exists as MFS Investment Management. Another venerable firm, Putnam Investments, began in 1937, and still exists today.

How many people own mutual funds?

Of the 78 million households in the United States, 44%, or more than 90 million people, invest in mutual funds.

How much money is managed by mutual funds?

The mutual fund industry currently manages $12.2 trillion. This number fluctuates every moment, as the share prices that comprise each fund's portfolio change every second.

What is a "turnover rate"?

A portfolio's turnover rate is a measurement of a fund's trading activity, describing what percentage of the total portfolio is traded each period. Low turnover rates suggest the portfolio is holding on to assets, expecting higher returns. High turnover rates mean the fund is trading very actively, trying to realize positive returns, minimize losses, or manage the inflow and outflow of cash into the fund effectively, and over shorter periods of time.

What has been the average turnover rate of an equity mutual fund?

During the period 1974 to 2009, the average equity or stock mutual fund had an average turnover rate of 58%.

Does the size of the companies that compose a mutual fund portfolio really matter when deciding what type of mutual fund to purchase?

Yes, size does matter. In each broad category, you have the choice to buy mutual funds that invest in small companies. They may have a higher potential return, but also may have more risk. Medium-sized companies may reduce the risk over time since they are not so small, are better established than small companies, and may have the ability to generate profit growth over time. Large-company stock funds may have fewer risks, as these very established companies have proven track records, dividends, and earnings growth, and are thought to be less risky than small company funds.

What is the median age of the owner of mutual fund shares?

The median age of the owner of mutual fund shares is 50.

Who invests in mutual funds the most?

People aged 35–64 invest in mutual funds more than any other age group.

What is the median number of mutual funds an individual owns?

In 1958, the median number of mutual funds an individual owned was one. Today, the median number is four.

How much money does the typical investor in today's market have in his mutual fund accounts?

The typical investor has about $80,000 in his or her mutual fund accounts.

What percentage of a household's financial assets are in the form of mutual funds?

Twenty-one percent of a household's financial assets are in the form of mutual funds.

How do I buy a mutual fund?

You can buy mutual funds in many ways. You can buy a mutual fund directly through a mutual fund company, a broker, a full-service bank, or through the company that manages your 401(k) or retirement plans.

What financial goal does the typical investor in mutual funds desire when making an investment?

Seventy-six percent of mutual fund investors have the financial goal of investing and saving for their retirement years.

How many people are employed in the investment company business?

In 2009, 157,000 people worked in the investment company business.

How do I decide which funds to choose?

This question is very complex because it involves so many variables. You must analyze the performance of many periods (one year, three years, five years, ten years, and life of fund). Experts also believe that you should find funds with lower expense ratios and stable management teams in place.

What does the phrase "past performance is no indication of future performance" mean?

Most mutual funds advertise a disclaimer that states "past performance is no indica-

Predicting the furture performance of a mutual fund is problematic, to say the least. Improve your odds by finding funds with stable teams and low expense ratios.

tion of future performance." It means that just because a mutual fund was number one last year, that does not necessarily mean it will be number one this year, or even in the top ten.

What other considerations exist when attempting to choose the right mutual fund?

Another consideration is how well the fund performs in comparison to its peers. Is it the best, or is it among the worst? Consider also the actual manager, and the time the manager has been managing this portfolio, since it is his stock picks that will create the returns you will realize. Has the manager been in the job for a few months, years, or decades? Does the manager have a great track record over time?

What are some other key considerations when deciding in which mutual fund I should invest?

Try to find out how well or poorly the mutual fund performs in the best and worst of times. Ask yourself: If the fund loses 25% in its worst decline, but its peers lose 50% in their worst decline, can I live with that scenario?

What does the Securities and Exchange Commission recommend investors do when considering investments in mutual funds?

Experts at the SEC recommend that before you invest in a mutual fund, you should not focus entirely on a fund's past performance. Compare such factors as the fund's sales charges (fees or loads), tax implications as it generates gains (or losses), the size of the fund, how many years the fund has been in operation, the risks and volatility of the fund, and any recent changes to the fund's management or trading and investing goals. You can discover this information by scrutinizing the fund's prospectus and annual (or quarterly) reports, and by using reports published by mutual funds rating research organizations.

How can I protect myself from fraud when I am considering investing in a mutual fund?

Many mutual funds use the services of outside companies to manage their funds, sometimes known as "investment advisers" that are supposed to be registered with the SEC. The SEC always recommends that you scrutinize this registration to ensure that the investment advisers are registered with the SEC by going to the SEC's website and doing some background checks.

What has been the average annual return of the S&P 500, a good indicator of the performance of listed stocks that frequently make up mutual fund investments?

The average annual return of the S&P 500 was 11.69% from 1926 to 2011, 9.07% from 1992 to 2011, and 10.05% from 1987 to 2011.

DIFFERENCES BETWEEN
TYPES OF MUTUAL FUNDS

How many mutual funds exist?

There are 8,624 mutual funds. If you add in closed-ended funds, ETFs, and unit investment trusts, the number reaches 16,120.

What types of mutual funds exist?

Mutual funds can be divided into three broad categories: equity funds (stocks), fixed income funds (bonds), and money market funds (cash/cash equivalents).

What other subdivisions of mutual funds exist?

Mutual funds are broadly divided into three classes of investment types: value, blend, and growth.

What are "value funds"?

Value funds attempt to find stocks in companies that are trading below their inherent value because they are out of favor in the markets, but still have great products and services. Over time, the stocks that compose the portfolio should appreciate faster.

What are "growth funds"?

Growth funds identify stocks that have high potential for growth in their profits and share price.

What are "blended funds"?

Blended funds seek to combine value stocks and growth stocks, reducing an investor's risk over time.

What other types of mutual funds exist?

There are also international funds that invest exclusively in companies outside the United States; global funds that invest in companies both outside the United States and in the United States if they have strong sales and operations located worldwide; and regional funds that invest in a portfolio of companies in various regions of the world, such as Europe, Asia, and South America.

What about sector/specialty funds?

Sector funds seek to invest in companies in various specific sectors of our economy, such as health care, manufacturing, oil and gas, financial services, information technology, bioengineering, and the Internet. Because of their specificity, these funds tend

125

Investing in an oil refinery would be an example of putting money into an energy sector fund.

to have higher risks—but also higher rewards—if the mutual fund company finds the right basket of winners.

What is the final category of funds?

The last category of funds is index funds. Index funds purchase a share in each of the stocks that compose a certain index, such as the S&P 500 or the Dow, and seek to mimic the returns the index may obtain. These funds have the lowest management fees, since there is very little management needed to maintain the portfolio; the managers are merely buying shares weighted exactly as the index. This enables an investor to minimize his risk by having the volatility of the portfolio distributed over dozens—if not hundreds or thousands—of stocks. Ultimately, the return you receive is the same as the return of that index in any given period of time.

What is an "open-ended fund"?

An open-ended fund is a mutual fund that has no restrictions on the number of shares it issues to the public, and is continuously buying and selling shares of its portfolio of stocks to both new and current investors. Most mutual funds are open to investors.

What is a "closed mutual fund"?

The managers of a closed mutual fund may decide that the number of investors and portfolio value is of a certain size, and they wish to limit the inflow of new capital into the fund. In this case, while the fund may be closed to new investors, current investors may continue to purchase or sell shares.

NO–LOAD AND LOADED MUTUAL FUNDS

What are "no-load mutual funds"?

No-load mutual funds do not charge any fee to investors for purchasing or selling (redeeming) shares of that fund.

What are "loaded funds"?

Loaded funds are mutual funds that charge a fee for purchasing (front loading) or selling (back-end loading) shares in the fund. They have the highest expenses associated with them, and are offered by brokers who receive commissions on your transactions. Because of the fees associated, an investor in loaded mutual funds may experience lower returns.

What is a "level load"?

The term level load refers to a load paid for a mutual fund that is dependent upon how long the investor has held shares in the fund. These loads are often deducted annually from the shareholder's account, and are computed as a percentage of the fund's assets. So, even if a the load percentage does not change over time, and if the net asset value of the fund increases over time, the value of the level load will become more expensive, and will erode the potential returns to the fund's investors. Level loads are often concealed within a fund's operating expenses.

Can a fund claim to be "no load," and yet still charge a load to investors?

Yes. Mutual funds may claim in their marketing literature to be "no load," and yet still charge up to one percent for a load. It is important to scrutinize all loads and fees associated with investing in any mutual fund, whether pre-tax or after-tax, as these fees and loads will greatly impact returns over time.

How is simplification an important aspect of investing in no-load mutual funds?

According to editors at *The Wall Street Journal*'s MarketWatch, experts assert that in their quest to cover financial news stories 24 hours a day, and financial services companies incessantly trying to create and market new financial investment vehicles, it is

For what do mutual funds use sales "loads"?

Mutual funds use sales loads to pay sales fees or commissions for additional compensation to sales representatives of the funds, including brokers, financial planners, investment advisers, etc., since they offer expertise, knowledge, and training on the funds' benefits to their clients.

difficult for an individual investor to adhere to a simple, long-term diversified strategy of investing. Younger investors seeking higher returns may choose relatively complex mixes of investments, when choosing simpler investments may work just as well.

What is a "tax-cost ratio"?

Most individual investors who invest in mutual funds are not sensitive to the tax consequence of their investments, especially for holdings not included in before-tax 401(k), IRA, or other before-tax retirement plans. Mutual funds that trade in and out of equities—buying and selling dividend-producing investments—tend to generate more gains that expose an investor to tax consequences that are the investor's responsibility on his income taxes each year. Morningstar reports the tax ratios of mutual funds in order to see the tax efficiency of a fund, compared with its peers. Ultimately, you can see how a fund's total return is diminished by taxes that ultimately are paid on gains realized by the fund. Since mutual funds, through their trading activity, are regularly distributing stock dividends, bond dividends, interest payments, and short-/long-term capital gains to investors, taxes must be paid by the investors for each filing year. A fund with a 2% tax-cost ratio means that during a particular year, the investors in the fund lose 2% of their assets to taxes. Tax-cost ratios may range from 0% (very tax efficient) to 5% (very tax inefficient)

What are typical tax-cost ratios for mutual funds?

Tax-cost ratios for mutual funds will often depend on the category of investment predominant within the portfolio. Typical tax-cost ratios for municipal bond funds are approximately 0.05%, but for the typical high-yield corporate bond fund it may be approximately 3.29%. Depending on the portfolio turnover rate, a fund can generate greater gains than other funds, even higher than 5% per year, so it is important to understand these costs before investing. It is important to note that under guidelines established by the SEC, after-tax returns for funds should be calculated based upon the highest taxable income brackets; if investors fall inside a lower tax bracket, their tax costs will be lower.

Why are tax-cost ratios important to our understanding of mutual fund expense loads?

You need to understand the taxable consequences of investing in mutual funds because after-tax returns for a particular fund reflect both tax effects and sales loads. It is very important to know what loads are being charged to enter a fund, and to redeem or sell shares of a fund.

Under what circumstances might I pay more in management fees or loads, instead of targeting lower-expense funds?

There are many reasons why you may wish to include (higher-fee) actively managed funds over (lower-fee) index mutual funds or other lower-fee alternatives. According to experts at *Forbes*, if you cannot identify a lower-cost fund that offers you diversification in a specific category of investments, you may have to invest in one that does, even if it charges relatively more in expenses. If the manager of the fund is very good at identifying and investing in a properly diversified portfolio, investors may have to pay higher fees to benefit from these selections.

INDEX FUNDS

What is a "market index"?

A market index is a collection or grouping of stocks that tracks the price performance of this selection of stocks. Indexes may cover any aspect of our economy, and may be quite broad or specific in focus, depending on the index. Some indexes use a market capitalization of individual stocks in order to weight each stock component of the index. Others, such as the Dow, use a special calculation in order to weight each stock component of its average.

What is a "capitalization-weighted" index?

A capitalization-weighted index uses market capitalization (the current value of all stock outstanding) to give proportionate weight to these stocks in relation to the total market capitalization of the index. Stocks that are highly valuable, with a large market capitalization, can influence the performance of an entire capitalization-weighted index by pulling the overall market prices either up or down.

How many index funds exist?

According to experts at *Kiplinger's Personal Finance,* in 2003 there were approximately 419 index funds in which to invest. Today there are more than 1,732 index fund choices for an individual investor, with assets increasing by 70% over the past five years to over $2 trillion. Money invested in bond index funds has increased to approximately $510 billion. In contrast, money invested in actively managed stock portfolios declined by 18% during the same period.

Why are index funds attractive to many investors?

Kiplinger's Personal Finance experts assert that index funds are a popular form of investment because some index funds have better returns than actively man-

The number of index funds in the United States has more than tripled in the last decade, and investment in bond index funds is now over $500 billion.

aged portfolios and have very low expenses related to managing the fund, so that the returns will be less impacted by expenses than actively managed funds. For example, typical index funds have expenses in fractions of a percent, whereas the average expense ratio of typical actively managed funds is 1.2%. *Kiplinger's* also cited transparency as a main reason why individual investors seem to like index funds. When an individual investor decides to acquire shares in an index fund, he knows exactly what makes up the investment.

What is an interesting strategy when it comes to investing in actively managed funds and passively managed index funds?

Some experts believe it may be wise to use active managers for some special sectors while still using more passively managed index funds for other sectors. In one example cited by *Kiplinger's*, one might use a passively managed index fund for large company investing, but use an actively managed fund for small company investing.

What are the important market indexes for mutual funds in which I may invest?

There are many different indexes in which you may invest. You may invest in a mutual fund or an exchange traded fund that mimics the performance of the index. The DJIA is an index of thirty top blue chip companies covering many segments in our economy. The index includes representative companies from various sectors of the economy, such as financial services, computers, and retail companies. The specific group of thirty stocks does not include sectors such as transportation or utilities, as they may be given special attention under another index. The index itself is not weighted by market capitalization, and it represents a good snapshot of how "the market" is doing at that moment.

- The New York Stock Exchange Composite Index tracks the price movements of all listed stocks on the NYSE, and is capitalization-weighted. The Standard & Poor's 500 Composite Index is a selection of key stocks in a variety of industries that are selected based upon such variables as market capitalization, liquidity, and the industry or market segment in which the company competes.

- The Wilshire 5000 Total Market Index measures the price performance of the entire U.S. stock market, containing all U.S.-based publicly traded companies, and is weighted by market capitalization.

- The Russell 200 Index is capitalization weighted, and represents some of the smallest publicly traded companies by market capitalization.

- The NASDAQ 100 Index is a modified capitalization-weighted index in which the hundred stocks listed are selected based upon such criteria as having average trading volume greater than 100,000 shares, and must have been listed on NASDAQ or any other major exchange for two or more years. The NASDAQ 100 tracks the 101 largest and most actively traded non-financial U.S. and foreign securities listed on The NASDAQ Stock Market.

What are some of the other key indexes in which to invest?

There are many other indexes in which to invest. Some of the key indexes include: The NYSE Amex Composite Index (including the former Amex Composite Index); Dow Jones Transportation Average (large capitalization stocks that represent the transportation sector of the economy); Dow Jones Utility Average (large capitalization stocks that represent the utilities segment of the economy); the Russell 3000 Index (largest companies, representing 98% of the U.S. stock markets); and the S&P MidCap 400 Index (representing mid-sized companies, reflective of the performance of most of the broader mid-cap equities available to invest in the United States).

Why do some experts believe in investing in indexes instead of investing in individual stocks?

Many experts, some of whom contributed their knowledge and opinion in a recent *Forbes* article, cited several longitudinal studies of investment performance of key index investing and the performance of actively managed mutual funds that may invest in individual stocks and other investment vehicles. The experts found, during the period 1984 to 2002, mutual fund managers, who regularly have staff and expert assistance in

The NASDAQ building is located in Times Square in New York City. The NASDAQ 100 is currently one of the most important market indices.

identifying and investing in stocks, generated a return of approximately 9.3% compared with an average annual return of 12.2% for the S&P 500 index. Another study, cited in an article published by Morningstar, analyzed the performance of all mutual funds, selecting only the top 30 funds to study and dividing their time period of analysis from 1976 to 2002 into five four-year windows in order to find out how many funds that were doing well for four years also were doing well during the subsequent four-year period. What they discovered was that while the top thirty funds generated returns of 28.3% during the first four-year period, these same funds dropped out of the top list in the next four years, and only averaged returns of approximately 1.8%.

Why are index mutual funds or index ETFs preferred by many over buying individual stocks and actively managed mutual funds?

Aside from being able to ride the gains of the current economic cycle without having to spend a formidable amount of time to do so, many experts believe that by investing in index funds of different types, the expenses needed to manage these funds are relatively less when compared with other types of investments. Since expenses are lower, more of the gains of the index can go directly into an investor's pocket. You should compare expenses related to acquiring different investments, as they have a great effect upon your returns.

Why are indexes important to investors, even if we do not invest directly in them?

One of the most important purposes of following a particular index is to provide both large and small investors with a benchmark by which to compare the performance of investments in similar categories. If you own a combination of mutual funds and stocks of large U.S. companies, you may measure your performance against a similar benchmark index such as the Dow to gauge how you are doing each period.

What are some disadvantages to investing in an index fund?

Experts at *Forbes* note many reasons to invest in index funds. However, there can also be some disadvantages to investing in index funds. Some index funds have relatively high management fees. Other index funds purchased through a broker may require commission payments and fees when you first buy shares, acquire more shares, and sell shares. It is also important to note that buying index funds is not intended to replace

---

How might I circumvent the minimum investment requirement if I invest in an index fund?

Some investment firms, brokerage houses, or mutual funds waive the minimum investment requirement if you enroll in an automatic investment program, in which you automatically invest the same amount of money per period.

proper financial planning, asset allocation, and risk awareness. It is important to have a clear understanding of how you wish to have your portfolio properly allocated before you invest in any instrument, including an index fund.

What are some reasons not to invest in an index fund?

While there are certainly many advantages to investing in an index fund, with its low (or no) fees, broad market coverages, and good returns, some experts believe there are some distinct disadvantages to investing in index funds. As the market that your index fund tracks increases, so do your holdings. But the opposite is also true. As the market for your index or index fund declines in value, so will your holdings. Many individual stock investors believe in culling out the poorly performing available stocks in which to invest in favor of a refined selection of the top performers. This strategy is asserted by many who try to outperform a benchmark index through proper selection. Index funds do not remove poorly performing stocks, nor do they actively trade a selection of stocks. One expert argues that although many index funds may represent some perceived modicum of diversification to investors, usually as the general market declines in value, so do both index funds and actively managed diversified portfolios or sectors of mutual funds. This expert also argues that index funds provide some investors with a perceived false sense of security. Just because you are invested in an index that seems always to be increasing does not necessarily mean it will continue to do so.

What is a "collective investment fund vehicle"?

A collective investment fund vehicle is any investment that groups together individuals to enter into investments in order to benefit more than investing individually. The many advantages of investing collectively include: the ability to have professional money managers manage the buying and selling of individual investments; the ability for these same managers to mitigate our risk, and spread this risk out among more choices; the ability to share the costs inherent in investing, providing for proper diversification among asset classes; and providing extensive research and analysis. Collective investment vehicles can also be known as mutual funds (a term used in the United States), investment funds, or managed funds.

What are the three main types of mutual funds?

The three main types of mutual funds are equity or stock funds, fixed income or bond funds, and money market funds. Stock or equity funds try to deliver positive returns to investors or shareholders by investing in the stocks of companies. Stock funds may be in one of several different subgroups, such as large capitalization, middle capitalization, small capitalization, and micro capitalization, depending on the size of the companies in which the management team is investing. Equity stock funds may also be grouped into various types of styles: growth, blended, and value. Growth funds typically try to deliver performance by investing in companies with very high earnings or profit growth that reinvest these earnings into areas that help continue to grow the business, includ-

133

ing sales and marketing, product development, research and development, acquisitions, etc. These investments typically pay out little or no dividends or income; rather, they reinvest this income to fuel their longer-term growth (beyond five years). Blended funds have no fixed income or bond funds in their portfolios. They do have various equities that may generate returns to investors by increasing share prices, comprising both growth stocks (high-earnings growth companies) and value stocks (with share prices that may increase in value once the market realizes this). Bond or fixed income funds deliver returns to investors and shareholders by investing in a variety of fixed income or debt-driven investment vehicles and money market funds.

What is a "style box"?

A style box is a graph with sectors that display the different types of investment styles or characteristics of typical mutual funds. On the vertical axis, there are several classes representing the size of companies in which the mutual fund may invest. On the horizontal axis, there are several classes representing the degree of aggressiveness in the portfolio, that describes whether the fund seeks to invest very aggressively, generate income for the investor, or provide a combination of the two strategies.

What is the typical organization of a fund?

Typical investment funds have organizations that may include: a fund or investment manager who helps drive the fund's investment decisions, researchers/analysts who as-

A typical investment fund includes a board of directors who ensure the fund is complying with regulations and laws, as well as the general mission of the fund, and safeguarding shareholders' interests.

sist in providing analysis on investment ideas and trades; a fund administrator who manages trading activity, redemptions, account reconciliations, valuations, and pricing; a board of directors who ensure the fund is complying with regulations and laws, as well as the general mission of the fund, and safeguarding shareholders' interests; the actual shareholders (who may be individuals, trusts, corporations, or even other mutual funds); and marketing and public relations teams who may be employees or outside companies engaged in creating demand for and sales of the fund's assets. Behind the scenes, there may also be many financial and accounting professionals, both internal and external, who ensure the capital flows and taxes are correctly accounted for and paid regularly.

How much money is currently under management by investment companies?

According to researchers at the Investment Company Institute (ICI), by the end of 2012 an estimated $14.7 trillion will have been under management, representing a $1.7 trillion increase over 2011 levels. The increase in this value may be due in part to the overall increase in the values of the major stock indexes in the United States, as well as very strong increases in stock prices in various key international markets. And because of the overall weakness in the U.S. dollar relative to other foreign currencies, some foreign stock prices recorded double-digit growth rates. Also in 2012, for the first time since 2008, investors contributed approximately $196 billion into mutual funds. Additionally, in 2012 investors reinvested $194 billion of income dividends and $93 billion in capital gains distributions back into the markets.

What is "gearing," or "leverage"?

Gearing, or leverage, occurs when a fund borrows money against its own assets in order to create capital that is then used to invest. The amount of leverage can be seen from the fund's reported indebtedness. The principal thinking here is that a fund with more debt is perhaps leveraging more than other funds, and therefore may be riskier over time than a fund with less debt. It may be good for some funds to leverage, especially to take advantage of upturns in markets, allowing the fund to benefit from these positive moves with more cash than current investors' proceeds would allow in order to generate better performance for shareholders.

Who is investing in mutual funds?

ICI researchers found that American households continue their reliance upon mutual funds, as 23% of all households' financial assets are currently being managed by registered investment companies.

What are some important points to consider before investing in a mutual fund?

According to the SEC, there are some key considerations before you invest in a mutual fund. It is good to look at the fund's service charges, fees, and loads, as well as the fund's expenses, to see how it compares to other similar funds. Funds with higher expenses will have to perform much better in order to generate a good return on their investments than lower-cost funds of the same type and return.

It is important to note that even small differences in a fund's expenses may translate into many thousands of dollars in costs, that in turn may affect the return an investor desires. It is also important to note how a mutual fund may affect your tax bill at the end of the year, as a mutual fund must distribute capital gains to shareholders if it sells a stock at a profit that cannot be offset by a loss. And you must pay taxes on any capital gains, even if the fund's return has been negative since you began investing in it. One way around this is to contact the prospective fund to find out when capital gains will be distributed, so you may avoid this burden immediately upon investing.

It is also important to consider the size and age of the fund. A "newly created" fund with a relatively small number of companies in its portfolio may show a higher return in the short term than other similar funds, and may still be small enough to generate quick profits. Over the long term, however, the results may be considerably different as the fund expands, and has more years of results to analyze. The SEC also notes that potential investors should look at a portfolio's turnover rate, the frequency with which the fund buys and sells securities. Each time a mutual fund buys and sells securities it generates capital gains and losses. This usually translates to higher costs for the investor in fees and in capital gains taxes.

You should also look at the volatility of a fund, since two funds may record the same average return over a long period of time, but one may have many years of losses offset by a few stellar years. This makes the fund more volatile than a more stable fund that may, year-over-year post smaller, more stable, and thus relatively less volatile gains. As mentioned above, it is important to read prospectuses to understand the risks of each fund choice, and understand that funds with very high rates of return may, in fact, be engaging in relatively riskier investments. You should also consider the management of the fund, whether there have been any changes, and how long the managers have been in place before investing.

Last, you should see how investing in such a fund affects the overall diversity of your portfolio. For example, if you have heard about a new small company or international fund, but already have a large percentage of your portfolio invested in this type, you should consider what may happen (both good and bad) if you increase our concentration in this fund type. You need to consider the overall diversification of your investments before you invest.

What percentage of the total dollars invested in investment companies are in each type of investment company?

According to researchers at the Investment Company Institute (ICI), in its 2013 study, of the approximate $14.7 trillion invested, 88% is invested in mutual funds, 1.8% in closed-ended mutual funds, 8.8% in ETFs, and less than 0.1% in unit investment trusts.

What percentage of mutual fund assets is typically invested in each mutual fund category by American families?

The Investment Company Institute also found that 55% of mutual fund assets are invested in stock funds, 23% are invested in cash or money market funds, 15% are invested in bond funds, and 6% are a hybrid of both bond and money market funds.

When looking at comparisons of mutual funds, what is "performance"?

Mutual fund performance is the appreciation of the current assets of a fund, plus the reinvestment of the earnings of the portfolio, less any fees related to this activity.

Who invests in mutual funds?

According to researchers at the ICI, citing its own data and data from the U.S. Census Bureau, in 2012, 92 million individual investors owned mutual funds and held 89% of all mutual fund assets. This represents a total of approximately 53.8 million households or 44% of all U.S. households. The ICI researchers note that the ownership percentages have remained rather stable over the past ten years. The researchers also note that the median amount invested in mutual funds is approximately $100,000; that 48% of these investors are college graduates; and that 72% of investors worked full- or part-time. They also note that 93% of these investors are investing for retirement, 27% are investing for education, and 63% invested in their first mutual fund through their employer.

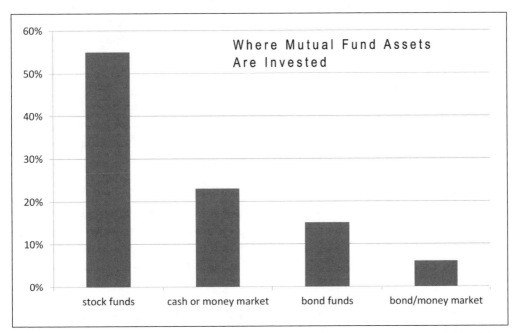

55% of mutual fund assets are invested in stock funds, 23% are invested in cash or money market funds, 15% are invested in bond funds, and 6% are a hybrid of both bond and money market funds.

How do mutual funds provide for diversification?

By their nature, mutual funds provide diversification, even within their specialty segments, because they hold many different investment instruments that may or may not be correlated. Some investments may go up and others may decline, but overall, the portfolio manager wants the portfolio to be sufficiently diverse that its performance is positive, exceeding its peers (other similar mutual funds) and "the market" at large. If some of its positions are not performing well, this can be offset by others that are doing well, providing investment diversity.

Why can a mutual fund provide for more diversity of investments than any one individual investment?

A mutual fund that pools together large amounts of capital from many investors can choose many more investment vehicles, thereby providing much more diversity within the portfolio.

CLOSED-ENDED MUTUAL FUNDS

What is a "closed-ended mutual fund"?

A closed-ended mutual fund is similar to an open-ended mutual fund. Both sell shares to investors and use the proceeds to buy securities or investment vehicles, depending on the investment goal of the portfolio. But the main difference between an open-ended and closed-ended fund is that an open-ended fund can sell an unlimited number of shares in the fund, depending on variables such as investor demand, investment performance, and the size of the fund that the fund manager desires, etc. The share price of an open-ended fund, or its net asset value, can be derived by dividing the market value of the portfolio by the number of shares outstanding and held by investors at the end of each trading day, when managers can assess the value of the holdings of the portfolio and the amount of purchases and redemptions of the fund on any given day. Closed-ended funds (a set or fixed number of shares) issue in an initial public offering, and invest the proceeds into investment vehicles, given the fund's objective.

How do closed-ended funds differ from exchange traded funds?

Both closed-ended funds and ETFs trade their shares on various exchanges. But ETFs generally track and try to mimic the performance of some benchmark exchange, such as the performance of the Dow, or the Standard & Poor's 500, making them comparatively more diverse than some closed-ended funds, and giving them relatively lower fees, since the ETFs are not trading as actively as closed-ended funds.

What are some other differences between closed-ended funds and ETFs?

Many experts believe closed-ended funds are more prone to change their original investment objective in order to pursue better returns. ETFs really cannot do this, since

Do closed-ended funds ever trade at a discount?

Many closed-ended funds trade at a discount, meaning the share price may be lower than the net asset value of the fund, in which case an investor may see a gain in a relatively short period of time. If the share price at any given moment is more than the net asset value of the shares in the fund, the investor may pay a premium to invest in the fund. But if the closed-ended fund generates many trades in order to outperform some benchmark, the investor may have to pay higher fees and capital gains taxes if the investments are not in some form of retirement account.

they usually invest in market indexes. This means that ETFs tend to be more transparent to the investor in terms of what is in their portfolios than are closed-ended funds that may change the mix of their investments at any time. Closed-ended funds may also use leverage to try to enhance the performance of their portfolios, whereas ETFs generally do not use leverage to enhance their portfolios. Closed-ended funds tend to have more activity in trades related to buying and selling its underlying shares, generating more taxable events than ETFs.

What are some important steps to take when considering investing in a closed-ended fund?

Before you invest in a closed-ended fund, you should consider what sector or type of closed-ended fund matches your investing goals. You may also see how the fund compares with similar funds by looking online at websites such as Lipper and Morningstar, as well as industry reports from popular news organizations such as *U.S. News & World Report* and *Money*. The next step is to check the size of the discount or premium the fund is currently trading against its net asset value. If the fund is trading at a discount (as opposed to a premium), you stand a better chance of having good performance after you invest. You may see the fund's average one-year discount since its inception, and compare it to today's current discount. Even though it has been stated many times that one should never base a decision to invest solely upon a fund's past performance, it may indicate how well the fund may do in the future. It is a good idea also to review a potential fund's historical performance, to see how consistent it is, how it compares to other similar funds, and how it compares to various market indexes. According to experts at *The Wall Street Journal*, it is important to note the debt of a closed-ended fund, since more debt means the fund may be taking out loans to leverage its portfolio's investments, inherently making the fund riskier.

What are some other important considerations when evaluating closed-ended funds?

Like any mutual fund in which you are considering investing, you should consider the expense ratio of the fund, covering costs such as management fees and expenses related

139

to trades. It is good to invest in funds with relatively lower fees, since these fees ultimately can depress the funds' gains. It is also important to note the yield of the funds, since closed-ended funds generate relatively more income than other types of funds, and the gains are taxable on investments in funds that are outside your retirement plans. Also, some experts suggest avoiding IPO closed-ended funds, as the discount between the initial offering and the net asset value typically becomes larger following the offering. It is also important to see how long a fund's management team has been in place. If a fund has had a great deal of turnover or change in its team, one may experience decreased returns as a result.

What percentage of closed-ended funds actually trade at a discount to their net asset value?

According to research experts at Lipper, as reported in May 2013, 81% of all closed-ended funds traded at a discount to their net asset value, while 19% traded at a premium to their net asset value.

EXCHANGE–TRADED FUNDS

What is an "exchange-traded fund"?

An exchange traded fund is an investment vehicle or security that behaves like a stock in that it can be regularly traded on any number of exchanges, but specifically tracks an index or indexes, commodities, bonds, or other assets. Its daily price may change during the trading day, as its shares are constantly being bought and sold by investors, so its net asset value is not calculated on a daily basis, as occurs with a mutual fund that determines its net asset value at the close of the market each day. ETFs tend to trade near their current net asset value during the course of a trading day.

Why are ETFs attractive to some investors?

ETFs are attractive to investors because they tend to track an index or indexes, have relatively lower costs than some mutual funds, and do not incur the same type of tax consequences as a typical mutual fund.

How long have ETFs been available to investors?

ETFs have been available to investors in the United States since 1993, and to European investors since 1999. Although index funds from their inception were allowed to

An exchange-traded fund behaves like a stock, while tracking specific bonds, indexes, commodities, or other assets.

track various market indexes, it was not until 2008 that the SEC allowed ETFs to be more actively managed, allowing managers of ETFs to purchase investments that appear to be undervalued or to sell short investments that may be overvalued, as indicated by share prices that may be falling in the near term.

How do I purchase shares in an ETF?

You may purchase shares of various ETFs by contacting your investment broker, or by using any number of online brokerage firms. Although ETFs may track a benchmark index and have low management fees, investors still must pay commissions when purchasing or selling shares.

What are some notable ETFs?

Some of the more notable ETFs include the NASDAQ "Cubes" (tracks NASDAQ–100), Dow "Diamonds" (tracks the DJIA), and various "Spiders" (tracks Standard & Poor's 500 or a component of the index).

What are some influential stocks used as components of many ETFs?

Some of the most influential stocks used as components within many ETFs include Apple Computer, Exxon/Mobil, Microsoft, Google, and Chevron.

Why do ETFs experience volatility in prices and liquidity?

Since exchange traded funds generally try to mimic the holdings and performance of various market indexes, if any heavily weighted individual share within an index experiences a severe drop, the market in general may experience a severe drop, and the ETF may experience an even worse drop. Since the prices of the underlying exchange drop precipitously, the prices of the ETF may also drop, and few buyers of the ETF may be found, further deflating the price of the ETF, thus affecting its liquidity.

UNIT INVESTMENT TRUSTS

What are "unit investment trusts"?

Unit investment trusts are one of three investment company types. A unit investment trust issues redeemable shares or units, and may buy back those shares at their approximate net asset value. Unit investment trusts typically make a one-time public offering of a specific number of shares. As opposed to a mutual fund that may continue well into the future, a unit investment trust will have a termination date established when it is created that indicates when the entire fund will terminate. For a unit investment trust that invests primarily in bonds, the termination date may be when the bonds mature. After a unit investment trust terminates, all remaining securities and positions in the portfolio are sold at the current market value, and all the proceeds are paid to investors (less any service charges or loads) at the time of sale.

What is a principal difference between a unit investment trust and a mutual fund?

One of the principal differences between a unit investment trust and a mutual fund is that a unit investment trust does not actively trade its investment portfolio. Rather, a unit investment trust buys relatively fixed securities (such as corporate and/or municipal bonds) and holds them for relatively long periods of time, with little or no trading. Since the portfolio is fixed, investors know exactly what they are investing in by reading the prospectus. Unit investment trusts also do not typically have boards of directors, corporate officers, or investment advisers. Unit investment trusts are also regulated under a specific Congressional act, the Investment Company Act of 1940, Sections 4 and 26.

What are some differences between a unit investment trust and an open-ended fund?

Unit investment trusts are more restricted in terms of how they manage their portfolios than open-ended funds. Unit investment trusts typically do not immediately reinvest dividends that may be paid or distributed to shareholders, but hold the dividends, and at some future point in time distribute these dividends to all investors. Unit investment trusts may not loan out securities that make up their portfolios, and must reproduce the index they are replicating. A unit investment trust has a specific expiration period when the trust is terminated, something an open-ended fund does not have to do. The time when a unit investment trust might terminate may be in a range of several years to several decades.

RATINGS COMPANIES

What is Morningstar?

As one of the most successful and credible ratings companies, Morningstar is a financial analytical firm that provides research services worldwide. Founded in 1984, it currently tracks the performance of 437,000 investment vehicles, including stocks, bonds,

---

Where can I find information pertaining to mutual fund ratings?

You can find a great deal of information by looking at various websites that offer performance data, research, rankings, and various online tools that may help you understand your mutual fund investment choices. Some websites will even report the best-performing funds and the worst-performing funds, along with analytical reports. Some key websites you should consider include Morningstar, U.S. News & World Report, www.theStreet.com, www.MSN.com, www.Bloomberg.com, www.CNNMoney.com, and www.Lipperweb.com.

and mutual funds, as well as real-time data on more than 10 million equities, indexes, futures, options, commodities, and precious metals, in addition to foreign exchange and treasury markets. Morningstar also offers investment management services, with over $176 billion under management. It maintains offices in 27 countries and employs approximately 3,490 people.

What is Lipper?

Lipper is a financial research firm founded in 1973 and owned by Thomson Reuters. Lipper tracks the performance of over 213,000 share classes and more than 117,000 funds located in sixty countries. Lipper ranks various funds on a scale of 1 (worst) to 5 (best) on a variety of criteria important to investors related to the funds' performance and expenses, carefully comparing funds to their peers. This gives potential investors in these funds added perspective and the means to wade through and compare similar investment choices in an unbiased fashion. When possible, funds are ranked based upon three-, five-, and ten-year performance. Lipper also tracks the performance of various indexes and sectors.

What is the "Lipper Average"?

The Lipper Average, or Lipper Index, is a number based on a series of indexes that include actively managed funds divided into various categories, such as large cap or small cap growth funds. The Lipper Average does not track the performance of passively managed funds, and only tracks the performance of current funds, so historical performance comparisons may be adjusted if a fund terminates. Since the comparisons are only between similar funds, and not any index or benchmark, some experts believe that some conclusions drawn from the Lipper Average performance data may mislead investors. An example could be one fund that declined by 20%, and another similar fund that declined by 10%. The fund that declined by 10% may seem attractive compared with a similar fund, but if a benchmark closely correlated to the fund declined by only 5%, then both funds' returns are pretty weak.

What is the Standard & Poor's Indices Versus Active (SPIVA) funds scorecard?

The Standard & Poor's Indices Versus Active funds scorecard is a research study published every six months. It measures the performance of actively managed U.S. equity funds, international equity funds, and fixed income funds. The data is corrected for various inherent inconsistencies, such as survivorship bias (as funds liquidate or merge with other funds), similarity of comparison (to compare the fund with the correct index, given its portfolio and objective),

Standard & Poor's, founded in 1860, is one of three major rating companies.

asset-weighted returns (so large funds with great returns are treated differently than small funds with great returns), style drift (when a fund develops a portfolio outside its core objective), and data cleaning (excluding indexed funds, leveraged funds, and inverse funds).

In the period 2008–2010, how many funds that SPIVA tracks either liquidated or were merged?

In the period 2008–2010, 17% of U.S. domestic equity funds, 13% of international equity funds, and 10% of all fixed income funds were merged or liquidated.

HEDGE FUNDS

How are hedge funds different from other types of mutual funds?

Hedge funds are not governed by the Investment Company Act of 1940, and are not required to register with the SEC.

What is a "hedge fund"?

It is a collective investment, similar to a mutual fund, that tries to make positive returns on invested capital whether the markets are rising or falling. In order to invest in a hedge fund, an investor needs to be a qualified investor or purchaser, as defined by U.S. regulations. Since a hedge fund limits the number of participants in the fund, hedge funds are not sold to the general public, and may therefore be exempt from certain regulations that affect how the fund is structured and managed. But the fund must comply with any regulations within the countries in which it operates.

In what kind of investments do hedge funds invest?

Most hedge funds employ a strategy and make investments around that strategy, but may rapidly change strategies when markets change. One type of hedge fund, "global macro," may take a position in an equity, currency, or bond of a country in anticipation of a large event that may positively affect the price, thus generating returns that are favorable to investors. Hedge funds may employ software and use mathematical models to generate returns. Other times, investment managers and analysts identify likely candidates according to their trading objectives, and try to make returns. Many hedge funds use a combination of both approaches.

Another type of hedge fund, "directional," may try to provide returns through understanding and placing bets on the general direction of markets, no matter where they are located. For example, a hedge fund manager may think a market is undervalued, and may engage in long equity positions, hoping the market will increase and realize its true value, and make positive returns. Hedge funds may also employ the opposite strategy, acting as a hedge, and employing short sales in case the market moves in the opposite direction, and make returns if the market falls.

Some hedge funds employ an event-driven strategy that may involve the merger, bankruptcy, or acquisition of a corporate investment. This may also include the default of a country on its debt obligations, and the effects that such an event may have on the price of the country's equities or currency. Wars, regional conflicts, disruption of oil, and other inputs may also be used to help drive profits for the fund.

Other hedge funds may try to profit from discrepancies in prices of investment vehicles such as currencies, equities, and bonds. The hedge fund may employ sophisticated mathematical models and software in order to identify these price discrepancies, and may try to take positions both long and short in order to provide maximum return to investors.

What is a "short position"?

A short position occurs when an investor or investment company borrows shares of stock from a broker and sells them on the open market at a later time. Since the stock must be returned or sold back to the broker at some future date, if the investment price falls, the investor may then buy it for less than the price he originally paid, earning a profit.

What is a "long position"?

A long position may be the purchase of an equity in expectation that the equity will increase in value, thus generating a profit. If the price falls, the investor loses.

SOCIALLY RESPONSIBLE INVESTMENTS (SRIs)

What are "socially responsible investments"?

Socially responsible investments are made in order to generate some financial gain while doing societal good. Some buyers enjoy investing in companies perceived to be "green" and engaged in environmentally sound practices, offering protection to consumers and defenders of human rights. For example, a typical socially responsible mutual fund may choose not to invest in tobacco companies, polluters, or weapons producers.

What about corporate governance issues? What role do they play in socially responsible investing?

Corporate governance, or the way in which corporate organizations are managed (or mismanaged) also plays a role in socially responsible investing, as more people believe that corporations need to be more responsible and take into consideration underlying supportive social values when making many broad decisions about the strategies of their companies. For example, a socially irresponsible corporation would have no issue using child labor in China, as long as the corporation continues to hit profit targets. Another example may be the high compensation of executives, even after a company fires thousands of employees and teeters on bankruptcy. The full disclosure of information on ex-

"Green roofs" are a growing (pun intended) trend in many cities. Companies that encourage such practices may get the added benefit of attracting investors concerned with the environment.

ecutive compensation is an important measure that many believe is often a sign of sound corporate governance. Socially responsible firms align themselves with and support certain broad values, both bottom-up and top-down.

How old is the concept of socially responsible investing?

The original concept of socially responsible investing may have its roots in mid-eighteenth century America. In 1982, Trillium Asset Management was founded to advise investors specifically in sustainable and responsible investing, as SRI is also known.

What is an example of socially responsible investing having an effect on changing a society?

Many experts believe the divestiture of companies doing business in apartheid-practicing South Africa played a large role in helping to end apartheid there.

How much money is now tied to socially responsible investing?

According to experts at The Forum for Sustainable and Responsible Investment, as of the end of 2012, $3.74 trillion has been invested in socially responsible investments through SRI-type mutual funds. In the period 2007 to 2010, total assets in SRIs grew 13%, compared with other professionally managed funds, which only grew less than 1%.

> ## How is socially responsible investing growing?
>
> According to experts at Morningstar, around 1995, approximately 55 SRIs managed $12 billion in assets. By 2010, that number increased to 250, investing in more than $569 billion. Additionally, 26 exchange-traded funds mirror the performance of investments in socially responsible companies

What is the "US SIF"?

The US SIF is the Forum for Sustainable and Responsible Investment, a membership organization serving professionals, firms, institutions, and organizations engaged in sustainable and responsible investing by considering environmental, social, and corporate governance criteria in order to generate long-term competitive financial returns with a measurable positive societal impact. Members include investment management and advisory firms, mutual fund companies, research firms, financial planners and advisers, broker-dealers, banks, credit unions, community development organizations, non-profit associations, pension funds, foundations, and other asset owners. Members in the organization seek to expand the concept that they may generate good financial returns while investing in social values they support.

What is the "KLD 400 Social Index"?

The KLD 400 Social Index consists of top socially responsible mutual funds. Some funds that compose the index can generate high returns, even compared with other non-socially responsible funds.

How has SRI generally changed other areas of investing?

Because many investors believe such environmental issues as global warming may have a direct negative impact on their investments, they are seeking more environmentally sensitive companies in which to invest.

Why do individual investors like to invest in socially responsible forms of investing?

Many investors like to invest in SRIs as a way to protest and give voice to their shared beliefs about a social cause, and feel that by making a certain investment, they are supporting their shared beliefs for a particular cause. Many unions and large pension funds that invest retirement money for millions of individuals have made investments or offered these types of investments to effect change through the pooling of resources of millions of members, as both members and managers of these investments want more socially impactful investments as part of their overall portfolios.

What is another form of sustainable or socially responsible investing?

Another popular form of sustainable or socially responsible investing is impact investing, whereby investors hope to make a positive impact on society by investing in com-

Some companies that might insist they are socially responsible will, upon closer investigation, be revealed as following unethical practices, such as employing child labor in other nations.

panies, organizations, and funds. The investments, as in traditional investing, are made to pursue profits, returns, and financial growth, as well as to make investments that lead to positive and measurable results or impacts on society.

Are there any conflicts when it comes to SRI?

There can be many philosophical conflicts when you choose to invest in a socially responsible fund. Morningstar cites the example of an investor desiring to make an SRI in an emerging market fund that purports to be "socially responsible." The conflict arises because perhaps one or more of the countries targeted by fund managers may be involved in many activities that are antithetical to socially responsible investing, such as engaging in child labor, unfair labor practices, broad violations of human rights, environmental disregard, etc. It is important to consider all facts about the strategy of a fund before investing.

What other major concern might investors have while investing in socially responsible funds?

Another major concern while you invest in SRIs is ensuring that the funds actually are acting socially responsibly when deciding what companies to include in the portfolio. Morningstar, through research conducted by MarketWatch, found that out of 20 large socially responsible funds, half invested directly in oil companies that may not be acting in a socially responsible manner. Morningstar also reported that only 27% of socially responsible funds file shareholder resolutions, or have activist shareholders who try to influence the fund's management into making correct investment choices.

EXPENSE RATIOS

When I consider investing in mutual funds, why are expenses so important?

Expenses are important to the basic evaluation of mutual funds because, although the percentage derived in the expense ratio may appear small, over time, as we look at historical returns of the fund, it can suppress the returns we want or need from our investment. When a mutual fund has an expense ratio of 0.5%, it means that 0.5% of the fund's assets are used to offset expenses to manage the fund every year.

What are a mutual fund's expenses?

The mutual fund's expenses may include management fees, offices and staff, and taxes.

What happens to the expense ratio if a mutual fund is small or new?

When a mutual fund is new, or when a fund has a relatively smaller amount of total assets under management, the fund must allocate its expenses across a smaller pool of investors, making the expense ratio appear high.

What are typical expense ratios of mutual funds?

According to experts, typical actively managed U.S. equity mutual funds may have expense ratios of approximately 1%, while many passively managed index funds may have expense ratios of approximately 0.06%.

How do I compare expenses of mutual funds?

The SEC website provides a mutual fund expense calculator that allows you to compare expenses related to mutual funds. Many websites provide information regarding the expense ratios of funds, so that investors may compare expenses in order to make a better-informed decision before purchasing.

What is the trend in mutual fund expenses and fees?

According to the ICI, the fees mutual funds charge their investors has fallen by half since 1990. This is due in part to the popularity of passively managed funds, as well as cost-cutting activities of actively managed funds.

Why are fees and costs of mutual funds so important in deciding which fund to choose?

The size of the expenses or fees that a mutual fund charges may lower your annual return. Mutual funds with the highest returns and lowest fees will give investors very good

Why does the expense ratio matter?

If your fund has an annual return of 5% this year, and has a 2% expense ratio, your annual return is actually only 3%. The return could have been nearer 5%, but high expenses make it lower. The same type of fund with a lower expense ratio would put more money in your pocket over time, since it spends less of your money administering the fund. This is why expenses matter.

returns over time on their investments. Funds with average returns and high expenses may perform much worse over time.

How do mutual funds justify high fees and expenses?

Some mutual funds justify their high fees because of the cost to employ the many hundreds of managers and analysts who work to bring the high returns investors desire. But these same managers may be no better than managers of funds with fewer expenses. All things being equal, it is best to find funds with the highest returns, the least risks, and lowest fees.

What is an "expense ratio"?

The expense ratio, or management expense ratio, is the total amount of expenses divided by the average net asset value of the portfolio of stocks that compose the fund, expressed as a percentage. A mutual fund with a 1% expense ratio means that 1% of the value of the entire portfolio is used to operate the mutual fund. An expense ratio is an important metric used by many experts to evaluate the relative costs of any type of mutual fund. It allows investors the opportunity to determine if a fund is more expensive to own. This ultimately cuts into returns, and illuminates how well the fund is managing its expenses as it tries to generate returns for investors.

What types of expenses are typically included in an expense ratio calculation?

Although there are many different expenses related to managing a mutual fund, typical expenses used when calculating an expense ratio include: administration, management fees, advertising expenses, accounting fees, rent, and staff. The expenses included in the expense ratio do not include loads for sales or brokerage commissions paid for trades. Many experts assert that once a mutual fund is running for a time, its expenses become fairly predictable. Some mutual funds pay a management company to manage the fund, and are paid a flat percentage per year based upon the fund's net asset value. So as the fund grows, some significant expenses may grow as well. In other cases, the fund's expenses are relatively fixed, so that as the fund grows in asset value, its expenses may stay the same or decrease.

INVESTING IN CASH

Isn't my money still at risk if it is invested in cash?

Yes, your money is still at risk in some ways, as the inflation of prices may erode the value of your money over time. And if prevailing interest rates are especially low, your risk of inflation exposure may actually be much greater than what you perceive.

How is investing in cash different from other forms of investing?

Investing money in cash, or holding a certain percentage of your portfolio in the form of cash, means investing into some investment vehicle with a very short duration (less than 90 days). This may provide a return on the investment in the form of interest rate payments.

What percentage of mutual fund assets are typically invested in cash by American families?

According to researchers at the ICI, 23% of American families invest a portion of their mutual funds in cash or money market funds, and 6% of families invest their portfolio in a hybrid of both bond and money market funds.

Why are returns I generate from investments in cash relatively less than those in other investments, such as stocks or bonds?

The returns for investments in cash-based investment vehicles will generally be less than those of other types of investments because your money is exposed to less risk, and the duration of some of the obligations may be very short term.

What are some examples of typical cash investments?

Typical cash investments that investors generally favor include savings accounts, checking accounts (that may pay interest), certificates of deposit (of a term less than three

151

months), money market funds (that may invest in a variety of different instruments in order to generate returns), and treasury bills.

Why are money market funds attractive to investors?

Besides the fact that money market funds are highly liquid and carry little relative risk, they also have very low (if any) costs or loads. There may also be some additional benefits for investors if the fund invests in tax-free municipal bonds (that may be exempt at the federal and/or state level for income tax purposes). Some money market funds also help a cash investor diversify his portfolio to include such investments as short-term U.S. Treasury securities ("T-bills"), certificates of deposit ("CDs"), and corporate commercial paper (of short duration).

What are some problems with money market funds?

A problem with money market funds is that they are not insured by the FDIC. Other investments with similar returns, such as money market deposit accounts, online savings accounts, and certificates of deposit, are covered by the FDIC.

Why do some people invest strictly in cash?

Some people have a very low tolerance for risk. That is, these investors may not be willing to lose any of their investment, and may decide to invest their money in federally protected investments, such as cash, that earn interest over time. People may also have a shorter time horizon in which to use cash, and may want a less risky investment during this time.

BANKS AND CREDIT UNIONS

What is a "bank"?

A bank is a financial institution licensed by the government that provides a variety of financial services, including: accounts in which to save (savings accounts, retirement accounts such as IRAs and 401(k)s, and certificates of deposit), spending accounts (checking accounts, debit cards, and ATM cards to make transactions), and loans (mortgage, equity, car). These institutions are profit-making entities that seek to give the highest possible return on investment to its investors, who can be both those who initially created the bank, and in the case of publicly traded banks, those who invest in ownership of the banks by purchasing its stock or shares.

What other services do banks provide?

Banks are also a great source of capital for account holders or those who have a relationship with the bank. You can take out loans for notable capital purchases such as house mortgages, automobile loans, home equity loans, small business loans, and large commercial loans for corporations. Banks also manage credit and debit card transactions. In short, banks provide the place to save money, the means to spend that money, and wholly new sources of money by way of loans that provide the fuel for our economy.

Can banks sell stocks and mutual funds?

Yes. Many banks also provide financial stock exchange trading services, enabling account holders to purchase stocks on all major exchanges and invest in mutual funds, as well as providing portfolio management and advice.

How many Americans do not have a bank account?

According to an FDIC survey, 7.7% of all U.S. households—or nearly 17 million Americans—do not have any kind of bank account.

According to the FDIC, about 17 million Americans do not use banks. Not a great idea, because banks provide a safe, insured way to keep your money, as well as providing a variety of useful loan and investment services.

Where do people who do not use banks obtain cash?

According to the same FDIC survey, 18% of all U.S. households rely on pawn shops and paycheck cashing businesses to provide themselves with cash.

Why use a bank?

A bank gives us a secure place to hold our cash. It allows us to keep track of the growth of our most important assets, the product of our work, and gives us a means to make this asset grow. Bank use also contributes to your credit history, and may open up many financial opportunities from the ability to seek advice, to managing your retirement plans, to helping you secure a loan for a major purchase such as a house or car. Banks also give you the means to write checks against your cash in the form of a checking account, so that you may easily make purchases without the need to carry cash. And banks pay interest on your deposits (in your savings accounts and certain types of checking and money market accounts) and CDs.

What percentage of banks offer mutual funds to their customers?

According to the Federal Reserve Bank of St. Louis, Missouri, nearly one-third of all banks in the United States, or approximately 3,500 banks, offer mutual funds to their clients. Some banks may refer customers to other brokerages, while others offer the funds directly to clients.

What is the Federal Deposit Insurance Corporation (FDIC)?

The FDIC was created in 1933—during the Great Depression—to fight the effects of thousands of bank failures that happened in preceding years. It protects depositors up to $250,000 per account holder at each institution, and guarantees this amount for every depositor at every FDIC-insured institution in the United States. If a bank fails, the FDIC is the receiver entrusted to pay all eligible depositors up to this amount, as well as handle the liquidation of all assets owned by the failed institution, combining them with healthier banks when possible, or selling them off entirely. This insures that all Americans have complete trust in the banking system and liquidity, and know their deposits are backed by the U.S. government.

What else does the FDIC do?

The FDIC also examines the health of the banking system by analyzing 5,160 banks—more than half of all banks in the banking system—to ensure they have enough cash on deposit, and to assess the quality of assets and loan repayments. If a bank is having difficulty, the FDIC may intervene to help it move toward a healthier state. If this doesn't work, the FDIC may take over the bank or merge the bank with another, healthier bank.

How is the FDIC funded?

Although an independent agency of the U.S. federal government, the FDIC is not funded by any congressional appropriation. It is funded entirely by insurance premiums charged to member institutions, and from earnings by investing in U.S. Treasury Securities.

What doesn't the FDIC insure?

If your bank offers stocks and mutual funds, these are not insured by the FDIC. Your bank must disclose to you everything that is and is not insured when you open up an account.

How much money does the FDIC protect?

The FDIC protects $4 trillion in deposits of every bank and savings institution in the United States.

Will my money always be protected by the FDIC up to $250,000?

Until this law is changed, all deposits are insured by the FDIC for up to $250,000 per depositor. Any single account with a bank-

When you see the FDIC logo at your bank, you know that the money you keep there is insured and safe.

ing institution is insured up to $250,000. All joint accounts have equally proportionate ownership for each account holder, and is insured up to $250,000 for each individual on the account.

What is the success record of the FDIC?

Since the start of FDIC consumer insurance protection on January 1, 1934, no depositor has lost any insured funds as a result of a bank failure.

What is a "credit union"?

A credit union is a not-for-profit institution that provides many financial services of traditional banks, including: allowing members to hold deposits; clearing checks against checking account deposits; and providing members with credit in the form of loans. In order to become a credit union member, a prospective client should belong to the group the credit union is chartered to service. Many credit unions are organized by professions, employers, geographic location, or other associations. Prospective members are then allowed to make a nominal deposit, giving them access to all the other services available at the credit union, including obtaining home loans, car loans, short term construction loans, etc.

When did the first credit union appear?

During the Great Depression, President Franklin D. Roosevelt signed into law the Federal Credit Union Act, enabling the creation of available credit to members all over the United States in order to stimulate savings and prevent usury (charging exorbitant fees for loans) by making reasonable interest-rate loans to its members. This enabled the United States to set up a nationwide network of non-profit, cooperative, member-owned credit unions.

Why use a credit union?

Consumers use credit unions because they charge very low or no fees, since they are not profit-making entities. Whatever profits are made during the course of the year are paid back to members in the form of interest (dividends) on their savings and/or checking accounts, as well as better terms and conditions on loans.

What are some other reasons to use credit unions?

Credit unions have lower interest rates than banks for loans, lower or no fees for using ATMs, overdraft protection, low- or no-fee checking accounts, and low- or no-minimum balance accounts, as well as personal and local services.

How substantial is the difference between interest rates for loans and savings accounts at credit unions compared with interest rates for loans and savings accounts at banks?

In a study by the National Credit Union Administration, using interest rate data from Datatrac, loans are from 0.66% to nearly 2% better at credit unions than at banks. And interest rates on savings accounts are between 0.09% and 0.72% higher at credit unions than at banks.

What is the difference between fees charged by credit unions and fees charged by banks?

Most credit unions charge $25 for overdraft fees, compared with $30 that many banks charge. And many credit unions charge $20 for credit card late fees, compared with $35 at banks. On mortgage closing costs, credit unions charge about 1% less than banks.

How much do American credit union members benefit from higher savings interest rates, lower interest rates on loans, and other lower fees?

America's credit union members' benefits total $9 billion per year.

How do I join a credit union?

In order to join a credit union, first check with your employer to see if your company belongs to a group covered by a credit union. You may also ask family members, check the Internet, or visit the National Credit Union Administration online, to find a credit union near you. After comparing fees, interest rates, services provided, and benefits to members, and you select a credit union, you may complete an application and make a small initial deposit.

People join credit unions because they tend to have lower fees and interest rates on loans. They can do this because credit unions because they are non-profit, member-owned institutions.

What is the minimum amount I need to open a credit union account?

Some credit unions require as little as $5 to initiate an account.

Is my money safe in a credit union?

Yes, through the protection of the federal government's National Credit Union Share Insurance Fund, each depositor is insured up to $250,000 for individual accounts and $500,000 for a joint account. This fund protects all depositors across the United States, and ensures that every depositor will be paid up to the maximum in case the credit union ever becomes insolvent.

How many people have money saved in credit unions?

Eighty-two million people regularly use credit unions to save.

How much money do Americans save at credit unions?

More than $520 billion is saved in credit unions today.

How many credit unions are in the United States?

There are more than 7,000 federally insured credit unions in the United States.

How much money have credit unions lent to members in 2013?

Credit unions lent approximately $631.5 billion to members in the year 2013.

What is an "overdraft"?

An overdraft occurs when you write a check or make a withdrawal from your account for an amount in excess of your current balance.

How many people overdraw their accounts?

Over 50 million people overdraw their accounts each year, and 27 million overdraw their accounts more than five times each year.

How much money do banks and credit unions earn from overdraft fees?

Banks and credit unions earn more than $24 billion per year from overdraft fees.

Americans spend more money on overdraft fees each year than they do on buying vegetables.

Do people spend more money on overdraft fees or vegetables during a year?

According to the Center for Responsible Lending, American families spend $22.8 billion on vegetables every year, and $24 billion on overdraft fees.

How much have overdraft fees been growing over the past few years?

From 2006 to 2009, overdraft fees charged by both banks and credit unions have grown an average of 35% per year.

Why do account holders put their accounts in overdraft situations?

Account holders put their accounts in overdraft situations because of the wide availability of debit cards and their (mis)management of these expenses. People are becoming accustomed to making many small purchases with debit cards, instead of using cash. Even one purchase for a few dollars, when it arrives at an account short of cash, will cause the account holder to be charged nearly $35 at some institutions.

MONEY MARKET FUNDS

What are "money market funds"?

Money market funds, also known as money market mutual funds, were developed during the early 1970s as an investment vehicle that allows investors to put their capital resources together to acquire assets that would provide a better return than an interest-bearing cash account at a bank. They were originally conceived as alternatives to bank accounts; during this time, banks were limited in what interest rate they were allowed to give to account holders. Money market funds maintain a stable net asset value of $1.00 per share, and are able to pay dividends to shareholders.

What different types of money market funds exist?

Although many types of money market funds invest in many types of asset classes, the principal types of money market funds invest in government securities, tax-exempt municipal securities, corporate securities, or combinations of the above. Most securities held in a money market fund are short term, consisting primarily of debt-based securities such as U.S. Treasury Bills and short-term commercial debt.

Are money market funds a safe way to invest cash?

Money market funds are generally regarded as a relatively safe way to invest cash, as the short-term nature of the obligations exposes account holders to less risk, and as money market funds are supported by large institutional investors.

Who regulates money market funds?

The SEC regulates money market funds, monitoring such items as the quality, the term, and the underlying combinations of investments to ensure liquidity of the investments.

Are money market funds taxable investments?

The income generated on money market mutual funds may be taxable or tax free, depending on the types of securities that make up the fund's portfolio. For example, investors in a money market fund that purchases tax-free municipal bonds may not have to pay taxes on the dividends generated during the filing year. Money market funds that invest in corporate bonds could generate taxable income to the investor.

Of the thousands of money market funds, how many have ever fallen below a net asset value of $1.00?

Since money market mutual funds are a safe way to invest cash assets, their guiding purpose is always to provide a relatively safe place to invest short-term cash assets, and maintain a $1.00 net asset value. Since their inception in 1971, only three money market mutual funds have ever had their net asset value fall below $1.00 per share.

What types of specific regulations guide the establishment of a money market fund?

Money market funds are required by law to have a weighted average maturity of 60 days or less, and not concentrate any single investment greater than 5% of the total portfolio, except in the case of purchasing government securities and repurchase agreements.

What investments are similar to money market funds?

Individual investors may invest in a number of money market fund-type accounts. Many banks typically offer account holders money market bank accounts. They offer higher interest rates than traditional savings accounts, but attach conditions on the number of transactions that may be initiated, as well as larger minimum balance requirements and associated penalties. Ultra-short bond funds behave similarly to money market funds, but they invest strictly in bonds of very short duration, although these securities may have more risk associated with them, and often have net asset values below the $1.00 per share benchmark. They are largely unregulated, and may invest the money in a variety of financial instruments in order to generate stated returns to account holders, but are inherently exposed to more risks than money market funds.

CERTIFICATES OF DEPOSIT (CDs)

What are "certificates of deposit"?

Certificates of deposit (CDs) are a type of savings account that may hold a certain amount of money for a specific amount of time. The amount of time the money may be held ranges from six months to five years. Banks pay interest to the CD holder.

Are CDs a safe method to invest my cash?

Yes, certificates of deposit are a very safe way to invest your cash, as each account holder at the bank is insured up to $250,000, including any CDs at that bank. Your money is always safe in a bank or CD, as bank and credit union accounts are protected and guaranteed up to the maximum amounts per account holder by the federal government. However, the rate you earn may not be safe or protected if the bank or credit union is sold and then merged with another lower-paying entity. In that case, you may actually earn less interest than before the merger or sale of your bank. You can track the health of your bank online at www.Bankrate.com or many other reputable reporting sites.

How and when do I get paid my interest on a certificate of deposit?

CD owners receive their principal (the amount of the CD they originally deposited) and any interest due when the CD's term expires.

How do I know the terms and rules for a CD?

Each CD issuer has a disclosure statement that outlines all the terms of the certificate, including any risks associated with the investment, the interest rate, and the term of the certificate. The disclosure statement will also describe whether the interest rate is fixed or variable for the term of the CD. If variable, the disclosure statement will also describe the benchmark rate of interest upon which the CD interest rate is based, and how it is computed.

What else is included in a disclosure statement?

Other items often included in a disclosure statement include how often interest will be computed and paid, and whether the interest will be paid in the form of a check or an electronic fund transfer. The disclosure statement will also describe any penalties that must be paid if the CD holder requires the cash before the term expires.

What is the biggest risk in holding cash in the form of a CD?

The biggest risk in holding a CD is inflation. If the rate of inflation is higher than the interest rate you may earn on the CD, then it will decline in value over this period of time.

Should I ever buy CDs from a broker?

Since CD brokers outside of a bank or investment firm are largely unlicensed and unregulated by any state or federal authority, you should avoid purchasing CDs from a broker. However, if you want to purchase a CD from a broker/dealer, you should investigate the broker, and see if the company he represents has had any complaints, charges, or litigation.

ONLINE BANKING

Why use an online bank?

Online banks compete intensely for new customers by offering some of the highest interest rates for savings accounts. They do this in part because some are Internet-only banks, without physical locations and thousands of employees to staff the branches of traditional brick–and-mortar banks. They pass these savings to their customers in the form of very competitive interest rates, and reduced loan rates, such as mortgages and home equity loans. Online banks can be completely paperless, sending you your monthly statements by e-mail.

Why else should I use an online bank?

Increasingly, we are turning into a cashless society. We pay our bills online, get our entertainment online, and pay for purchases online, so it is only natural that we also desire a virtual bank account. Maybe we are tired of having to drive to a branch location, park, and wait in line just to make a deposit. With an online bank, making a deposit is as easy as making a few mouse clicks. The time savings alone is enough to make people switch to an online bank, since you can do all the same things with an online bank as with your local bank, but much faster.

What is a "virtual bank"?

A virtual bank is another term for an online bank, with no physical branch locations. A virtual bank exists completely online.

How do I know if a prospective online bank is legitimate?

The FDIC has a bank locator tool that allows you to go online to see if a prospective bank is covered by the FDIC. If the prospective bank does not show up with the exact name and address of the bank in question, do not submit an application. You may also read bank reviews online, and ask family or friends if they have used the bank. Most people will know someone who uses an online bank.

Mobile banking is possible now at any bank, but you can go a step further and open an account at an online bank that has no brick-and-mortar office.

How can I compare the interest rates of different banks?

The website www.Bankrate.com offers many tools to compare banks, from savings interest rates to loan interest rates. You can select from a variety of criteria and compare fees to determine the best bank for you.

How do I open an online account?

In order to open an account, go to the online bank of your choice and complete its application. This takes only a few minutes. Then you associate or tie one of your checking accounts with your new account, and your Internet bank makes two small transactions into your checking account. Once you receive these, go back online and enter the dates and amounts of the two transactions, and your account is then opened. Now you may make your initial deposit. Afterwards, you may move money in and out of your account with a mouse click.

Is my money available when I want it?

Your money is not immediately available. When you make a deposit, the bank holds it for three business days before the money appears in your account. If you make the request on a Friday, you may have to wait until Wednesday before your money appears in your account. At the same time, this forces customers to become savers, as their money is just a bit more inaccessible and therefore less prone to impulse withdrawals or purchases.

Is my money protected the same way in an online bank as in a traditional bank?

Yes. The FDIC's coverage is the same for online banks as for brick-and-mortar banks, protecting each account holder up to $250,000 per account.

Can I open an online checking account?

Online banks offer checking accounts that are truly paperless. Your statements and your check register are entirely online. You can set up automatic payments for regular monthly bills, and can easily transfer money to them in the form of an electronic check. You can also write checks for people the same way. The money is either automatically transferred into their accounts, or a paper check can be printed and sent. Since so much of what we do today is centered around online services, it is natural to use online banking.

Why do people like online banks?

People like online banks because they are always open. One can see all the transactions updated every second. Online banks also allow users to manage many different types of accounts, including savings and checking accounts, as well as IRAs, CDs, mutual fund accounts, and even individual stock transactions. Your money is readily available, either by using your ATM/debit card or by electronically transferring your money to your associated checking account. Your accounts are truly paperless, with no need to file statements in folders and deal with physical mail deliveries.

Why do people dislike online banks?

Sometimes, depending on the bank, you may have trouble communicating with foreign customer service operations. To cut costs, online banks tend to use call centers located

Banking online gives you a lot of flexibility to make transactions and check balances anywhere you go.

in countries where English is not the native language, making communications sometimes more difficult. You want to find an online bank that has excellent customer service, one with highly trained representatives who will always be there to help you should you have any questions. Online banks tend to put holds on online deposits and withdrawals from three to five days. Online banks may have a simple or complex user interface that may change with each new version of the website, so it may require a user to learn how to navigate it. Users of online banks no longer have the local human presence of the teller who greets them; for some, the human touch and trust factor are important considerations. These are just some variables that users must consider when deciding which bank to choose.

How popular is the use of online banks?

According to a survey by Gartner, more than 47% of all adults in the United States are using online banking. More than 50% of all adults with incomes higher than $30,000 use online banking; only 25% of adults with incomes less than $30,000 use online banking.

How fast is online banking growing?

In another survey by Forrester Research, the use of online banking is growing at an annual rate of 5.4%, with 48 million users today, growing to over 63 million users by 2014.

REAL ESTATE

THE BASICS

What are some considerations I should think about before investing in real estate?

According to experts at *Forbes*, potential real estate investors need to consider the amount of risk to which they may be exposing themselves (and their cash), as well as the amount of time required to manage this investment.

What about the liquidity of a potential real estate deal?

When you use liquid assets such as cash, money market funds, or CDs to fund a real estate deal, you may be pulling money from a very liquid investment, and re-investing the proceeds into one that is not very liquid. At the very least, the potential real estate investor needs to ensure that his real estate investment is earning at least the same amount of return that it would receive if he left his money in a cash-based account.

What are some general factors that affect house prices?

Many factors affect house prices. On a macroeconomic level, house prices follow the basic economic principle of supply and demand: The more houses available for sale, the lower the price; the more buyers in the market, the higher the price.

If I am thinking of buying a house in a certain city, how can I find information about my target city online?

Many websites offer information about the specific characteristics of cities, including www.city-data.com, www.neighborhoodscout.com, and https://homes.yahoo.com. Each site provides valuable information on your future city, including house prices, unemployment rates, education quality, and crime statistics. You should investigate these sites before buying or selling a house.

What is "shadow inventory"?

Shadow inventory is the inventory of houses that most likely will move into foreclosure, thus increasing the supply of houses and depressing house prices.

What is the percentage of households that owned their own homes?

According to a 2014 release of U.S. Census data, 65.2% of all households owned their own homes at the end of 2013.

Why is affordability important when it comes to selecting a home?

In order to make a successful investment when purchasing a home, it is important to buy as much house as you can afford. This means you must take a hard look at your current expenses to decide what you can live without in order to determine how much house you can afford. A larger house may require much more monthly cash for utilities, maintenance, and property taxes.

How can I find out how much house I can afford?

Many financial calculators are available online. They allow you to enter information about your income and expenses, and will roughly compute how much you can afford. Only a bank or mortgage adviser will really be able to tell you how much you can afford.

What factors should I consider when thinking about affordability?

You must look at such factors as your current income; your debts and the payments for each of them each month; your current monthly expenses; and what money remains to go to your mortgage payment. The second big factor that will affect your mortgage payment is the amount of your down payment. The larger your down payment, the less money you must borrow, reducing the amount of interest you pay. You also may be able

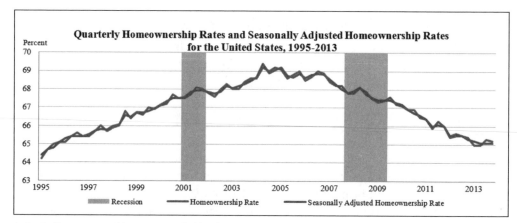

A chart of home ownership rates compiled by the U.S. Census (source: http://www.census.gov).

Location, location, location is the mantra of real estate agents. A house by the beach is highly desirable, but what if there are no schools nearby for your children? Consider many factors before buying.

to secure better terms for the mortgage amount. For further information, consult a mortgage lender.

What are the most important rules to follow when buying a house?

You have probably heard the answer before: Location, location, location. This means the place where you purchase your house is one of the most important factors to help you maximize the return on your investment.

Why is location so important?

Your house needs to be in an area where there are excellent schools, where taxes are used to support great city services, where upkeep and maintenance of neighboring homes is excellent, and near your place of work. It is great to live in a walkable community, a place with a sense of belonging, security, and friendliness. It is important that there be very little crime, as this will greatly increase your home's value, and make it easier for you to sell your home in the long term.

What if your potential home is in an area with only one major industry or employer?

If this is the case, it means that if something were to happen to that industry or employer, it could become very difficult to sell your house, or even earn any appreciation on your investment.

What about buying houses in "up-and-coming" locations?

This really depends on your preference for risk and the amount of time you wish to wait for the house to appreciate. Some buyers prefer to find a great house in a changing location, where they feel the area is growing and desirable. In that case, they may realize a high return on their investment, even though it has more risk.

What about great deals on newly created subdivisions?

If you buy a house in a newly built subdivision, the builder could run out of money and not complete the project, leaving the initial buyers with houses in an incomplete area, making them very difficult to sell. Also, newly created subdivisions greatly change the available inventory of houses, making them much more difficult to sell in the short term.

What is another general rule about location?

Some people believe you should consider buying the worst house on the best block, since high home prices on the street may already demonstrate that it is a very valuable area in which to live. And with some hard work—and perhaps cash invested to improve it—the house will be far more valuable over time than buying "the best" house on the block, one that requires no work or additional changes but already commands a premium price, as there is less potential for appreciation.

How much did real estate prices decline between 2006 and 2009?

The average home lost 33% of its value during this period of economic decline.

What percentage of Americans saw their house equity decline from 2006 to 2009?

Twenty-seven percent of all Americans saw their home value cut by at least half from 2006 to 2009.

How much real estate value disappeared during the decline of 2006 to 2010?

During the decline of 2006 to 2010, $6 trillion in home values was wiped out.

What percentage of online economic users use the Internet to find information on their homes' value?

Eighteen percent of users use the Internet to find current home prices, trends, and data pertaining to the value of their homes.

What are some top real estate websites I can use to analyze current and past listings on my own?

Thousands of websites enable users to search for homes across the United States and many parts of the world, especially as more real estate companies and organizations publish and tie together electronic records of current home listings online. Some real

> ## Why is the speed of selling a house so important?
>
> **M**ost online real estate sites allow users to see how long a house has been available on the market. The longer the house is on the market, buyers may perceive there is something wrong either with the house or the price, and may be more reluctant even to look at the house.

estate companies use mapping software such as Google Maps that enables users visually to see the homes, nearby parks, streets, and areas; to have an aerial view of the property; or even see the prices of all houses for sale on a map. This makes it much easier for sellers to price their houses properly, and for buyers to have the proper expectation as to the market price of all houses in a specific area or even geographic radius. The sites below consistently rank very high based upon unique monthly views by website usage experts: Experian's Hitwise study, which uses sophisticated monthly sampling data to support its conclusions and rankings; homes.yahoo.com; Realtor.com; Zillow.com; HGTV FrontDoor; Trulia; Rent.com; MSN Real Estate; Homes.com; ZipRealty; and Mynewplace.com.

How often do sellers reduce their prices?

In July 2010, according to Trulia, 25% of all U.S. sellers cut their prices in order to sell their houses.

If home mortgage debt rises, does that signal a turnaround in the real estate market?

According to experts at CNBC, when home mortgage debt rises, it usually means the real estate market is turning around, as more people seek loans to acquire real property of all types. Recently, it means that mortgage debt grows as banks foreclose on fewer homes, clearing less debt off their books. Goldman Sachs researchers found that by August 2013, 57% of all residential home sales were all-cash deals in which buyers obtain no financing. This is up from 19% in 2005.

What actions of the Federal Housing Administration (FHA) will affect the housing market in 2014?

The Federal Housing Administration, which guarantees and insures many home loans, will drop its limit of what it will loan by more than $100,000, from $729,000 to $625,000. The FHA has instituted increased premiums and fees, and requires a much higher average credit score for its borrowers. This may further suppress demand for purchases, especially loans to first-time home buyers, who typically use FHA loans for housing purchases.

HOME OWNERSHIP AS AN INVESTMENT

Why should I buy a house?

When you buy a house, you own an asset that can appreciate over time. You will experience a sense of pride when you own your own home. You no longer have to pay rent, or live with roommates or family. It is one of the first steps to financial security, allowing you to begin to create a credit history. It is a form of forced savings (since you must make monthly payments if you purchase your home with a loan or mortgage), and this money is going both to you (in the form of equity) and the bank or mortgage company (in the form of loan payments). It is also a good way to diversify your portfolio through real estate ownership. You can get tax deductions for a home office and deduct the interest on your mortgage. You may also qualify for special loan programs at lower interest rates to purchase a home. You may also sell the home at a profit without paying capital gains tax (up to a limit), and use the proceeds to pay cash for your next home, thus saving the money you would have used for mortgage and interest payments on your future house.

Why else should I buy a house?

Home ownership also represents a major aspect of the American Dream: To be independent financially, and to increase your wealth. This has been aided in part by many federal programs that make credit available, act as an incentive for house buyers through tax deductions, and provide mortgages and other credits for home purchase.

What about all the foreclosed houses flooding the market?

The number of distressed mortgages or foreclosures in the area you are considering will have a depressing effect on all house prices. It not only increases the supply of available houses, it increases the supply of very inexpensive available houses, since the banks or lenders that own them want to receive any cash they can, and are not willing to wait for a premium offer.

How much cheaper are foreclosed houses than currently occupied houses on the market?

According to investment services provider Moody's, foreclosed houses sell for nearly 40% less than occupied houses today.

How important are property taxes in deciding to purchase a home?

Property taxes could be a determining factor in choosing one area over another. Check what percentage of a home's sale price will be paid in taxes before you decide to buy a house. A city with very high taxes will charge you a larger percentage of the home's selling price than a more affordable city.

What is a "down payment"?

A down payment is the amount you can comfortably pay in cash to purchase a house. This down payment, plus the mortgage amount, is the price you pay for your house (plus some additional fees and expenses). The larger your down payment, as a percentage of the home price, the less your mortgage amount, and therefore your monthly payment.

How do I know how much to put down on a house?

This is a tough question because it touches on purchaser sentiment. You should already have at least four to six months of living expenses saved in a cash account as an emergency fund, in case something should happen to your employment situation. This money should not be touched, not even to purchase a house. The money you have saved in addition to that—money you may have invested in other ways—should be used for your initial down payment.

What are general guidelines for down payments?

Most lenders would prefer you to put down 10–30% of the house price as a down payment. This may enable you to get better interest rates, pay fewer fees or points, and reduce your monthly payments and interest over the life of the loan. Banks offer many programs, including federal incentives for the purchases of homes, especially for first-time home buyers. Check with your bank or mortgage adviser.

What is an "appraisal"?

An appraisal occurs when your bank or mortgage company inspects a house to see if the amount of money it wishes to loan equals what it sees as the house's current market value.

What does the term "appraise out" mean?

If a house "appraises out," this means the bank or mortgage company feels the value of the house is at least equal to the current sales price, and that it is safe for the bank to make a loan to a purchaser.

What if a house doesn't appraise out?

If a house doesn't appraise out, you have two options. You can put more money down, if you really love the house. Or you can try to negotiate down the price of the house, and get it nearer to what the bank feels is the house's "real" market price.

Make a home inspection part of the conditions in agreeing to buy a home. Inspectors can sometimes find serious problems with a house that you were unaware of.

What is an "inspection"?

An inspection is paid for and arranged by a buyer before he purchases a house. A home inspector will check every physical aspect of the house, letting the buyer know all the faults of the house, as well as an exhaustive list of all items that need to be repaired in the house.

How can I use this information when purchasing a home?

A buyer may use the results of a home inspection in several ways. You can use the information to reduce the offer price, or to reduce the price after you have made an offer. A buyer can also use an inspection to tell a seller what items need to be repaired before he will buy the house. In other words, the buyer and seller negotiate either to make the necessary repairs, or to reduce the price to accommodate the buyer, who will have to make the repairs later.

What if I discover something about the house that makes it unacceptable to me?

You may write in your purchase agreement "offer contingent upon satisfactory inspection," allowing yourself the protection that if the house doesn't pass inspection, you don't have to purchase the house.

If I walk away from the deal before closing on a house, won't I be penalized?

Probably. Another offer may come in that has no such terms, perhaps at an amount equal to your bid. Naturally, the seller will choose the better deal. You could also lose a portion of your "earnest money" deposit, which you have given to initiate the transaction. Check with your bank or mortgage adviser to discover its practice, and at what point you can walk away from the deal without losing any money.

How do real estate agents work?

A real estate agent is hired by a seller, and is paid a commission after the home is sold. Real estate agents who work on behalf of buyers understand both buyers' needs and the available listings in the desired areas. Their expertise is essential in guiding you to the right house.

What is the multiple listing service (MLS)?

The multiple listing service is an electronic database of every property for sale nationwide. Realtors access this information to help search for all properties listed by realtors in order to identify specific choices for their clients.

What are "comparables"?

Comparables, or "comps", are houses that are physically similar to your house in a specific radius from your target house that have sold recently. You can gain intelligence as to the "market price" of a house by reviewing the price at which comparable houses actually sold. Real estate appraisers will identify comps in order to ascertain the current market value of any real estate.

How can I use comps to negotiate a better house price?

You can use comps to negotiate a better house price by discovering what is deficient about your target house compared with the comps, and telling the seller and your realtor when you make your offer. You might say, "We are offering $5,000 less than your sales price because all the comps had central air conditioning, and this one doesn't." If the seller is motivated to sell, he may accept your offer, and reduce the sales price. Comps are usually provided by each client's realtor.

What else can I learn from comps?

Perhaps all the recent comparable houses sold for $30,000 more than the offer price of your target house. Knowing for what price comps have sold may indicate that you are getting a very good deal. It could also indicate that real estate prices in this area have fallen precipitously, and perhaps the price may go even lower. You may reconsider buying or investing in the area, since home prices are not appreciating.

What is "curb appeal"?

Curb appeal is the impression your house makes to buyers when driving by, or as they first approach your house on the way in. Many buyers make instant decisions on whether or not to buy your house based upon these initial minutes or seconds.

One of the best ways to increase your chances of selling your home is to make sure it has curb appeal.

What are some of the most important things you can do to prepare your home for sale?

Some of the most important things you can do to prepare your home for sale include making the most important repairs that may increase the curb appeal of your house, as well as necessary improvements inside that may sway a buyer to purchase your house. Sellers may invest in exterior landscaping, kitchens, and bathrooms in order to improve their chances of attracting a buyer.

What is "staging"?

Staging is the act of changing the furnishings either by buying, renting, or rearranging the layout of each room in order to present your house for sale in the best possible manner.

Why are neutral colors so important when selling a house?

Neutral colors are important when selling a house because one wants to give a buyer the least number of reasons to dislike the house. Even if you really love your red-walled kitchen, consider painting it white or beige so that potential buyers do not use the color of the room as a reason not to buy the house. Also, neutral colors allow a potential buyer the ability to see how big the house is, how spacious the interior is, and better allows them to imagine living in the house.

Should I move out of my house when I am trying to sell it?

Absolutely not. Unless your job forces you to move before selling the house, it is very important that your house look as if someone is currently living in it. Nothing detracts more from the sale price of your house than walking through a series of empty box-like rooms, with no signs of life. Your house is much more valuable when you are still living in it.

What about all my clutter?

One of the best things you can do when trying to sell your house is to go through and de-clutter every room. This means taking a very minimalist approach, and removing all but the most essential items. This means you should display no stacks of anything in any room, and should have no toys in view.

What about photographs and personal art?

Again, if you want to make your house appeal to the largest number of buyers, do not display personal artwork and photographs, unless they are completely neutral. Your house should be perfectly clean and orderly.

How quickly do people form first impressions?

The speed with which we are able to decide whether something is good or bad is measured in tenths of a second. With our ability to use the Internet to see pictures of houses, we are deciding whether we like a house or not in seconds. This means a seller must take extra care to make his house as attractive as possible.

What does the expression "priced to sell" mean?

Priced to sell means your house is competing with many other houses for sale, and you want to price the house low enough so that it will be among the first houses that people consider buying. That means pricing the house lower than its rivals at the onset. But it really depends on personal preferences and factors, including how long the seller wishes to keep the property on the market, the minimum and maximum price the seller desires, and how much the seller wishes to profit on the transaction.

Why is it important to pick the right agent to sell your house?

Picking the right agent to sell your house is important because the agent will deliver potential buyers to you. Your agent should be knowledgeable in the area in which you are selling, and he should know the community and its characteristics. He has many contacts, and is an expert at showing your home in the best possible manner. Since he is compensated by earning a commission on the sale price, he is naturally motivated to try to get the highest reasonable price for you.

What is a "depressed" or "down" real estate market?

A down market, or downturn in the real estate market, occurs when average prices are falling relative to some baseline measure.

Should I consider selling my home during a down market?

People may consider selling their homes during a down market because of some life change, perhaps an employment/marital change or the desire to pull equity from their original investment in the property. If you have owned the house for a long time, and wish to monetize the equity in the house, it may be the time to sell. However, in thinking of your home as a long-term investment, some would argue it is best to wait out market cycles, and sell when prices are high or higher than they currently are. Each individual seller must evaluate his tolerance for losses, target for gains, and appetite for risk, and decide the best time to sell.

What about buying in a down market?

If you are selling your current home in a down market in order to purchase another home, you will benefit from the low prices

Get yourself an experienced realtor to sell your house. He or she will bring the most qualified potential buyers to your door.

of your potential new home by purchasing when prices are near their historic lows. You will greatly benefit from the appreciation of the new property, which may help compensate for selling your current home for less than you would like.

If I stay in my home, what should I do during a down market?

You may think about refinancing the original mortgage loan, hoping to get a better mortgage interest rate and thus lower your monthly payments. You may also consider reducing as many discretionary expenses as possible, and delaying purchasing big-ticket items, in order to continue to grow cash savings during these uncertain times.

What else should I do if I stay in my home during a down market?

You should also focus on reducing or eliminating all credit card debt, and delaying or eliminating all non-essential purchases.

OWNING VERSUS RENTING

How does owning a house improve my net worth more than renting?

Owning a house may improve your net worth in more ways than if you are renting a home because, if you own a large appreciating capital asset, even if you borrowed a portion of the sale price to own it, you benefit from the appreciation of the house over time,

An advantage of renting a home is not having to deal with house maintenance or coming up with a downpayment, but you also don't get a tax break and you accrue no equity in the house.

even after factoring in inflation, interest payments, tax deductions, etc. The more expensive the house you can afford to purchase, the higher the amount of dollar equity you eventually get to use when computing your net worth. Simply put, a $100,000 home appreciating 10% generates $10,000 of equity, while a $500,000 home that appreciates 10% generates $50,000 in equity. When you rent, you have no investment and no appreciating asset.

What are some important factors when I decide to rent instead of owning my own home?

When you are evaluating whether to buy or to rent, you should consider a few important variables. According to real estate editors at *The New York Times*, you should consider how much and how fast real estate purchase prices and rental prices are increasing or decreasing, and for how long you plan to stay in the house. According to *The New York Times* rent calculator, assuming such factors as your income and deductions available to purchase a house (such as deduction of mortgage loan interest), a nominal 2% annual house price increases, and nominal 3% annual rent increases, if you plan to stay in the house for five years or longer, you should make the investment and purchase the house. If you decrease the time to four years or less, you should rent.

What other assumptions does the rent versus own calculator make that we should consider?

When you try to evaluate renting versus owning, you also should factor in such items as real property taxes you might have to pay each year if you purchase the house, homeowner's insurance, moving costs, rental deposits, and rental insurance.

How do I accurately compare the expenses to rent compared with owning a similar house?

Look at all cash costs by year for the time you plan to live in a new place, and try to compare these costs to see what choice makes more sense from a cash outlay perspective. You also should consider the tax advantages of using a mortgage, the lost opportunity for holding the money you would use for a down payment in some other form of investment, the cost of utilities if you buy a house compared with being (sometimes) included in the rental lease, and the ongoing house maintenance for which you would not be responsible if you chose to rent.

What are some examples of renting costs that I should anticipate?

When you rent a place to live, you may expect to pay for moving costs, furnishing costs, possibly some or all utility costs, rent, a broker's fee for finding the rental, and renter's insurance. You should also consider the lost opportunity if you used some of the expenses in some other way. Remember to add back into the equation the return of your security deposit, typically 1½ months' rent paid upon signing the lease.

What are some examples of house purchase costs that I should anticipate?

You should consider the price paid for the house if you pay cash, or the amount you put down if you obtain a mortgage, closing costs, appraisals and fees, moving costs, and furnishing costs (if necessary). For costs you might incur during the course of a year, you might expect to pay for maintenance, property taxes, homeowners' insurance, homeowners' association fees (HOA fees for a condominium), utilities, and any renovation work that needs immediate attention. If the house appraises out for more than you paid for it, congratulations on earning an immediate benefit to purchasing the house! You will know this quite some time before you actually close on the purchase of the house. Also consider the lost opportunity of having to redirect money from other investments such as mutual funds that may have been earning a certain decent return per year in order to purchase the house.

You also should consider the tax advantage of the interest on the mortgage deduction. Consult your tax adviser or real estate professional, who can give you a rough idea of the benefits, depending on your status and income during that year. As for determining the approximate cost of your property taxes, you may contact your local tax authority, give them the house's address and sale price, and ask for a tax estimate. Remember that local property taxes may be quite different from what is reported on the real estate listing information; they are based upon the last sales price, as well as local tax codes that may have changed over time.

If you plan to sell the house after a relatively short period of time, you need to consider many expenses, such as broker/real estate sales commissions and payment of the original mortgage balance due.

Are there other "rent versus own" tools or calculators available online that may assist me in making these types of analyses?

Dozens of sites offer rent-versus-own tools or calculators that use different variables in their models (some quite detailed), allowing you to enter comparative data into each field and quickly see the effect of changing the amount of rent or the price of a house so you may decide whether to rent or own. Some calculators may consider such factors as rapid increases or decreases in home prices over the years, current mortgage interest rates, and changes to tax codes. Investigate the currency of the data each calculator uses.

Why do some people prefer to rent rather than own?

Some people prefer not to devote time for maintenance and fixes that home ownership requires. Other people may live on their own, and would prefer not to own a house until they are married or living with another person to share the responsibilities. Others need to continue to rent to improve their financial position so they may afford to purchase a home one day, according to experts at the *Chicago Tribune*.

What key factors can make a real estate purchase attractive as an investment?

A real estate purchase may be even more attractive as an investment, if you work with a competitive mortgage company in order to find a lower fee-based mortgage, combined with lower interest rate loans and buying the property at the right time. Most homeowners prefer to "pay themselves first," and earn equity or return on their investment, rather than let a landlord benefit from the income and appreciation of a rental investment.

COMMERCIAL REAL ESTATE

What is "real estate development"?

Aside from acquiring real property for the benefits of providing income and appreciation, some investors choose to develop real estate with a view to increase the value of the asset or the income generated from the asset; they use a specific real estate investment strategy by correctly applying capital in order to achieve their goals.

Why is real estate investment considered by many a relatively risky investment?

Real estate investing is viewed by many as a relatively risky investment because it is relatively illiquid compared with other forms of investing. It may require large cash resources in order to participate. Also, the long-term nature of how the investment appreciates over time may require an investor to commit his money for years or even decades before finally receiving the proper return on the initial investment.

What are two main concerns that investors must consider before investing in any real estate deal?

The two main concerns every investor in real estate must consider is the risk he is taking with his initial and ongoing capital investment (how much he risks losing), and the time spent to manage the investment.

How sizable an effect does commercial real estate development have on the U.S. economy?

The commercial real estate industry contributes approximately 2.3 million jobs in the United States, and contributes approximately $303.4 billion to the U.S. gross domestic product (a 16% increase from 2011). Since 2011, real estate development investment in construction and other real estate development spending has been growing at 10% per year, according to researchers at the Commercial Real Estate Development Association (NAIOP).

What are other names for commercial real estate?

Commercial real estate is often referred to as investment real estate, investment property, and commercial property.

Commercial real estate comprises a large chunk of the U.S. economy, supporting over two million jobs and over $300 billion to the gross domestic product annually.

Does commercial real estate fall into many sub-categories?

Commercial real estate is divided into many sub-categories or classes, including:

- Office buildings (both large and small, multi- or single-tenant, professional office buildings and multi-story buildings)
- Industrial (including research and development buildings, warehouses, manufacturing buildings)
- Retail/restaurant (retail strip buildings, single-/multi-tenant retail spaces, shopping centers) or big-box retail centers (anchored by regionally or nationally recognized brands)
- Multi-family (any multiple unit development larger than four units)
- Land (developed or undeveloped, rural/urban with intent for future use)
- Miscellaneous property (hospitality, health care, rehabilitation centers, and self-storage)

What are some other important areas of commercial real estate development?

According to NAIOP, some other important areas of commercial real estate investment include mixed use, brownfield regeneration or development, wind energy development, and urban waterfront development.

What are the most basic elements to understand and evaluate the success of commercial real estate investments?

The most basic elements of commercial real estate investment are similar to those elements used to analyze many investment opportunities, including cash inflows/outflows, the timing of receivables, and capital risk.

What about cash flow and real estate deals?

In the short term, most real estate deals are quite cash-intensive investments, with little room to recover these costs in the near term, or until the property is sold or leased. They require cash to purchase, to use for a down payment, to repair, to maintain, for taxes, homeowners fees, emergency repairs, utility bills management, and marketing fees, among many other costs. In your initial analysis, you should recognize that nearly all real estate deals will require a considerable amount of cash. Ultimately, because of this large, chronic cash requirement, you should ensure the reward for such an investment outweighs the risks you must take to enter into this type of investment.

What are some typical types of real estate investments?

In addition to the investment in and purchase of your principal place of residence, typical real estate investments may include: real estate developments; land developments; private real estate fund investments; rental real estate acquisitions; purchasing a "fixer-upper" and "flipping" it for profit, etc. Each real estate investment type involves a certain amount of risk based upon the amount of cash needed to finalize the transaction. You may also need to spend cash after the transaction, spend time managing the project, and spend time holding the asset, so you must analyze each potential investment to see what return you may earn on the investment, as well as the hidden cost of using your time to manage the investment.

Why is this a good time to consider investing in real estate?

When interest rates are low and available property inventories are high, you may find a more attractive climate in which to invest, as you stand a better chance to recover your cash investment from the real estate deal. According to experts at www.MSN.com and www.Bankrate.com, real estate values plummeted $3.6 trillion in 2008, but "only" $489 billion in the first 11 months of 2009. So the base prices of real estate generally are at or near all-time lows, thought by many experts to be a great time to purchase.

What questions should I ask myself before I invest in real estate?

Before you begin to invest in real estate, you should answer some questions to narrow your focus and make a proper acquisition:

What are some examples of more time-intensive real estate investments?

Some more time-intensive real estate investments may include vacation rental property, rental properties in declining areas, self-managing multi-unit properties, and rental properties in college and university communities.

- Do you wish to be a landlord?
- Do you wish to renovate and resell a dilapidated house?
- Are you interested in commercial multi-tenant properties?
- Are you interested in investing in raw, undeveloped land and holding it for future development?
- Are you interested in buying land that can be developed?

What other tips should new real estate investors consider?

Some experts assert that new real estate investors should at the very least partner with a real estate professional experienced in the type of real estate investment you are considering making, and you should ensure the property is well located.

What are some other important steps experts also suggest you should consider when planning a real estate investment?

Most experts agree that you should factor in the cash necessary to accomplish the deal, as well as enough cash on hand after completing the deal to cover unforeseen expenses. Many experts also advise you identify potential service providers, such as contractors, handymen, electricians, plumbers, and cleaners after consummating the deal.

What are typical cash inflows in a commercial real estate investment?

Some important cash inflows, or revenue, for a commercial real estate investment may include rent, expense reimbursement, various tenant-related fees, income generated by the initial purchase of the property, and long- and short-term tax credits and deductions you may be entitled to receive.

What are typical cash outflows in a commercial real estate investment?

Some important cash outflows for a commercial real estate investment may include your initial cash investment to acquire the property, operating expenses on the property (including taxes and utilities), debt/loan servicing, capital expenses such as maintenance and refurbishing, commission on the transaction, leasing commissions, and property management fees.

Why is timing my cash inflows and outflows critical to analyzing and ultimately investing in commercial real estate?

Accurately projecting and correctly approximating the way cash flows into and out of a commercial project allows you to see if an adequate return on an investment can be made, and within what time frame you will realize gains. Perhaps after analyzing near-term cash flows, a commercial deal does not make a great deal of sense in the short term, but you may realize gains if the property is sold five years later.

What is my risk when investing in commercial real estate?

Some risks may include not having tenants, or not having tenants pay as much rent as you initially assumed; a sudden change in supply of similar properties, affecting demand for your property; delay of receipt of income due to unforeseen or unplanned events; and broad economic market risk affecting the area of investment.

How much did developers pay for six parking lots in downtown Los Angeles in a recent commercial real estate deal?

Developers paid $82 million to purchase six parking lots, intending to develop the land into 1,500 apartments to meet demand for urban housing and participate in revitalizing the downtown urban community.

What types of macroeconomic variables contributed to the developers' ultimate decision to invest in the project?

Aside from the positive return the project may provide, experts at *The Wall Street Journal* suggest developers are trying to ride the wave of downtown and urban revitalization projects, as well as take advantage of specific market conditions. During 2008 to 2013, developers constructed approximately 3,400 units, while 5,100 units remained under construction, and 3,000 units were approved for construction. In Los Angeles, a city of approximately 3.8 million people, only approximately 14,000 apartments were available to rent. In late 2013 only a reported 17 condominium units were for sale, and only 68 under construction. According to a report obtained by *The Wall*

Urban renewal is a growing trend in the United States, with companies investing billions to create lofts, townhouses, and apartments in cities. The price of land is higher, so urban homes tend to be smaller.

Street Journal, the downtown vacancy rate is only 3%, and average rents are approximately $1,970/month, while national vacancy rates average 4.2%, and average rents are $1,073/month.

What other types of macroeconomic variables might a potential investor use to evaluate the success of a downtown Los Angeles real estate development, such as the example above?

In addition to favorable loan interest rates, potential investors may be interested to know some interesting market and demographic facts about this real estate investment. Almost 77% of the population is above age 18, and thereby eligible to rent. Los Angeles is the second-largest center of government employment (after Washington, D.C.); the largest fashion industry employer (employing 87,000 people); home to a burgeoning biotech industry; and the second-largest city in the United States. More than 40 million tourists visit each year, supporting nearly 372,000 people employed in the tourism and hospitality industries. Also, the five-county regional area represents the sixteenth largest economy in the world, and plenty of college students need to rent in the area, given 113 colleges and universities in Los Angeles.

What are some downsides to investing in commercial real estate, especially urban development projects?

According to experts at *The Wall Street Journal,* there are downsides to commercial urban real estate investment transferable to many areas of real estate investing, including an over supply of housing; office or retail space; slow velocity of growth of rental demand for any systemic reason; increasing building costs; and a general trend toward increasing real estate prices.

Why do commercial real estate deals often fail?

Commercial real estate deals may fail for several reasons, including: lack of proper analysis; overpaying for the property; cash flow/income problems; large macroeconomic events that affect the ability to rent and/or sell the property; and making incorrect assumptions or overstating positive assumptions when computing potential return models.

SECOND HOMES

What is the difference between a second home and an investment property?

According to experts at the legal website www.Nolo.com, an investment property cannot be your primary residence. It is real property used to earn income through direct rental agreement or lease, through appreciation over time, or for certain tax advantages. Typically, interest rates and conditions on investment property loans are higher and more stringent than loans for second homes. You may occupy a second home in addition to using your primary residence, and it typically may be used as a vacation home or for business trips. Only the borrower may use the property. It may not be part of a timeshare agreement or rental pool, may not fall under the terms of any rental agreement or lease, and may not have a company managing the property's occupancy or use. Second home loans may have more favorable rates and conditions than loans for investment properties.

Why do some experts believe owning a second home may not be a relatively good investment?

Experts at the real estate site Zillow argue that a second home may not be a great investment over the long term because of many cash outlays, and because the owner receives very little income.

How do I realize any gains on my investment in a second home?

Unfortunately, with the exception of tax benefits, such as mortgage interest deductions, the only income you can make is long-term capital appreciation if home prices increase and outpace inflation during the period of ownership. You can realize a gain only if you sell it for more than what you originally paid, minus interest and other fees.

What are typical cash outlays I should consider when owning a second home?

You should consider several typical cash outlays when owning a second home. You must use cash for such items as your initial down payment (if you get a mortgage in order to purchase the property), all fees associated with obtaining the initial mortgage, property taxes, homeowners insurance, homeowners fees, furnishings, repairs, renovations/ rehabilitation, ongoing maintenance, cleaning, monthly mortgage payments, and transportation costs.

What is a hidden cost involved in second home ownership?

One hidden cost involved in second home ownership may be the lost opportunity of moving money out of interest- or income-bearing investments and into an investment that may potentially result in losses over a long period of time (depending on how long you choose to keep the second home).

What is the S&P/Case-Shiller Home Price Index?

The S&P/Case-Shiller Home Price Index tracks repeat sales of houses in many mar-

Many well-to-do people like the idea of owning a second, usually vacation, home, but it might not be a good investment, practically speaking.

185

kets, allowing for comparisons in house prices and how they may change over time. There are a diverse number of Case–Shiller Home Price Indices, including a national home price index, a 20-city composite index, a 10-city composite index, and twenty individual metro area indexes.

What are some examples of data I can use from Case-Shiller Indices to understand a potential second home investment?

You may use reports emanating from Case-Shiller Indices to discover if the price of a target property is high, low, or stable, and perhaps you may also discover whether you should buy or sell. For example, using data collected in September 2013, the S&P/Case-Shiller Indices shows that U.S. home prices rose 3.2% in the third quarter of 2013, and 11.2% over the past four quarters. In order to confirm this trend, you must analyze data near your target property, but national results indicate an increasing price trend.

How well has the second home market performed in recent years?

According to researchers at the National Association of Realtors, second home sales jumped 7% in 2011, with more than 502,000 second homes listed and sold.

Why might I want to own a second home?

Many experts agree the time may be right to purchase a second home because home prices are rising throughout the United States after decreasing by as much as 50% from their highs only a few years ago. Inventories for houses available for sale are also down in many markets, keeping prices buoyant. Mortgage interest rates are relatively favorable for prospective buyers, as they remain near their 40-year low of 3.37% for a thirty-year fixed interest rate, and near their all-time low of 2.65% for a fifteen-year fixed loan.

RENTAL PROPERTIES

Why is location so important for rental investments?

Many factors may influence your success rate with rental investments. Some important factors include: population density (avoid rural areas); excellent school systems; obvious demographics (high employment equals better tenants); proximity to jobs and public transit; public safety; and proximity to shopping.

What can I discover from U.S. Census data that supports demand for rental housing?

On a macroeconomic level, you can see why future prospects for housing rentals may continue to grow. Age groups that showed the greatest increase (from 2000 to 2010) are people in their twenties seeking their first home, and people in their sixties who may be selling their primary residence and renting.

Why are real estate analysts cited by *The Wall Street Journal* worried for small college town rental property owners?

In a recent article, real estate experts warned that, with the glut of college rental housing construction fueled by private equity investing and investments made by real estate investment trusts, small private owners of aging college rental units will find it difficult to keep and attract clients.

On a macroeconomic level, how much building of college rental beds has recently occurred?

Citing a recent real estate research report by AXIOMetrics, *The Wall Street Journal* states there have been approximately 310,000 off-campus beds constructed during the past decade, 51,000 constructed in 2013 and more than 50,000 slated for 2014.

What other factors point to difficulties in the college rental market?

Experts have published research that shows rent increases in this market at only 0.5%, or essentially no increase, as the markets adjust to the new supply of available rental options.

Why has the college rental market been historically stable compared with other types of rentals?

The college rental market has always been stable historically because, regardless of the general economic conditions, students will attend colleges and universities, and will at some point require rental housing.

What is the vacancy rate for rental housing in the United States?

In a 2013 report cited by the news service Reuters, the national apartment vacancy rate hit a ten-year low at 4.2%. Forty-seven out of seventy-nine markets—or nearly 60%—reported decreases in their vacancy rates. Annual lease rate increases for rentals are quite low, barely matching the rate of inflation. But experts feel the reason rent charges cannot increase, aside from the new building and construction of rental beds, is a basic lack of job and income growth within the economy, preventing people from having more disposable income to pay apartment or housing rents. For comparison purposes, after the economic collapse in 2008 and 2009, the rental housing vacancy rate was 8%.

What is another factor leading to more demand for rental housing?

Another factor that contributes to rental housing demand may be that banks and mortgage brokers have instituted more stringent requirements in order to obtain or qualify for a mortgage loan. Instead of purchasing a house, many people delay this purchase in favor of renting. As mortgage interest rates tick upward, more people also rent instead of purchasing a home.

Apartment vacancy rates in the United States are at a 10-year low after so many people lost their homes in the real estate bubble.

Where is the most expensive place to rent in the United States?

The most expensive place to rent in the United States is New York City, with an average monthly rent of $3,049.37.

Where is the least expensive place to rent in the United States?

The least expensive place to rent in the United States is Wichita, Kansas, with an average monthly rent of $528.95.

What is a rent-to-income ratio?

A rent-to-income ratio is used to test housing affordability. The ratio is computed by taking your monthly rent and dividing it by your monthly income. For rental housing to be affordable, your rent-to-income ratio should not exceed 30%, meaning your monthly rent and utilities should not exceed 30% of your monthly gross income and wages. These numbers may need adjusting; in some markets, you may exceed this affordability ratio because of the relatively high cost of housing.

What are some differences between investing in a rental home and investing in a rental apartment complex?

Experts assert some notable differences between investing in a house for rent and investing in an apartment complex for rent. Single-family houses require fewer inspections and regulations, and require less capital to repair and renovate in order to increase their value. Also, there are more houses than apartments available, a relatively large pool of house buyers makes that market more liquid, house tenants may rent for a longer du-

> ### How do some property owners make their rentals more attractive to potential renters?
>
> To compete with other property owners, in addition to cutting monthly rental prices or including utilities in the monthly rental charges, some landlords waive application fees (used to run credit checks or verify such factors as employment and income), offer such rewards as gift cards, or include several months' free rent in exchange for longer-term rental agreements with tenants.

ration, house mortgage requirements are less stringent, and house utility bills may easily be assigned to one tenant.

What are some disadvantages to investing in a single-family house for rental purposes?

Some difficulties that many real estate professionals anticipate in investing in single-family houses for rental purposes include an increased risk, since you require 100% occupancy to earn any income, or you have zero percent occupancy, and therefore receive no return on your investment. Single-family rentals are heavily dependent upon maintaining a successful landlord-tenant relationship, and may expose the landlord to more liability, since rental houses typically include tenants with children who are prone to accidents, for which the landlord may incur legal responsibility. And the individual unit cost of a single-family house is much higher than the individual unit cost of a multi-family apartment building.

What are some benefits of investing in multi-family apartments?

One benefit of investing in multi-family apartments is better cash flow than a single-family house, especially if the apartment has a good occupancy rate, and was originally purchased at a favorable price. Apartments may have other hidden values that come not necessarily by way of appreciation, but may come by increasing income (rents), renovating, and rezoning (for example, converting the property to condominiums). If the investor buys a poorly managed complex and turns the business around, he may be able to earn more income and increase the value of his property over time.

RETURN ON INVESTMENT (ROI)

How do I calculate my return on investment for real estate transactions?

You can calculate your ROI of a real estate deal in several ways. Generally, ROI may be calculated by taking the capital gains from the investment, subtracting all expenses and losses, and dividing this difference by the cost of the investment. Although the computation is quite simple to understand on the surface, it does not consider many other variables.

189

What is the cost method of calculating ROI on a real estate transaction?

The cost method of calculating your return on an investment focuses attention on understanding all costs associated with the real estate transaction and ownership, as well as the owner's equity in the real property. For example, if you purchase the property for $100,000, renovate it for $50,000, and then sell it for $200,000, your equity is $50,000. If you divide the equity ($50,000) by the costs associated with owning the property ($100,000 + $50,000), your ROI will be 0.33, or 33%.

What is the out-of-pocket method to calculate a return on investment in real estate?

When you purchase real property using a loan, you leverage the use of the bank or mortgage company's capital in order to invest. In so doing, your cash outflow to acquire the property may be lower than if you paid cash for the property, and your ROI may be higher as a result. Using loans or leverage enables you to obtain the returns you require when you eventually sell the property. Using the same values as in the above example, if you purchase a property for $100,000, make a down payment on a loan for $20,000, and spend $50,000 in additional capital to renovate the property, your total out-of-pocket expenses are $70,000. If you sell the property for $200,000, your equity is $130,000. Accordingly, your ROI will be calculated as above, $130,000 (equity) divided by $200,000 (your sales price), which equals 0.65, or 65%, improving your ROI.

When computing potential returns on investments in real estate, with what assumptions should I be concerned?

When you are analyzing any real estate deal, you need to concern yourself about your assumptions, such as what you believe is the value of the property, and what the market says the property is worth. You can review a bank appraiser's appraisal, but ultimately a buyer and a seller determine a property's final price or value. So you should underestimate a house's value when analyzing possible return models.

What other costs should I include when computing my return on an investment?

There are many costs inherent in real estate investing that you should capture in order to calculate your returns accurately. Those additional costs may include: property taxes paid; insurance costs; costs to advertise the sale of the property; sales and listing fees and commissions of the real estate agent or broker; and financing charges related to discharging the loan. You should

When calculating your Return on Investment (ROI), divide the money you get back (return) by your total costs into the investment to get a percentage or ratio.

discuss the transaction with an accounting professional to understand fully all the expenses related to a real estate transaction.

What are some limitations to using ROI models in order to understand my returns on real estate investments?

You can further complicate the simplistic return models by using variable interest rate loans or interest-only loans, by refinancing the original loan, or by extracting equity from the property by obtaining a second mortgage.

What is a cash-on-cash return, and why is it so important?

According to experts at Zillow, returns on any type of real estate investments fundamentally depend on two important factors: operating the investment so that it generates cash and income to the owner, and the property's appreciation over time. Since it is difficult to know in advance when you might sell a property, or at what future price you may sell it, experts generally agree that potential investors should focus their analysis on the cash flow and income-producing characteristics of the investment.

Cash- on-cash analysis allows you to understand the income compared with the amount of cash invested before making any tax considerations. To calculate your cash-on-cash return, first add all income generated from the investment, such as monthly rents and fees, and subtract your monthly expenses to give you a rough estimate of the income the property may generate. You should also subtract your monthly loan payments to compute your annual income.

If you purchase the property with a loan, if you use a down payment, and if you make one-time renovations, add these numbers to estimate the initial costs associated with purchasing the property (the property's "equity cash.") Then divide your annual income by your equity cash figure and multiply by 100 to see the cash-on-cash returns as a percentage.

Zillow notes that many real estate investors fail to make these and many other basic calculations, preferring to "wing it" when investing in real estate. Relatively simple calculations will remove much of the mystery and luck from the equation, and improve your chances for success.

Are there any online calculators that will allow me to calculate returns on potential real estate deals easily?

There are many online calculators available on websites that will allow you to see and understand potential returns from a real estate transaction. However, each calculator may use different variables in its equation, including such important items as calculations and terms of amortization, depreciation, mortgage interest paid, interest rates, property taxes, occupancy rates, analysis duration (the duration of time over which you review the data may greatly influence your results), and your tax bracket information.   **191**

The more variables you try to capture, the more accurate your estimate will be regarding your potential returns.

When discussing real estate returns, what is a "cap rate"?

Many real estate investors use a cap rate to understand the amount of income generated, compared with the amount of cash expended to acquire the investment. It is computed by dividing your net operating income assumptions by your cost of purchase, expressed as a percentage. If your investment property earns $12,000 per year, and you purchased it for $100,000, your cap rate would be 12%.

REAL ESTATE INVESTMENT TRUSTS (REITs)

What is a "real estate investment trust"?

A REIT is a company that may own or operate, by way of direct investment, a portfolio of income-generating real estate properties. A REIT may be publicly traded on an exchange, or may be a privately held consortium comprising investors or investor groups that pool their resources, expecting to generate a return. Typical REITs are categorized as equity based, mortgaged based, or a combination of both classes of investments. REITs were created to allow individual investors the opportunity to invest in real estate in a fashion similar to the way in which individual investors invest in the equities of companies through the use of a mutual fund.

When did Real Estate Investment Trusts begin?

Real estate investment trusts have existed for more than fifty years, and became an investment option by act of Congress during the Eisenhower administration in 1960.

In what types of commercial properties might a REIT invest?

REITs may invest in many types of commercial properties that have the potential to generate income, including: office space; rental housing/apartments; warehouse space; medical facilities; shopping centers; and raw land that may be held, developed, or sold to generate income and profits. REITs may also purchase mortgages and invest in various debt obligations related to financing real estate. In this way, REITs pool large amounts of capital to finance the development and ongoing ownership of many classes of real property investments.

In what other interesting types of commercial real estate might a REIT invest?

The effects of investments made by REITs may be found in every segment of your life. Some less noticeable investments made by REITs include investments in land used to grow trees for commercial application, wind farms, student housing, and cell phone towers.

Shopping centers are one type of commercial property in which Real Estate Investment Trusts may invest.

How much real estate do REITs control today?

REITs own more than $1 trillion of real estate.

How many REITs exist?

Approximately 414 REITs exist globally, of which 300 are listed with the SEC. These include mutual funds and ETFs in which individual investors may invest. Approximately 160 REITs are traded regularly on the New York Stock Exchange.

What percentage of corporate-sponsored 401(k) plans include REITs as an investment option?

REITs have grown as offerings for individuals seeking pre-tax investment options from 5% ten years ago to over 30% today.

How many Americans invest in REITs?

According to the National Association of Real Estate Investment Trusts, nearly 50 million individual Americans invest in real estate investment trusts today.

How do REITs generate their stated returns?

Many factors contribute to a REIT's income-producing characteristics, including: generating income through efficiently collecting rents from tenants; purchasing and selling real property; realizing income from owning mortgage debt and the interest income it produces; and adding value by developing real property and selling it for profit.

How do investors profit from owning shares in a REIT?

Investors hope to profit from owning stock in a real estate investment trust by enjoying the benefits of profit and income distributions from their stock ownership (and the overall gains of the REIT itself), as well as the appreciation (if any) in the value of the stock from the time of purchase to its ultimate sale.

What makes REITs desirable investments?

Many individual investors invest in REITs because they allow you to take advantage of the growth of the real estate market without the daily work necessary to manage a direct real estate investment. Investors do not have to find, analyze, and purchase property directly, but merely buy shares in a REIT and hope to make gains from their investment.

What percentage of real estate investment trusts are equity REITs, and what percentage are mortgage REITs?

More than 90% of all REITs are equity-based REITs that earn income primarily through collecting tenant rent payments. The remaining 10% earn their income through receipt of interest payments on mortgage debt and obligations owned by the REIT.

How does a company become classified as a real estate investment trust in the United States?

In order to be classified as a REIT, a company must invest at least 75% of its assets in real estate; make at least 75% of gross income from collecting rents from real property it owns, from earning interest on mortgages financing real property, or from selling real estate; must distribute at least 90% of its taxable income in the form of shareholder dividends each year; must be legally organized as a corporation; must have a board of directors or trustees; and must have a minimum of 100 shareholders, with no more than 50 percent of its shares held by five or fewer individuals.

SMALL BUSINESS INVESTING

THE BASICS

What impact does small business have on the U.S. economy?

Small business, defined as all companies employing fewer than 500 people, accounts for 88.7% of all firms that employ people, according to researchers at the Small Business Administration (SBA). In addition, small business employers account for approximately 64% of net new private sector jobs, 49.2% of all private sector employment, 42.9% of private sector payroll, 46% of private sector output, 43% of all high-tech employment, 98% of all exporters, and more than a third of the value of all exports.

How many small businesses exist in the United States?

As of 2010, approximately 27.9 million small businesses existed in America, compared with 18,500 firms employing more than 500 people. But according to SBA researchers, over 75% of all small companies have no employees, a statistic that has been trending upwards for a decade.

What percentage of small businesses are home-based businesses?

Fifty-two percent of small businesses are home-based businesses. This may illuminate a trend, as technological innovations make it possible for more individuals to create and manage businesses from the comfort of their own homes.

How successfully do small businesses create jobs?

Between 1993 and 2011, SBA researchers found that small businesses created 64% of new jobs. More importantly, since the recession in mid-2009, small businesses created 67% of all new jobs.

What effect do the unemployed have on the self-employed?

Unemployed people have had a great effect on the self-employed. Instead of seeking similar work after losing a job, many people launch a new business. The trend for this dynamic has increased for many years. In 2001, 3.1% of unemployed people became self-employed; in 2006, 3.6% became self-employed; in 2011, 5.5% became self-employed.

Of all small businesses in the United States, how many are owned by women and various minorities?

As of 2007, women owned approximately 7.8% of all small businesses in the United States, and minorities owned approximately 6.1%.

What is the most widely used legal form of corporate organization for firms that employ people?

The most widely used legal form of corporate organization for firms that employ people are subchapter S corporations, which account for 44% of all small businesses. This is followed by 22% of businesses that are organized as C corporations, and 18% of corporations that are organized as sole proprietorships.

Even today, women only own less than eight percent of all small businesses in the United States.

What is the effective tax rate for a small business?

The effective tax rate for a small business is the amount of tax paid divided by the amount of income made in any tax year. For example, a company that paid $45,000 in taxes on $180,000 in net profits would have an effective tax rate of 25%.

FINANCING SMALL BUSINESSES

How do small businesses use loans to finance their operations?

According to researchers at the SBA's Office of Advocacy, in the second quarter of 2013, commercial, industrial, non-farm, non-residential, and non-commercial real estate loans accounted for 94.1% of all loans, while commercial real estate made up the largest percentage of dollar volume or capital loaned, at 50.7%.

Why are business loans increasing?

Many experts believe that as loan restrictions relax and interest rates improve, more small businesses will be inclined to accept loans made available to them.

Why do small businesses borrow money?

Small businesses turn to outside sources to fund their businesses for many reasons, including: financing the business's initial start-up cost; purchasing inventory; expansion; and improving the financials and/or cash position of the business.

How large an effect do small businesses have on borrowing in the United States?

The SBA reports that small businesses accounted for approximately $1 trillion in borrowing (for the most recent year tracked, 2010). This borrowing activity may be categorized further to outright loans worth $652 billion, and lines of credit extended ($460 billion).

On average, how much money do new companies require to start their operations and activities?

According to the Kauffman Foundation, in a sampling of many new companies (that may be larger than the national average), new companies require approximately $80,000 per year. The median or middle amount required to start a business is approximately $50,000. New companies tend to require capital from owners directly and bank credit, when possible or required to fuel their beginning operations. In its rigorous data collection set, Survey of Business Owners, the U.S. Census Bureau found that one-third of all non-employer firms and 12% of employer firms required no start-up capital. Furthermore, twenty percent of all employer firms required less than $5,000 in start-up capital.

How do start-up businesses engaged in franchise activities use credit?

Almost 38% of new franchising companies in start-up mode use lenders to finance their operations, compared with the national average of 23.1% for all small businesses that employ people.

How does the SBA assist small business owners?

The SBA provides many financial assistance programs to help small business owners become successful. These programs include loans, grants, venture capital, and bonds. The SBA also provides information on its website to help potential business owners plan the launch of their business and receive business management information.

Owners of franchise companies tend to rely more on lenders to start their operations.

How does one obtain an SBA loan?

The SBA creates the guidelines used by banks that offer SBA loans. Because the SBA has worked with the business owner to understand the business in order to secure the loan, the SBA guarantees repayment for the loan, making banks more secure when providing these loans.

Is an SBA loan a commercial loan?

Yes, an SBA loan is a type of commercial loan, structured according to SBA requirements.

What if I have other business loans available, such as a line of credit?

You will not receive an SBA-guaranteed loan if you have access to other forms of financing at reasonable terms.

What types of loans does the SBA offer?

There are many loan programs available, depending on your business, your location, your ownership, whom you serve, etc. Some programs include: the 7(a) Loan Program (loans for businesses with special requirements, such as exports assistance, companies affected by NAFTA, rural business loans, and loans in underserved communities); the CDC/504 program (long-term financing that helps develop communities); and the Microloan Program (small, short-term loans for certain types of businesses).

What is the SBA CAPlines Program?

This short-term loan program helps small businesses gain access to working capital when they need it. The different types of CAPlines available include: Seasonal Line (for businesses that need to adjust their capital because of their seasonality), Contract Line (capital needed to fulfill a contract); Builders Line (for general contractors and builders); and Small Asset Based Lines of Credit (based upon the assets of the company, up to $200,000).

What are the typical loan maturities for the lines of credit?

The loans can mature anywhere from a few months to five years, depending on the business's needs.

Who guarantees these short-term loans?

Anyone who owns more than 20% of the business may guarantee the loan.

What about other sources for small business loans?

Contact your local bank loan officer for information on business loans and lines of credit. Check with your state, city, and county economic development authority to find out what funds are available from these entities. Many cities, especially those in distressed areas, have set up programs that mix both private and public funds to help small businesses succeed. You may also search the Internet for sites that provide more specific information on local or regional programs.

How do small businesses finance their operations?

According to a survey by the SBA, 59% of small businesses finance their business through credit cards. 23% of those surveyed used four or more credit cards during the past year to finance their business.

How else do small business owners fund their companies?

In the same survey, 51% of respondents funded their business through the company's earnings, 45% had access to a bank loan, 30% received credit from a vendor, 19% obtained a private loan through friends or family, 7% used leasing, and 5% obtained an SBA loan.

What percentage of a small business owner's debt is credit card debt?

Thirty-four percent of respondents have more than 25% of their business debt on credit cards. Twenty percent of those surveyed paid interest rates of 20% or more per year to finance this debt.

Are small business owners happy with their credit card terms (interest rate, fees, credit limits)?

Seventy-nine percent of all respondents said that over the past five years, their credit card terms have worsened.

STARTING A BUSINESS

What percentage of America's entrepreneurs are "ethnic"?

According to researchers at the Kauffman Foundation, 39.8% of the approximately 11.5 million entrepreneurs in the United States are not Caucasian, and 22.9% are classified as Latino.

How many new businesses are created every month in the United States?

According to reporters at *Forbes*, citing recent research published by the Kauffman Foundation, 320 new businesses per 100,000 people start each month in the United States. This equals approximately 543,000 new businesses created each month, or more than 6.52 million businesses per year.

How many entrepreneurs exist in the United States?

The same researchers at *Forbes*, citing "multiple estimates," approximate the number of U.S. entrepreneurs at 11.5 million, with male entrepreneurs outnumbering their female counterparts two to one.

Who are these business creators?

According to researchers and experts interviewed by *Forbes*, 25% of all entrepreneurs are age 20–34, but surprisingly, more than 35% of all entrepreneurs are age 55–64. The report asserts that from 1996 to 2007, Americans age 55–64 created more new businesses than any other age group, and 33% more businesses than the 20–34 age group.

Why do so many older Americans start businesses?

The Kauffman Foundation, in a landmark study on understanding entrepreneurship, believes older Americans are starting companies in record numbers because their life expectancies continue to increase; they are working fewer years for an employer; they live healthier, longer lives; they can afford to create a company; and they encounter fewer barriers to enter a given business market.

How old are people who typically start technology-related companies?

Kauffman Foundation researchers discovered the average age of people starting technology companies in the United States is 39, with twice as many people over age 50, as under age 25.

Older Americans are starting new businesses in record numbers these days. Some reasons include the fact that people are living longer, and older people tend to have more money available to invest; they are therefore able to be productive longer.

What are the different types of business structures?

There are many different types of business structures that assist the IRS to determine what taxes and proper documents need to be filed with the taxpayer's return. The different types of business structures include: Sole Proprietorships; Partnerships; Corporations; "S" Corporations; and LLCs (Limited Liability Companies).

What is a sole proprietorship?

A sole proprietorship is an unincorporated business owned by an individual. The owner or taxpayer is responsible for such federal filings as income tax, self-employment tax, estimated taxes (paid monthly or quarterly), Social Security and Medicare taxes, income withholding taxes, information on Social Security, Medicare, and income tax withholding, FUTA (Federal Unemployment Tax Act) tax, and the the filing of information returns for payments to non-employees and transactions with other persons, and any excise taxes.

How many sole proprietorships exist in the United States?

Today there are approximately 19.4 million sole proprietorships.

What is a partnership?

A partnership is a business structure between two or more persons who join to carry on a trade or business, contributing money, property, labor, and/or skill, and expect to share in the profits and losses of the business. According to the IRS, a partnership must file an annual information return to report the income, deductions, gains, losses, etc., from the operations of the business, but it does not pay income tax. Instead, it "passes through" any profits or losses to its partners. This means each partner includes his or her share of the partnership's income or loss on his individual tax return for each tax year. Partners are not employees, and should not be issued an IRS Form W-2. The partnership must furnish copies of IRS Schedule K-1 (Form 1065) to the partners by a predetermined filing date. According to the IRS, the actual partnership itself is responsible for filing such documents as an income tax return, employment taxes for employees such as Social Security and Medicare, FUTA taxes, and for depositing employment taxes and any excise taxes due. If you are a partner in a partnership, you are responsible to file such items as income taxes, self-employment taxes (since you are paying yourself with the money earned from the partnership), and estimated taxes throughout the course of the tax year.

How many partnerships exist in the United States?

There are approximately 1.6 million small companies organized as partnerships in the United States.

What types of corporations does the IRS recognize?

The IRS recognizes two types of corporate entities: a "subchapter C" corporation and a "subchapter S" corporation.

What else is a corporation?

A corporation conducts business, realizes net income or loss, and pays taxes and distributes profits to shareholders.

What is a "C" Corporation?

In a C corporation, shareholders (people who own the company) exchange money, property, or both for the corporation's capital stock, issued either initially when the corporation is formed, or at different times during the year, according to the company's laws and shareholder agreements. A C corporation may generally use the same deductions as a sole proprietorship to figure its taxable income. A corporation may also take special deductions. For federal income tax purposes, a C corporation is recognized as a separate tax-paying entity.

Why do C corporation shareholders pay double taxes?

C corporation shareholders pay double taxes because they must pay taxes for the corporate entity they own, and they must pay personal income taxes on any profits or dividends the corporation distributes. Shareholders cannot use any C corporation losses against their income on their personal tax returns.

Why would someone want to own a C corporation?

C corporations allow owners to have more than one hundred shareholders, to issue different classes or types of stock to shareholders, and to have foreign shareholders. This makes the corporate entity more attractive to a broader group of people, helping the C corporation attract more capital (by selling different types of shares) without having to borrow money from other sources to fund its growth in exchange for partial company ownership. But this also obligates the company to provide a certain level of return on its shareholders' investment, and listen to many more voices when managing the company. Because of its broader appeal and more activity, the company can be perceived as having more value, since there is very little commingling between individual owners and the corporation.

What federal filings must corporations file?

Corporations are responsible to file such items as income taxes, estimated taxes paid at certain intervals throughout the year, and employment-related taxes (such as Social Security and Medicare taxes), as well as FUTA taxes. They are also responsible for excise taxes (taxes paid for buying certain types of items, such as fuel).

What is an "S" corporation?

Under their bylaws, S corporations elect to pass through corporate income, losses, deductions, and credit to their shareholders for federal tax purposes. S corporation share-

Corporations hold annual shareholder meetings, during which they typically elect board members and often discuss and vote on other issues affecting a company.

holders report the flow-through of income and losses on their personal tax returns, and are assessed taxes at their individual income tax rates. This allows S corporations to avoid double taxation on the corporate income. S corporations are responsible to pay tax on certain gains in the value of their equity and passive income they may realize throughout the year.

What are the requirements to create an S corporation?

In order to qualify for S corporation status, a corporation must meet the following requirements: It must be a domestic corporation; it must have only certain types of shareholders (such as individuals, certain types of trusts, and estates, but not partnerships, corporations, or non-resident aliens); it must have no more than 100 shareholders; it must have only one class of stock; and it must not be what the IRS calls an ineligible corporation, including certain types of financial institutions, insurance companies, and domestic international sales corporations.

How do I create an S corporation?

To begin to create an S corporation, you must submit Form 2553, "Election by a Small Business Corporation," to the IRS.

What is the biggest difference between an S corporation and a C corporation?

The biggest difference—and the main reason why people who start companies elect to create an S corporation instead of a C corporation is to avoid paying the double taxes that shareholders of C corporations must pay.

What is an "LLC"?

An LLC, or limited liability company, is a business structure allowed to exist by state statute. Accordingly, each state has different laws to regulate its LLCs. It provides limited liability to its owners in most U.S. jurisdictions. LLCs do not need to be organized for profit. People who own LLCs are referred to as members, and there is no limitation to the number of LLC members. Members may include individuals, other corporations, other LLCs, and foreign entities. LLC members cannot be held personally liable for the company's debts or liabilities, providing a degree of protection for the owners' personal assets outside the LLC. Also, members are not taxed twice on their profits. The IRS has special rules regarding LLCs; consult with a tax adviser for more information.

What are some early steps I should consider before starting my own business?

According to entrepreneurship expert Alan Hall, if you are a prospective business creator you should keep your "day job" as long as possible (especially if you intend to use income from your employment to fuel your start-up company); give yourself a time frame or goal (for example, one year), as this will allow you to focus your energy in order to attain the goal; honor your signed non-compete agreement, if your employer has required this; try specifically to create the purpose, vision, and strategy of the idea; test assumptions on the market; know your market size and the portion of the market that best matches your idea; consider all aspects of competitive offerings; evaluate the viability of your product or service; determine how the product will be sold and purchased; how you will collect revenues; and create a plan and budget on the profitability of your product or service.

What are some key steps to take in creating my business, after I consider the information above?

While starting a business may be complex or simplistic, depending on the nature of that business, many experts assert that some early steps include: having a store of capital available for a long period of time while in start-up mode; deciding the location of the business; its corporate and legal structure; creating your company name; obtaining licenses or certifications; obtaining a federal tax identification number to properly file IRS documents and taxes; forming a relationship with an accountant; and creating a business plan/strategy document.

What are some guidelines for creating a business, according to the IRS?

According to the IRS, you should determine whether your business is a business or a hobby. If indeed it is a business, then the IRS will expect to receive various forms, reports, and returns. Ask yourself the following questions to determine how the IRS will treat your new business entity:

- Does the time and effort put into the activity indicate an intention to make a profit?

- Do you depend on income from the activity?

- If your business incurs a loss, is it due to circumstances beyond your control, or did it occur in the business's start-up phase?

- Have you changed methods of operation to improve profitability?

- Do you or your advisers have the knowledge necessary to carry on the activity as a successful business?

- Have you made a profit in similar activities in the past?

- Does your business make a profit in some years?

- Can you expect to make a profit in the future from the appreciation of assets used in the activity?

There are many legitimate business expenses that can be written off on tax returns, such as the purchase or upgrading of essential computer equipment.

205

Can I deduct expenses to offset taxes if I own my own company?

In general, you may deduct many categories of ordinary and necessary expenses to conduct a trade or business. An ordinary expense is one commonly used and accepted in your trade or business. A necessary expense is one that is appropriate for your business. Generally, an activity qualifies as a business if you operate it with a reasonable expectation of earning a profit. For more information on business expense deduction guidelines, see IRS Publication 535, Business Expenses.

INVESTING IN A SMALL BUSINESS

What important disclaimer must every investor in a small, privately held business consider before making an initial investment?

The disclaimer considered by many experts to be essential is that an investor should not make any investment of this type without being prepared to lose all of his investment. Although the potential for gains may be very high, the potential for losses is also very high for a variety of reasons, as described in earlier answers above.

What must an investor first consider before deciding to invest in a small, privately held company?

When deciding to make any investment, an investor must first specifically determine his principal motivation to make the investment. Is it to earn current income? Is the investment expectation to generate long-term capital gains? Is it to free yourself from the confines of your previous career? Is it to work with someone with whom you wish to work? Each individual investor is unique, and has unique reasons to make an investment. By looking at your motivations, you may create filters that enable you clearly to find the target company that makes the best fit with your investment goals.

After I decide my motivations for making the investment, what is the next logical step in deciding to invest in a small, privately held company?

The next logical step is to decide what area of competency is best suited for you by answering many questions. Some typical questions might include: What experience in specific verticals match my experiences? What industries inspire in me the most passion? What industries do I wish to avoid?

What are some important dynamics of investing in a business that every investor should consider before making the investment?

A component of both the downside and upside risk is that when you invest in a small company, you are actually making an investment in and with the business's founder or partner, who may remain, so the financial success of the company may be heavily dependent upon this person's personality, and the dynamics of your relationship. Of course, as a new partner, after making the investment, you hope to add some value to the business and assert changes that might make the business more profitable over time. But the dynamics, positive relationship, and communication abilities of the partners is important to the success of the new entity. Partners need to share the same or similar short- and long-term goals for the business. If these goals are not shared and explicitly stated and agreed upon, risk of financial underperformance increases. It is very important to consider with whom you are partnering as much as what you are buying.

How do I identify a small company in which to invest?

Good fortune plays a great role in finding the right company in which to invest. It is best to focus on a specific industry, and find candidates in that industry and competitors to those candidates, in order to have a large list of prospects, as many will not be for sale. The ones that are for sale may have specific reasons to sell that may involve substantial risk or impossible conditions to create a turnaround investment situation, in which, after making the investment, you fix problems to make the investment perform better financially. By looking deeply at each target company, you can see the problems and identify paths to make the company more profitable or financially successful. Not all private companies have good financial reports. Many companies will not disclose proper information even if they are interested in selling, so it is difficult to have a fully transparent transaction. And investments in small businesses are highly illiquid, as it is very difficult to match buyers with sellers in order to convert equity to cash.

What are some red flags that may warn potential investors of problems when making a private investment?

According to experts interviewed by Fox Business, many investors initially identify an investment from friends, family, or word of mouth, but this might not be a great idea, nor the most successful method to identify a target company. Some experts assert that if a small company wants to sell equity in order to get cash, it may be a sign that the entity cannot obtain financing from a bank.

What does the phrase
"Some of the best deals are those you walk away from" mean?

Even after you identify opportunities to invest in target companies, for whatever reason, often the transaction is not consummated. It is best to find companies in which the transaction can happen, and not feel attached to deals in which the seller is not motivated, or if the numbers do not support making the investment. Remember, you may be walking away from a deal in which you could lose hundreds of thousands or even millions of dollars. By walking away, you may use those same funds for a better potential candidate.

Some companies may be averse to taking on any debt, or dealing with the often stringent financial reports that banks or lenders require. If a company has a great cash flow and a solid client base, a bank typically will make a secured loan (with some form of collateral) of approximately 70% of the company's current accounts receivable without an exchange of equity, but with interest and strict repayment/default terms.

Some private company owners may prefer to give up equity rather than obtain a loan. Or perhaps the business owner cannot qualify for a loan, a fact that will be apparent when you see the company's financials. If the business cannot qualify for an external loan, it may be a red flag of a rather large problem, or indicative of a large opportunity in which to invest, depending on your analysis of the target company.

What are the two principal ways to acquire a private company?

The two principal ways in which an investor may acquire a company are to acquire stock or equity in the company, and to acquire a company's debt. In many cases, investors could use a combination of both acquisition methods.

When I buy an equity position in a company, what exactly am I buying?

When you buy equity or stock in a private company, you acquire a percentage of the ownership of the company (both its assets and liabilities), depending on the mutually agreed valuation of the company and the terms of the transaction, in exchange for a percentage of the profit, usually equal to the percent of ownership of the new entity. For example, if the buyers and sellers agree to a valuation, that the price of the company is $500,000, and 50% of the company is sold, the new buyers would control 50% of the company, and would share in 50% of the company's earnings, in exchange for a cash payment of $250,000. Most private transactions to acquire private companies require considerable cash as an initial payment.

What will the former owner of the company typically do with the cash received from the transaction?

Businesses may use the capital generated from a sale of equity, if the sellers so intend, to finance necessary capital expenditures to expand, pay down debt and/or other obligations, buy out equity of other owners or partners, increase the seller's cash position or liquidity, hire new employees, or invest to expand the company.

Must the sellers pay capital gains tax to the IRS?

The sellers will be responsible for some form of capital gains tax, depending on how long they owned the shares and how much they have appreciated, since they ultimately will receive a sum of money at the transaction's closing.

Why is the acquisition of a company a highly risky form of investing?

Acquiring a private company is a highly risky form of investing because such investments offer nearly no protection to the downside risk of owning a business. If the company has a bad month and requires additional capital to stay afloat, owners of the business typically must provide this capital immediately. If the company is not making a profit, and therefore is not distributing earnings to shareholders, the new owner will not generate any return on the initial investment. Private ownership may also require an inordinate amount of time to see returns, much more than usually assumed when analyzing the transaction. Depending on the unique circumstances of the company, it could run out of cash and file for bankruptcy. In this case, the investor loses all of his initial investment.

Even large, formerly successful companies, such as Circuit City, which closed its brick-and-mortar business in 2009, can go bankrupt.

Why can acquiring a company be a great investment?

Acquiring a company can be a great investment for a multitude of reasons. If the business has a proven track record of adapting to all market conditions, consistently generating profits, distributing those profits, and growing its client base over time, the downside risks can be reduced, and high returns on the initial investment can be realized. The valuation of the company and the price paid for the initial investment materially affects the investor's returns, so you should base the sales price such that the investor does not overpay for the equity, as it may stretch the time it takes to earn a decent return by months or years.

What is an investment in a private company's debt?

When an investor invests in a private company's debt, the investor is making a loan to the entity in exchange for some form of interest plus the initial principal of the obligation. The investor is the financier, or bank, to the company. Typically, debt obligations are made as direct loans to the entity, with a regular amortization schedule based upon a mutually agreed-upon interest rate. Collateral may be used to secure the loan. Or the business entity may issue a corporate bond, wherein interest is paid semi-annually and all principal is paid when the bond comes due.

Why do investors like to acquire a company's debt?

Investors like to acquire a company's debt for many reasons, including the fact that the debt of a company is first in line to be repaid—in front of all equity shareholders—if the company becomes insolvent. If the investor also is given a lien on real property or assets of the company, and the company becomes insolvent, then the debt owner may force the sale of these assets in order to be repaid. So there is more security associated with investments in debt. However, the returns that may be realized could be far less than if the investor acquired equity in the company.

If the target company has no debt, isn't an investment in equity less risky?

To a degree, if you are investing in a company with no debt (now), it may appear to be less risky. But the new company may require capital in the future, and may expose itself to debt obligations, for which the equity owner will be responsible. And as stated above, debt holders are normally first in line to be repaid, followed by equity holders, so the risk may present itself in the future, and should be included in your valuation of a company before completing an acquisition.

Why is it important to have a thoughtful exit strategy before I invest in a small company?

It is very important to define how you will or can exit before investing in a small company for a variety of reasons. Because of the illiquid nature of the investment, and the very fact that you cannot just go online to redeem your shares, you must consider how you could exit the investment after some time. The investment may not see any returns or dividends for many years, according to many experts, and may be rather difficult to sell. It is best to discuss and agree on several different exit strategies for a liquidity event, such as the eventual merging with another company, the selling of shares at a specific

When investing in or purchasing a business, it is an excellent idea to get an attorney who specializes in corporate law to help with the paperwork.

valuation to another partner or to the company itself, an initial public offering of equity on the public markets, opening up investment opportunities to new partners, selling equity to employees, etc.

Why is it important to have proper documentation and legal agreement when I invest in a small business?

Investors often conclude a private deal with family and friends with nothing more than a handshake, exposing themselves to many potential risks. It is best to pay for the services of an attorney, and perhaps even share the costs of all legal expenses related to the transaction with your investment partner. You should especially attend to such details as what the corporate structure will be, dilution clauses, capital calls, board voting rules, share buyback rules, share valuation rules, liquidation, payment of earnings, cost and expense control, and legal jurisdiction. You should also ensure the purchase agreement is balanced, and does not favor the buyer or the seller. These and many other considerations must be of high priority to protect both buyer and seller, so you should seek the guidance of a lawyer who specializes in small company transactions.

What are some other benefits to investing locally in a small business?

In an interview published by the site www.Mint.com, author of the book *Locavesting* (2011), Amy Cortese, cites many reasons why investing locally is beneficial, beyond obtaining returns and gains from the investment. Her top reasons include: creating and maintaining local jobs; keeping local capital in circulation; the local multiplier effect (local money helps other ancillary businesses that employ people, who then spend locally, etc.); the effect local businesses have on the local community (because they are based locally, they care about the local community, and are not interested in exporting jobs and capital outside the community); and the use of local banks (that, in turn, lend the money locally and reinvest in the community).

Why is it good to be a "silent partner" in a business?

There are some distinct advantages to being a silent partner when you make an investment in a private business. Assuming you paid the right price for the equity, and assuming you have very good, aligned, competent management in place to run the day-to-day operations, many think being a silent partner is a great choice. It allows you to play a supporting role in managing the company on an as-needed basis, and greatly limits the amount of time you must devote to the business, so that you can focus on other projects and investments. According to experts interviewed by *The Houston Chronicle*, acting as a silent partner allows you to step out of the way of competent, knowledgeable partners, yet share in the income/benefits generated by the company without the daily operational hassle. An active partner may earn a management fee as compensation for his time. A company may also create a compensation scheme in which the passive partners earn less and the active partners earn more.

211

What are some key methods to evaluate a target company?

Experts generally agree that, in order to analyze a target company for investment purposes, you should compare the target against its local competitors, especially the business model. You should evaluate the current management of the company and its strategy; make an intensive analysis of the company's financials; and note how much money the company spends to acquire and keep its clients.

When I invest in a private company, on what type of financial information should I focus?

When investing in a private company, you should look at such financial information as to how well the company generates profits, how well it manages cash and expenses, how well it acquires new clients and keeps old clients, how well the company gets paid, and how well the company performs year-over-year in generating revenues. You should also see how much cash flows from one calendar year to the next, as companies will often manipulate the income received at the end of a year in order to improve its subsequent year's stated financials. You should also understand the current return on invested capital. If you think of all cash used to fund the business as an annual investment with a return, it is good to investigate if this return is increasing or decreasing over time. Also pay close attention to the pricing models used by the business, and compare them against other competitors to see if they are accurate or deficient in some way. Since the greatest expenses of small companies tend to be employees and benefits, you should analyze its per-employee profitability as well as its per-employee productivity. Also review the costs of health care and retirement benefits.

MANAGING A SMALL BUSINESS

Why are small businesses so important to the U.S. economy?

Despite media impressions that large companies seem to wield a great deal of influence on the U.S. economy, according to the SBA's Office of Advocacy, 99.7% of all companies in the United States are small companies that employ over 50% of the available private labor force, or approximately 120 million people.

How many small businesses exist in the United States?

Approximately 27.8 million small businesses exist in the United States, and 22 million small businesses employ only one person.

Just how small is America's small business?

Although nearly 55 million people depend upon small business, 79.4% of all small businesses have no employees, and the majority of the remaining small businesses have fewer than twenty employees. Sixty-five percent of all new jobs were created by small businesses since 1995.

Why is it difficult to see the survivability rates for new businesses?

It is difficult to calculate the survivability rates for new businesses because many statistics merely use the raw number of new companies started in a year and the number of companies that failed during that year to compute the rate. A more accurate method to determine the survival rate would be to track all companies—or a statistically significant representative sample of all new companies—and ask if they survived for subsequent years, and note the distribution of these results.

What is the survival rate for new companies?

Actually, the survival rate of new companies is much higher than what you have heard in the past. Seventy percent of new employer firms survive at least two years; approximately half of all new companies survive five or more years; approximately one-third survive ten or more years; one-quarter survive longer than 15 years. So the success rate for new business start-ups is quite good.

What percentage of small businesses in the United States are actually home-based businesses?

Approximately 52% of all small businesses are home-based businesses, without an external office location.

What are some more typical reasons why small businesses fail?

While most businesses celebrate their fifth birthday and beyond, some businesses can and do fail for a variety of reasons, including: lack of experience by owners and employees; insufficient capital; bad location decision; poor inventory management; too much capital spent on fixed assets; insufficient access to credit; withdrawing too much capital; failing to keep up with growth; competitive business climate; and poor sales.

What are some other reasons why a small business might fail?

According to small business experts and editors at *The New York Times*, small businesses may fail because: demand for the product or service and price assumption is incorrect; owner incompetency; inability to manage growth; poor financial attention and accounting; no cash cushion; average (rather than exceptional) abilities to operate the business; insensitivity to cost

Over half—52%—of all American small businesses are now based out of people's homes.

control and expense management; management dysfunction; no succession plan or exit strategy; and declining markets.

As an investor or owner of a small business, why does proper management help me increase the return on my investment?

As an investor or owner in a small business, one great benefit is the ability to make corrections in the company to help improve its financial picture (and ultimately its ROI). You have a unique opportunity to be able to invest in a business and then directly affect any part of it that materially affects the company's financials. You cannot exert that sort of influence when you are one of perhaps hundreds of thousands of shareholders in a mutual fund. At best, you may be able to call the toll-free customer service line when you have a question about your account. But you cannot request any kind of change to any of the companies in the portfolio of holdings of the fund. When you invest in a small business, you can improve the financials considerably by properly managing the investment. If you make the correct combinations of changes, you may increase your earnings and returns of the business.

How do I generally decide on what issues to focus when managing a small business?

Like any investment, you must begin with your original investment goal. If that goal is to earn a stable earnings growth in the company over some time period, or triple your revenue (and increase your profits), then this requires specific focus on the drivers of those outcomes.

How do I determine what component or functional area of my business affects the drivers the most?

To decide what part of the existing business needs the most attention in order to achieve our goals, it is best to see how this functional area is performing, and how it should perform. If your goal is to increase earnings, then there are a finite number of actions you can take in order to do this. If your end goal is to sell the company for a profit to another company, then you must identify ways to increase the inherent value of the company, such as by efficiently using cash, productively using people, properly managing expenses, taking care of employees and clients, increasing sales or repeat business, managing taxes properly, and/or patenting or trademarking.

Why is understanding financial metrics, and corrections made as a result of understanding these metrics, important to successfully manage or invest in a small business?

According to experts at www.Inc.com, owners need to focus attention beyond simply looking at the profits and losses of a business, since many metrics may tell the owner what may happen in the near future. Certain metrics indicate warning signs that may illuminate a potential problem weeks, months, or years in the future. If you correct these problems as soon as you identify them, you can continue on a path of financial success.

What are some key metrics that a small business owner should analyze to grow his business?

According to management experts at www.Forbes.com, entrepreneurs and small business owners may be very adept at creating a business, but may lack the skills or discipline and attention to detail that proper management of the financial aspects of the business requires. There are many different financial metrics a small business investor or owner should track, including: sales revenue; customer loyalty and retention; cost associated to acquire a customer; staff productivity; profit margins/earnings; monthly profit/loss; overhead expenses; fixed/variable costs; inventory control; and hours worked per functional process. Experts interviewed by *The Washington Post* would also specifically include pre-tax net profit margin, current ratio/quick ratio (assets divided by liabilities/cash plus accounts receivable divided by current liabilities), and accounts payable days/accounts receivable days (how long it takes to pay and receive payment).

What are additional key metrics that require the focus of small business owners and investors?

Experts at *Inc.* offer four additional metrics that allow owners/investors a view inside a business that may indicate success or trouble in the near future. These include cost to acquire customers (all costs associated with sales and marketing divided by number of clients); lifetime value of a customer (assuming a period of time, how much each customer spends with the company); revenue percentages (analyzing each discrete source of revenue and profit of the business); and churn rate (what percentage of new clients and repeat clients for each period, expressing this revenue as a percentage, for each service or product offering).

What is one the biggest challenges of small business ownership?

One of the biggest challenges of small business ownership is that the owner/investor must be highly competent in many areas of management. If the owner/investor lacks skills, knowledge, or expertise in a certain area, or does not have an employee well-versed in that area of expertise, it may be challenging to correct problems within the company in order to achieve financial goals.

Why do many small business owners struggle with financial management of their business, or pay little or no attention to it?

Many small business owners pay little attention to analyzing key metrics and struggle with financial management of their business because they spend an inordinate amount of time working directly for the business in order to increase sales or create product, and find it difficult to delegate authority, responsibility, and control to subordinates to man-

If you dedicate part of your home to office space for your business, you have the option of writing that off on your taxes.

age daily activities, which would then allow them to focus on big-picture financials that may have a greater effect on the business's overall financial performance. Other owners/investors may simply dislike dealing with financial information, and may ignore this aspect of management altogether.

How do self-employed business owners pay their income taxes?

According to the IRS, as a self-employed individual, generally you are required to file an annual return and pay estimated taxes quarterly, but some business owners may pay monthly.

If I own a home-based business or a business that requires me to maintain a home office, may I deduct expenses related to this office?

If you use part of your home exclusively and regularly for the sole purpose of conducting your business, you may be able to deduct expenses related to the use of that room from your taxes. Depending on what percentage of your house is actually being used for business purposes, you may deduct that same percentage of your bills such as mortgage interest, insurance, utilities, repairs, and house depreciation. For further information, please consult a tax professional.

What percentage of small businesses are ultimately approved for a loan either to start or manage them?

According to the SBA, approximately 49% of small businesses are approved for business loans or other financing needs.

What are "Small Business Administration loans"?

The SBA backs loans to small businesses through commercial lenders, as long as SBA guidelines are followed. Although the SBA does not loan money directly to businesses, it partially guarantees the loans, acting as a co-signer, since many small businesses often have not established a long credit history or do not have access to collateral to guarantee the loan. This makes the loan less risky for lenders, and allows for economic expansion and employment.

ROIs AND SMALL BUSINESSES

Why is Return on Investment an essential measurement standard for businesses?

ROI is an essential measurement for businesses because it allows the business owner/ investor the opportunity to see how effectively the business is using its cash and equity resources. Experts at *The Houston Chronicle* point out that this important metric can be used by both small and large companies, since both types of companies generally have scarce financial resources, and small companies are more limited in what they may be able to do with their financial resources, since they lack the myriad financing options that large companies may access.

What is the main purpose of using ROI calculations or techniques?

The main purpose of using ROI calculations or techniques is to measure how much money is earned (profit) for every dollar of expenses. If a company is earning more than 0%, it is earning more money than it is spending. If the company is generating very high ROI, and increasing its ROI each month, quarter, or year, it is very efficient at deploying its capital.

How else do businesses use ROI in their decision-making process?

ROI enables the business to see what capital investment option might generate more returns for the business. In this way, businesses may make relatively safer, more profitable decisions. For example, a company may use ROI to analyze whether the company should hire sales people, with all of the inherent costs, or use an outside firm to generate sales, but give up a certain percentage of the income to cover the outsourcing expense. By accurately projecting or budgeting the expenses related to a direct sales activity, as compared with an outsourced sales activity, the company may make a proper financial-based decision.

What are some limitations to ROI analysis?

As with many metrics used by businesses to analyze their success, each metric does have its limitations. With ROI, especially forward-looking projections of possible returns, you must make accurate assumptions. When you want to use ROI accurately, you should be careful not to overstate the income generated by the idea, or understate the expenses re-

217

No. In the real world of business, many activities cannot be modeled using ROI analysis. There is also nearly no practical way to control the many variables that influence a company's ultimate earnings, so it is not practical to use ROI analysis to see whether you should, for example, subsidize employee health club memberships, if doing so does not directly or greatly affect your company's earnings. It may be a great idea, and may be just what the company needs to do to retain or attract employees, but it would be difficult to analyze the return on this type of investment.

lated to the idea. Businesses also may not capture all sources of expense, or all future sources of income. Businesses also typically overstate the time frame needed to generate the return, and may understate the amount of time needed to actually implement the idea so that it may begin to generate a return, so it is prudent to estimate this time accurately. If your assumptions and numbers are accurate, you can see if the possible return justifies the investment. ROI calculations also do not take into consideration the risk inherent in the idea or investment. When a company considers several options, it may include a probabilistic factor for the assumptions, such as a 90% chance of hitting the revenue targets if the idea is implemented.

How do I easily calculate return on investment?

You may easily calculate ROI by dividing the profit attributable to the investment by the total investment made. For example, if you decided to invest in a new server for a discrete group of clients for $10,000, and after all the income was received from the clients and expenses were paid you received $2,200 in profit, the ROI would be 2,200/10,000, or 22%.

How might a small business use ROI analysis for strategic planning purposes?

A business may have several products or services, each with distinct costs and income. Each product or service generates a return for the capital used to support the product or service in a given time period. A business can run ROI analyses to decide to improve or eliminate lagging products or services. If the business sees line items with better ROI, it may seriously consider investing more money and expanding this area of the business.

How else do small business owners mistakenly use ROI analysis?

Some experts assert that business owners may mistakenly use ROI analysis by not accurately including their own time in the expense (investment) side of the equation. Many business owners may not formally pay themselves regularly, and typically would not factor in or include the use of their own time, since they feel their time is "free." If the owners are actually conceiving, funding, and implementing the idea, as well as selling the idea to clients and collecting income from the idea, their time and energy should be captured and not understated, as is often the case.

How can I use ROI techniques to analyze a small company's social media campaigns?

It may be challenging to use ROI techniques to analyze social media campaigns of a small company. When you try to calculate return on investment to analyze the successfulness of less tangible activities, such as marketing, advertising, public relations, or social media, there are successful ways to achieve this. According to experts at www.steamfeed.com, computing the return on an investment in social media activity is an important step for large companies to justify the cost, budget, consultants, and additional support personnel needed to implement the campaign. But because of the limited number of staff and financial resources available to a small business, the decision to use ROI techniques may be difficult.

If I can't use ROI analysis to decide whether or not to engage in a social media campaign, how can I analyze the effectiveness of the campaign?

The same experts at www.steamfeed.com suggest you look at other metrics, such as how many clients are coming to your blog or Facebook page (or website), or how many clients are discovering your company's product or service through websites/applications such as

Social media sites such as Twitter, Facebook, and LinkedIn are increasingly being used to help with business advertising and public relations.

Yelp. For consumer products, you can review how many repeat customers you might obtain. You can use key performance indicators that the company may decide are important to your business success, track these indicators, and see how they compare to a goal or target established prior to launching the campaign. You can track important performance indicators using such tools as Google Analytics to see the baseline of potential client/customer activity before and after your campaign. You can compare this activity with your daily, weekly, or monthly sales to see if there is a real connection between the social media campaign and your sales success. Experts suggest that after one quarter, you might begin to see how effective the campaign really is. If the campaign is not successful or meeting targets and goals, then it may be the right time to change the tactics or try a new idea.

How might I attribute costs associated with social media campaigns?

You can estimate costs for a social media campaign by analyzing the costs and time of the people responsible for managing the campaign, as well as what percentage of their time (and expenses) is used to maintain the social media activity. If you spend time generating content for websites/blogs or other social media sites, then this time needs to be captured as well, as it is never free. You may also want to factor in the lost opportunity of the person or people who may be pulled away from another activity in order to engage in the social media activity.

PRIVATE EQUITY

What is "private equity"?

Private equity is an asset class or investment vehicle in which the investor purchases all or part of a company's equity or stock and debt or obligations, using capital either to assist in the expansion, develop new initiatives, continue profitable initiatives, restructure the company to improve profitability, or improve the value of the company for later sale or merger.

What else is private equity?

As the term implies, there is a private component to the words "private equity." But there are many cases in which private equity firms may acquire part or all of a public company, take the company private, and even sell shares and ultimately make the company public again. Normally this type of activity is but one of a number of strategies of private equity firms decide upon at the onset as a way to create liquidity from a very illiquid investment.

What is "private capital"?

Private capital is used to support private equity investments. Since private equity may tie up capital used to fund an acquisition for many months or years, experts generally assert that it is a highly illiquid investment strategy. It may take a very long time for private equity investors to earn back their principal or receive distributions on the profit generated by the target company.

What is "private" about private equity investments?

Private equity investments involve using a variety of sources of private capital from other investors or groups of investors with the intent of acquiring a notable percentage of a privately held (not publicly traded) or publicly held company.

What is a "leveraged buyout"?

A leveraged buyout is one form of private equity, whereby investors may come together and use a percentage of the target company's current cash flow in order to obtain loans to acquire the target company at an agreed-upon valuation. By working with the current management of the company, the leveraged buyout private equity investor may turn around the target company and assist the company to realize its full profitable potential.

How do companies use private equity investments to improve their financial picture?

Many companies improve their financial picture and unlock value within their organizations by spinning off or selling parts of the company to private equity firms, who then attempt to manage and turn around the new company. Perhaps the company did not fit the overall strategy of the parent company, or market conditions forced the sale of a weaker-performing division. The private equity firm acquires the division from the parent company, hoping to improve the new stand-alone company and receive financial rewards for doing so. The parent company may also benefit from the influx of capital for the sale of the division, as well as the savings from not having the expenses related to the acquired company on its books. In some cases, the parent company may also invest in the new venture, hoping to make a better return by reorganizing or merging the new entity.

What is the main purpose of private equity investing?

The main purpose of private equity investing is to buy all or part of a company and use the company's new earnings to repay the original investment, plus provide for a return on that investment over time. Sometimes the liquidity event may be the ultimate sale of the newly reorganized company to another buyer or group of buyers, or eventually offering shares to the public for the new entity.

Who are some of the biggest lenders for private equity deals?

Some of the biggest lenders for private equity deals include such banks as Bank of America, Citigroup, and JPMorgan Chase. Other players include investment banks such as Goldman Sachs, Merrill Lynch, and Morgan Stanley.

How many private equity deals in the information industry alone happened in 2013?

In one of hundreds of market segments, the information industry—including virtually all content created, edited, published, and sold, according to experts at Berkery Noyes Investment Bankers—experienced approximately 336 separate transactions, valued at approximately $33.5 billion through the third quarter of 2013. The largest individual transaction was valued at approximately $1 billion.

How does a valuation multiple help me understand the price paid to acquire a company, or to value a target company?

A valuation multiple is a key metric used to express an asset's current market value. The metric used must be highly correlated with the financial performance of the company, and although quite simplistic, comparing this multiple to other peer companies and/or transactions will give prospective buyers a rough idea if they are underpaying or overpaying for an asset. For example, a company that creates $1 billion in sales might be sold to a private equity firm for $2 billion (or valued at a multiple of two times sales). In another example using earnings, if this same com-

JPMorgan Chase is one of the largest lenders for private equity in the United States.

pany generates $200 million in profit per year (or valued at a multiple of ten times earnings), and we compare this multiple value with other similar transactions, again we may see if the target company is selling at a premium or a discount to the private equity investors.

OTHER INVESTING OPPORTUNITIES

GOLD AND OTHER PRECIOUS METALS

Why invest in gold?

Gold is said to be a hedge against inflation, and is perceived by investors as a safe haven from the fluctuations in values of currency, such as the U.S. dollar. So investors believe that, at certain times, it may be better to keep a portion of an investment portfolio in gold, as it may appreciate better than holding the same amount in cash, currencies, bonds, or other investments.

What affects the price of gold?

As in all aspects of the economy, supply and demand affects the price of gold. As supplies of gold become scarce, prices tend to increase. As demand for gold decreases in favor of other investments such as stocks, the price of gold tends to decrease.

What is the biggest component of demand for gold?

Jewelry accounts for roughly 68% of the demand for gold. This leaves 32% of the demand emanating from technology and manufacturing needs, as well as investors purchasing physical bullion and holding it, hoping it will appreciate in value. Gold plays an important role in the electronics industry, where it is an important component for its conductive, heat resistance, anti-corrosive, and chemical stability properties.

Why do investors invest in gold?

Most experts agree that gold is often included in portfolios as a hedge against economic, social, or political uncertainty.

What country is one of the largest buyers of gold?

From 2004 to 2008, the United States accounted for 11% of all gold purchases.

In what other places is the demand for gold high?

Fifty percent of the worldwide demand for gold in the form of jewelry comes from India, China, Turkey, and the Middle East.

What percentage of world gold sales comes by way of investments?

Twenty percent of world gold demand comes in the form of investments, with India, Europe, and the United States leading the world.

When stocks are down or there is economic turbulence, some investors turn to gold as a safer way to protect their money.

What else can affect the price of gold?

Central banks of countries are also big consumers of gold, and may buy or sell large amounts at any given time, affecting the global price of gold.

What are the different ways to invest in gold?

The most popular way to invest in gold is through purchasing gold jewelry. Other ways include: purchasing gold coins, bullion or bars, buying stocks in companies that extract gold, selling gold jewelry, or buying mutual funds that invest in precious metals, including gold. Investors may also buy exchange-traded gold funds that may represent a certain holding or portfolio of gold purchases. They may also purchase gold certificates that are issued by some banks, representing a certain quantity of gold held by the bank.

What are a few examples of coins as investment vehicles?

Some of the types of coins used for investments in metals include: antique coins (because the inherent collector value may exceed the meltdown value); newly minted gold coins, such as the American Eagle, Canadian Maple Leaf, South African Krugerrand, British Sovereign, Vienna Philharmonic, Mexican Gold 50 Pesos, and U.S. Mint 24K Gold Buffalo; minted platinum coins, such as the American Platinum Eagle, Australian Koala, and Canadian Maple Leaf; minted palladium coins, such as the palladium Canadian Maple Leaf; and minted silver coins, such as the Canadian Silver Maple Leaf, Silver American Eagle, and the Austrian Vienna Philharmonic. Some investors prefer to acquire bullion or bars of precious metals that are minted by some governments and companies, such as Johnson Matthey, Wall Street Mint, Credit Suisse, Engelhard, Produits Artistiques Métaux Précieux (PAMP), Sunshine Minting, and Pan American Silver.

Where else might I invest in precious metals?

Experts at *Forbes* suggest that investors may also purchase shares of stocks and mutual funds in mining companies, or ETFs that hold bullion, including Gold SPDR, Platinum SPDR, Palladium PALL, and Silver SPDR.

How big is the SPDR Gold Shares ETF?

SPDR Gold Shares is one of the largest ETFs in the world by market capitalization, valued at approximately $32 billion.

Should I include gold as part of my investment portfolio in the form of mutual funds?

According to the American Association of Individual Investors, you most likely should not, for a variety of reasons. Gold sector funds often invest in the underlying mining companies that produce gold bullion. Very few funds invest in physical bullion itself, and some funds invest in commodity contracts, hoping to reap a reward as prices increase. The volatility in the price of gold as an investment exposes your portfolio to risk. And although gold is used as a hedge against many future conditions, even as the stock market portion of a portfolio may decline, the gold portion of the portfolio may also decline and behave in tandem with the broader market.

What other precious metals are used as investments?

Experts at *Forbes* say investors also favor platinum, palladium, and silver. These metals also have industrial applications, contributing to their demand and usage.

Where is platinum used, besides in making jewelry?

Platinum is used as a component to many parts found in medical equipment and computers.

What has been the historical return on investing in gold?

Although most experts disagree on the ROI for gold (because many analyses do not take into account the effects of inflation, or look at different periods of time), American business magnate Warren Buffett, in an interview with *Fortune*, and re-published on the site www.Dailyreckoning.com, stated that since 1965, the historical return on gold investments has been 4.45% (not adjusted for inflation). If you consider inflation and average income taxes, the returns may be far less.

Where else might I find palladium being used?

Palladium can be found throughout the auto industry. It is an essential component for catalytic converters within an automobile's exhaust system, because it can stand up to high temperatures and oxidation-provoking environments. In the electronics industry, palladium may be used instead of gold. Palladium is integral to many other applications, including raw material processing, photo processing, water purification, fuel cells, and the refining and purification of oil and natural gas.

FUTURES AND OPTIONS

What is a "commodity"?

A commodity is a marketable or saleable item that is produced without many differences across a market. It has very little brand differentiation, and consumers have little concern regarding precisely where the item was produced. Typical commodities include petroleum, coffee beans, iron ore, copper, sugar, and wheat, and may also include various financial instruments, such as cash or currencies, bonds and stocks, or even other intangible financial assets and instruments, such as indexes of stock exchanges and interest rates.

What are some of the most U.S. important markets for futures and options trading?

Some of the most important futures and options trading markets in the United States are the Chicago Board of Trade, the Chicago Mercantile Exchange, the New York Board of Trade, and the New York Mercantile Exchange. Other smaller exchanges exist, including the Minneapolis Grain Exchange and New York's Coffee, Sugar and Cocoa Exchange.

What is a "derivative"?

A derivative is a sellable or marketable financial product or investment vehicle that derives its price from an underlying product or investment vehicle. Copper or oil futures contracts derive their price from, among many other factors, the underlying market price, supply and demand, and future perceptions of supply and demand.

Coffee beans are one example of a commodity, a marketable or saleable item. Not all commodities are crop or mineral products; some are financial assets.

What is the "spot market"?

The spot market is a financial market in which financial instruments—including currencies or commodities such as gold, copper, and petroleum—are traded by investors, with an obligation for immediate delivery of the financial instrument or commodity.

What is an "option"?

An option grants the investor the right, but not the obligation, to buy an investment vehicle—such as stocks, bonds, stock indexes, commodities, or currencies, among many other choices of possible investments—at a defined future date.

Can anyone advise me on trading commodity futures?

According to the SEC, all firms and individuals that trade futures with the public must be registered with the National Futures Association.

What is a "commodity future"?

A commodity future is a contract between two parties to buy a commodity at an agreed-upon price today, with delivery and payment at a later date, and with a stated obligation between the parties to sell and buy at a certain point in time.

What is a "futures price"?

A futures price is the agreed-upon price today of a commodity futures contract, and is often called the "strike price".

What does being "long" or "short" in commodity futures trading mean?

After two parties agree on a price for the futures contract, the buyer is said to be long (meaning he expects the price to increase), and the seller is said to be short (meaning he expects the price to decrease).

What is the purpose of a futures exchange market?

A futures exchange market brings buyers and sellers together to efficiently transact futures contracts, and to minimize default by a seller or a buyer

Why do producers of commodities use futures markets?

Many producers use futures markets as a hedge against dramatic price fluctuations, to raise cash for what they produce, and to make their financial affairs more predictable. In terms of pricing, producers of all sizes are on an equal footing, and may come together with a common product to take advantage of the more favorable prices afforded to larger players by being a part of a larger pool of available product.

What is a "financial future"?

A financial future may not be a classically defined commodity, such as beans or petroleum, but may be derived from a financial vehicle, such as a stock market index, interest rates, currency basket, etc.

What is a "margin"?

An exchange obligates sellers and buyers to deposit cash in the form of a margin, and to clear differences in price between the future price of the contract and the current or daily price, as it changes, until the future contract is settled. This cash is then deposited into either the buyer's or seller's account, depending on the direction of the price movement. This margin may be between 5–15% of the contract's value, and is sometimes referred to as a "performance bond".

What is "marking to market"?

Marking to market is when either the buyer's or seller's account must have additional cash deposited to cover the price difference between today's price and the future price agreed upon in the contract. On the delivery date, when the futures contract is settled, the spot value or spot price is paid.

What is the "spot value"?

On the delivery date of the contract, the amount of money that changes hands is not the specific price of the contract, but the original value agreed upon, since all gains or losses have been previously settled by marking to market.

What are some fraudulent websites that purport to trade in futures and options?

The SEC, through its Commodity Futures Trading Commission (CFTC), regularly monitors and investigates fraudulent companies that attempt to steal money from unsuspecting investors. Some of these sites include Global Financial Private Capital, Colfax Trading International, Forex4You, White, Truman and Fischer, Excaliber Precious Metals, and www.CommodityProfits.com. For more information, you may visit the Commodity Futures Trading Commission's website.

When did futures contracts first emerge?

As early as the eighteenth century, Japanese rice farmers needed a way to collect money in expectation of future harvests. In the United States, the Chicago Board of Trade emerged in 1848 as an exchange to bring buyers and sellers to a marketplace to trade grains.

> ## If I am dealing with a well-respected, global firm, am I immune to fraud in futures or commodity trading?
>
> No. In a period of 18 months, the CFTC imposed $1.765 billion in penalties involving manipulation of interest rates on such globally recognizable firms as Royal Bank of Scotland, UBS, Rabobank, and Barclays. Large-branded financial companies may still have employees who engage in fraud or abuse.

How does the CFTC protect participants from fraud and abuse?

The CFTC assists participants in trading futures by providing educational resources, protecting futures traders, and investigating complaints from traders on fraudulent acts.

What does the CFTC recommend I do to limit my exposure to fraud?

The CFTC recommends that you be wary of any company that purports to offer extremely high profits with little risk, firms that offer to pool your money with other people's money to trade in commodities, and, in general, firms that promise easy profits from trading metals, currencies, petroleum, or agricultural products; any unsolicited phone calls from trading companies; any firm asking you to send cash immediately; and any company asking for your bank information so that funds may be wired in or out of the accounts. You should never invest in futures contracts without first seeking expert outside advice, and investigating the firm you are considering using.

How may I investigate if a firm is legitimate and properly licensed to trade in futures?

You may investigate the legitimacy of potential trading firms by contacting the National Futures Association, checking out the disciplinary history with the CFTC, or contacting your state's securities commissioner or attorney general's office, among many other sources for information about fraud and abuse.

What are some basic principles that the CFTC recommends I follow when I am beginning to invest in commodities and futures?

The CFTC recommends that you follow a few basic principles before you begin trading in commodities and futures: the money you choose to invest is considered "risk capital," meaning you should be able to lose all of it without a detrimental effect on your total portfolio; you should investigate all the risk disclosure documents of the firm, and you should decide whether you will depend upon the advice of a broker or make your own decisions on trading activity. Additionally, the CFTC recommends you fully understand any financial obligations inherent with your trades in commodity futures and option contracts, that you fully understand sources of fraud and abuse exist within the firms that you may encounter (and that they may attempt to steal money from unsuspecting investors and traders), and that you should contact the CFTC if you have any problem or additional questions.

How might I participate in commodity trading without having to trade commodities directly?

Experts at www.Investorplace.com, citing a Lipper database, found there are more than 94 broad commodity mutual funds that allow investors to earn returns on commodity trading without having to trade directly in the commodities. Because these funds continually trade in commodity contracts, they tend to have relatively high expenses that may ultimately eat into your profits and returns over time.

What drives the trends in commodity prices?

According to experts at the ICI, important fundamental economic factors—not the least of which are market supply and demand—may cause changes in commodity prices. Experts also believe the relative value of the U.S. dollar and the world business cycle greatly influence prices. The effects of players in key emerging markets, such as China, India, Brazil, and Russia, who are both buyers and producers of many commodities, influence commodity prices. The same report states that the flow of funds into index-based investment vehicles has not created price volatility, that investing in commodity mutual funds helps investors hedge against movements in the basic prices of such items as food and energy, and that the flows of capital into commodity mutual funds have little effect on the overall growth rate of commodity prices. According to the experts, this may be because the mutual funds are diverse in the commodities in which they invest, and because the size of the commodity markets is so large that the effect caused by capital flows into commodity mutual funds is relatively small by comparison.

What is the "Dalian Commodity Exchange"?

The Dalian Commodity Exchange is the largest mainland China commodities exchange, founded in 1993. Its significance is derived from capturing much of the Chinese domestic market share of futures contracts, and is a major player in the global futures industry. The Dalian Commodity Exchange captures approximately 2% of all global market share futures. In 2006, the trading company Louis Dreyfus became the first foreign member of this important exchange, with more than 160 brokers representing approximately 160,000 investors among its members. Typical commodities exchanged at Dalian include soybeans, soy meal, soy oil, corn, palm oil, and linear low-density polyethene.

What does the term "stockout" mean, when I trade in commodities?

In commodity trading, scarcity of physical product leads to price volatility, as some investors see scarcity pushing prices up, and others see that production will eventually compensate, pushing prices in the opposite direction. When available tradable inventory of a commodity is exhausted, it is termed stockout, or "out of stock." Information as to the stock inventory held by companies and governments is not easily available, and requires much research to discern how much output of a commodity is currently being stockpiled by any one entity.

INVESTING IN ART

Why do investment experts at JPMorgan Chase say that investing in art is considered an "investment in passion"?

JPMorgan Chase experts assert that when you invest in art, it is an investment in passion because, along with the return you might get on the investment, it allows you to benefit because of the "aesthetic utility" of what you are collecting.

Are there mutual funds that allow investors to diversify their portfolios and participate in the world of art investing?

JPMorgan Chase advises clients that over 40 funds invest approximately $700 million in various art-related investment vehicles, including the outright purchase of collectible art. The trouble with art mutual funds is that they generally have very high minimum initial investments, some starting as high as $250,000.

Why do experts at JPMorgan Chase feel that art as an investment may offer good, uncorrelated returns over a long term?

Experts at JPMorgan Chase believe art may prove to be a good, uncorrelated, long-term investment because wealth created recently in such places as China, Russia, and the Mideast has increased the number of participants in the art market, ensuring there will be an ever-increasing market for art trading and investment. And for very costly works of art, collectors globally are now paying record amounts.

Why is it said that the art market is not transparent?

Many experts agree that the art market is not transparent because most people are unaware of where to buy or sell fine art, since many art transactions happen privately be-

---

Why is art a relatively bad investment?

Art collecting and investing is a relatively bad form of investing because the markets are illiquid, idiosyncratic, cost a considerable amount to enter, and are not transparent.

tween rather secretive buyers and sellers. Most former sales prices are seldom reported by auction houses, since they do not have to report sales prices. And the long-term nature of the investment may not allow for a known history of pricing on the art itself, since it may take decades before a particular piece is ever bought and sold.

Who is buying and selling art?

JPMorgan Chase experts describe buyers and sellers of art generally as high-net-worth individuals, combined with collectors, dealers, auction houses, museums, and corporations.

What percentage of high-net-worth individuals invest in fine collectible art?

Citing a study by The European Fine Art Foundation, JPMorgan Chase informs clients that approximately 50% of high-net-worth individuals invest in art, and that art often constitutes 4% of their portfolios.

Who sells art?

In addition to wealthy individuals and private collectors or their representatives, auction houses, dealers, small galleries, and artists themselves sell art.

Why do people buy or collect art?

People buy and collect art for a variety of reasons, including for the prestige and social status it confers on the purchaser; philanthropic reasons (supporting an artist or a particular art style); and to obtain some type of return on their investment, if their strategy is to hold the asset until it appreciates adequately.

Collectible fine art is an investment that is usually more appealing to people with deep pockets who can afford better pieces that are more likely to increase in value.

In order to understand the price changes of art, why can't we trust historical auction prices for art?

The reason why we can't use auction prices historically in order to compute a valuation on a work or works of art is because so much of the market for selling art occurs in a secretive, private world, where sale prices are nearly never disclosed.

What is the Mei Moses Art Index?

The Mei Moses fine art indexes seek to provide information on historical performance of the fine art market as a distinctive asset (investment) class, developed from the analysis of the purchase and sale price of over 30,000 works of art that have sold at public auction more than once.

How does the performance of collectible art compare to other investments over time?

According to Beautiful Asset Advisors, LLC, publishers of the Mei Moses World All Art Index, fine art as an investment has shown positive returns for the past fifty years, having approximately equal compound annual returns to the S&P 500 stock index, but lagging behind the performance of stocks in general for the past 25 years. In the past five and ten years, the Mei Moses index has outperformed equities.

How volatile are the returns generated by art as an investment?

The volatility of returns for art as an investment has been lower than international and U.S. equities over the past 25 years. An investment in art is highly illiquid, meaning it is very difficult to convert your purchase to cash now or in the future.

With what investments does art correlate?

Some investment advisers believe art is an interesting investment because it has nearly no correlation to the movements of prices of equities, and moves inversely to REITs and fixed income (bond) investments.

How do different sectors or genres of the art world perform as investments?

If you think of different genres of art as different sectors, each one may have more or less demand and returns. For example, according to the Mei Moses Index, post-war contemporary art has outperformed the impressionist and modern art genres.

What do experts at CNBC feel are benefits to art and antiques as investments?

Experts at CNBC believe that if you hold these tangible possessions for a very long time, they may appreciate in value. For example, you may have purchased an antique piece of furniture that you appreciate, love to look at or use, hold for thirty years, and sell it. You may make a profit. You may also not be able to give it away at any price. But you are able to enjoy using it while you have it. If you focus on a specific genre or period of art, antiques, or other collectibles, you may realize a return if you purchase it with the intent to hold it for a very long term. However, these investments are highly illiquid, meaning they cannot be easily or quickly converted to cash.

Why do prices of art and antiques vary so widely?

According to many experts, art and antique prices vary so widely because each is unique. And prices are not easily discerned, so it is difficult to assess if you are paying too much or too little for the investment.

What are some other hidden costs to art or antique collecting and ownership?

There are many other costs related to developing any kind of art collection, including costs of insurance, proper storage, appraisals, shipping, and consignment sales commissions.

TAXES

INVESTING AND TAXES

How does the IRS define an investor?

The IRS defines an investor as anyone who buys and sells securities for the purpose of generating income from dividends, interest, and/or capital appreciation. As long as you are not conducting a trade or business with these securities, the IRS considers you an individual investor.

What types of factors do investors normally consider when trying to choose between tax-exempt and taxable investments?

Investors often have to choose between investing in tax-exempt securities such as municipal bonds, and taxable investments such as equities. But because of the tax-free nature of certain investments, investors are willing to part with higher returns in order to take advantage of the lower tax consequences of tax-free investing. So each individual's tax status may determine how attractive a tax-exempt investment may be.

How do I compare the yields of tax-exempt investments and their taxable investment equivalents?

You may compare the difference between the yields of tax-exempt investments and taxable investments by performing a calculation. First, find the yield of your tax-exempt investment (say 5%). Then subtract your tax bracket from one, and express it as a decimal (if your tax bracket is 25%, then 1.0 minus 0.25 equals 0.75). Then divide the tax-free yield by the tax bracket computation (5% divided by 0.75 equals 6.67%). This means an investor in the 25% tax bracket would need a taxable investment to pay at least 6.67% in order to receive an equivalent amount of income from another taxable investment.

Must I pay taxes on savings bonds?

Savings bond investments are taxable. You must pay federal income taxes—but not state or local taxes—on the income generated. If the savings bonds are part of an estate or inheritance, you must also pay inheritance taxes on it.

Does the IRS give special tax exemptions to people who use the savings bonds to fund educational endeavors?

Yes, the savings bond education tax exclusion permits qualified taxpayers to exclude from their gross income all or part of the interest received upon the redemption of eligible Series EE and Series I Bonds issued after 1989 when the bond owner pays qualified higher education expenses at an eligible institution. But there are additional requirements that must be met. Qualified higher education expenses must be incurred during the same tax year in which the bonds are redeemed. You must be at least 24 years old on the first day of the month in which you bought the bond(s). When using bonds for your child's education, the bonds must be registered in your and/or your spouse's name(s). Your child can be listed as a beneficiary on the bond, but not as a co-owner. When using bonds for your own education, the bonds must be registered in your name for use at a college, university, or vocational school that meets IRS standards. If you are married, you must file a joint return to qualify for the exclusion. You must also meet cer-

The IRS has special tax exemptions for people who use savings bonds to pay for their children's education. Many rules apply, so consult with a tax adviser.

tain income requirements. Your post-secondary institution must qualify for the program by offering federal assistance (such as guaranteed student loan programs). Please consult your tax adviser for more information.

According to the IRS, what is a "capital asset"?

The IRS defines a capital asset as nearly everything that you own and use for personal and investment purposes. It could include the value of a rental house, your home, furnishings, cars, vacation properties, and your portfolio of stocks and bonds.

How does the IRS define the length of time that I hold assets or the age of my assets?

The IRS determines the age of the asset by counting the date after you purchased the asset for a period up to and including the day that you dispose of the asset.

Can I deduct expenses related to my investment income?

Yes, you may deduct expenses related to your investment income, according to the IRS. Investors can generally deduct the expenses of producing taxable investment income, including expenses for investment counseling and advice, legal and accounting fees, and investment newsletters. You may report these expenses on IRS Form 1040, Schedule A, "Itemized Deductions", as miscellaneous deductions, as long as the expenses exceed 2% of your adjusted gross income. Interest paid on money to buy or carry investment property that produces taxable income is also deductible on Schedule A, but the deduction cannot exceed the net investment income.

What about my commissions for executed trades? Are they deductible?

No, commissions and other costs of acquiring or disposing of securities are not deductible, but must be used to figure gain or loss when you dispose of or sell the securities. Please see IRS Publication Topic 703, "Basis of Assets", for additional information.

What is the "net investment income tax"?

The net investment income tax applies a rate of 3.8% to specific net investment income of individuals, estates, and trusts with annual incomes above certain threshold amounts, ranging from $125,000 to $200,000, depending on your filing status. If you are an individual who is exempt from Medicare taxes, you still may be subject to the net investment income tax if you have net investment income and also have modified adjusted gross income above the applicable thresholds.

What are the statutory amounts?

The statutory amounts depend on your filing status. These amounts are $250,000 for married filing jointly, $125,000 for married filing separately, $200,000 for single filers,

$200,000 for heads of household, and $250,000 for qualifying widows/widowers with dependent children. Please consult a tax professional for further information.

What does the IRS consider "net investment income"?

The IRS classifies net investment income as interest, dividends, capital gains, rental and royalty income, non-qualified annuities, income from businesses involved in the trade of financial instruments or commodities, and income from purely passive business activities.

What happens with my taxes if I fail to report foreign financial assets?

The IRS will impose a 40% penalty, in addition to any taxes owed, for any abusive tax shelters or unreported investments held in foreign countries.

LONG-/SHORT-TERM CAPITAL GAINS/LOSSES

What effect does changing the capital gains tax have on our economy?

According to researchers at the American Council for Capital Formation Center for Policy Research, in a study by the accounting firm Ernst & Young, a change in the capital gains tax has dramatic effect on the U.S. economy. For every $1 billion increase in investments, approximately 15,000 jobs are created. If capital gains tax rates increase by 5% (from 15% to 20%), some researchers believe that real growth in our economy declines by 0.05%, and employment declines by 231,000 employed people per year.

What are "capital gains"?

In order to understand what a capital gain is, we first assume that everything we own, for personal use, pleasure, investment purposes, and private uses is treated by the IRS as a capital asset. When you sell this asset for a profit, the difference in the price you paid (its cost basis) and the sales price is the capital gain. You have a capital gain if you sold an asset for more than what you paid for it, and a capital loss if you sold the asset for less than your basis. If the difference is positive—meaning the asset's value increased—it is called a capital gain. If the asset's price decreases from the time of purchase, then it is called a capital loss. Both situations are given attention when you file your taxes each year, and must be reported to the IRS for each filing year.

What is a "long-term capital gain"?

The IRS defines a long-term capital gain as the profit gained from the sale of an investment asset that has been owned for more than one year, beginning the day after you purchased the asset. Typical long-term capital gains tax rates may range from zero percent to 20 percent, depending on your tax bracket. The previous maximum long-term capital gains tax rate was 15 percent.

Restoring and selling a valuable antique car for profit is one example of a taxable capital gain.

What is a "short-term capital gain"?

A short-term capital gain is the profit gained from the sale of a capital asset that has been held for less than one year, and may be taxed at ordinary income tax rates ranging from 10 percent to 39.6 percent, depending on your tax bracket. A short-term gain is taxed as ordinary income.

Is there a difference in how long- and short-term gains are treated on my taxes?

Yes, if the gain is a long-term one, it is currently taxed at different rates, depending on your marginal tax bracket. The gain is taxed at 0% if your taxable income falls in the 10% or 15% marginal tax brackets; 15% if your taxable income falls in the 25%, 28%, 33%, or 35% marginal tax brackets; and 20% if your taxable income falls in the 39.6% marginal tax bracket. It is best to consult a tax professional about your liability.

What is a "capital loss"?

Capital losses are also divided into two categories, depending on how long you held the asset, either less than one year (short term), or more than one year (long term). If the sale price is less than the price for which you acquired the asset, then the difference in price is treated by the IRS as a capital loss.

Can I deduct capital losses?

Yes, the IRS allows you to deduct capital losses. If in any one year your capital losses exceed your capital gains, the excess losses may be deducted on your tax return and used

239

to adjust other income sources, such as wages, up to an annual limit of $3,000 per year, or $1,500 for couples who are married and filing separately. These deductions appear on IRS Schedule D, "Capital Gains and Losses," and on Form 1040. The IRS is only concerned with the "net" gain or loss you may realize during the course of the year. For example, if you make $100 on one investment and lose $100 on another, your net gain or loss would be zero. No tax would have to be paid, nor could any loss be deducted. For real estate, you can only deduct capital losses on investment property, not on property categorized as personal or pleasure.

What are some examples of typical investments that may yield capital gains and/or losses?

Typical investments that may yield capital gains and losses include equities or stocks, mutual funds, bonds and bond funds, precious metals, and real property. Investments may generate income through price changes, dividend distributions, interest, rents, or royalties. It is also important to note that you do not generate capital gains while you hold an asset. The gain or loss is triggered only when you sell the asset.

What about high-income taxpayers who earn short- or long-term capital gains? Are there additional considerations?

Under current tax laws, depending on your income, you may also be responsible for an additional 3.8% unearned income Medicare contribution tax (net investment income tax) applied to capital gains, so it is best to understand the tax consequences for any investment, and speak to a competent tax professional when you incur gains and losses from your investments.

Where do I report capital gains and losses when I file my taxes?

When you file your taxes and report any capital gains or losses during a tax reporting year, you file IRS Form 1040, Schedule D, "Capital Gains and Losses," and Form 8949, Sales and Other Dispositions of Capital Assets, along with your tax return.

Under what circumstance could I pay more than a 20% capital gains tax?

According to the IRS, you may be responsible to pay more than 20% capital gains tax if you fall under any of three exceptions: The taxable part of a gain from selling Section

---

Must I pay capital gains tax on the sale of my principal residence?

No. The Internal Revenue Service still allows homeowners to exclude gains ranging from $250,000 to $500,000 depending on your filing status under the Internal Revenue Code, Section 121. Because this gain is excluded for regular income tax purposes, it is also excluded for purposes of determining net investment income.

1202 qualified small business stock is taxed at a maximum 28% rate; net capital gains from selling collectibles (such as coins or art) are taxed at a maximum 28% rate; and the portion of any unrecaptured Section 1250 gain from selling Section 1250 real property is taxed at a maximum 25% rate.

What are some additional considerations?

The IRS recommends you make estimated tax payments (either monthly or quarterly) on your capital gains. Please see IRS Publication 505, Tax Withholding and Estimated Tax, for additional information.

What is a "cost basis"?

A cost basis is the amount of money you use to purchase an item or asset that you own.

May I deduct capital losses on the sale of my personal property?

No. You may only deduct capital losses on the sale of investment property, not on property purchased for personal use.

What is the maximum I can claim in a year as a capital loss?

After you total all your capital losses for a year, you may only apply $3,000 each year for a loss until the total loss is fully utilized. For example, if you lost $9,000 on a stock investment, you may claim $3,000 in losses each year for three years.

What happens if my losses are larger than my gains in any tax year?

If your losses are greater than your gains, you may claim the lesser of either $3,000 ($1,500 if you are married filing separately) or your total net loss as shown on line 16 of IRS Form 1040, Schedule D. If your net capital loss is more than this limit, you may carry the loss forward to later years. Please use the Capital Loss Carryover Worksheet found in either IRS Publication 550, "Investment Income and Expenses", or IRS Form 1040, Schedule D Instructions, "Capital Gains and Losses", to figure the amount eligible to carry forward.

SMALL BUSINESS TAXES

What is the first question the IRS wants to know if I am interested in starting a business?

The first thing the IRS would like to know if you are interested in starting a business is whether your activity is a hobby or a business. This means you need to decide whether your income and livelihood will depend on this business, or if the business merely supplements your income.

How much money does the IRS figure it loses each year because of incorrect filings of deductions and expenses related to small businesses that are, in fact, only hobbies?

The IRS figures that approximately $30 billion in taxes goes unpaid each year because many of these activities are supporting hobbies, but are being claimed as supporting businesses.

A business is only considered to have a loss when legitimate expenses exceed total income for the year.

What are some factors the IRS considers when allowing for certain types of expenses and deductions associated with a business?

The IRS considers many factors when allowing certain expenses and deductions, including: whether or not the time and effort to create and run the business indicate that it is trying to make a profit; whether the taxpayer depends on the activity of the business; whether there are profits or losses; whether losses are related to start-up expenses or whether they are due to circumstances beyond the taxpayer's control; whether the taxpayer improved some aspect of his business process in order to return the business to profitability; whether the taxpayer or his advisers and team have the knowledge and skills to be able to manage a business successfully; whether the taxpayer made a profit from similar activities in the past; whether the business is profitable in some years; and whether the business can make a profit in the future because of the appreciation of assets used in the business.

What is another big assumption the IRS makes when determining whether to allow certain business-related expenses and deductions?

The IRS will allow certain types of business expenses and deductions if the business makes a profit in three of the preceding five years, including the current year.

What is a "loss"?

The IRS defines a loss as when related business expenses exceed the amount of income reported by a business entity during a filing year.

RETIREMENT TAXES

What is the biggest change with regard to paying taxes when I enter retirement?

The biggest change with regard to paying taxes is the need for retirees to pay estimated taxes. Generally, while you are working, your employer withholds a certain amount of your income, and remits the appropriate amount to the IRS and your state's treasury for your taxes due. But when you retire, you must begin to make these remittances yourself. You do this by paying a tax estimate, depending on your retirement income, and filing an IRS Form 1040-ES every quarter.

What is a benefit to me when I retire?

When you are working, you are required to contribute a portion of your income into the Social Security system, and then you may draw upon those funds during your retirement years. After you retire, you no longer make Social Security payments, representing a rather major savings to all retirees.

What are some other post-retirement benefits?

Once you retire, the current tax laws assist you in several ways. You pay less in income taxes because generally you earn less during retirement than during your working years. You may also take a larger standard deduction if you are over age 65 when you retire. If your income is lower than certain IRS thresholds, you may be eligible for certain tax credits that are deducted directly from the amount of tax you owe. Certain states do not tax your post-retirement income, or they tax it at a greatly reduced rate. Please check with your state tax authority or accounting adviser.

What are some strategies to reduce my tax burden when I retire?

Some experts suggest you buy tax-exempt municipal bonds to limit the state taxes you may pay on your investment interest. However, you remain responsible for capital gains taxes. Please consult your tax adviser for further information.

Do tax-exempt investments pay more or less interest than taxable investments?

Generally, tax-exempt investments pay less interest than their taxable counterparts. In order to estimate the tax consequence and compare to a tax-exempt against a taxable investment, subtract your current federal tax bracket from 100, and then divide your tax-exempt yield by this number, giving you the equivalent taxable yield of your taxable investment.

Do I have to pay taxes on my 401(k) account?

No, you do not have to pay taxes on a 401(k) account. The 401(k) account can grow tax free until you begin making withdrawals after you retire. At that time, you will pay taxes on the amount of income that you have during your retirement years.

Why are some mutual funds more tax efficient than others?

Some categories of mutual funds are relatively better for individual investors in terms of taxes because of the current tax codes. The dividends you may receive for bond funds may be taxed at a higher rate than dividends from equities, yet municipal bond funds may be exempt from federal and/or state taxes, depending on the holdings within the portfolio.

What are "hardship distributions"?

The IRS defines hardship distributions from a retirement plan as when a participant has an immediate and heavy financial need to access his retirement plan account in order to satisfy that need. The IRS may limit how much of your account may be accessible. For further information, please talk to your plan administrator or tax professional.

What types of events may qualify as "immediate and heavy financial needs"?

Some expenses that qualify under the IRS hardship definition may include: medical expenses of a participant, spouse, or other dependents; costs related to the purchase of a principal residence (excluding mortgage payments); tuition payments; educational fees, room, and board for the subsequent 12 months of post-secondary education for the participant, spouse, or any dependents; any expenses necessary to prevent eviction from the participant's principal residence or mortgage foreclosure; funeral expenses incurred by the participant or dependents; and certain expenses that may be incurred because of damage to the participant's principal residence. The IRS rules also allow for some of this early distribution to be used to pay taxes on the distributions related to the above hardship events.

What does "pre-tax dollars" mean?

When you contribute to your 401(k) or retirement plan, you make contributions before you pay taxes on the amount of your contribution, and you pay taxes on what remains of the income or wages, less the amount of your annual retirement plan contribution.

When you retire and begin to withdraw money from the retirement account, you must pay taxes on this ordinary income at that time. In this way, you are able to contribute to your retirement plan using pre-tax dollars instead of after-tax dollars.

But what happens if I make a withdrawal from my retirement plan before I reach age 59½?

If you make withdrawals from a retirement plan before you reach age 59½, the IRS assesses a 10% penalty on the amount you withdraw. Some retirement plans allow you to pay taxes now on contributions, instead of when you retire.

The advantage of a 401(k) investment is that money goes in before taxes, so you can earn interest on all of that cash until you actually withdraw it.

FEDERAL TAXES

When it comes to dividends that I may earn, how do I determine what taxes to pay?

As of 2013, dividends from companies are usually divided into two categories: qualified and nonqualified. Depending on this qualification, your income tax due may be different. Please consult your tax adviser.

What IRS form do I use to report dividend income from my investments?

The form you use to report dividend income from investments is IRS Form Schedule B, "Interest and Ordinary Dividends." On this form, you report any interest that you have earned on your bank deposits, as well as any dividends that may have been distributed to you during the tax reporting year.

When am I supposed to file Schedule B?

You file Schedule B whenever you receive more than $1,500 in interest income from banks/credit unions, or if you ever receive dividends on your investments. You may also use this form if you accrue interest from a bond, unless that bond is tax exempt. Please see your tax adviser for further information.

Must I pay taxes on my investments held within my 401(k) or retirement plan?

Depending on what type of plan you have, and whether you have made withdrawals prior to the allowable date, the earnings on your retirement plans are not taxed. Please consult your tax adviser for specific filing information.

What are some of the most important rules regarding obtaining distributions from my 401(k) plan?

According to the IRS, you generally cannot take distributions from your 401(k) plan unless one of the following events occurs: the death of the plan participant; termination of the plan without establishment of a successor plan; reaching age 59½; or incurring some sort of financial hardship.

What are some important IRS forms that I should know when I am managing the tax implications of my investments?

Some important forms you should know regarding managing the tax responsibilities of your investments include: 1040 U.S. Individual Income Tax Return; 1040A U.S. Individual Income Tax Return; 1040EZ Income Tax Return for Single and Joint Filers with No Dependents; Schedule B—Interest and Ordinary Dividends; Schedule D—Capital Gains and Losses; 1099—General Instructions for Certain Information Returns; 2439—Notice to Shareholder of Undistributed Long-Term Capital Gains; 3115—Application for Change in Accounting Method; 6251—Alternative Minimum Tax—Individuals; 8582—Passive Activity Loss Limitations; 8615—Tax for Certain Children Who Have Unearned Income; 8814—Parents' Election to Report Child's Interest and Dividends; 8815—Exclusion of Interest from Series EE and I U.S. Savings Bonds Issued After 1989; 8818—Optional Form To Record Redemption of Series EE and I U.S. Savings Bonds Issued After 1989; and 8949—Sales and Other Dispositions of Capital Assets.

What are some additional important IRS publications that may help me understand more fully the tax implications of my investments?

The IRS publishes many documents that may provide you with great information on tax consequences and responsibilities regarding your investments. Some of these

The 1040 income tax form is the most important one to fill out when you file federal taxes.

publications include: 525—Taxable and Nontaxable Income; 537—Installment Sales; 590—Individual Retirement Arrangements; 925—Passive Activity and At-Risk Rules; and 1212—Guide to Original Issue Discount Instruments.

What types of deductions will the IRS not allow on IRS Form 1040, Schedule A?

The IRS does not allow such deductions as federal income taxes, Social Security taxes, stamp taxes, transfer taxes on the sale of property, homeowners' association fees, estate and inheritance taxes, and service charges for water, sewer, or trash collection. You may be subject to a limit on some of your itemized deductions, including non-business taxes. Please refer to the Form 1040 Instructions available at www.irs.gov for the limitations.

Must I pay taxes on earnings from my investments?

If your investments are made using after-tax dollars, meaning they are not held within any retirement accounts, then you may be exposed to two types of taxes: a tax of up to 20% on any dividends distributed to you, and, if you buy and sell a stock, a capital gains tax of 20% on any profits made while you bought and sold the stock or investment. But if you hold the stock for less than one year, you may have to pay taxes on the gain as part of your ordinary income, which is usually higher than the 20% tax rate.

What about mutual funds?

If you own mutual funds for even one minute during the tax filing year, and the mutual fund distributes a dividend, you must pay taxes on this distribution, even if you still hold the shares in the mutual fund and have the dividends reinvested.

STATE TAXES

Do I have to pay special capital gains taxes at the state level when I file my state income taxes?

Most states do not have a separate line on tax returns for "capital gains," as such. Instead, any income you make outside of normal payroll is calculated at the ordinary income rate. Please consult your tax adviser for further information.

Are there certain investments that provide tax exemptions on gains at the state level?

There are investments that offer tax benefits at the state level, if the investor is interested in holding tax-exempt municipal bonds in the state in which he resides. Municipal bonds originating in the state in which you live are free of state taxes.

Are there any deductions I may take that help me with my yearly state income taxes?

The IRS allows filers to deduct any state taxes paid during the filing year.

What federal tax form must I use to claim state income tax deductions?

The IRS requires Form 1040, Schedule A to itemize your deductions, including any state tax payments.

How many states impose a state tax on capital gains?

Nearly all states impose some sort of capital tax (although it might be called something else) on income generated from investments. The tax imposed may be as high as 13.5% (New York). Taxes paid on gains must be considered when investors compute their real rate of return on their investments.

What states have no income tax or capital gains tax?

The nine states with no state income tax or capital gains tax are Washington, Nevada, Alaska, Wyoming, South Dakota, Texas, Tennessee, Florida, and New Hampshire.

Which states' residents create the most capital gains from their investments?

California residents are responsible for investments that create approximately 13% of all capital gains. Investments made by New York residents are responsible for 12.5% of all capital gains.

Which states have unusual tax laws regarding gains on investments?

Many states have unusual ways of treating investment gains, according to editors at *Forbes*. New Jersey does not allow taxpayers to carry forward capital losses from year to year, as is allowed for federal tax purposes. Tennessee taxes its residents on capital gains earned from the sale of mutual funds, but not on the sale of individual stocks. New Jersey, Connecticut, Kentucky, and Ohio grant tax exemptions to residents on gains made on the sale of their own state's bonds.

Which states have the highest income tax rates (based on the highest tax brackets)?

New Jersey, New York, Connecticut, Maryland, and Hawaii.

Which states have flat-rate income taxes?

The seven states that have a flat-rate income tax are Colorado, Illinois, Indiana, Massachusetts, Michigan, Pennsylvania, and Utah. All other states either have no income tax or use a marginal or bracket system, depending on income, similar to the federal marginal tax system.

How many states increased their taxes from 2009 to 2010?

According to the National Conference of State Legislatures, 12 states increased their taxes by more than 1%, 37 states made no notable changes to their state's taxes, and one state actually decreased its taxes by 1%. The good news is that, for the most part, states decreased the personal income tax, but increased taxes on many consumption items, such as fuel and tobacco.

Do I need to file my state income tax each year?

Depending on which state you live in, and if your adjusted gross income is higher than the personal exemption amount on your state's form, if you file a federal tax return, you should also file your state's tax return.

How do I find out if I have been delinquent in paying for my state taxes in previous years?

You may write to the customer inquiries department at your state's treasury department, or check the website for the state in which you live to find out if you owe any past due amounts.

What is a "sales tax"?

A sales tax is a tax levied by a state on the sale of goods and services.

Do all states have sales taxes?

Five states do not have a sales tax. In others, the sales tax can be anywhere from 2.9% to 7.5%

What state has the highest sales tax?

California has the highest state sales tax rate, at 7.5%.

What states have no sales tax?

The five states with no sales tax are Oregon, Alaska, Montana, Delaware, and New Hampshire.

Depending on the state you live in, sales taxes can range from nothing on up to 7.5%.

LOCAL TAXES

What types of taxes can cities impose?

In addition to the normal property taxes cities and counties impose on residences, approximately fourteen states have allowed cities within these states to impose many different forms of taxes that may affect the earnings you make from investments. These taxes may include local flat income taxes, local school district taxes, local bracketed income taxes, resident and non-resident income taxes (for people who work and earn income in the city subject to the tax), transit/transportation taxes, and education-related taxes on income.

What is a "mill levy"?

A mill levy is the method used by most local governments (cities, counties, school districts), whereby one mill represents one tenth of one cent, to raise needed capital. As an example, for every $1,000 of assessed value of your property, one mill is equal to one dollar. Since various local government entities have the power to levy taxes on properties within their jurisdictions, the total of all individual mills are used to compute your tax responsibility.

What is "property tax"?

Property tax is a general term meaning the taxes levied on the value of your principal residence. The proceeds go to finance local services, education, and operational costs for the city and county in which you live, the financing of special projects such as sewers, streets, and parks, and—depending on the state you live in—state services as well.

What other local taxes are deductible?

If you live in a community where other personal property, such as a boat or car, is taxed at its present value, you may also deduct those payments, regardless of their frequency. You must pay the tax annually, whether or not it is collected more or less than once per year.

When do I pay my property taxes?

Property taxes are normally paid twice per year, in the winter and summer.

What is "equalized value"?

Equalized value is the value of your property after assessment that is then adjusted so that all similar properties are equally and uniformly assessed. This ensures that a school district, city, or township in which property is underassessed does not get more than its fair share of state aid or funds. In some states, the state equalized value represents 50% of the true cash value of the property, although this may or may not be the same as the market value (the value for which the property would sell).

What affects the assessed value of a property?

If a house has recently sold, or if you have made any major improvements to the property, this will affect your city's current assessment on your property's value.

Do I have the right to appeal my city tax assessment?

Yes. When your assessed value statement is sent to you (with your tax bill), you have the right to appeal the assessment, and have a local hearing at which you can state why the value should be changed. If you are still unsatisfied, most states provide an opportunity to appeal at the state level, in a hearing at your state's tax tribunal.

What states have laws that allow cities to impose an income tax?

As of 2010, the fourteen states that allow cities to impose an income tax are Alabama, Arkansas, Colorado, Delaware, Iowa, Indiana, Kentucky, Maryland, Michigan, Missouri,

New York, Ohio, Oregon, and Pennsylvania. The District of Columbia has a bracketed income tax system.

Which major cities have the highest local taxes on capital gains?

Because many of these cities have a local- or city-imposed income tax, gains on such investments realized during a filing year may be subject to local taxes. Some of the highest taxing cities/municipalities include: Indianapolis, Indiana; Baltimore, Maryland; Montgomery County, Maryland; Detroit, Michigan; and New York City.

INSURANCE

THE BASICS

What percentage of Americans are covered by some type of life insurance?

According to experts at the Insurance Information Institute, citing a survey published in 2013, 62% of all Americans are covered by some type of life insurance.

At what age do people typically purchase life insurance?

More than 50% of all people who own life insurance are age 25 to 34, while only 18% are under age 25.

What percentage of employed consumers own some form of disability insurance?

Thirty percent of employed consumers have some type of disability coverage that will pay them a percentage of their current income should they become disabled while working.

In what investment vehicles do life/health insurance companies readily invest?

According to the Insurance Information Institute, approximately 74% of life/health insurance companies' portfolios are invested in bonds, 9.8% are invested in mortgage loans, and approximately 2% are invested in stocks.

How can I find out if I am dealing with a legitimate insurance company?

The National Association of Insurance Commissioners (www.naic.org) keeps track of all complaints lodged against insurance companies in each state. You may investigate an insurance company by going to its website to see if it exists, if it has any complaints against it, and if it is a legitimate company with which to do business. You should never pay any company or website to view its reports, as this information is available for free on many websites.

What percentage of renters are uninsured?

According to a study released by www.apartments.com and reported by Allstate Insurance, 67% of the 81 million renters in the United States do not have renters' insurance. This means if there is a catastrophic loss, they would not receive any money toward replacing their lost possessions while renting.

If I already have a well-funded IRA or 401(k) retirement plan into which I automatically invest each month, do I really need life insurance?

If your retirement plan is well funded, your mortgage nearly paid off, and you are nearing retirement age, it is probably a good idea to save the money on expensive insurance premiums and insurance investments that may have less of a return on your retirement plan. The older you are, the more expensive your insurance premiums. It may be more prudent to redirect the money you would invest in an insurance policy into your retirement fund.

INSURING YOUR HOME

What is a "deductible"?

A deductible is the amount of money a homeowner must pay toward a loss in order to collect on a claim.

What is a "premium"?

A premium is the amount you pay each month for your insurance coverage. Insurance companies take your premiums, invest them, use the proceeds to pay claims from other insured members, and use the returns to help generate profits for the insurance company and provide a return on the investments for its shareholders.

How does homeowners' insurance work?

Mortgage companies and banks that finance your loan to purchase a house require you to have a homeowners' insurance policy. The policy protects your investment (your house) in case of loss due to damage from a catastrophic natural event, such as a hurricane or earthquake, as well as damage because of snow, ice, or fallen trees. You may get a policy covering the replacement cost of your home at current market rates. Your premium is paid monthly, and remains in force as long as you continue to pay the premium and retain ownership of the house.

Why are dwelling coverage limits tricky?

Dwelling coverage limits, or computing a replacement value, may be difficult if your house either increases or declines in value from the time that you purchased your policy. If your home value has increased, or appreciated, you may not have enough coverage to replace your house. If your home value has declined, or depreciated, you may be paying for too much coverage. You should reassess these amounts every year, and adjust your policy according to today's real estate market conditions.

What does my house insurance policy cover?

In general, your policy covers the costs to repair or rebuild your house and any other structures on your property, such as garages or work sheds, from such events as a fire, water damage from a broken pipe or heating system, fallen trees, and damage due to wind or snow. If there is damage, the insurance company will send out an insurance/claims adjuster to your house within a few days. He will investigate the claim, and provide you with an estimate of the cost of repair. The policy then allows you to pay a small deductible and use the insurance company's contractor to do the repairs necessary to

Home insurance should cover, among other things, damage caused by storms.

bring your house back to its former condition, or allow you to use your own contractor to complete the repairs. If you live in a flood plain, or hurricane- or earthquake-prone area, your initial policy may not cover these occurrences. Your insurance company will tell you what additional coverage you may need to be properly insured. Most home-owners' policies cover personal property and effects in your house from damage or loss, such as artwork, clothing, jewelry, electronics, appliances, etc. Your policy may also cover personal injury and liability from such claims as someone falling or injuring him-self on your property. You may pay for certain amounts of coverage, depending on how much protection you need. Your coverage should equal or exceed your net worth, so that you will not lose any of your assets if you are sued.

Should I document certain items I would like to have on my homeowners' insurance policy?

It is a good idea to keep copies of receipts of big-ticket items, and record them on video, room by room, so that you have a record of what you own. Be sure to store this infor-mation in a fire/waterproof safe place. Your insurance company can provide you with specifics on documenting the purchase and ownership of such items.

How can I save money on my homeowners' insurance?

The easiest way to save money on your insurance is to increase your deductible, from say $500 to $1,000 or higher. This will lower your monthly premiums by as much as 25% for your coverage. You may also consider obtaining several quotes before you decide on an insurance company. You may save even more if you group several different policies together with the same company. Check with your insurance agent to see what kinds of discounts are available if you move all of your policies to one company. Many insurance companies offer additional discounts for installing burglar alarm systems, fire alarms, and smoke detectors, retrofitting your house with storm windows, or fire-retardant bar-riers to minimize damage due to fire. Check with your insurance agent to see if these additional discounts are available.

What should I look for in deciding which homeowners' insurance company to use?

You should look for a company that provides excellent service, pays claims promptly, is financially solvent and in good standing, has a long history of serving clients, and, of course, provides a competitive price.

Can I be overinsured on my homeowners' policy?

If you insured the replacement cost of your house to match what you paid for it, you are most likely overinsured, since the price of your house included the price of the physi-cal land beneath it. Since your land does not incur damage, you should insure your house only for the cost to rebuild the same size and type of house you originally pur-chased. The property appraiser you used to buy the house can give you an exact figure for the land, given today's real estate market rates in your area.

RENTERS' INSURANCE

What is "renters' insurance" or "tenants' insurance"?

The owners of your apartment carry some form of insurance that also covers the physical building from loss. But their policy does not cover the loss incurred by tenants for their possessions.

How does tenants' insurance work?

You can make a list or electronic record of the possessions and their values inside your apartment, and have a file of receipts for these items. You may then contact an insurance company to purchase a policy covering your possessions, choose a deductible, and pay premiums each month. If there is a fire in your building, you will be able to collect the replacement value of your possessions.

How expensive is renters' insurance?

A typical policy, depending on the value of one's possessions, may be $100–$300 per year.

What does my renters' or condo insurance cover?

Your policy likely covers damage due to fire or lightning, windstorm or hail, explosion, riot or civil commotion, aircraft, vehicles, smoke, vandalism or malicious mischief, theft, damage by glass or safety-glazing material that is part of your building, volcanic eruption, falling objects, weight of ice, snow, or sleet, water-related damage from home utilities, and electrical surge damage. It does not cover flooding or earthquakes, as these disasters need to be covered under separate policies.

What is the difference between "actual cash value" and "replacement cost coverage" in my renters' insurance policy quote?

Actual cash value means the insurance company will pay you what your possessions were worth at the time of the claim, less your deductible. Replacement cost coverage is the value to replace the possessions as new at the time of the claim.

If I own a condominium, am I covered under the condo association's policy?

No. The condo association's policy covers the physical property itself, not the possessions within. Check with your condo association to see exactly what is covered under its policy, and what coverage it recommends before you purchase a condominium. Most condominium owners believe their possessions are covered, when in fact they are not.

INSURANCE AS AN INVESTMENT

What is "life insurance"?

Life insurance represents a contract between an insured and an insurance company whereby, in exchange for premiums paid by the insured (whether at regular intervals or in one lump sum), the insurance company will pay the value of the insurance policy, at the end of life of the insured, to his beneficiary. There are two main types of life insurance products, term and permanent.

How do I know how much insurance to buy?

It really depends on your goal, and how you and your beneficiaries will use the money. People often purchase life insurance to cover their outstanding mortgage balance; in the event of their death, their house can be fully paid, and their family can live comfortably without having to worry about incurring a great debt. Other people buy insurance policies that allow them to take income or provide income to their family upon the insured person's death. Experts at *Forbes* believe that, before you invest in an insurance policy as an investment, you should determine the amount you actually need, and the ultimate purpose for acquiring the policy.

Is purchasing an insurance policy ever a good investment?

According to experts at CNN Money, it would be a good investment if an insurance policy did not have so many fees and charges, often hidden from prospective buyers. For example, a cash value policy may have such fees as marketing and sales commissions, a surrender charge if you stop paying the premium before approximately ten years (often more than one year of the premium), investment fees that can top 2% per year (on some variable life policies), and a "mortality and expense" fee, often hidden, that can be one percent or more. This can be compared with the average management fee of many passively managed mutual funds of less than 0.5%, and management fees of actively managed funds of approximately 1%. This will depress any returns you hope to receive while your policy is active and invested.

Can you buy too much insurance?

Yes. The amount of insurance you should purchase depends on the value of your assets, your debt situation, the amount of income you wish to have in retirement years, and the amount of income you wish to leave your spouse upon your demise. Many insurance companies have calculators available on their websites that allow you to see how much insurance you need to purchase in order to meet your goals.

What is "term life insurance"?

With term life insurance, the insured is covered for a certain period of time such as ten, twenty, or thirty years, and pays a benefit to a beneficiary when the insured person dies.

The policy also expires when the term ends; if no death occurs during the term period, no payout is made.

What if I outlive the term of my term policy?

An insurance company will give you the option to continue your policy (for a much higher premium), convert it to a permanent policy, or just let it expire.

Why do some people favor term life insurance policies?

They are favored because they are relatively inexpensive. You can buy a policy for a specific period of time, such as until your children are financially independent. And you may not incur taxes as a beneficiary of the policy. Some also buy a term life policy to supplement other insurance policies, and to cover the value of their home mortgage upon their death.

When selecting life insurance, research the differences between a term life and a permanent life policy to make sure you pick one that is right for your needs.

What is "permanent life insurance"?

It is an insurance policy that, in exchange for regular premiums paid throughout the lifetime of the insured, pays a benefit upon the death of the insured. Part of the money you pay in premiums is set aside in an account to grow in cash value that you can later access by borrowing against it, and part of the premium is used to pay the death benefit.

Why are permanent life insurance policies relatively more expensive?

According to experts at www.Forbes.com, permanent life insurance policies are expensive because they are intended to cover the insured for the duration of his life, as compared with less expensive term policies that tend to cover you when you are young and do not readily need the money. Forbes asserts that most people will not require insurance when they retire, as they will not have any dependents, and may rely on retirement plans, Social Security income, and assets from a deceased spouse or family member.

What if the investor would like to use an insurance policy as a tool to enable passing on a large (greater than $5 million) estate?

The tiny fraction of people with high net worth assets that are part of an estate that may be passed to survivors may use an insurance policy to help defray the cost of estate taxes

259

that a beneficiary might be responsible to pay. You should discuss this strategy with a tax professional before taking any action.

When I am considering an investment in an insurance policy, what are three issues with which I should be concerned?

Financial experts at *U.S. News & World Report* note that the investments used by your insurance policy may not do as well as the marketing literature states, that the policy-holder may not be able to initially fund the investment adequately, and when the policyholder requires cash from the policy, he withdraws too much money, increasing his exposure to higher-than-expected taxes due.

Since it is difficult to analyze or even know the typical sales commissions we must pay on an insurance policy, how can I identify the sales commissions?

Experts at www.Bankrate.com suggest getting a competing quote from a commission-free insurer such as TIAA-CREF and comparing the prices of the policies in order to identify the commissions. Experts further note that sales commissions on a whole life policy could be as high as 85% of your first-year premium, and 7% per year of your premium for the first ten years of your policy term. Insurance companies are not required to readily and easily disclose fees and charges to potential clients.

Do I need to take a medical exam to get life insurance?

You do not have to take a medical exam to get life insurance, but it depends on the company you choose; many insurance companies require it. If you convert a term life insurance policy to a permanent policy, sometimes the insurance company will not require a second exam. Experts at www.Bankrate.com assert that the larger the value of the insurance policy, the more scrutiny and attention is given to a medical examination.

BUSINESS INSURANCE

Why would I need business insurance?

Since operating a home-based business may involve a significant financial investment, a business owner needs to protect himself and limit the financial risks of events such as lawsuits that may arise from the operation of that business.

What types of insurance do I need if I operate a home-based business?

There are many types of insurance coverage available for a small, home-based business, including contents insurance, general liability insurance, product liability insurance, professional liability insurance, errors and omissions insurance, and disability insurance.

What is "contents insurance"?

Contents insurance pays for loss or damage to possessions on the premises of your home-based business. Your homeowners' insurance will not cover the loss or damage of equipment in your home-based office under your homeowners' policy; this needs to be covered under a separate policy.

What is "general liability insurance"?

General liability insurance covers a home business operator from general claims of liability or injury due to negligence, and protects against claims as the result of bodily injury, property damage, medical expenses, libel, slander, the costs to defend lawsuits, and settlement bonds or judgments required during an appeal procedure. If a client injures himself while visiting your office, general liability insurance will cover the expenses related to this claim. Your homeowners' policy will not cover these types of claims.

What is "product liability insurance"?

Companies that manufacture, wholesale, distribute, and retail a product may be liable for its safety. If your home-based business sells physical products to people, product liability insurance will cover you for lawsuits that arise from injuries or damages caused by the product that you sell, and its use or misuse.

What is "professional liability insurance"?

Also known as professional indemnity insurance, professional liability insurance protects professionals such as architects, accountants, and lawyers from injuries or damages caused by the services they provide, and may be available through the professional association/society to which the professional belongs. Depending on your profession, you may be required by your state government to have such a policy.

What is "errors and omissions insurance"?

Errors and omissions insurance is used by people in service and consulting businesses. It covers the insured from claims arising from a client who holds such company or individual responsible for a service that was provided, or failed to be provided, that did not have the agreed-upon results.

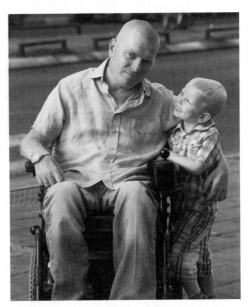

Disability insurance can cover temporary or permanent loss of income when you suffer a severe injury or illness.

What is "disability insurance"?

Disability insurance covers you for temporary or permanent loss of income, enabling you to continue earning income for a period of time as specified in the policy. Typical policies may have enough coverage so that income is being earned until you can get back to work.

Where can I purchase insurance for my home-based business?

You should obtain several quotes from reputable insurance companies or brokers, as prices for these and many other policies may vary greatly.

How do employers react to rate increases by medical insurance companies?

According to an annual survey by the firm Mercer, 40% of companies pay for the increases by having employees pay a larger percentage of the premiums, while 39% will increase the employees' share of deductibles, co-pays, co-insurance, or out-of-pocket maximums.

What is a "health savings account"?

A health savings account is a medical savings account that offers you a tax advantage, since you pay no federal income taxes at the time of deposit. The money can be used to pay for out-of-pocket health expenses related to your medical care. The funds in the account can also be rolled over from year to year.

What is a "flexible spending account"?

Similar to an HSA, a flexible spending account allows you to set money aside in an account to be used during the plan year plus 2 ½ months for medical expenses, free from payroll taxes. The money must be used during that time, and any unused funds can be used for future plan administrative costs, or returned to the employee as taxable income. The maximum allowed per plan year in contributions is $2,500.

THE FUTURE

SAVING FOR RETIREMENT

What percentage of Americans do not have enough money saved for even six months of living expenses?

According to personal finance experts at *The Huffington Post*, citing a recent telephone survey of a representative sample of the U.S. working population, 75% of all Americans do not have an emergency savings fund capable of funding six months of expenses to be used for emergency purposes, such as a sudden job change, health issue, or other unexpected event or expense.

What percentage of people have less than a three-month expense cushion?

According to editors at CNN Money, citing the same www.Bankrate.com study above, 50% of all working Americans lack even a three-month savings cushion.

What percentage of Americans have no savings at all?

In a survey by www.Bankrate.com, 27% of all Americans have no savings at all.

How many working households have no money saved for retirement?

According to financial editors at *USA Today*, citing a 2013 survey conducted by the Washington, D.C.-based National Institute on Retirement Security, 38 million working households have no money saved for their retirement.

What is the median retirement savings balance for people ten years away from retirement?

Experts at the National Institute on Retirement Security found that the median retirement savings for people who are nearing retirement is $12,000.

Among people who are retired, what percentage have no money to use for their retirement?

One-third of all retired people have no money to use for their retirement.

What is a participant-directed 401(k) plan?

If an employer-sponsored plan is participant-directed, it means that the employee can choose from a variety of stocks, mutual funds, and bond funds, as well as the company's own stock (if the company is publicly traded), and invest a sum of money before taxes each pay period.

If I am self-employed, is there a similar program to save for retirement?

A self-employed person may open an individual retirement account (IRA) and contribute up to $5,000 per year if under age 50, or $6,000 per year if you are over age 50.

How do I know if I will have enough money saved for my retirement?

It is important to understand your financial picture today, what kind of income you will want to live on in your retirement years, and what other sources of income you will have (such as Social Security, pensions, insurance investments, and other after-tax investments). It is equally important to know if you will have any large debts, such as mortgages, college tuition payments, or student loans, as those will also affect your expenses. With compounding of investment income, reinvesting dividends, company matches, and getting an early start on investing for retirement, it may be easier to reach your retirement goal than you think.

What are some of my main concerns as an individual investor when I think about managing my retirement portfolio?

When you analyze your portfolio in order to achieve a long-term goal, such as having enough invested to provide resources into your retirement years, you generally must

---

What is a "retirement calculator"?

Widely available on the Internet, a retirement calculator allows you to input important variables, such as your income, how much money you have in retirement savings, and your expected Social Security income, to see where you would be today if you were to retire, and how much you need to start saving in order to retire and live comfortably some years into the future. The actual results of your savings plan depend on how early you start saving, how much you contribute to your plan, the rate of return of your investment choices, and how long you will live.

think of several considerations: How to make your investments grow and exceed the rate of inflation; selection of appropriate income-producing investments; and methods to preserve your investable principal or capital.

What are some strategies I can employ that may help me reach my post-retirement income goals?

Aside from the commonly held belief that you should begin investing for your retirement early on, in order to grow your money in early years, it is generally accepted that you should invest your money in equities (individual stocks or equity mutual funds), and manage your portfolio so that you may mitigate risk through proper diversification. In the medium term—and perhaps even during our retirement—you may require certain types of investments that produce income, such as interest-producing bonds or even dividend-paying stock investments. For more astute investors, purchasing bonds that have certain expiration dates is a prudent method to generate income during retirement. As the bonds mature, and the bond is paid to the bondholder, income is generated. As we reach our retirement years, many prudent investors look to investments that grow, but are of a more conservative investment type, as the cash alternative may erode because of inflation. This may be one of the biggest threats to maintain enough capital to fuel your retirement needs.

How much income do I really need for my retirement?

It is generally accepted that you need approximately 80% of your pre-retirement income in order to live comfortably during your retirement years.

INVESTING FOR RETIREMENT

What percentage of workers earn retirement benefits at work?

According to the U.S. Department of Labor, nearly 57% of all workers earn some sort of retirement benefit as a result of their employment. This means that over 40% will have to rely on Social Security benefits, plus whatever savings they manage to put aside for retirement.

What are the most important components to my retirement income that will allow me to enjoy a good retirement?

According to the U.S. Department of Labor, some components that might help you enjoy a relatively comfortable retirement include: income from Social Security, income generated by your employer-based retirement plan benefits and pensions (for some retirees), and income generated by your personal savings and investments. The amount you might have available will depend upon the amount you have saved by the time you retire, the annual return these investments may provide, whether your expenses draw on your principal, and your life expectancy, among many other factors.

Saving enough for retirement so that you can live comfortably takes considerable planning and management of your current income.

What are three common misperceptions about retirement?

Many people feel they have saved and invested enough to enjoy a comfortable retirement. However, most people believe their daily expenses for living will drop during their retirement (they won't), they will be responsible for paying less in taxes (not necessarily), and they will not have any extraordinary health care or family financial expenses during retirement (not necessarily).

At what rate are people retiring in the United States?

Every day, approximately 10,000 people enter retirement. Thirteen percent of all Americans are of retirement age, and this number is expected to jump to 18 percent by 2030, making our need to invest for retirement more important than ever.

How has the age of retirement changed over time?

The age of retirement and our attitudes toward retirement have fundamentally changed over time as our life expectancy has changed, and as our cultural attitudes toward work have changed. In the late nineteenth century, approximately 78% of men over age 64 were still productively working. But by the late twentieth century, only 30% of men age 64 and above were still productively working. Because of the need for more income in retirement, the increase in life expectancy, and the desire to continue fulfilling employment, the trend has been to delay retirement. So the need for additional sources of income to help finance our retirement has become more apparent.

At different ages, what should I do to help fund my retirement and other savings goals, such as acquiring my first house, car, etc.?

One of the most important generally accepted principles to help you finance your retirement is to begin investing early. So in your twenties, you should set up an IRA or 401(k) retirement account, and participate in your employer's retirement account matching program, if available. It is probably also a great idea to set up after-tax investment accounts. In your thirties, while you plan for such long-term goals as retirement, financing children's education, and short-term goals such as changing houses, realize that having investment accounts—indeed, any substantial savings accounts—may help you access capital, such as for a mortgage, and allow you more choices later in life. At later stages in your life, many people begin to switch from riskier or higher-growth investments to those that may provide more predictable returns. Many people in their sixties and beyond reinvest earnings on investments so as not to spend the proceeds of previous investments, and time the maturity dates of certain bonds or other fixed income investments such as CDs so that when better investment opportunities present themselves, capital is available to take advantage of them. At this stage, because your income is reduced, your tax liabilities are also reduced, so you can earn returns for many years without having tax liability as your principal grows (for pre-tax retirement accounts). When you need the money, you may withdraw it from your pre-tax accounts and pay reduced taxes at that time.

How much should I save for my retirement?

It is difficult to establish a hard rule about the amount you should save for your retirement: it depends on how much you depend on your current income, the amount of your daily living expenses, what you want your expenses to be, and what kind of lifestyle you wish to lead upon retirement. It also depends on when you begin saving for retirement. If you start very early (in your twenties), you won't have to save as much of your after-tax income per year, as compared with starting to save in your forties or fifties. There are no strict rules regarding saving for retirement because people's lifestyles, expenses, and income are quite different. For people with highly variable annual incomes, it is more difficult to set a "one-size-fits-all" rule. Some experts suggest you should save approximately 10% of your after-tax income per year, putting it into a diversified portfolio so it can grow while mitigating the erosive effects of inflation, and therefore having enough savings stockpiled for a comfortable retirement.

What is the biggest consideration when it comes to saving for retirement?

The most important consideration when it comes to saving for retirement is the age at which you start saving. This is because if you start early enough, the compounding effect of your returns allows your savings to grow over time, and allows you to save relatively less money in your later years. The other important consideration may be having the discipline to save regularly (and invest in some way), for the long-term discipline of saving leads to good financial health.

What is another key behavior that will help me in my retirement years?

Before you retire, it is important to adjust the amount you save as your income changes. This means if you make more income during your pre-retirement years, you should save more of this income.

What kind of expenses can I try to reduce before I retire?

Many experts believe you should reduce your debt payments by retiring loans such as mortgages and home equity loans, as they tap your monthly income, taking away money you would otherwise use for retirement living expenses and savings that would later be used for such endeavors.

What is an "asset income multiple"?

An asset income multiple is the product of an equation in which you divide your net assets available for such items as retirement by your current income. The larger the result, the better your chance to accumulate enough to fuel your retirement. If the result is low, you need to make some adjustments if at all possible, including reducing your expenses, saving more, or delaying your retirement age in order to obtain more income.

How might I analyze what I need for my retirement?

Many websites offer online calculators to help you see where you are, and where you need to be financially in order to hit your retirement goals. *Money* has devised and offered such an online calculator. Similar websites generally allow you to input a few pieces of information, such as your age, your current salary or income, and your current savings available for retirement. Some of these calculators even take into consideration at what age you wish to retire, and what income you wish to have while retired.

What percentage of a typical person's retirement plans is in mutual funds?

For 401(k) and related plans, 51% of a typical person's retirement plans is in 401(k) mutual funds. For IRAs, 46% of a typical person's retirement plans is in mutual funds.

IRAs

What are the main reasons why people delay retirement?

There are many reasons why people delay the age at which they choose to retire. In recent surveys, 29% of respondents cite the weak economy as the underlying reason. Other reasons include a change in employment situation (22%), inability to afford to retire (16%), need to make up for stock market losses (12%), lack of faith in Social Security (7%), need to pay current expenses first (6%), increase assets to retire well (6%), uncertainty about stock market (5%), health care costs (4%), and changes in the minimum retirement age (4%).

What is an "IRA"?

An IRA, or Individual Retirement Account, was created in 1974 under an act of Congress called ERISA, or the Employee Retirement Income Security Act. An IRA gives individuals who do not have access to an employer-sponsored retirement plan the means to have one, and gives individuals the ability to preserve the tax advantages and growth opportunities of having a retirement plan when they leave a job.

How many different types of IRAs exist?

There are six different types of IRAs: Traditional, SEP, SARSEP, Simple, Roth, and Educational.

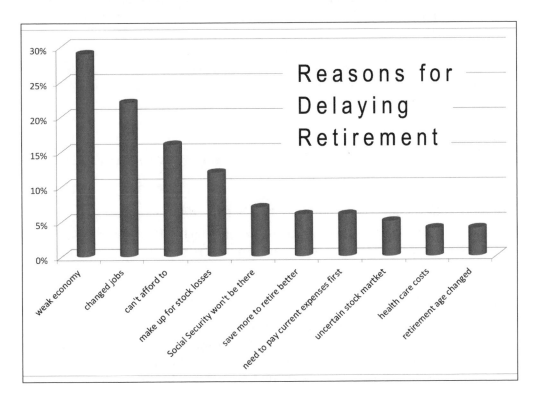

What is a "Traditional IRA"?

A Traditional IRA allows an employee to make tax-deductible contributions up to a certain limit each year for the duration of his working life until he retires. The earnings and balance of the account, together with the employer's match, are then taxed at the retiree's tax rate when he begins to withdraw this money at retirement.

What is a "SEP IRA"?

A SEP IRA is a Simplified Employee Pension plan that allows employees and small business owners the ability to save for their retirement. It allows employers to contribute into an employee's SEP IRA account up to 25% of his annual earnings. The employee may also contribute to this account, and all contributions are tax deductible. Sole proprietors, partnerships, and corporations—including S corporations—can set up SEPs for their employees. You cannot take out loans against your balance. If you withdraw money from the account as income prior to retirement, you will pay a 10% penalty on this money. When you retire, you may make withdrawals from the account, and pay tax on this amount as ordinary income at that time. You may move a SEP into another IRA any time you like.

What is a "SARSEP IRA"?

A SARSEP IRA is a Salary Reduction Simplified Employee Pension plan that is used in companies with fewer than 25 employees. In order to set up such an account, the employer must have at least 50% of the eligible employees contribute to this plan. Employees may make contributions in pre-tax dollars and deduct these amounts from their current income through salary reduction, thus reducing their current tax burden while saving for their retirement. After 1996, these plans were replaced by Simple IRAs. Some employers still use pre-1996 plans.

What is a "Simple IRA"?

A Simple IRA allows employers with fewer than 100 employees who earned $5,000 and above to save for their retirement.

How much may an employee contribute to a Simple IRA?

In 2013 and 2014, employees may contribute (or defer) up to $12,000 of their salary per year, and set this money aside for retirement. Employers may also match up to 3% of each employee's income into this account.

What is a "Roth IRA"?

In a Roth IRA, contributions are made with after-tax dollars, meaning the income of your paycheck after your employer deducts income taxes. You may make these non-tax-deductible contributions to a Roth IRA up to a certain limit each year. Under certain circumstances, you may withdraw money from this account tax free before retirement, and you can withdraw all of it tax-free after age 59½. You may continue to add to this account up to the annual limit for as long as you like. You currently do not have to pay taxes on any distributions from this account, so that your money may grow tax free.

What is the difference between a Roth IRA and a Roth 401(k)?

A Roth 401(k) allows people to divert up to $17,000 annually (as of 2014) if they are under 50 and $22,500 if they are over 50, while a Roth IRA allows for $5,500 a year for those under 50 and $6,500 for those over. A Roth IRA may exist indefinitely and be passed down to the next generation, while you must start taking distributions for a Roth 401(k) beginning at age 70½.

What is an "Education IRA"?

An Educational IRA, which was renamed in 2002 to Coverdell ESA, allows funds to be withdrawn tax free for educational expenses. It was created as an incentive to help parents provide educational funds to their children. Contributions to this account cannot exceed $2,000 per year, according to the IRS, and are not deductible from the taxpayer's taxes, but the contributions do grow tax free until distributed. Even the beneficiary will not owe taxes on the distributions, as long as the distributions are less than the qualified education expenses at an eligible institution.

What percentage of our IRAs are invested in mutual funds?

Forty-six percent of all IRAs are invested in mutual funds.

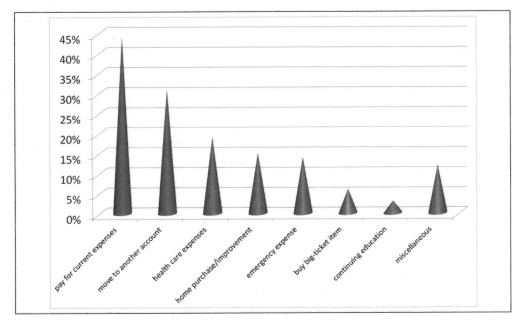

How people use their IRAs after retirement.

How much money is invested in IRAs?

$4.2 trillion in assets is invested in IRAs, of which $1.9 trillion is invested in mutual funds.

How many households own IRAs?

Forty-six million American households are currently invested in some form of an IRA.

What do people do with their IRAs after they retire, when they begin to access their holdings?

Forty-four percent of retirees use the money in their IRAs to pay for current living expenses; 31% moved it into another account or reinvested it; 19% spent it on health care expenses; 15% used it for a home purchase, remodeling, or repair; 14% used it for an emergency; 6% used the account to purchase a big-ticket item; 3% used it for education; and 12% used it for miscellaneous purchases.

What percentage of people are not likely to withdraw funds from an IRA before age 70½?

Thirty-seven percent are not at all likely to withdraw funds from an IRA before age 70½; 27% are not very likely; 20% are somewhat likely; and 16% are very likely.

What is "vesting"?

Vesting in a retirement plan means that, after working for a defined period of time, an employee may own and keep whatever account balances and employer matching funds have been deposited into his "vested" account. A company may decide that an employee must be employed by the company for, say, five years in order to have 100% ownership in his retirement plan or pension.

Why do companies have a vesting period?

This vesting period allows a company to reward long-term employees, and penalize employees who may not remain long with the company. Some vesting is immediate, while other plans follow a graduated period, increasing ownership in the plan by 20% each year for five years. This is all determined in the fine print of your employer's retirement plan document.

401(k)s

What is a 401(k) plan?

A 401(k) plan is a corporate retirement plan that allows an employee to set aside a certain percentage of his income, tax deferred up to a limit, and withdraw from this account when he retires. Under the tax code that created the 401(k) Plan, the company is also allowed to match a certain percentage of an employee's income up to a limit, and contribute to the account.

Do I have to pay taxes on my 401(k) investments?

All earnings on any investments held within your 401(k) are not taxed while you are contributing until you reach the minimum retirement age. You begin to pay taxes only when you retire.

When did 401(k) plans start?

The 401(k) plans began in 1978, when Congress revised a section of the Internal Revenue Code, by adding a section called 401(k), whereby employees would not be taxed on income they direct as deferred, but only on the direct income they receive today. As a result of this important legislation, employees could now set aside a portion of their income and not pay any taxes on it until they retire. The law went into effect in 1980.

How much should I save for retirement?

Many retirement professionals believe it depends on your retirement savings goal. For example, if you manage to accumulate before-tax retirement savings consisting of 5% of your income each year for 30 years, assuming an annual growth rate of 8% per year, you may retire with almost half the income that you were making before retirement. If you save 10% of your income per year, you will be very comfortable in retirement. But if the portfolio's inflation-adjusted annual return is only 2–3% per year, you would need to save almost 40% of your current annual income just to have half your current income in retirement.

What makes 401(k)s great?

401(k)s are great because they compound investment returns over time and have the ability to grow tax-free over the long term. You don't have to pay current taxes on the amount of income earned from these investments as you contribute into your 401(k), so it shields your income from taxes. Since you will most likely make more money now (and pay more in taxes now) than when you retire when you begin to withdraw from your 401(k), it will be taxed at the rate of your income bracket when you are earning much less, thus allowing you to pay less taxes on that money in the future than you would pay on it today. You receive retirement savings, company matches, tax deferrals, and tax-free earnings, just by deducting a small percentage of your income each year.

Can I withdraw money from my 401(k) before I retire?

Yes, you can withdraw money from your 401(k) before you retire, but you will pay rather severe penalties to do so if you are younger than age 59½. Although the penalties may also include employer penalties in addition to IRS penalties, you will most likely have to pay 10% additional taxes on the money withdrawn.

In what ways are participant-directed 401(k) plans more choice-centered?

Participant-directed 401(k) plans are more choice-centered because many employers give the employees many investment choices, allowing an employee to choose how he wishes to invest his retirement savings, either through investment vehicles such as stocks and mutual funds, bonds and bond funds, and even the purchase of his employer's stock.

Why is purchasing your employer's stock a risky investment?

As with all investments, you may obtain great benefits or losses from investing in your own company's stock. But in a bad economic year, if your employer has severe financial difficulties, you may lose not only your job, but also your retirement savings, if a large percentage of your retirement account is invested in your company's stock.

When must I begin to withdraw money from my 401(k)?

You must begin to withdraw money from your account on April 1 of the calendar year after turning age 70½ or on April 1 of the calendar year after you retire, whichever comes later.

What percentage of people do not invest in their company's 401(k) program?

According to researchers at the Employee Benefit Research Institute, 64% of employees save money for retirement, while 36% do not. More than 30% of all employees do not invest in their company-sponsored retirement programs.

What percent of Americans who are saving for retirement do not understand their investment choices?

According to researchers at TIAA-CREF, 28% of respondents to their survey stated that they do not understand the investment choices for their retirement plans, and 40% of those surveyed feel that they have the right investment choices and are not afraid of running out of money during retirement.

What percentage of employees actively trade or manage their retirement funds?

According to one study, only 17% of employees made transfers within their funds. Eighty-three percent showed no trade activity.

What is a "matching program"?

A matching program provides an opportunity for millions of Americans to obtain free money from their employers, deposited directly into their 401(k)s. An employer will match a percentage of what you put into your 401(k), as long as you set aside a certain minimum amount each year, with a limit on the amount per year. For example, if a company matches 5% of your contribution, this means that for every $100 you contribute to your retirement account, your employer contributes $5.

What percentage of employees who learn of their employer's matching program actually direct enough money into their 401(k)s to obtain the matching funds?

Only about 15% of all employees direct enough money to obtain the matching funds from their employers. This seems quite low, considering the match is free.

What percentage of employees know about investing in their 401(k) program at work?

About 66% of employees know what investment choices their company offers; the remaining 34% have no idea that they can invest in their 401(k) program at work. Another 25% are very knowledgeable, actively managing their own investments.

Do people in their twenties manage their 401(k) portfolios the same way as people in their sixties?

People in their twenties manage their 401(k) portfolios quite differently than people in their sixties. Younger people have a much longer view of the market, and have many years in which to make both great financial moves and mistakes. People in their sixties tend to have a shorter investment horizon, and desire more security and less risk.

So how does this understanding translate to their investment behavior?

When it comes to their 401(k) retirement plans, twenty-somethings invest nearly 46% of their total portfolio in equity mutual funds and company stock, and only about 23% in stable fixed income, bond, or cash funds. People in their sixties tend to invest only about 36% in equities or stock funds, and 47% in stable fixed income funds or guaranteed investment contracts.

What else can we see from these two groups of investors?

Fifty-three percent of all twenty-somethings have more than 80% of their 401(k) portfolios invested in equities; the majority of sixty-somethings have only about 23% of their 401(k) portfolios invested in equities.

What percentage of 401(k) assets are in mutual funds?

Fifty-five percent of all 401(k) assets are invested in mutual funds.

What percentage of a typical person's retirement plans are in the form of mutual funds?

For 401(k) and related plans, 51% are in the form of mutual funds; for IRAs, 46% are in the form of mutual funds.

How do I begin to save for retirement?

The easiest way to begin saving for retirement is through your employer's 401(k) program. Companies will match the amount you contribute up to a certain limit (typically between 4–6%). The money may appreciate by the combined effect of your contributions, your employer's matching funds, and the growth of your investment choices over a long period of time.

What is the maximum amount I may contribute each year into a 401(k) plan?

The maximum amount you may contribute each year into a 401(k) plan today is $17,500 per year, and may change each year with inflation, in $500 increments. If you are over age 50, the 401(k) program allows employees to make additional catch-up contributions of $5,500 into their accounts.

Should I ever borrow from my 401(k)?

According to the IRS, some 401(k) plans allow participants to borrow from their plans, but this comes with quite a number of conditions, especially if the participant is below age 59½. The amount can be no more than $50,000; the loan must be repaid within a certain time frame (unless it is to purchase your primary residence); interest rates on the loan must be "reasonable"; loan payments must be made on a regular (at least quarterly) basis; you may be responsible for a 10% penalty; and you must report this loan as income. Please contact your tax adviser or the IRS for further guidance on 401(k) loans.

What is the frequency of 401(k) distributions?

How often you receive distributions or income from your 401(k) or other retirement plan depends on the plan's rules. You may receive non-periodic distributions, a lump sum amount, or periodic or annuity/monthly installment payments until the money is exhausted. For further information, please consult your plan administrator/manager or tax adviser.

LIFE STAGE INVESTING

Why do we use the term "life stage investing"?

As you age, your financial resources and financial needs change, as does the risk profile of your investments. At different periods in your life, you may have to consider different types of investment profiles to adjust to your changing circumstances.

What is a "life stage" or "life cycle" investment?

Typically, life stage or life cycle investments are investments in mutual funds or other investment vehicles in which as you age, your portfolio gradually shifts from predominantly equities of varying types and risk factors to predominantly bonds of varying types and risk factors. The fixed income attributes of investments such as bonds carry relatively less risk.

What is the main purpose of life stage investments?

The main purpose of life stage investments is to limit potential losses from market fluctuations as you approach your retirement years.

In what investments do life stage funds typically invest my money?

Life stage funds will usually begin investing in many broad-based market indexes such as the S&P 500 Index, and gradually balance the portfolio to more broad-based bond indexes such as the Lehman Brothers Corporate Bond Index.

Why do life stage funds prefer to use indexes?

Life stage funds prefer to use indexes as investment vehicles because they tend to have relatively less risk associated with them than less-diversified individual stocks and bond investments.

What is a major factor in deciding how to invest as I near retirement?

A major factor in deciding how to invest your money as you near retirement is how much risk you are willing to tolerate in exchange for the return you wish to make. Some investors prefer portfolios that carry a considerable amount of risk, whether the investments are in equities or bonds. Other investors prefer more conservative portfolios, and are willing to sacrifice higher returns in exchange for peace of mind.

What is one important consideration when I am thinking of investments at different points in my life?

There is one certainty you must accept as you age: Your income will change (and hopefully increase) over time. But this income will come to you at a price; as you make more income, you inevitably have less time to spend analyzing and managing your investments.

Why does my age play such an important role in determining what types of investments I make?

Your age plays an important role in determining what types of investments you make because, when you are younger, you may have many more years of increasing income, and many years in which to correct for poor performance in your investments. As you age, your ability to generate income decreases, and there is less room for error if you make improper investment choices or experience market downturns.

What factors do I need to contemplate when planning for different stages in my investing life?

In order to plan the different stages of your investing life appropriately, you should contemplate several factors, including your savings goals, risk tolerance, income, age, what you have managed to save, and how much income you will need in retirement. Since each factor or groups of factors may require different investment ideas, it is important to be flexible to invest successfully for your retirement.

When I am young and just beginning my career, what is the most important behavior that will help me when I am older?

When you are young, perhaps earning income from your first job, most experts agree that you should create healthy financial habits and practice the discipline of saving—no matter how small—on a regular basis. Since some investments require minimums in order to invest, you should explore investment options available through your employer (such as 401(k)s) or through local financial institutions. When you are young, you can afford to learn and explore different investment strategies, since you have a long time horizon in which to realize gains from our investment choices.

What is a basic assumption of life stage investing?

Life stage investing assumes that as you age—especially as you near retirement—your risk profile changes from high to low, so investors often reduce their exposure to higher risk investments as they age. Typically, by your retirement year, you are entirely invested in a low-risk money market or bond portfolio, gradually reducing more risky investments in preceding years.

What are some limitations of life stage investing?

While adjusting your portfolio over time, some experts believe there are some limitations inherent with the approach. People do not always share the same feelings about their exposure to risk, they do not always retire at the same age, and they may not require the same amount of income produced by investments in retirement, among many other limitations.

What are some typical allocations of investment portfolios as we near retirement?

There are many different opinions among experts as to the proper allocations of portfolios for investors nearing retirement. The main differences in opinion stem from how near to retirement age you are, and your tolerance for risk, among many other factors. For example, one retiree may require much more income from investments than another retiree, and therefore may require higher-producing investments before and during retirement. Generally, most experts use the rule of your age subtracted from 100 to determine what percentage of your portfolio should be allocated to equities; the remaining amount is allocated to bonds and cash. Some experts believe you can adjust the rule to 110–125 minus your age to help you decide what percentage of your portfolio should be allocated to equities, and the remainder to bonds and cash, if you want a more aggressive portfolio.

In the most simplistic terms, what is the proper allocation for my retirement portfolio?

The most simplistic way to consider the proper mix of assets for your retirement portfolio is to understand that when you allocate more of your portfolio to equities, this asset class may provide more opportunity to grow the value of your portfolio while also exposing it to more risk. A portfolio more heavily weighted toward income-producing investments such as bonds will provide some annual income—hopefully better than inflation, at less risk—but the portfolio will not increase very much in value over time.

Why is the allocation or mix of my investments so important to me as I near retirement?

Your allocation is so important as you near retirement because your income sources may be limited. Investments that are based solely on cash may offer you some security and peace of mind, but may not provide enough income—compared with bonds or stocks—over time.

What can I learn about my investment behavior, depending on my time horizon?

A 1999 study conducted by Schooley and Worden in *Financial Analysts Journal* asserted that people with longer time horizons, or long-term investors willing to invest for at least five years, have portfolios consisting of 50% equities. By contrast, investors with shorter time frames—perhaps one year or less—have, on average, portfolios consisting of only 12% equities.

What else can I learn about the behavior of people who are very near retirement?

The same study found that 50% of people who are only a year away from retirement are unwilling to take any risk with their assets. Only 25% of people who are ten or more years away from retirement are unwilling to take any financial risk with their investments, but 75% are willing to take some risk.

Do life cycle funds deliver appropriate returns to investors who are trying to invest for their retirement?

In a 2005 study by Case-Shiller published by the National Bureau of Economic Research, the author found that people who invest in life cycle mutual funds are still exposed to significant risk, with very little opportunity to earn returns. Using a nominal 3% return for the investment, based upon portfolio allocations typical of life cycle funds, the author found that only 32% of hypothetical funds could outperform the 3% benchmark. This contrasts with his finding that if an investor purchases 100% of his portfolio in equities based upon the S&P 500, the portfolio would outperform the benchmark 98% of the time.

Why should I consider using a moderate portfolio allocation for my retirement investments?

You should consider using a moderate mix of stocks, bonds, and cash if you will not need much current income from the portfolio. You want solid growth and tolerance for some fluctuation in the value of your portfolio, but less than in the overall markets.

Why would I consider a moderately conservative allocation mix in my retirement portfolio?

You should consider a moderately conservative allocation mix in your retirement portfolio if you want current income from your investments, and you may want the ability to increase the value of those investments.

Why would I consider a conservative approach to my retirement investment portfolio?

You should consider a more conservative approach to the allocation of your retirement portfolio if you think you will need current income generated from your investments, and you are not really concerned with trying to increase the value of your portfolio.

What types of questions should I ask myself in order to determine how much of my portfolio I should allocate to equities?

According to experts at Morningstar, the following questions may help you determine your allocation of equities in your retirement portfolio. More "yes" responses mean you can devote more assets to equities; more "no" responses mean you should devote fewer assets to equities. The typical questions are:

- Do you expect other sources of income during retirement?
- Do people live a long time in your family?
- Do you expect to need a lot of income during retirement?
- Have you already saved a large amount of money for retirement, or are you just beginning?
- Is the rate at which you save very high?
- Will you have to use some savings prior to retirement?
- Do you wish to leave any assets for your children or other loved ones?
- If you are still employed, is there any chance of a disruption in your income?

Why is longevity risk an important consideration when I consider the asset allocation of my retirement portfolio?

Morningstar experts assert that you must consider your own longevity risk—the risk you may outlive your assets—and weigh this risk more heavily than any short-term fluctuations in your portfolio's value.

SAVING FOR EDUCATION

How much has the cost of a higher education increased?

College tuition and room and board have increased more than 500% since 1980 to $20,435 per academic year, according to the National Center for Education Statistics.

What percentage of undergraduates receive any type of financial aid to attend universities or colleges in America?

According to the National Center for Education Statistics, 68% of all undergraduates receive some form of aid to attend university or college.

What is the average amount of student aid that students in undergraduate programs receive?

In the same study, the average amount of aid that an undergraduate student receives is $9,100.

One of the most expensive U.S. colleges to attend is New York University (business college shown here), where tuition, room, board, and fees run about $60,000 a year.

What types of programs are available to help fund my child's education?

If you are eligible, the federal student aid office has myriad programs to help parents and students fund their college or university expenses, including grants, campus-based aid, Stafford Loans, PLUS loans for parents, PLUS loans for graduate or professional degrees, and loan consolidation. More detailed information on each of these programs is available at http://studentaid.ed.gov.

What is the first step to obtain federal assistance for education?

The first step is to fill out the FAFSA (Free Application for Federal Student Aid) application form and submit it, along with the required documentation, in order to demonstrate the need for assistance. Avoid any website that charges you to submit this application; there is no charge to submit this form.

What does the FAFSA application cover?

The FAFSA application covers all types of student aid—from grants, loans, and work-study programs to sources of non-federal aid and assistance.

Which colleges and universities use the FAFSA application to help finance a college or university experience?

Nearly every college and university in the United States uses FAFSA to assist with funding a student's education.

Why are there so many questions on the FAFSA application?

The questions on the FAFSA application are designed to help families demonstrate a financial need to receive financial aid. It ensures that students who have real financial need get the most assistance available to fund their college or university experience.

What is an expected family contribution?

After filling out the FAFSA form, the authorities will determine how much the student's family should contribute to the educational expense—the expected family contribution—and how much financial aid the student will receive to cover the gap. As each institution has different fees and expenses, the amount of financial aid may differ between institutions.

What if I have had some unusual expenses that make my ability to pay for my child's education more difficult?

If you have had unusual medical expenses, or dramatic changes in income, these circumstances should be noted on your application and discussed with the financial aid office of the school at which your child is applying.

How does the financial aid actually come to me?

Generally, the financial aid will be paid directly to the institution to cover tuition and room and board, if necessary. Any remaining amount may be remitted to you to cover other additional living expenses or educational materials.

If I am applying to different schools, must I submit a separate FAFSA application to each one?

No, your printed application may be used at up to four schools that you specify on the application. If you intend to include more than four, you may add up to ten schools by completing an online application.

What is an "educational grant"?

An educational grant does not need to be repaid. An educational loan needs to be repaid, with interest.

What types of educational grants are available?

There are many types of educational grants available for students, some based on financial need, and others based on the student's academic ability, subject interest, or whether he has served in the armed forces. Some of the more popular grants include TEACH grants, Federal Pell grants, FSEOG grants, ACG grants, National Smart Grants, institutional grants, and Iraq/Afghanistan Service Grants.

What is a "Federal Pell Grant"?

A Pell Grant, the most popular grant, is awarded to undergraduate students who have not yet earned a bachelor's or professional degree. The Pell Grant can be used in conjunction with other forms of financial aid as well. The maximum amount of the grant changes from year to year, and most recently was $5,500. It is dependent upon your financial need, the costs associated with attending your school, whether you are a full- or part-time student, and whether you plan to attend the school for the full academic year. You may receive up to two Pell Grants in a single academic year for up to 18 semesters.

What is "campus-based aid"?

Campus-based aid is designed to help a student fund his education based upon financial need, how much other aid he currently receives, and the funds available from the institution when application is made. It is available on a first-come, first-served basis. Several federally funded campus-based aid programs are available to students, including Federal Supplemental Educational Opportunity Grant (FSEOG), Federal Work-Study (FWS), and Federal Perkins Loan Program.

What happens if the university runs out of campus-based aid funds?

Once the pool of funds is allocated, no additional funds are available; you should apply early for these programs. As each school determines the deadlines to apply for these funds, the cut-off period may be earlier than your FAFSA application. Be sure to check with the institution regarding its deadline for campus-based aid, and apply accordingly.

What is a "Federal Supplemental Educational Opportunity Grant" (FSEOG)?

FSEOGs are grants for students with exceptional financial need. They fund between $100 and $4,000 per year, depending on when you apply, so apply early. The money will be paid either directly to you, the school, or a combination of the two.

What is a "Federal Work-Study grant"?

A Federal Work-Study grant provides part-time employment opportunities to students in undergraduate and graduate programs, allowing them to defray the costs of education and gain valuable work experience at the same time. The institution will pay the student directly, and the minimum hourly wage you can earn must be equal to or greater than the federal minimum hourly wage. You are not allowed to earn commissions or fees in this work, and you are limited in the amount that you can earn by the size of the grant.

Can I work anywhere in a work-study program?

Most on-campus work-study jobs will be at or near the institution you attend. You may also opt to work off-campus, at private not-for-profit organizations, or with private companies that have special work-study programs sanctioned by your institution.

Students who obtain a Federal Work-Study grant can pay for part of their tuition by working certain jobs.

What is a "Federal Perkins Loan"?

A Federal Perkins Loan is a low-interest (5%) loan made available through your institution's financial aid office to undergraduate and graduate students who have demonstrated exceptional financial need. The school actually lends the money, and therefore the loan is repaid to the institution directly, although the funds issue from the government.

How much may I borrow under the Federal Perkins Loan program?

You may borrow $5,500 per year for each year of undergraduate study, up to a maximum of $27,500. If you are pursuing graduate studies, the maximum amount is $8,000 per year, up to $60,000 (including the $27,500 for your undergraduate study). The amount available to you depends on your financial need, when you applied, and the funds available at the school you attend.

When must I repay school loans?

In general, you must begin to repay the loans nine months after you graduate, or drop below half-time status. You may be given a grace period to repay these loans, so check with your school's financial aid office.

What is a Direct Stafford Loan?

Direct Stafford Loans, from the William D. Ford Federal Direct Loan Program, are low-interest loans for eligible students to help defray the costs of undergraduate education at a four-year college or university, community college, or trade/career/technical school.

285

Eligible students borrow the money directly from the U.S. Department of Education at all participating schools.

How many types of Stafford Loans exist?

There are two types of Stafford Loans: direct subsidized loans, and direct unsubsidized loans. Subsidized loans are based on financial need, and the amount is determined by your FAFSA application. No interest is charged on the loan as long as you are enrolled in school at least part time, and during grace periods and deferment periods. Unsubsidized loans do not require you to show financial need. The amount of this loan is also determined by the institution you attend, and interest will accrue from the time you actually get the loan. While you are in school, you may opt to pay only the interest on this loan, or let the interest accumulate over time, and then have this amount added to your original loan amount for repayment. If you choose this option, the original loan amount will be larger, since you will be adding the amount of interest you must repay.

What are the interest rates for these subsidized and unsubsidized loans?

Both loan types give borrowers the option to have a fixed interest rate or a variable rate. As interest rates change from year to year, check with your school's financial aid office for specific rates.

How much money may I borrow under the Stafford Loan Program?

The amount varies, depending on where you are in your educational journey, what other loans or aid you have, and whether you are in graduate school.

What is a PLUS Loan for Parents?

A PLUS Loan enables parents of dependent students to seek financial aid in the form of a low-interest loan to help fund their dependent's education. Parents must meet certain eligibility requirements in order to receive the aid, and as with many of these loans, only the amount of the educational expense (minus any other financial aid you might already have) will be the maximum allowed for the loan.

What are some of the requirements for a Direct PLUS Loan?

The parents must be the biological or adoptive parents of the dependent student. The student must be enrolled at least half time at a participating school. The parent borrower must not have an adverse credit history, and must be a good credit risk. The student and parents must be U.S. citizens or eligible non-citizens, and must not be in default on any other federal educational aid.

What is a "529 Plan"?

A 529 Plan, also known as a Qualified Tuition Plan, is designed to make higher education more affordable for families by helping parents save for college or pre-pay college and university tuition for their children. It is named after Section 529 of the Internal Revenue Code.

What types of 529 Plans are available?

These plans are divided into two types: college savings plans, and prepaid tuition plans.

What is a "college savings plan"?

A college savings plan allows people to contribute into an account, grow the money tax-free, and then make withdrawals to pay for their dependent's higher education expenses. Some states also exempt earnings from 529 accounts from state taxes, as well as allow state tax deductions for contributions.

How does a college savings plan work?

You set up an account similar to your retirement account. It may offer you investment options and choices as to the amounts you wish to invest and the frequency of those investments. Some people like to fund these accounts with several large payments, whereas others may fund it each month over many years. When your child begins to attend college, the money can be withdrawn from the account to be used for room, board, tuition, and books.

May I change the name of the beneficiary on a college savings plan account?

Yes. When you set up a college savings plan account, you must name a beneficiary for the plan, but you may also change beneficiaries later if you choose.

Do I have to select a 529 Plan in the state in which I live?

No, you do not have to select a 529 Plan in the state in which you live. You may choose any state's 529 Plan, even if you or your dependents do not reside in that state. As each 529 Plan is sponsored by a different state, there is some variability in the plans and benefits each state offers.

Are there any income restrictions for a 529 Plan?

No, a 529 Plan contains no income restrictions.

How much may I contribute to a 529 Plan?

States restrict the total amount you may contribute to a 529 Plan to a maximum of $300,000.

What if I don't want to tie up my child's educational savings in the stock market?

Many states offer investment choices that do not invest in the stock market.

Are there any tax advantages to having a 529 Plan?

Yes. Earnings accumulate tax-free while in the account, and no tax is due on a distribution used to pay higher education expenses. The beneficiary does not have to include in income any earnings from a 529 Plan unless the amount distributed is greater than the beneficiary's higher education expenses. However, contributions made to a 529 Plan are not deductible on your federal tax return. Each state offers different tax incentives, and even matching programs. Check your state's 529 Plan website for more specific state tax benefits.

How does a prepaid tuition plan work?

Each state has its own method to administer a prepaid tuition plan. Some states allow parents to make tuition payments over four, seven, ten, or fifteen years. The money can be spent at an in-state or out-of-state college, depending on what plan you select. If you do not use the money, it is refunded to you.

How much is tuition increasing?

Using the value of a dollar from 2009–2010 as a baseline, the most recent analysis by the National Center for Education Statistics found that, in the period from 1980 to 2011, college tuition (both private and public, including universities) increased on average more than 4.46% per year. Between 2000–2001 and 2010–2011, prices for undergraduate tuition, room, and board at public institutions rose 42 percent, and prices at private not-for-profit institutions rose 31 percent, after adjusting for inflation. The inflation-adjusted price for undergraduate tuition, room, and board at private for-profit institutions was 5 percent higher in 2010–2011 than in 2000–2001.

What does it cost to attend a degree-granting college or university today?

As of the 2010–2011 academic year, annual current dollar prices for undergraduate tuition, room, and board were estimated to be $13,600 at public institutions, $36,300 at private not-for-profit institutions, and $23,500 at private for-profit institutions.

Why is prepaying tuition such a great deal?

Prepaying tuition is a great deal because you are able to pay for tuition when your earning power is very high, and using today's dollars, you pay a lot less than if you decided to pay at the time you go to college.

What is the biggest difference between a prepaid tuition plan and a college savings plan?

The biggest difference between a prepaid tuition plan and a college savings plan is that a prepaid tuition plan locks in the price of tuition at eligible public and private colleges or universities; a college savings plan does not. All prepaid tuition plans cover tuition and mandatory fees associated with tuition, and some plans include such items as room and board or other defined expenses; college savings plans cover the costs of tuition, room and board, fees, books, and computers. Most prepaid tuition plans set lump-sum and installment payments prior to purchase based upon the beneficiary's age and number of years of tuition to be purchased; many college savings plans impose limits that exceed $200,000. And while your money may be guaranteed by the state in which you live if you choose a prepaid tuition plan, money directed toward a college savings plan is subject to market risk, may increase or decline in value over time, and is not guaranteed by the state.

Tuition costs in America are crippling graduates' ability to get by after they finish school. The average student graduates with about $25,000 in debt.

What did Jack Bogle, founder of the Vanguard Group, do to save and invest money for his children's college education?

In a CNBC interview, the famous investment manager stated that when his six children were very young, he opened up investment accounts for them. Ultimately, some of his children used the money for their higher education. Some years later, his children used what remained of the money to purchase their first houses.

TEACHING CHILDREN ABOUT INVESTING

According to the Visa International Financial Literacy Barometer 2012 survey, how do Americans rank when it comes to financial literacy?

According to a survey of parents from many countries, commissioned by Visa International, in conjunction with Kiplinger's, Americans ranked fourth overall when it comes to financial literacy, finishing behind Mexico, Brazil, and Australia. In the study, which surveyed residents of 28 countries, respondents were asked questions to measure how often parents discuss financial matters with their children, whether teens and young adults under their care were adequately prepared to manage their own money in adulthood, and how well parents manage their own financial affairs. A majority of respondents believed their children did not understand basic financial management practices such as expense budgeting, savings, debt management, and responsible spending habits. Over 70% of U.S. respondents agreed they could do a better job of teaching their children these basic financial lessons.

How much time do American parents spend discussing financial matters with their children?

According to the same Financial Literacy survey, American parents spend approximately 26 days a year discussing financial matters with their kids. In comparison, Mexican parents spend an average of 42 days per year, and Brazilians spend approximately 38 days per year.

How often do parents engage their children in discussing financial matters, such as saving and spending?

According to the Fourth Annual Parents, Kids & Money Survey published by T. Rowe Price, 76% of parents and 67% of children report that they have had conversations on the importance of saving and spending at least somewhat often, but only 32% of parents are having these types of conversations very often.

What percentage of parents never discuss financial matters with their kids?

Nearly one-third (32%) of parents never discuss financial matters with their kids.

Why do some parents spend more time discussing financial matters with their children?

The T. Rowe Price survey also measures the change in the amount of time that parents spend discussing important financial matters with their children. Some reasons cited for the increased time is attributable to such factors as the child's age and ability to understand more, changes in the family's financial situation, the child's desire to spend more money, and the child's success saving his own money.

What financial topics are older children most interested in discussing with their parents?

The Fourth Annual Parents, Kids & Money Survey found that 20% of children are interested in talking about saving, 18% are interested in discussing how to make money, 12% are discussing allowances, and 7% are discussing investing.

With whom do children prefer to discuss money matters, Mom or Dad?

The same survey found that 54% of children prefer to discuss financial matters with Mom, and 40% of children prefer to discuss financial matters with Dad.

Why bother to teach children about financial matters?

Many family financial experts agree that it is important to help children become financially capable before they leave home so they can live independently later. We educate our children in financial matters so that as adults, they have a capable and successful attitude toward managing their money, and to impart financial values, such as having personal responsibility, developing a saving mentality, delaying gratification, and practicing charity.

Why is it important for me to set an example for my children about how to value money and investing?

Many experts believe it is important to teach our children the value of money before we teach them about investing because financial literacy and values toward money are greatly influenced by what we observe from our parents from childhood through adulthood. After a child learns about financial values, he will be ready to learn about investing.

At what age are children capable of understanding financial concepts such as the value and purpose of money?

According to academic research dating back more than 70 years and pioneered by Jean Piaget, children are quite capable of understanding what money is, and for what it can be used, at a very early age. This research has been debated in academic literature for decades, and supported by many researchers subsequently. To understand what a child is capable of comprehending, academicians break a child's financial understanding into four distinct stages: At age four to five, a child understands that money can purchase any object; at age five to six, that the amount of money to be used must exactly match an object's price; in a range of ages between three and six, that he can pay with money greater than the price of the object; and at age seven to ten, full understanding of all of these concepts is achieved. At this point, the child understands fully what "change" is, as a result of a transaction.

What is the earliest age that I should begin to introduce financial concepts to young children?

According to Paul Solman, an economics correspondent for the *PBS NewsHour*, who analyzed a famous longitudinal study of children in New Zealand, adult financial habits may be determined as young as age three. Children who have difficulty with self-control by age three may have the most difficulty managing their money in adulthood.

What is the first step in teaching my children about money?

Perhaps the first step in teaching your children about money is that you and your spouse share similar attitudes about money, and common goals about saving and investing for the future. Children need to see parents speaking with one voice, with little conflict, on financial matters.

Teaching children about money and saving can begin surprisingly early, as young as three years old.

Why should we be positive and neutral, as opposed to negative and emotional, when it comes to speaking about money with our kids?

You want to be positive and neutral because you want your children to associate saving money with something positive so that they can carry these feelings over into their adulthood. It is important to be balanced in your outlook and explanation so that they may approach financial talks from a neutral rather than an emotional point of view.

What is the next step to teaching a child about money?

Many experts believe the next step to teaching children about money is to begin to reward them, in some small way, for chores done around the house, and encourage them to save by opening up a bank account in their name in which to make deposits. The act of encouraging saving at a young age will greatly boost their self-esteem, even if they only deposit a few dollars at a time. Each time he goes to the bank, the child begins to think positively about saving, and these feelings may last a lifetime.

How else can I teach my child about money?

It is important to teach your child the value of delaying a purchase, not impulsively buying an item just because he wants it. Show your children that you are saving every week for experiences such as vacations, or other big-ticket items such as a car. Let them see that when you are in a store, you may look at items to buy, but when you don't need it right now, you decide not to buy it. Experts say that children learn by observation. If you believe in delaying purchases and not using your credit card to buy something that you do not have cash to pay for, your children will begin to do the same.

What is another way to encourage children to save money?

As with your employer's matching program for your 401(k) retirement plan, you can also match what your child puts into his account. Some experts have suggested making this match for a long-term goal, such as the purchase of some new game or clothes. The match will allow your child to see how fast his money has grown, which will boost his self-esteem as well.

With today's paltry interest rates, will it not be hard for a child to see his money grow, even if he looks at a physical or online statement from a bank?

With today's interest rates near zero, it may be difficult for your child to see his money grow quickly by looking at monthly savings account statements. However, the Internet has various online calculators, such as www.moneychimp.com, that allows you to enter an amount in a savings account, as well as an interest rate, and the amount of time that the money is in the account, to see how his savings account may grow because of compounding interest.

How do we make children's savings goals easier to understand?

Experts in child financial literacy believe that, in order to teach children to save, parents should give them easily attainable savings goals, such as saving specifically to buy a toy, game, music, or a computer application. One expert at www.Kiplinger.com suggests showing a child a photograph of the desired item to make the savings goal more tangible. As a child grows, it is important to show him bank statements, so he can begin to see how his money grows in a savings account. Finally, it is essential to let the child spend the money he has saved, so he can start the process over again.

After a child has mastered the concept of saving to meet financial goals, what else can I do to educate my child on the value of investing?

The AICPA also suggests that parents should teach children the basic concept of risk compared with reward—that in order to achieve higher returns on your money, you may have to tolerate considerably more risk.

What does the American Institute of Certified Public Accountants (AICPA) feel is the most important step that parents should take to help their children to understand investing?

The AICPA recommends that before you try to explain complex concepts such as options and short selling, you should first teach children to understand the concept of

Why is hands-on training important to teach investing concepts to young children?

By giving children age-appropriate, hands-on training, letting children play with real companies and real money, a child can choose companies or investments that interest him, and follow the price movements of these investments, so he can put the concepts to work in practice. The more your child practices investing, the easier it will be for him to incorporate these concepts in later life.

making money grow by understanding short- and long-term financial goals, using examples a child can understand. You can achieve this by giving a child a goal, such as saving for a new game. If your child needs to save for something that is more expensive, then you can teach him why investing in other choices, such as equities or mutual funds, may help him achieve this goal.

As my child grows, how can I encourage him to continue to learn about money, finances, and investing?

Encourage your child to get a job, whether babysitting, cutting lawns, or working in a restaurant. Encourage him to have some goals in mind for what he wishes to save, and show interest in his pursuit, always encouraging him, no matter how small his success. Success breeds more success when it comes to creating wealth, and it begins at a very young age.

What does Warren Buffett think about teaching children about investing?

Warren Buffett, aside from being one of the most successful investors in our time, is participating in creating an animated series designed to help teach kids about investing. In an interview with www.Forbes.com, he recently said, "It's never too early to help kids understand about money. Whether it's understanding the cost of the new toy they want, or the value of saving money. Kids are exposed to money matters from a very young age, so why not help them understand it and develop healthy habits early on?"

What is the minimum age for a child to open a bank account?

There is no minimum age requirement to open a bank account for a dependent child. Some banks will allow a child to open a direct account in his own name, and others allow someone to open a custodial account for that child.

What is a "custodial account"?

A custodial account is an account in the name of a child, but the main signatory and responsible party on the account is the child's custodian, normally a parent.

What is the Uniform Transfers to Minors Act (UTMA)?

The Uniform Transfers to Minors Act was created in 1986. In keeping with the IRS Code, UTMA allows for the tax-free transfer of funds to a child or multiple children up to an annual limit of $13,000.

What two states have not yet adopted UTMA?

Only Vermont and South Carolina have not adopted the Uniform Transfers to Minors Act. Some states have altered UTMA by making changes to such items as the age of termination for certain types of transfers, or provisions that permit a donor to change the age of termination before the gift is made.

When can my child have access to his UTMA account?

Most states allow a child to begin drawing from this account at age 21, although some states allow children to do so at age 18. Some states require a child to be between the ages of 18 and 25 to use the funds in the account.

Why do experts at www.Forbes.com feel that opening UTMA accounts may not be such a great idea?

Experts at www.Forbes.com feel that creating UTMA accounts for children may not be such a great idea because, over the long term, the account may incur a large tax burden. Before UTMA replaced the Uniform Gifts to Minors Act, parents could enjoy a sizable tax advantage by transferring money to their kids. But under UTMA, a child will enjoy the first $1,000 of earned income tax-free but the second $1,000 of earned income is taxed at 15%. Please consult with a tax adviser to further understand the tax implications of gifting or transferring money to minors, including any updates to the current code.

What does the term "irrevocable" mean?

The term "irrevocable" means a custodial account cannot be changed. The person for whom you originally created the account must remain the same, and cannot be changed after the account is initially created.

What if my bank doesn't allow accounts for kids?

If your bank doesn't allow accounts for kids, shop around until you find one that does. It is important to obtain comparison information from each bank, including the minimum age, interest rate, and minimum deposit to open an account.

Can I give money to my children without incurring any tax liability?

A parent may give a gift of $14,000 or less to a child without having to pay a gift tax and filing form 709 for the filing year 2013. Additionally, a spouse may also give a minor $14,000, and "split" the gift for a total of $28,000. In this case, you must file a form 709,

Not all banks allow minors to open accounts, but shop around for one that does. It's a good way to teach them about financial responsibility.

and the spouse needs to sign the form. Please consult your tax adviser for more information, as these amounts may change from year to year.

Why is it important to teach children about risk and reward when they begin to learn about investing?

Many experts agree that a child needs to grasp the concept of risk and reward in order to realize that having investments may provide rewards, but that those investments are also exposed to a certain degree of risk.

What are six ways experts at *The Wall Street Journal* feel will help children begin to understand how to invest?

Experts at *The Wall Street Journal* believe that, in order to successfully teach children about investing, parents need to start having conversations about investing when children are young; have children invest in companies they understand; teach children about the effects of inflation before they invest; let older children share in managing their investments; let children learn from making wrong choices in their investments; and always reinforce charitable values.

How do I begin to select individual stocks that would interest a child?

In order to select stocks that interest a child, begin by asking the child what products he likes, retail stores he frequents, food he likes, and restaurants he enjoys. The main purpose for this initial assessment is to create a list of brands in order to find out which ones are most interesting and relevant to the child. Then you should check to see if any of the companies are publicly traded, and on what exchanges they are listed.

How do I find out if a company is publicly traded?

The easiest method to identify if a company is publicly traded is to enter the name of the company into your favorite search engine, and go directly to its main corporate website. Normally, if a company is publicly traded on any stock exchange, its website will include a navigation tab that will say "investor relations" or "about." In these pages of the website, you can see if the company offers its shares to the public, and on which exchange it is traded. You may also see if a company is listed when you look up its name on many general financial websites, such as Google Finance or Yahoo! Finance.

How else might I find out if a company offers shares to the public for purchase?

You may also look on the website of many online equity trading companies, and enter the name of the company into its search box. From there, you will see if the company has shares available for purchase, as well as information about the company and its performance, such as fundamental information and stock price performance.

After I have identified the names of the companies my child might be interested in acquiring, what is the next step?

After you have made an initial assessment of the list of your target companies, many experts feel you should select those stocks with high quarterly earnings, low P/E ratios, low debt, and strong product quality and demand. Perhaps your child may have some intuition regarding the future prospects of success with a particular brand, even though its current performance may not support the decision to select this particular stock. This may be an opportunity to teach the child about owning riskier investments, and the reasons why a company with certain attributes may not be such a great investment today (such as high debt, higher than normal stock price, low earnings, etc.).

Should I actually purchase the shares of these companies, or just monitor the prices of the shares, and show these price movements hypothetically?

Many people opt just to select a basket of companies, and begin tracking their performance on a spreadsheet, by looking up or updating the current stock price. Many sites such as Google Finance or Yahoo! Finance will automatically track the performance of a hypothetical portfolio of stocks, after you enter the name or symbol of the stock into its interface. Each time you look at the portfolio, the prices are updated automatically. You can see what you initially "paid" for the stock, and its current performance.

What is another important point to teach children so they may begin to understand some basic principles of investing?

Bogle suggests teaching and showing a child the value that is created simply by compounding interest. He uses the example of a $10 investment, earning only 7% interest, that will double in ten years. He also suggests opening an investment account with your child's saved money, and purchasing an index fund. This index fund and its performance can teach your child how an investment may grow (or not) over time.

What is one of the most important lessons I need to teach my children for them to incorporate investing ideas into their own lives?

Children observe the behaviors and values of their parents, such as delaying immediate gratification, saving regularly, and patience. Bogle feels that if parents' actions match their words, children will learn by observing good behaviors over time.

What do experts at Kiplinger's say is the best approach to teach children about investing?

According to experts at www.Kiplinger.com, in order to teach children about investing effectively, it is best to understand this is an ongoing practice that occurs in small steps. It is best to engage children at different points in their lives, when they are ready to learn important lessons.

Into what three groups can we categorize children who actually own stock?

Experts at www.Kiplinger.com assert that children who own stocks in companies are a minority, but may fall into one of three categories: children who start a traditional savings account, notice they are earning only a few cents in interest on their accounts, and wish to see this amount grow; children who have significant adults in their lives who have an interest in the markets, such as grandparents, parents, aunts, and uncles, or other friends and relatives; and entrepreneurial kids who have managed to earn and save money from their odd jobs or business ideas at a young age, and wish to earn more money on their savings, rather than earning only interest on their money while deposited in a bank.

To help your children understand money better, you can play games with them to familiarize them with different coins and denominations.

What are four steps we can take to introduce investing concepts to children?

Experts at Kiplinger's, who have been writing about this subject for decades, suggest you explain investing concepts in a simple way; assist your child in buying stock in some of his favorite brands or companies (by either purchasing a stock or tracking its performance); mentor your child by teaching him, and taking an interest in what he is doing; and include both sons and daughters in all early investing ideas (since surveys show that women feel less confident than men when it comes to investing).

What are some other activities parents can do with their young children in order to teach them the value of money and investing concepts?

Family financial expert Neale Godfrey, co-author of *The New York Times* best seller *Money Doesn't Grow on Trees: A Parent's Guide to Raising Financially Responsible Children* (2013), suggests parents play money games with kids so they begin to understand the value of different coins. She suggests setting up three or four jars and a pile of assorted coins with which parents can teach young children about the value of money, reinforcing such skills as math, counting, and sorting. The parent then shows the child how to divide the money into each jar that has a specific purpose, such as charity, quick cash, short-term savings, and long-term savings.

What are some tips experts at Kiplinger's suggest for reinforcing saving concepts with young children?

Experts at Kiplinger's suggest that parents can better reinforce financial concepts in young children by helping the child set short-term goals because children do not have a long time frame or conceptual image developed. So the experts suggest that parents should encourage children to set goals that are short term in nature and easy to achieve. They even suggest that children specifically save money for a trip to their favorite toy store, a goal that is both short term and easily attainable.

Why should we not think about investing only as a subject for adults?

Many people erroneously think that investing—or any financial discussion—is most appropriate when a person is technically an adult. But experts believe we are doing a disservice to our children by waiting until they reach age 18 before we begin teaching them about investing. Many kids can understand basic financial concepts much earlier in life, so it is best to expose them to financial and investing concepts when they are quite young.

What if my child is not too interested in learning about investing?

In the same CNBC interview, Jack Bogle stated that not all of his children were interested in investing, and only one of his six children became a hedge fund manager some years later. For those children who are less interested in learning about investing, Bogle feels we should find a way to communicate with them about investing, depending on their level of interest. For his grandchildren, who range in age from their late teens to early twenties, Bogle briefly discusses the performance of the investments in their individual portfolios at the end of each year.

Why can teaching children about investing be so challenging?

To many parents, the investing world is filled with so many terms and definitions that it can be a daunting task to engage a child without having him get lost in understanding the complex concepts and definitions. Most experts on educating children about investing believe the best approach is to keep the definitions simple, and spend only a short time on each concept so you can keep the child interested in the concept. Parents can also use real examples from their own financial experiences, since children identify and understand more easily when the topic relates to someone they know and love.

Why is it important to start teaching kids about financial matters when they are young?

According to family financial experts at www.CNN.com, it is important to introduce children to basic financial concepts because, as they get older, they will more likely have created many habits related to spending, and will not have the time to learn about basic financial matters once they become teenagers.

What are four concepts that will help older kids increase their financial literacy?

Experts at Kiplinger's distill four important concepts that older kids need to understand in order to increase their financial literacy: Even small amounts of money when saved in a bank account earning only 2% interest will continually grow, because of compounding interest; when you obtain a 30-year loan to buy a house, you may have to pay less each month for principal and interest payments, while a 15-year loan will require higher monthly payments, but you pay less in interest; there is generally more risk associated with buying an individual stock than in buying a mutual fund, because the fund may be properly diversified; and when interest rates increase, bond prices decrease, because newer bonds may be issued with higher rates and will be more attractive to investors.

Why is it important to use allowances to teach older kids proper financial management?

Family financial experts at www.CNN.com suggest parents use an allowance—whether for work completed around the house or not—as a tool to teach older children the value of money because it will help prepare them for when they begin to work and earn much more money. As they get older, they will be better prepared for such necessary financial activities as opening a checking and/or savings account, and using credit or debit cards wisely.

How do parents use allowances for their children?

In a recent national survey of 2,000 families, experts at the site DoughMain.com, an organization committed to encouraging parents to teach their kids about money matters, found that 89% of all families assign chores for their kids to do, and 51% of all families give an allowance, but only 21% give an allowance as compensation for chores. They also found that only 21% of the families that pay an allowance actually pay it in recognition for the completed task. Forty-seven percent of all families stated they pay the allowance in order to teach their children about financial matters, but not in connection to the completion of chores. The study further found that 26% of parents now give privileges such as computer or television access instead of a monetary allowance. And only 4% of parents require their children to deposit saved money into a bank account.

What are some creative ways in which parents may use allowances to educate their children on financial matters?

The DoughMain survey shows that 38% of parents match the deposits made by older kids in their savings account. This helps to

Parents can teach kids about working for money by giving them an allowance as compensation for chores and sometimes requiring them to save some of that allowance.

301

show older kids that their savings can grow, giving them further incentive to save. Since many teens are given responsibilities such as paying for cell phones, music, and entertainment, they will become more accustomed to and interested in saving.

What are some other findings from the DoughMain study?

The study also showed that although 63% of families have opened savings accounts for their kids, only 43% of parents ever look at those same account statements with their children, and only 28% of children have ever looked at their account statements online.

What are some top books on children and financial literacy?

A quick search of the Internet reveals dozens of books related to children and financial literacy. Some popular titles include: Robert T. Kiyosaki's *Rich Dad, Poor Dad: What the Rich Teach Their Kids About Money—That the Poor and Middle Class Do Not!* (2011); Nancy Holyoke's *A Smart Girl's Guide to Money* (American Girl Library) (2006); Eno Sarris and Masaaki Aihara's *My First Book of Money: Counting Coins* (2007); Gail Karlitz and Debbie Honig's *Growing Money: A Complete Investing Guide for Kids* (2010); Larry Burkett's *Money Matters for Teens* (2001); Katherine R. Bateman's *The Young Investor: Projects and Activities for Making Your Money Grow* (2010); Brette McWhorter Sember's *The Everything Kids' Money Book: Earn It, Save It, and Watch It Grow!* (An Everything® Series) (2008); and Hollis Page Harman's *Money $ense for Kids* (2004).

What are some interesting websites that parents may use to help educate their children about financial literacy?

According to experts at the non-profit Alliance for Investor Education, parents can benefit by visiting several websites that introduce children of varying ages to financial matters. Some of those sites include 360 Degrees of Financial Literacy at http://www.360 financialliteracy.org/; Gen i Revolution at www.genirevolution.org (Council for Economic Education); Tips for Teaching Students About Saving and Investing at www.sec.gov (SEC); and Great Minds Think at www.federalreserveeducation.org (Federal Reserve Board of Governors).

THE FUTURE OF INVESTING

What are some trends that indicate a changing international landscape for investors?

According to experts interviewed by *Businessweek*, developing countries that were responsible for contributing 37% of the world's global output in 2000 are now responsible for more than 50%. Because of the global nature of the economy, the location of a company will become less apparent and, according to a Wharton School expert, will lead to less-than-adequate diversification by investors, as many markets will be correlated, and the location of a company will not necessarily be the primary driver to influence a stock's price.

Will a global stock exchange emerge?

Stock exchanges themselves merge with other stock exchanges in order to capture more profit from the trading activity in other markets. Experts expect this trend to continue, since it will be harder to attribute a company's activity to any single country, and more countries will adopt similar accounting standards.

What is one limitation of the trend toward the emergence of similar individual investors and investment products located in other parts of the world?

One limitation to the trend toward having similar investors and investment products located in other parts of the world is that much of the developing world lacks the legal protections and codes that protect individual investors. Until these laws are in place, according to experts at Northwestern University, the developing world will have a difficult time competing with the developed world in making investment products available to more of their population, who may either invest a portion of their income into financial products or use investment products such as mutual funds to fuel their retirement.

Will investment banks become deposit banks?

Some experts feel that since the U.S. government has helped investment banks by backing up money invested by private individuals, allowing the investment banks to use the Fed's discount window (lending system), policies may change and allow for an FDIC-like organization to protect individual depositors with the investment bank.

Will the growth of ETFs and index funds replace actively managed mutual funds?

Stanford University professor of finance Darrell Duffie, who was interviewed by *Businessweek,* acknowledged the explosive growth of ETFs, which grew from only 80 funds in 2000 to more than 1,400 in 2013. Actively managed funds, which charge a fee to manage investment portfolios, may decline in popularity, as ETFs become more prevalent. Many mutual funds will also launch their own ETFs to capture more of the market share for mutual funds that they would otherwise lose to new, cheaper, passively managed products.

Will actively managed funds disappear?

Some experts argue that, although passively managed funds that use indexes for their underlying investment product will continue to grow, people will still need access to the myriad investment products available to a market. As the sophistication and knowledge of the individual investor increases, the need for financial products to match these needs will also continue to grow.

How will the use of software help individual investors to analyze their portfolios?

Stanford professor Darrell Duffie also believes that as individual investors become more capable of managing their own financial affairs, improvements in software and online tools will enable investors to visualize changes to their portfolios, allowing them to see the effects of changing the allocations of their investments, and the returns they might experience. They will also be able to alter the risk of their portfolios and see many different possible scenarios and correlations with just a mouse click.

What are four reasons why long-term investing may be diminishing?

Experts at the World Economic Forum—in workshops and interviews of 150 participants (academicians, policy makers, and professionals)—found several factors leading to the decrease in long-term investing: decline of the period in which investors actually hold stocks or positions in equity investments; high frequency computer-assisted trading; the brevity of tenure of CEOs of publicly traded companies; and the intense focus on companies' quarterly earnings.

Why will capital markets continue to need both short- and long-term capital?

Capital markets will continue to need short-term capital to provide the liquidity necessary for the smooth functioning of our markets as well as accountability by responsible managers. Long-term capital investment provides the capital to create long-term industries of the future, such as clean energy, advanced technological infrastructure, advances in health technology, and new forms of transportation, among many other uses. As an example, the World Economic Forum sees that by 2020, the world will need an annual investment of $500 billion in order to reduce CO_2 emissions. This investment is usually supported by the long-term investment community by the investments made in bonds that may finance projects and in the stocks of companies developing this technology.

What are some future trends that we can see in the mutual fund business?

Expert authors at Investopedia believe that with the explosion of low-cost ETFs, and the popularity of index funds by the individual investing community, mutual funds will be under pressure to eliminate higher-expense classes of funds in favor of lower-cost investment products in order to survive.

How will mutual fund companies cut costs, in order to compete with ETFs and offer more lower-cost investment products?

Experts at Deloitte believe mutual funds will outsource much of their administrative functions, consolidate their technology platforms, and reassess their physical locations in order to reduce expenses that are passed on to individual investors.

Deloitte Touche Tohmatsu Ltd., the world's largest professional services network, expects mutual funds to outsource administrative functions and consolidate technology platforms to save investors money.

By 2015, how big will the value of the market for ETFs be?

Experts at the Deloitte Center for Financial Services believe the market for ETFs will be at least $2 trillion by 2015.

What is the future of investment advice?

Experts at CNNMoney believe that online discount brokerages will continue to offer advisory services to account holders, in order to continue to compete with traditional, brick-and-mortar investment companies. Individual 401(k) investors will have access to advisory services that will be subsidized by their employers. More than 30 million people use these outside financial services to seek advice today. Many online tools will be available to help individuals model and balance the allocations of their portfolios with a mouse click. Mutual fund companies, discount brokers, and traditional investment companies will continue to compete by offering the very best web-based tools for account holders.

What is the future of sustainable investing (investing in businesses that take into account social factors, clean energy, and corporate governance)?

According to experts at The Motley Fool, citing a study conducted by Mercer for the philanthropic organization Ceres, investment opportunities in such sustainable areas as

305

clean energy and climate adaptation may be worth more than $5 trillion over the next 15 to 20 years. For example, individual companies such as Apple would like to power 100% of their data centers using renewable energy, and are working with many companies to accomplish this goal. Apple currently operates the largest solar array in the United States. Furthermore, the State of California, seen by many to indicate future trends in action, increased its solar installations by 26% during 2012 and 2013.

What future trend can we see in the near term about the cost for discount brokers?

The future trend in the near term is for brokerage firms, both new and old, to greatly reduce their fees. According to investment editors at Thomson Reuters, individual investors will benefit from much lower costs of investing because of two technology trends playing out today: greater use and access to the Internet, and an improvement in investing-related software that enables users to build and analyze what used to be rather complex investment portfolios. New start-up online brokerage firms are beginning to offer super-discounted fees, and now may compete with some of the largest online discount brokerage firms.

What is a trend in the use of social networking in the individual investing industry?

New start-up brokerage firms are offering within their online trading and investing interfaces the ability for individual investors to share information about their own portfolios. This will help to share ideas and information on popular social networking sites.

What is the future trend for socially responsible investing?

As new industries such as clean technology continue to develop and require capital from markets, the entire category of socially responsible investing will continue to grow. According to the Forum for Sustainable and Responsible Investment, capital under management in socially responsible investments grew 22% from 2010 to 2012, and will continue to do so. The number of firms and community-investing organizations involved in socially responsible investing doubled during the same period.

How will the use of benchmarks change how individual investors perceive their financial goals and objectives in the future?

Many individual investors use index-based benchmarks to measure the success of their investment choices and to decide fundamental investment objectives. The future trend, according to experts at *Financial Advisor Magazine*, will be the use of personal benchmarking. Traditional benchmarking uses returns of certain benchmarks to decide an investor's portfolio allocation, diversification, and risk objectives. Personal benchmarking uses the individual investor's personal goals, objectives, and desired returns to achieve these results. Because of the fallout of litigation of advisory and investment firms in 2008 and 2009—in part because of poor returns of recommended portfolios—more firms will continue to support personal benchmarking in the years to come.

INVESTING RESOURCES

INVESTMENT EXPERTS

Why do I need professional guidance when exploring exotic investments such as virtual currency, derivatives, and credit swaps?

There are many reasons why you need to seek professional guidance before you enter exotic investments. Many exotic investments are not transparent, meaning it is quite difficult for you to assess many key attributes of the investment, including how its underlying value is derived, what the demand may be, or even what the returns and risks may be. Exotic investments may also be quite complex, representing business models that require a great deal of expertise to understand what they do or how they create value. You should either avoid these investments entirely or seek the guidance of an expert in this investment area before deciding to invest.

Do brokers have any obligation to monitor the performance of investments they sell?

Brokers are under no obligation to monitor the performance of investments that they sell to you; as long as the investment was good at the time you purchased it, they are under no legal obligation to follow that investment or plot its course for you (although many do advise the best time to buy or sell). You must determine when to buy and sell, even if you use a broker or adviser.

Do brokers know all about the investments they tell me to buy?

Some brokers are well informed about the investments they sell, and are well trained in investment analysis. Some brokers sell clients exotic investments, investments inappropriate for the client's age, or investments that are far too risky without knowing the difference. To avoid this, you must do research to understand what you are investing in, and its potential risks.

307

What should I do if I wish to invest in an area in which my broker is unfamiliar?

Ask him to refer you to another broker who is an expert in this area, and who has the necessary credentials, education, and training to help you invest.

What should I do if my broker suggests an exotic investment?

If the investment is too difficult for you to understand, do not invest your money.

What factors should I consider when choosing a broker or firm in which to invest my money?

Some of the most important considerations include: the training and education of your broker; the fees or commissions on trades, both buying and selling; your broker's track record of performance, especially how well he does during both up and down markets; the firm's reputation; whether there have been any official complaints against the firm; whether the firm is solvent; whether the firm trades directly in the markets; and whether the firm is legitimate.

Does a stockbroker make money on the stocks he directs me to buy?

Stockbrokers are compensated in many ways to direct clients to purchase stocks—they receive commissions, bonuses, even gifts and vacation travel as incentives to purchase and sell stocks. You should ask exactly how your potential broker receives compensation for your trades.

What kind of research do I need to do before investing?

There are hundreds of ways to analyze stocks, but looking at very basic information about a company in several areas is a good way to start. These areas include analyzing a company's financial picture, especially its ability to generate profits consistently, its assets, its debt, and its obligations. You may also look at external factors, such as the company's market, how the company compares to its competitors, past stock performance, and the company's ability to create products or services in high demand.

What are the different distinctions between stockbrokers?

Stockbrokers are generally divided into two categories: regular brokers, who have relationships directly with investor clients; and stockbroker-resellers, who may represent larger brokers and investment companies. Since resellers may be compensated by some of the firms they represent, you should work directly with a regular broker.

What organizations provide accreditation to stockbrokers?

Several different organizations provide membership, training, and accreditation for stockbrokers, so we can be safer while investing. The key organizations include The Financial

Industry Regulatory Authority (FINRA), previously known as the National Association of Securities Dealers (NASD), and the Securities Investor Protection Corporation (SIPC).

What does FINRA do?

FINRA is a private, non-profit company that regulates its member stock brokerage firms and exchange markets, and is the largest independent regulator of securities firms in the United States. Its primary mission is to protect all investors by ensuring integrity within the investing community that now comprises approximately 4,215 securities firms and 633,000 brokers. FINRA is responsible for writing and enforcing rules, examining securities firms to ensure they are complying with those rules, supporting transparency in the markets, assisting investors by providing educational resources, and providing trade reporting. FINRA also administers the Series 7 examination that, when passed, allows brokers to be licensed to trade in securities.

What kind of actions has FINRA taken to protect the investment community?

In 2012, FINRA brought 1,541 disciplinary actions against registered brokers and firms, ordered $34 million in fines paid to harmed investors, and referred 692 cases of fraud and insider trading to the SEC and other U.S. government agencies for prosecution or litigation. FINRA also barred 294 individuals and 549 brokers from any association with member firms, and levied more than $68 million in fines to rule breakers. FINRA also provides an online BrokerCheck tool, that enables investors to check any broker's or securities firm's disciplinary history and professional background.

How many households in America benefit from FINRA's services?

According to its chairman, Richard Ketchum, FINRA helps the investments tied to approximately 53 million households in the United States. FINRA maintains 20 offices across the United States, and has a staff of 3,400 people to support its mission.

What does FINRA recommend that I do in order to begin investing?

FINRA recommends you check the background of anyone providing investment advice, determine your investment goals, evaluate what level of risk you are willing to accept, and understand fully every investment you might make by scrutinizing the investment's offering information, prospectus, regulatory filings, and research information. You

---

What percentage of people believe their stockbroker acts as a fiduciary, exclusively with their best interests in mind, when directing clients to a particular investment or trade?

In a recent study, 66% of all investors thought stockbrokers were, in fact, acting as fiduciaries.

should also fully understand all fees, commissions, loads, and/or service charges associated with an investment.

What does FINRA suggest I do after I have invested to work properly with my investment adviser?

FINRA recommends that you carefully review monthly account statements, order confirmations, and all other information regarding your trading activity. FINRA experts also recommend contacting your investment adviser immediately if you notice a trade you did not authorize, or information you do not fully understand.

FINANCIAL PLANNERS

How many financial planners are there in the United States?

Approximately 300,000 Americans call themselves financial planners.

How many of them are actually certified?

Of the 300,000 financial planners in the United States, only 60,000 have passed the rigorous examinations that allow them to be called "certified financial planners," or CFPs.

What is the difference between a financial planner and an investment adviser?

An investment adviser may offer advice on the many investment choices available to you, both from the company for which he works, as well as other choices outside the firm. A financial planner is a generalist who is experienced at looking at the big picture of your financial health and your entire portfolio (both assets and liabilities). He can guide you on the proper choices that will allow you to reach your short-term and long-term financial goals.

What does a financial planner do?

A financial planner can advise you how best to increase your assets and reduce your debt, help establish an expense budget and savings/investing budget, and help you develop a detailed strategy or financial plan to realize your short- and long-term financial goals.

Why do people seek the advice of financial planners?

People seek the advice of financial planners because they believe there is a sea of

Of the 300,000 financial planners working in the United States today, only 60,000 have been certified. Check to see if they are certified before hiring one.

information available to them and numerous acronyms that need to be learned, as well as many options available—so many that people think it requires much work to manage their portfolios, and they seek investment advice in order to save time. Many people believe they will never become experts in analyzing investment vehicles, and they pay others for this expertise.

What is the difference between stockbrokers, accountants, and insurance brokers?

Stockbrokers are specifically versed in helping clients invest and grow their wealth through purchasing equities and other specific investment instruments. Accountants are able to give advice on taxes and tax strategies that can affect how much you must pay in taxes, what types of tax credits and deductions are available to you, and what you can do to limit your tax exposure in a given year. Insurance brokers are interested in selling policies to you as part of a larger investment strategy. Both stockbrokers and insurance brokers may earn commissions on what they recommend.

Why should I use a financial planner?

If you are too busy to invest the time and energy involved in researching the many financial options available to you, a planner may represent the one-stop source of information that you need. Also, using an outside adviser may help enforce the sort of discipline needed to reach your financial goals, and may help steer you in the right direction.

How important is experience in identifying a financial planner?

It is very important. Many years of experience across a wide variety of clients assures you that a financial planner should be able to give you proper advice.

Are investment advisers or financial planners required to have credentials or certifications?

No state or federal authority requires specific credentials in order to give advice. However, many states do require that people advising clients on financial matters pass some proficiency tests.

How important are certifications when it comes to choosing a financial planner?

Certifications are very important when it comes to choosing a financial planner. They demonstrate that he has gone through the necessary courses, examinations and continuing education, as well as the ethical training involved in the certification process. You should never use a financial planner who does not have such credentials.

How many different financial planning certifications exist?

There are many different designations for financial planners. The most important are Certified Financial Planner (CFP), Chartered Financial Analyst (CFA), Certified Fund

Specialist (CFS), Chartered Financial Consultant (ChFC), and Chartered Investment Counselor (CIC).

What is a "Certified Financial Planner" (CFP)?

CFP holders are tested on their knowledge of over 100 areas of financial planning, including stocks, bonds, taxes, insurance, retirement planning, and estate planning. Candidates for this certification must also complete qualifying work experience, and adhere to the CFP Code of Ethics. The certification is granted by the Certified Financial Planner Board of Standards, Inc.

What is a "Chartered Financial Analyst" (CFA)?

People who hold this certification have passed rigorous examinations, have a minimum of three years' work experience, extensive knowledge in such financial areas as ethics, portfolio management, securities analysis, and accounting, and must demonstrate integrity. The certification is offered by the CFA Institute.

What is a "Certified Fund Specialist" (CFS)?

A certified fund specialist accreditation means the adviser is an expert in mutual funds and the mutual fund industry. He has studied and been tested for his knowledge in portfolio management, dollar cost averaging, and annuities. If he has a license to buy and sell funds, he will also be able to purchase funds on behalf of his clients. The Institute of Business & Finance oversees the accreditation of a CFS.

What is a "Chartered Financial Consultant" (ChFC)?

A Chartered Financial Consultant (ChFC) is an adviser who holds an accreditation from The American College of Financial Services and has successfully completed an examination covering all areas of financial planning, including income tax, insurance, investment, and estate planning. He must have a minimum of 3 years' experience in the financial industry.

What is a "Chartered Investment Counselor" (CIC)?

To be a Chartered Investment Counselor, one must first be accredited as a Certified Financial Analyst. Candidates must study more advanced concepts in portfolio management, adhere to a strict code of ethics, and provide character references.

What is The National Association of Personal Financial Advisors (NAPFA), and why is it an important resource when choosing a financial planner?

NAPFA is the nation's leading organization dedicated to the advancement of fee-only financial planning. This means financial planners who have earned a registration with NAPFA cannot charge clients a commission, and must go through rigorous examinations and continuing education.

Why else are the NAPFA standards so high?

NAPFA also believes it is on the leading edge of standards of education, training, and methods of practice. With these standards, NAPFA can help move people away from debt-crazed, undisciplined, and retirement-poor conditions that beset millions of Americans.

What is a conflict of interest in financial planning?

A conflict of interest occurs when a financial planner may benefit financially from the investment choices he offers you, because those choices may be subjective and biased. Bias occurs when a commissioned financial planner limits the choices offered to you and steers you toward only those financial investments that help him earn commissions.

So should I steer away from considering commission-based financial planners?

You should find an unbiased and objective fee-only planner who does not directly benefit from the ideas and strategies he presents to you.

Can I ask the potential planner if he or his firm has ever been involved in any litigation or disciplinary action?

Yes, you should ask if a potential planner or his firm has ever been involved in any litigation or disciplinary action, and obtain a letter from him stating they have not. You should disqualify any individual or firm that has had any disciplinary action.

How can I check the disciplinary history of a potential financial adviser?

You may check if there has been any disciplinary action taken against either the financial planner or his firm by going to the following websites: Certified Financial Planner Board of Standards, North American Securities Administrators Association, National Association of Insurance Commissioners, FINRA, or the SEC. You may enter the planner's or firm's name and state, and discover whether there have been any actions taken against either.

Should I ask the potential financial planner what services he offers?

Yes, it is important to know the range of services a potential financial planner offers, as well as whether he earns a commission on what he recommends, or if he only works based upon a one-time fee. A financial planner should not be able to offer advice without the proper licenses and registrations from state or federal authorities.

Why should I use a fee-only financial planner?

By using a fee-only financial planner, you remove the financial motivation of a commissioned planner who may be interested in making commissions on his advice, rather than seeking the best solutions for your circumstances.

What about the financial planner's approach? Should it be aggressive or conservative?

If your adviser is getting some financial benefit by recommending particular investments to you, that represents a conflict of interest.

Depending on your life situation and your short- and long-term financial goals, you should match your situation and style with that of your financial planner. It is important for you to discover his approach, and if it matches what you wish to accomplish. It is also important for your adviser to have clients in similar life situations, and a track record of success working with them.

Will the financial planner work with me alone, or with a team of other people?

This is an important question, as you should also check the backgrounds of anyone with whom your financial adviser partners, including his insurance representative, mutual fund company broker, or others whom he may bring on to work with you.

How do financial planners receive compensation?

Financial planners are compensated in many ways. Some charge an hourly fee. Others charge a monthly fee, no matter how much advice they give. Some charge a flat fee to draw up an annual financial plan. Others may charge a percentage of what you actually invest based upon the size of your portfolio. Still others earn a commission or percentage of whatever financial product they sell to you. So you should carefully consider how much you must pay in fees before choosing a financial planner.

Should I ask if the planner is benefiting in other ways by directing me into a certain investment?

Yes, you should ask how else he may be compensated, if he earns a referral fee for selling you a particular mutual fund or insurance policy, and if his company earns something as a result of the referral.

If my financial planner earns a commission, how could that harm me?

If your potential financial planner earns a commission, he may steer you in the direction of purchasing investments that benefit him, not you. You should, therefore, understand how the planner makes his or her money and stay away from those who work on commission.

What if my potential financial planner will not work with me because my portfolio is too small?

This is actually beneficial to you, since the financial planner is telling you that he specializes in higher-net-worth individuals. You should work with a financial planner who specializes in clients similar to you.

How can I determine if my financial planner has a criminal history?

Most states have a free, online criminal history or offender database. Check first with the main website for your state, and run a check to determine if your planner has a hidden criminal past.

What if I find a financial planner who says his clients make huge returns on their investments?

Any planner who boasts about the high rates of return for his clients is probably not telling the truth, and most likely is not suitable for you.

Should I ask my friends for referrals when identifying a potential planner?

Most likely not, since this is the principal way in which fraudulent planners ensnare new, unsuspecting victims. Many people think that by asking friends for advice, they will somehow escape the hard research they must do to identify the best financial planner for them. You should do the research yourself and be diligent in your interviews.

What types of questions might I ask a potential financial planner?

You might ask such questions as:

- Where did you go to school?
- What licenses do you hold?
- Are you registered with the SEC, a state or financial industry regulatory authority?
- Can you recommend only a limited number of products or services, and why?
- If you are a registered investment adviser, can you give me a copy of your Form ADV?

315

Why is a Form ADV important?

The SEC Form ADV is required by all licensed investment advisers who manage more than $25 million. Anyone who manages less than that must register with his state securities regulator. Part one of the form lists the adviser's education, business, and disciplinary history for the past ten years. Part two lists information pertaining to the adviser's fees and investment strategies.

My financial adviser mentioned that he is a fiduciary. What does this mean?

It means that in all circumstances your adviser will put your interests first—above his own, his firm's, or the investment companies he represents. You should ask if your adviser is a fiduciary.

Why is fiduciary responsibility important?

Under the current guidelines established by the SEC, an adviser merely needs to meet the "suitability standard," meaning that advice "needs to be appropriate for the client," rather than "in the client's best interest."

What percentage of people think "financial advisers" employed at a brokerage firm to sell are held to a fiduciary standard?

Seventy-five percent of those surveyed believe these sales reps act with their clients' best interests in mind, when, in fact, they do not.

Do I really need a financial adviser?

It really depends on your unique situation, your time, and the educational resources available to you. Some employers use very large companies to manage their employees' retirement plans, or mutual fund families that offer free advice on financial planning. For some, this information is sufficient to help guide them through the many choices offered in their retirement plans. Other people need more direct control over their portfolios, and wish to work with an adviser as they move toward their financial goals. The decision to use a financial adviser really depends on your own personal needs.

What is discussed in a financial planner's meeting?

A financial plan discussion might include such items as your financial goals (both short- and long-term), your net worth (all of your assets/savings/investments minus all of your liabilities/debts), your monthly budget (your income and expenses), a discussion on how comfortable you are with risk (how much you can afford to lose), and an action plan.

Under what circumstances should I decide to leave my financial adviser?

The decision to leave a financial adviser really depends upon each individual. Some people look at the annual return of their portfolio to make this determination. Others feel the financial planner's advice is too risky or too complex, or they feel he is just moving money around to make commissions on investment trades or sales.

If I use an adviser, does it mean I don't need to learn about investment options?

No. You should be as knowledgeable as possible about investing even if you use an adviser.

What are the biggest mistakes people make when using an adviser?

Not paying attention to the investment, and not being involved enough in the decisions. Your investment adviser must have your consent to make trades, but you need to be well informed in order to decide what to do. You should not blindly follow your adviser; you need to remain engaged and involved.

AVOIDING SCAMS

What does FINRA recommend we do to avoid scams and fraud related to our investments?

In order to avoid becoming a victim of fraud, FINRA recommends that you avoid any investments that have intense sales pitches that make exaggerated claims about the potential for returns and profits. FINRA also recommends that you avoid any investments in which you are pressured to buy by a certain time. Never send money to an individual or firm based upon a telephone call or an e-mail about an investment.

What is "investment fraud"?

Investment fraud, also known as securities fraud, is the practice of trying to deceive a potential investor into buying or selling a security by providing the potential investor with false, misleading, or exaggerated claims pertaining to the investment's return, profit potential, and/or price, among many other practices, in violation of various securities laws. Types of fraudulent activity may include stealing money outright from investors (embezzlement); manipulating a security's price; misstatements or false statements of a security's financial reports; and providing false information to a corporate auditor. They may also include insider trading, whereby someone closely linked to a security attempts to profit from information accessible only within the company. Another type of fraud and abuse may include the creation of a fake or "dummy" corporation, wherein the criminal attempts to sell shares in the fake corporation or investment scheme.

How does the Internet contribute to the prevalence of fraud within the investment community?

The Internet may help contribute to the prevalence of fraud within the investing community by providing sites and addresses where criminals may post information about an investment opportunity on bulletin boards, chat rooms, online communities, "legitimate" Internet advertisements, or e-mail alerts sent to millions of unsuspecting potential investors. The scammers may try to disseminate false information about a stock price in order to persuade thousands of investors to invest, taking the money before closing down the operation.

According to FINRA, what types of conduct within the securities industry are unacceptable?

While there are many rules that regulate and govern the securities industry, FINRA states explicitly that certain acts are prohibited, as they may indicate the existence of some form of fraud or abuse. These prohibited acts include: making unsuitable recommendations to an investor, given his age, financial background, objectives, and experience;

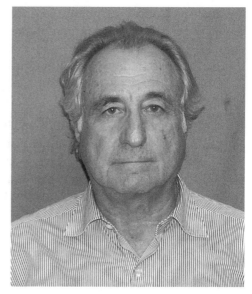

Former stockbroker, adviser, financier, and NASDAQ chairman Bernard Madoff was convicted of fraud in 2009 and sentenced to 150 years in prison for a Ponzi scheme that defrauded investors of billions of dollars.

trading securities in a client's account without being authorized to do so; switching a client from one mutual fund into another for no legitimate purpose; misrepresenting an investment; providing false information about an investment; taking funds from a client's account without his permission; charging excessive fees and commissions to clients; guaranteeing clients that they will not lose money on an investment; doing special deals or transactions without the brokerage firm's knowledge; failure to display limit orders by market makers; failure to be diligent in assuring that an order is executed at the best possible price; buying or selling securities while possessing non-public (inside) information; and manipulating, deceiving, or misleading the investor to effect the purchase or sale of a security.

How can I as an investor avoid fraud and scams while I am engaged in investing?

You may avoid fraud while engaging in investing by being skeptical of stock "tips" and advice posted on various online communities. Also, you should be skeptical about subscribing to or reading "free" investment advice newsletters that may falsify information pertaining to the potential change in a security's price in order to affect the price of that security without proper disclosure about the writer's relationship to that security. You should also ignore various online bulletin boards touting investment ideas, and delete e-mail spam attempting to entice you into parting with your money.

How many complaints does the SEC receive each year?

The SEC receives 82,000 complaints each year, growing at 2.7% per year.

> ## How can I find information on the legitimacy of a stock brokerage firm, and complaints against them?
>
> Visit www.finra.org, which allows you to look up the names of individual firms to see what actions have been taken against them. The SEC maintains a great source of investing information designed to protect investors at www.investor.gov, a portal site to many tools and information that potential investors may use before making an investment.

What are the top complaints individual investors make to the SEC?

The top complaints are liquidation/account closing issues; short selling; theft of funds/securities; manipulation of securities/prices/markets; advance fee fraud; inaccurate or incomplete disclosure of information; retirement/401(k) plan issues; bankruptcy/issuer reorganization; delivery of funds/proceeds; and failure to disclose relevant information about investments.

How can I protect myself from fraud?

Never invest any money in a stock based purely on a tip or advice from a friend, colleague, family member, or trusted source. You must do all the research first, with a very skeptical eye, in order to find a relatively safe place to invest a portion of your portfolio.

Why should I avoid investments with "guaranteed returns"?

According to the SEC, promises of high returns with little or no risk are classic warning signs of fraud.

What does the saying "If it sounds too good to be true, it probably is" mean?

It means that when someone tells you of a guaranteed investment that will give you incredible returns with little risk, it is likely not true. When something sounds too good to be true, be alert to the possibility that there could be fraud involved.

Further Reading

Books for Adults

Carret, Philip L. *The Art of Speculation*. New York: Barron's, 1927.

Cortese, Amy. *Locavesting: The Revolution in Local Investing and How to Profit from It*. Hoboken, NJ: John Wiley, 2011.

Crescenzi, Anthony. *The Strategic Bond Investor: Strategies and Tools to Unlock the Power of the Bond Market*. 2nd edition. New York: McGraw-Hill, 2010.

Falloon, William D. *Charlie D.: The Story of the Legendary Bond Trader*. New York: J. Wiley and Sons, 1997.

Fisher, Philip A. *Common Stocks and Uncommon Profits and Other Writings by Philip A. Fisher*. New York: Wiley, 1996.

Godfrey, Neale S., and Carolina Edwards, with Tad Richards. *Money Doesn't Grow on Trees: A Parent's Guide to Raising Financially Responsible Children*. New York: Simon and Schuster, 2006.

Graham, Benjamin. *The Intelligent Investor: A Book of Practical Counsel*. 4th edition. Harper & Row, 1973.

———, and David Dodd. *Security Analysis: Principles and Technique*. 6th edition. New York: McGraw-Hill, 2009.

Kiyosaki, Robert T. *Rich Dad, Poor Dad: What the Rich Teach Their Kids About Money—That the Poor and the Middle Class Do Not!* New York: Warner Business Books, 2000.

Lefèvre, Edwin. *Reminiscences of a Stock Operator*. Dallas: Books of Wall Street, 1976.

Loeb, Gerald M. *The Battle for Investment Survival*. New York: J. Wiley, 2007.

Lynch, Peter, with John Rothchild. *Beating the Street: The Best-selling Author of One Up on Wall Street Shows You How to Pick Winning Stocks and Develop a Strategy for Mutual Funds*. New York: Simon and Schuster, 1994.

———. *One Up on Wall Street: How to Use What You Already Know to Make Money in the Market*. New York: Simon and Schuster, 2000.

Mackay, Charles. *Extraordinary Popular Delusions and the Madness of Crowds*. Edited by Martin S. Fridson. New York: Wiley, 1996.

Malkiel, Burton Gordon. *A Random Walk Down Wall Street*. New York: Norton, 1985.

Porter, Michael E. *Competitive Strategy: Techniques for Analyzing Industries and Competitors*. New York: Free Press, 1998.

Rothchild, John. *A Fool and His Money: The Odyssey of an Average Investor*. New York: Penguin Books, 1988.

Schwager, Jack D. *Market Wizards: Interviews with Top Traders.* Hoboken, NJ: John Wiley and Sons, 2012.

Smith, Adam. *The Money Game.* New York: Vintage Books, 1976.

Train, John. *Money Masters of Our Time.* New York: HarperBusiness, 2000.

Books for Young Readers

Bateman, Katherine R. *The Young Investor: Projects and Activities for Making Your Money Grow.* Chicago: Chicago Review Press, 2010.

Harman, Hollis Page. *Money $ense for Kids.* Hauppauge, NY: Barron's, 2004.

Holyoke, Nancy. *A Smart Girl's Guide to Money: How to Make It, Save It, and Spend It.* Illustrated by Ali Douglass. Middleton, WI: American Girl Library, 2006.

Karlitz, Gail, and Debbie Honig's *Growing Money: A Complete Investing Guide for Kids.* New York: Price Stern Sloan, 2010.

Mayr, Diane. *The Everything Kids' Money Book: From Saving to Spending to Investing—Learn All about Money!* Holbrook, MA: Adams Media, 2000.

Magazines, Newspapers, and Journals

The Economist, www.economist.com.
Financial Analyst Journal, http://www.cfapubs.org/loi/faj.
Financial Times, www.ft.com/home/uk.
Forbes, www.forbes.com.
Fortune, www.fortune.com.
Inc., www.inc.com.
Investor's Business Daily, www.investors.com.
Kiplinger, www.kiplinger.com.
The New York Times, www.nytimes.com.
The Wall Street Journal, www.wsj.com.

Websites

Bloomberg, http://www.bloomberg.com.
Business Insider, http://www.businessinsider.com.
CNN Money, money.cnn.com.
FT Alphaville, http://ftalphaville.ft.com.
Google Finance, www.google.com/finance/.
Gurufocus, www.gurufocus.com.
King World News, www.kingworldnews.com.
MarketWatch, www.marketwatch.com.
Mauldin Economics, www.mauldineconomics.com.
Minyanville, http://www.minyanville.com.
Mish's Global Economic Trend Analysis, globaleconomicanalysis.blogspot.com.
The Motley Fool, www.fool.com.
MSN Money, money.msn.com.
The Street, www.thestreet.com.
Yahoo! Finance, finance.yahoo.com.
Zero Hedge, http://www.zerohedge.com.

Glossary

401K Plan—a corporate retirement plan that allows employees to set aside a certain percentage of their income, taxes deferred up to a limit, and withdraw from this account when they retire.

403B Plan—a retirement plan that is similar to a 401K retirement plan, except it is open to public education employees and employees of certain types of nonprofit organizations.

529 Plan—a retirement plan designed to make higher education more affordable for families by helping parents save for college or prepay college and university tuition for their children. Also called a Qualified Tuition Plan.

Adjustable rate mortgage—a loan that offers a fixed-rate of interest for a short period, usually 3, 5, or 7 years. At that point, the interest rate may change up or down, depending on what index is associated with the interest rate.

Appraisal—when your bank or mortgage company inspects the house to see if the amount of money that you wish to loan equals what they see as the value of the house.

Asset—tangible or intangible economic resource, which, when given a monetary value, has the potential to produce value.

Asset allocation strategy—a strategy adopted by many investors in which they buy and invest in a mix of investments that are believed to achieve the highest return for whatever level of risk with which they are most comfortable.

Asset income multiple—the product of an equation in which one divides net assets for such items as retirement by one's current income.

Back-end ratio—the sum of one's total monthly housing costs and all other debts divided by monthly gross income.

Bank—a financial institution that is licensed by the government to provides a variety of financial services, such as accounts in which to save, including savings accounts, retirement accounts like IRAs and 401(k)s, certificates of deposit, and spending accounts like checking accounts, debit cards, and ATM cards to make transactions.

Bear market—a period of time when the prevailing stock prices are trending downward by more than 20% for two months or more.

Behavioral economics—a new science that tries to help us understand why people make often irrational financial decisions because of their own perceptions and biases.

Beta—the result of a mathematical equation that measures the volatility of a stock or mutual fund when compared with some benchmark such as other stocks or funds of similar qualities or some benchmark index; it measures how the price of a stock or mutual fund might react to changes in the price of a benchmark.

Blended funds—mutual funds that invest by combing value stocks and growth stocks, which reduces the investors risk over time.

Blue chip stock—stocks that are nationally recognized as being issued by stable, profitably growing companies capable of weathering financial downturns. They are also publicly traded companies, usually very large ones, that may be distributing profits in the form of dividends for many years.

Bond—a financial instrument or debt security that is issued by governments (local, state, and federal), as well as corporations, large and small, that offer fixed-interest payments over a period of time greater than a year. The issuer of the bond promises to pay the bond buyer a specific and stated interest rate during the life of the bond and to repay the face value of the bond when the bond becomes due or reaches maturity.

Budget—the established limit of the amount of expected expenses during a defined future period.

Bull market—a period of time—usually averaging 2.7 years—during which there are more buyers than sellers of stocks, causing overall stock prices to rise; investor confidence is high in anticipation of rising prices, and investments increase over time.

Capital assets—everything that an individual owns and uses for personal and investment purposes.

Capital gain—the positive difference between your cost basis, or what you paid for an asset, and the sales price.

Capitalization weighted index—a market index that uses the market capitalization (the current value of all stock outstanding) and gives proportionate weight to these stocks in relation to the total market capitalization of the index.

Capital loss—when the sale price of an asset is less than the price paid for the asset when first purchased.

Cap rate—used by many real estate investors to understand the amount of income generated compared with the amount of cash used to acquire the investment. It is computed by taking the net operating income assumptions and dividing this number by the cost of purchase, expressed as a percentage.

Cash account—an account used by investors to pay for the full cost of acquiring or selling securities.

Cash cushion—a special savings in which enough money to cover expenses for three months to a year is kept; a "rainy day" fund.

Cash flow—how much money is flowing into (on the revenue side) and flowing out of (on the expense side) a corporation; its analysis is often a key metric in understanding whether or not a company is doing well.

C Corporation—shareholders exchange money, property, or both, for the corporation's capital stock, which is either initially issued when the corporation is formed, or at different times during the year, according to the company's laws and shareholder agreements.

Certificates of deposit—a type of interest-bearing savings account that may hold a certain amount of money for a specific amount of time ranging from six months to five years.

Closed-ended mutual fund—a type of mutual fund that offers a fixed number of shares on a public exchange during its initial public offering, and then is listed on an exchange with the price of the shares determined by the supply and demand for shares in that fund, as well as the underlying value of the stocks in the portfolio of the fund. These tend to be sector funds, or funds that seek to invest in specific aspects of the economy.

Closed mutual fund—a mutual fund that limits the inflow of new capital into the fund because the number of investors and portfolio value is of a certain size.

Collective investment fund—any investment that groups together individuals to enter into investments in order to benefit more than investing individually.

Commodity—a marketable or saleable item that is produced without many differences across a market with very little brand differentiation and with little concern for precisely where the item was produced.

Comparables—houses that are physically similar to a certain house on the market and that are in a specific radius of distance from the target house and have sold in the recent past. Comparables are used to calculate a "fair market price" for the house one is selling.

Concentration—when capital is invested in just a few investment classes or one class.

Conference Board—a nonprofit organization that releases authoritative research and reports on the state of the economy.

Consumer Price Index—created and published monthly by the U.S. Bureau of Labor Statistics, it represents data collected on the prices paid by urban consumers for a representative sample of a market basket of many goods and services in order to gauge the changes in prices over time.

Contents insurance—a type of insurance that pays for loss or damage to possessions on the premises of your home-based business.

Corporate bonds—corporations issue bonds in order to raise capital to fund projects, instead of issuing new stock to raise capital. Corporate bonds come in several forms, depending on the maturity: short term (less than five years), intermediate term (five to twelve years), and long-term (over twelve years).

Correction—occurrence in the stock markets when the trends of indexes show a decline in the prices of 10–20% over a short period of time (from one day to fewer than two months).

Correlation—two outcomes that are similar in reaction to some event or market condition.

Cost basis—the amount of money used to purchase an item or asset.

Coupon payment—when a bond issuer pays the bond buyer interest periodically on a bond investment during the term of the bond.

Credit card—a card issued by a company that allows the users to borrow money, with interest, from the card issuer in exchange for paying in full the provider of the good or service.

Credit counselor—a person employed by a credit counseling agency whose job is to help the client understand how spending and misuse of credit has created debt; such counselors should guide clients toward solutions to reduce debt and improve their overall financial situation.

Credit risk—the risk associated with investments for which a company is unable to pay its debt obligation.

Credit union—a credit union is a nonprofit institution that provides many of the same financial services as traditional banks, including allowing members to hold deposits, clear checks against checking account deposits, and obtain credit in the form of loans.

Curb appeal—the impression that a house makes to buyers first see a house from the street.

Custodial account—an account that is opened in the name of a child, but the main signatory and responsible party on the account is the child's custodian, usually a parent.

Cyclical investment—any investment that is highly correlated to some chronic economic event, condition, or pattern.

Cyclical stocks—stocks that signal recovery after a period of economic decline, since they tend to begin to grow early when a recovery is underway.

Dalian Commodity Exchange—the largest mainland China commodities exchange, founded in 1993.

Day trading—the action or strategy of buying and selling securities of all types, and holding the securities for seconds, minutes or hours, in order to profit from miniscule price movements during the session, often trading in and out of a security inside of a day.

Debit card—a card issued by a bank that allows the user to withdraw funds or purchase goods and services by immediately debiting the card holder's bank account for the purchase.

Debt consolidation—the act of taking out a loan in order to pay off several others loans or financial obligations.

Deductible—the amount of money that the insured must pay toward a loss in order to collect on a claim.

Debt consolidator—someone who is hired to look at a client's debt situation and create strategies designed to pay off the debt.

Debt equity ratio—measures how leveraged a company is and how wisely the company is using debt in order to finance its operations. It is calculated by taking the company's total liabilities (both short and long term) and dividing this number by the value of shareholder's equity.

Default risk—the risk associated with investments in which the company is unable to pay its debt obligation.

Depreciating asset—an asset that loses value over time.

Derivative—a sellable or tradable financial product or investment vehicle that derives its price from an underlying product or investment vehicle.

Direct Stafford Loans—low interest loans for eligible students to help defray the costs of undergraduate education at a four-year college or university, community college, or a trade/career/technical school. Money is borrowed directly from the U.S. Department of Education at all participating schools.

Disability insurance—a type of insurance policy that covers the insured for temporary or permanent loss of income, enabling one to continue earning income for a period of time as specified in the policy.

Discretionary expense—an expense incurred by choice rather than obligation.

Diversification—the act of making investments in different categories with the hope and expectation that the risk of losing money is spread out or diversified within the portfolio, thus reducing the overall risk of losing money on the whole portfolio.

Dividend—a product of the distributions of profits or earnings of a company to shareholders of record.

Dollar cost averaging—a simple timing strategy of investing in which an investor buys the same dollar amount of a stock at regular intervals (say, $100.00 per month of a certain stock).

Dow Jones Industrial Average—a price-weighted average of thirty blue chip stocks that are traded on the New York Stock Exchange; it is often seen as a barometer for the health of U.S. stock markets.

327

Down market—when average prices are falling relative to some baseline measure.

Down payment—the initial amount paid on the purchase of a home whenever the entire cost of the home is not paid up front.

EBIT—earnings before interest and taxes; it is used as a metric to understand a company's financial position and considers cash flow and net income or profits and the company's earnings before the company accounts for items like the payments of taxes and interest expenses to finance various aspects of an operation. To compute EBIT, take the revenue of a company and subtract its expenses; then add back the interest paid, as well as taxes paid, in order to get a clearer picture of the company's earnings.

EBITDA—earnings before interest, taxes, depreciation, and amortization; the net income of a company, with interest charges, depreciation, and amortization added back into the equation.

Educational grant—money given to a student that does not need to be repaid.

Effective tax rate—the amount of tax paid divided by the amount of income made in any tax year.

Equalized value—the value of your property after assessment, which is then adjusted so that all similar properties are equally and uniformly assessed.

Errors and omissions insurance—A type of insurance policy used by people in the service and consulting businesses; it covers the insured from claims arising from a client who holds such company or an individual responsible for a service that did not provide the agreed-upon results.

Exchange-traded—often abbreviated ETF, it is an investment vehicle or security that behaves like a stock in that it can be regularly traded on any number of exchanges, but specifically tracks an index or indices, commodities, bonds, or other assets. Its daily price may change during the trading day, as its shares are constantly being bought and sold by investors, so its net asset value is not calculated on a daily basis like a mutual fund.

Expense ratio—the total amount of expenses divided by the average net asset value of the portfolio of stocks that comprise the fund, expressed as a percentage.

FAFSA—the Free Application for Federal Student Aid covers all types of student aid, from grants, loans, and work-study, to non-federal aid; all U.S. college and university students must fill out this form to apply for financial aid.

FDIC—The Federal Deposit Insurance Corporation was set up in 1933, during the Great Depression, to fight the effects of the thousands of bank failures that happened in the years preceding. It protects depositors up to $250,000 per account holder at each institution, and guarantees this amount for every depositor at every FDIC-insured institution in the United States.

Federal funds interest rate—the price that the Federal Reserve charges member institutions for borrowing money.

Federal Perkins Loan—a low-interest (5%) loan made available through the educational institution's financial aid office to undergraduate and graduate students who have demonstrated exceptional financial need.

FHA mortgage—A loan backed by The Federal Housing Administration that provides mortgage insurance through FHA-approved lenders; often used by first-time home-owners because the loans require a smaller down payment than conventional mort-gages. FHA loans require the borrower to pay mortgage insurance for five years, or when the loan-to-value ratio is at 78%, whichever is longer.

Fiduciary—a legal or ethical trust between a client and an adviser, who must then put the client's interests before his or her own or the interests of the company for which he or she works.

Fixed-rate mortgage—a mortgage that has a fixed interest rate for the period of the loan, and that allows the purchaser to pay off the loan over a period of time, which is usu-ally 10, 15, 20, or 30 years; sometimes it's as much as 40 to 50 years.

Flexible-spending account—allows consumers to set aside money in an account to be used for medical expenses during the plan year, plus 2 months, free from payroll taxes.

Form ADV—a form required by the Securities and Exchange Commission for all li-censed investment advisers who manage more than $25 million. Part one of the form lists the adviser's education, business, and disciplinary history for the past ten years. Part two lists information pertaining to the adviser's fees and investment strategies.

Front-end ratio—total monthly housing cost divided by gross monthly income.

FSEOG—the Federal Supplemental Educational Opportunity Grant makes educational grants for students with exceptional financial need; grants range between $100 and $4,000 per academic year.

Full employment—the economic condition in which there exists no cyclical deficiency in the number of people required to sustain the economy.

Fundamental analysis—the analysis of the effects of various economic indicators and fi-nancial statements that have influenced or may influence the prices of stocks in finan-cial markets.

Futures price—the agreed-upon price of a commodity future contract; often called the strike price.

Gearing—when a fund borrows money against the assets of the fund in order to create capital that is used to invest. Another word for gearing is leveraging.

General liability insurance—a type of insurance that covers a business operator from gen-eral claims of liability or injury due to negligence; it protects against claims as the result of bodily injury, property damage, medical expenses, libel, slander, the costs of defending lawsuits, and settlement bonds or judgments required during an appeal procedure.

Goodwill—the assigned value of a company's intangible assets, including brand equity, outstanding customer relations, good employee relations, patents, and any proprietary technology.

Government bond—an interest-generating security, issued by a government, that promises to pay the investor a specified sum of money on a specific date.

Growth funds—mutual funds that invest in stocks that have high potential for growth in their profits and share price.

Growth stocks—stocks that have had, and may continue to have, good track records for growing revenues, profits, and market share, even as larger economic forces may depress the performance of other similar companies.

Hardship distributions—when a participant in a 401(k) plan has an immediate and heavy financial need to access the retirement plan account in order to satisfy that need.

Health savings account—a medical savings account that offers consumers a tax advantage, since they pay no federal income taxes at the time of deposit for the funds that are deposited. The money can be used to pay for health expenses, normally out-of-pocket expenses and co-pays related to medical care.

Hedge fund—a collective investment, similar to a mutual fund, that tries to make positive returns on invested capital, regardless of whether or not the markets are rising or falling, by employing a specific strategy and making investments around this strategy, but this strategy may rapidly change as the markets change.

Home equity—the current market value of a home, minus any mortgages or liens on the home.

Home equity conversion mortgage—another name for a reverse mortgage, a financial product for people aged 62 and older who have significant home equity and are able to pull out this equity in the form of a mortgage; the bank pays the homeowner a lump sum, monthly checks, or gives a line of credit up to the amount of equity that the homeowner has in the house.

Home equity line of credit—similar to a home equity loan, except that the lender gives the homeowner the opportunity to use all or part of the amount of accrued equity in a principal residence, in the form of credit, over a certain period of time.

Home equity loan—a loan that is financed by a bank, which allows one to receive a lump sum cash payment for the value of the equity that has accrued in a house, or leverage the accrued equity of a principal residence.

Index funds—an investment vehicle that purchases a share in each of the stocks that comprise a certain index—like the S&P 500 or Dow Jones Industrials—and seeks to mimic the returns that the index may obtain.

Individual investor—each individual person who directly or indirectly purchases stocks or bonds and invests in the market on his or her own account.

Insider trading—when corporate insiders (officers, directors, and employees) buy and sell stock in their own companies and must report their trades to the SEC.

Inspection—a physical assessment of a house, prior to purchase, in order to let the buyer know of all of the faults of the house, as well as an exhaustive list of all items that need to be repaired.

Institutional investor—large organizations that pool money together from other large organizations and individuals and invest this money in companies, both private and public.

Intangible assets—non-physical assets that can be patents that have been applied for, the name of the company, and its brand identity and logos, trademarks, or experience of the employees and management team.

Interest-only loan—a loan that allows a person to pay only the interest on a loan for a period of time. At the end of this period, the borrower must make a balloon payment on the value of the entire loan, or refinance the loan into a conventional loan.

Interest rate—the price of using some entity's money for a period of time, or the price of money that one uses to acquire goods and services.

Investing—the act of using money to buy a financial product with the expectation of making more money than what was used to initially buy the financial product over a period of time.

IPO—an initial public offering, which is when a company wishes to offer shares in the company to the public in hopes of raising capital for the first time.

IRA—An individual retirement account gives individuals who do not have access to an employer-sponsored retirement plan the means to having one; it gives individuals the ability to preserve the IRA's tax advantages and growth opportunities just like a corporate retirement plan.

Irrevocable—An account that cannot be changed. The person to whom one originally created the account must remain the same, and cannot be reversed.

KLD 400 Social Index—an index consisting of top, socially responsible mutual funds.

Laddering—is a strategy of staging the maturity dates of bonds in order to maintain fluidity of a portfolio.

Lagging economic indicator—an economic indicator that may capture what is or has been happening in an economy from a few months to a few quarters after a change has occurred.

Leading economic indicator—a statistic that one can use to illuminate the overall health of the activity of an economic system.

Level load—a fee paid for a mutual fund that is dependent upon how long the investor has held shares in the fund.

Leverage—borrowing money against assets in order to create capital that is then used to invest.

Leveraged buyout—when investors use a percentage of the target company's current cash flow in order to obtain loans to acquire the company at an agreed-upon valuation.

Life insurance—a contract between the insured and the insurance company in which, in exchange for premiums paid by the insured (at regular intervals, or one lump sum), the insurance company will pay out the value of the insurance policy at the end of the life of the insured to his or her beneficiary.

Life stage investments—investments in mutual funds or other investment vehicles where, as the investor ages, the portfolio gradually shifts from one that is predominantly in the form of equities of varying types and risk factors to a portfolio that may be predominantly in the form of bonds of varying types and risk factors. Also known as life cycle investments.

Limit order—allows an investor to buy or sell a stock at a specific price.

Lipper—is a financial research firm, owned by Thomson Reuters, that was founded in 1973. Lipper tracks the performance of over 213,000 share classes, and more than 117,000 funds, in sixty countries.

Lipper Average—are several indices that include actively managed funds, divided into various categories, like large capitalization growth funds or small capitalization growth funds.

LLC—a limited liability company, a business structure that is allowed to exist by state statute and provides limited liability to its owners in most U.S. jurisdictions; it does not need to be organized for profit.

Loaded funds—these are mutual funds that charge a fee for purchasing or selling shares in the fund. They typically have the highest expenses associated with them and are offered by brokers, who may then get paid commissions on your transactions.

Loan origination fee—fees or points that lenders charge for a fixed-fee mortgage, with 1 point representing 1% of the loan amount.

Loan-to-value ratio—the loan amount divided by the selling price of the house.

Longevity risk—the risk that we are living longer than people used to and therefore need more money for retirement.

Long position—the purchase of an equity in expectation that the equity will increase in value, thus generating a profit.

Long-term capital gain—profit gained from the sale of an investment asset that has been owned for more than one year.

Loss—when related business expenses exceed the amount of income reported by the business entity during a filing year.

Margin—an amount of money in cash used to clear differences in price between the future price of a contract and the current or daily price, as it changes, up to the time when the future contract is settled.

Margin account—an account used by investors who are able to borrow a percentage of money against the value of their account for the purposes of acquiring securities.

Market index—a collection of stocks, or grouping of stocks, that tracks the price performance and performance of this selection of stocks.

Market order—an order to purchase or sell a stock at the best available price.

Market Risk—is the risk of an investor in incurring losses due to movements in the prices in the securities that the investor is considering.

Matching program—employers match a percentage of what employees put into their 401(k)s, as long as they set aside a certain minimum amount each year, with a limit on the amount per year.

Medicare—the U.S. government's medical insurance available to people of retirement age.

Mei Moses Family of Fine Art Indexes—provides information on the historical performance of the global fine art market as a distinctive asset (investment) class, developed from the analysis of the purchase and sale price of over 30,000 works of art that have sold at public auction more than one time.

Millage—the number of tax dollars that property owners must pay per $1,000 of taxable value of their property. Also called a tax rate or mill levy.

MLS—multi list service, an electronic database of every property for sale nationwide.

Money Market Fund—allows investors to pool their capital resources together to acquire assets that would provide a better return than an interest-bearing cash account at a bank. Money market funds maintain a stable net asset value of $1.00 per share and are able to pay dividends to shareholders. The principal types of money market funds are ones that invest in government securities, tax exempt municipal securities, corporate securities, or a combination of these. Most of the securities held in a money market fund are short term in duration, primarily comprising debt-based securities, like U.S. Treasury bills and short-term commercial debt.

Morningstar—a financial analytical firm providing research services worldwide; founded in 1984, it currently tracks the performance of 437,000 investment vehicles, including stocks, bonds, and mutual funds, and provides real-time data on more than 10 million equities, indexes, futures, options, commodities, and precious metals, in addition to foreign exchange and treasury markets.

Mortality risk—the risk of dying earlier than expected.

Mortgage—the amount of money loaned from a bank, which is the agreed-upon price of the house that is purchased, and financed by the bank in the form of a loan to the buyer, less any down payment and closing costs at the closing of the transaction.

Mortgage fraud—a crime committed in order to secure or grant a mortgage, usually falling in two categories: misrepresenting information on a mortgage application or appraisal-related misrepresentation.

Mortgage insurance—a type of insurance that protects lenders from losses if a mortgage is not paid off in full.

Multiple—A ratio that measures the price of a stock relative to its earnings per share. A company with a PE ratio of 15 is also called "trading at a multiple of 15," meaning that someone who buys this stock is willing to pay $15.00 for every dollar of earnings, or a multiple of earnings.

Municipal bonds—a debt instrument issued and used by local municipalities in order to raise capital to fund the building of capital-intensive projects like water systems, road improvement, or to build a new school, etc.

Mutual fund—a professionally managed investment vehicle that pools the funds from many investors and collectively invests these funds in stocks, bonds, cash instruments, commodities, other mutual funds, real estate, and many other types of investment instruments that enable the investors to gain or lose from the performance of the fund.

Net investment income tax—a tax that applies a rate of 3.8% to specific net investment income of individuals, estates, and trusts that have annual incomes above certain threshold amounts, ranging from $125,000 to $200,000.

Net worth—the value of all of a person's assets, including cash, after tax, stocks and bonds, mutual funds, retirement accounts, including IRAs and 401Ks, home equity, precious metals (like gold, silver), minus all liabilities, which may include car loans, mortgages, credit card debts, student loans, significant health-related expenses, and any other financial obligations.

No-load mutual funds—mutual funds that do not charge any fee to investors for purchasing or selling (redeeming) shares of that fund.

Online trading—the buying and selling of securities using the Internet or some other electronic method.

Open-ended fund—a mutual fund that has no restrictions on the number of shares it issues to the public, and whose managers continuously buy and sell shares of its portfolio of stocks to both new and current investors.

Option—grants the investor the right, but not the obligation, to buy an investment vehicle—stocks, bonds, stock indexes, commodities, or currencies, among many other choices of possible investments—at a defined date in the future based upon a current contractual valuation of the price.

Overdraft—a withdrawal from an account for an amount in excess of what the current balance is; a fee is typically charged for each overdraft.

Participant directed—an employee can choose from a variety of stocks, mutual funds, and bond funds, as well as the company's own stock (if the company is publicly traded or makes stock available to employees), and invest a sum of money before taxes each pay period, with the money going toward retirement.

Partnership—a business structure between two or more persons who team up to carry on a trade or business, contributing money, property, labor, or skills, and expecting to share in the profits and losses of the business.

Pell Grant—money awarded to undergraduate students who have not yet earned a bachelor's or professional degree; it can be used in conjunction with other forms of financial aid up to a maximum amount of $5,500 based upon financial need.

Performance—the appreciation of the current assets of a mutual fund, plus the reinvestment of the earnings of the portfolio, less any fees related to this activity over time.

Personal capital asset—Nearly everything that you have purchased and use for personal purposes is a capital asset. It could be an individual stock, the value of your rental house, etc.

Personal finance—the management of income, expenses, and investments to reach personal financial goals.

PLUS Loan—enables parents of dependent students to seek financial aid in the form of a low-interest loan to help fund their dependent's education.

Points—loan origination fees that lenders typically charge for a fixed-fee mortgage, with 1 point usually being 1% of the loan amount.

Portfolio—a mixture of investments of different types and risks held by an individual, investment company, or mutual fund in hopes of making more money.

Pre-approved—when a lender has already investigated the client's credit worthiness and has established that the client can borrow up to a certain amount from the lender.

Preferred stock—stocks or equities issued by a company that combine some qualities of a common stock with some qualities of a bond.

Premiums—the amount paid each month for insurance coverage.

Pre-paid credit card—a credit card that allows consumers to add a small amount of money to the account and then use the card to pay for goods and services until that amount runs out.

Pre-qualified—the bank or mortgage company has looked at the borrower's income and debt to determine the approximate amount of the loan. It does not necessarily mean that the borrower has been approved for a loan.

335

Pre-tax dollars—the contributions to a retirement plan that are made before paying taxes on the amount of the contribution as income.

Price-earnings ratio (PE)—the current price of a stock divided by the amount of earnings per share.

Price-earnings-to-growth (PEG) ratio—the PE of a company divided by its annual earnings per share growth rate.

Price-to-book ratio—a ratio that describes what the investment community is spending to own a share of the stated value of a company's hard assets, less such intangibles as goodwill.

Principal—the face value of the loan or bond or the original loan amount, which is what is used to calculate interest payments. The principal and the accrued interest is what an investor receives when a bond is due or matures.

Private capital—capital used to support private equity investments.

Private equity—an asset class or investment vehicle in which an investor purchases all or part of a company's equity or stock and debt or obligations, using this capital to either assist in the expansion, development of new initiatives, continuation of profitable initiatives, restructuring of the company to improve profitability, or to improve the value of the company for later sale or merger.

Product liability insurance—a type of insurance that will cover lawsuits that arise from injuries or damages caused by a product and its use or misuse.

Professional liability insurance—a type of insurance that protects professionals—like architects, accountants, and lawyers—from injuries or damages caused by the services that they provide; it may be available through the professional association or society to which the professional belongs.

Property tax—the taxes levied on the value of a residence, with the proceeds used to finance local services, education, operational costs for the city and county, and the financing of special projects like sewers, streets, and parks, and, depending on the state, certain state services, as well.

Prospectus—a document, sometimes known as an offering document or official statement, that provides an explanation as to an investment's terms, features, and risks that all investors need to know before entering into the investment.

Qualified Tuition Plan—see 529 Plan.

Real Estate Investment Trust (REIT)—a company that may own or operate, by way of direct investment, a portfolio of income-generating real estate properties.

Renter's insurance—a policy that covers the loss incurred by the tenants in the building for their damaged or stolen possessions.

Rent-to-income ratio—a test of the affordability of housing that is computed by taking monthly rent and dividing it by your monthly income.

Retirement calculator—an interface that is widely available on many financial websites that allows you to input important variables— your income, how much money you have in retirement savings, your expected social security income—and see whether you are on track to save enough for a comfortable retirement.

Reverse mortgage—a financial product for people aged 62 and older, and who have significant home equity, to be able to pull out this equity in the form of a mortgage; the bank pays the homeowner a lump sum, monthly checks, or extends a line of credit for the amount of equity that the homeowner wishes.

Reverse stock split—when a company decides to consolidate its outstanding shares by doubling the price of each share, but cutting the amount of shares in half.

Risk—a quantifiable, probabilistic number that compares what an investment's actual return was with what was expected.

Risk/return trade-off—the principle that the higher the level of uncertainty as to the potential return, the higher the reward, and the investment with a relatively predictable, low level of uncertainty will have a lower return.

Risk/reward ratio—a comparison of the expected returns of any investment with the amount that the investor could lose with the same investment.

ROI—the return on the investment, usually expressed as a percentage; it refers to how much more money is made over a period of time as a result of buying an investment; expressed as a percentage.

Roth IRA—an individual retirement account; contributions are made with after-tax dollars, so money put into the Roth is not taxed again when it is withdrawn after retirement.

Sales tax—a tax levied by states on the sale of goods and services.

Savings—the act of putting aside a portion of money, liquid and accessible, after all consumption expenditures, for future use.

Schedule A—a tax form used in conjunction with form 1040 that is used to report itemized deductions for the tax year, including medical and dental expenses, taxes paid to state authorities, city taxes, charitable gifts, and interest paid on loans such as mortgage interest.

Schedule B—a tax form used in conjunction with form 1040 used to report the receipt of more than $1,500 in interest income from banks or credit unions, as well as interest from a bond, unless the bond is tax exempt.

S Corporations—corporations that, under their bylaws, elect to pass corporate income, losses, deductions, and credit through to their shareholders for federal tax purposes.

Second mortgage—see home equity loan.

Sector/specialty funds—mutual funds that invest in companies that are in various specific sectors of our economy, such as healthcare, manufacturing, oil and gas, financial services, information technology, bioengineering, internet, etc. Because of their specificity, these funds tend to have higher risks, but they also offer higher rewards.

Secured bond—a bond that is issued and backed by some form of collateral.

SEP IRA—a simplified employee pension plan, which allows employees and small business owners the ability to save for their retirement. It allows employers to contribute into each employee's SEP IRA account up to 25% of the employee's annual earnings. The employee may also contribute to this account, and all contributions are tax deductible.

Shadow inventory—the inventory of houses that most likely will move into foreclosure, thus increasing the supply of houses and depressing house prices.

Share buybacks—the purchasing back of outstanding shares from the open market.

Short-term capital gain—the profit gained from the sale of a capital asset that has been held for less than one year.

Small Business Administration—the SBA provides many financial assistance programs (loans, grants, venture capital, and bonds) to help small business owners become successful.

Socially responsible funds—mutual funds that invest in stocks of companies that do no harm to the world, the environment, or its people. Companies in the fields of renewable energy and recycling are two examples, as well as companies in general that are environmentally conscientious.

Sole proprietorship—an unincorporated business structure owned by one person.

S&P Case Shiller Home Price Index—an index that tracks repeat sales of houses in many markets, allowing for comparisons in the prices of houses and how these prices may change over time.

Speculation—when someone buys a share of an asset, believing that the market value of the share of this asset may rise, holds it for some period of time, and then sells it to someone else at a higher value.

SPIVA—the Standard and Poor's Indices Versus Active Funds Scorecard, a research study that is published every six months that measures the performance of actively managed U.S. equity funds, international equity funds, and fixed-income funds.

Spot market—a financial market in which financial instruments—such as currencies or commodities like gold, copper, petroleum, etc.—are traded by investors, with an obligation for immediate delivery of the financial instrument or commodity.

Staging—the act of changing the furnishings, either by buying, renting, or rearranging the layout of each room, in order to present a house for sale in the best possible manner.

Standard deduction—a deductible amount for people who do not itemize their deductions that is subtracted from income in order to compute the tax liability for the filing year.

Stock market—a place, whether a physical building or an online virtual environment, where stocks are bought and sold.

Stockout—when the available, tradable inventory of a commodity is exhausted and is out of stock.

Stocks—a way of owning the assets and earnings of a company. Companies that offer the opportunity for investors to own stock in the company place a value in the shares or pieces of the company based upon the value of all of the assets of the company and the value of the past, current, and future earnings of the company. A stock can be purchased, sold, or traded.

Stock split—when a publicly traded company decides to divide its outstanding stocks in half, or split, doubling the number of shares outstanding, while cutting the price of the shares in half.

Stop-loss order—also called a stop price, it is the point when one determines to buy or sell a stock at specific price.

Style box—a graph with sectors that display the different types of investment styles or characteristics of typical mutual funds.

Systematic risk—the risk associated with broad events that affect the entire market or market sector and cannot be mitigated through diversification.

Tangible assets—physical buildings, property, factories, stock of products sitting in a warehouse, stocks, or cash sitting in a bank.

Tax-cost ratio—a measurement of how tax efficient a mutual fund is. Since mutual funds, through their trading activity, are regularly distributing stock dividends, bond dividends, interest payments, and short/long term capital gains to investors, taxes must be paid by the investors in the fund for each filing year. The tax-cost ratio measures the amount of a fund's return that is lost due to taxes that have to be paid on capital gains distributions made by the fund.

Tax credit—an item that allows you to reduce the taxes that you must pay; it is generally more valuable to you than a tax deduction.

Tax deduction—an item that reduces taxable income that is used to compute the amount of taxes owed at the end of the year.

Tax-exempt bonds—bonds issued by a municipal, county, or state government with interest payments that are not subject to any state, local, or sometimes federal taxes, depending on the bonds and the state or municipality.

Tax preparer—a professional who prepares tax filings for a fee. They usually have had formal training, may have their own practice, or work at one of the nationwide tax preparation chains.

Tax schedule—a rate sheet used by individual taxpayers to approximate their estimated taxes due. It is also a term used to describe the addendum worksheets that accompany IRS Form 1040, and include Schedules A (itemized deductions), B (dividend & interest income), C (business profit or loss), and D (capital gains).

Technical analysis—a method of understanding the patterns and trends of the price of stocks; accurate analysis can lead to profit by learning from these trends.

Term life insurance—a type of insurance in which the insured is covered for a certain period of time or term, usually 10 or 20 years; benefits go to a beneficiary if the insured person dies within that time period.

Theoretical risk-free investment—the return that an investment may bring from an investment that carries no risk.

Ticker symbol—a unique series of characters, sometimes as many as four or more characters long, that identify the name of the investment actively traded on an exchange.

Timing the market—the act of using economic, fundamental, and technical indicators to predict future performance and to time one's decisions to enter or exit an investment position based upon this information.

Total return—the percent at which an investment grows, over time, including all interest, dividends, and capital appreciation, less any fees or commissions.

Traditional IRA—an individual retirement account that allows employees to make tax deductible contributions up to a certain limit each year for the duration of their working lives until they retire.

Treasury bill—a short-term debt obligation backed by the U.S. government that matures in one year or less; purchased for a price less than or equal to face or par value.

Turnover rate—a measurement of the funds-trading activity expressed as a percentage, representing how much of the total portfolio is traded each period.

Underwater—when sellers owe more on the balance of their home mortgages than they can make when they sell their properties.

Uniform Transfers to Minors Act—an act created in 1986, and adopted by most states, that allows for the transfer of funds to one's child or children up to an annual limit of $14,000, tax free.

Unit Investment Trust—a collective investment that issues a specific number of redeemable shares or units after an initial offering; investors may buy back those shares at their approximate net asset value after the termination date that is established when the trust is created.

Unsecured bond—a bond that is issued that has no collateral to provide investors protection against default and that offers a higher interest rate and return in exchange for this risk.

Unsystematic risk—the risk associated with a particular industry or market sector; it can be mitigated through having a diversified portfolio of stocks.

U.S.S.I.F.—the Forum for Sustainable and Responsible Investing, a membership organization serving professionals, firms, institutions, and organizations engaged in sustainable and responsible investing by considering environmental, social, and corporate governance criteria in order to generate long-term competitive financial returns with a measurable positive societal impact.

Value funds—mutual funds that invest in companies that are trading below their inherent value because they are out of favor in the markets, but that still have great products and services so that, over time, the stocks that comprise the portfolio will appreciate faster.

Vesting—after working for a defined period, an employee is able to own and keep whatever retirement account balances and employer matching funds that have been deposited into one's "vested" account.

Virtual bank—an online bank with no physical branch locations that exists completely online.

Volatility—the relative rate that the price of a stock or market index moves both up and down. If a price moves up and down over short periods of time, it is said to be highly volatile. If the price doesn't move very much, it has low volatility.

Wealth—the state of abundance of assets in terms of marketable or saleable value, minus any liabilities owed; it is often examined in comparison to others in some reference group.

Yield curve—A graph used to compare the yields of different bonds over time.

Zero-based budgeting—a method of budgeting in which one accounts for the spending of every dollar of income from all sources. If any one category must be revised upward, another must be revised downward, so that the net effect is zero on the total amount that is spent during the budgeting period.

Zero-coupon bond—a bond that does not make coupon payments on a regular basis, but instead pays all interest compounded when the bond matures.

An Interview with the Experts

Three investment experts, each with decades of experience, answer questions in the following round table discussion. There is some agreement in certain areas, and great perspective and points of view that may help the reader understand much of what has been described in this book in a practical sense. The participants are Nick Demopoulos (interviewed December 27, 2013), an investment sales and trading professional, who is originally from the U.S. and now lives in London; Zachary Savas (interviewed January 13, 2014), of Cranbrook Partners, is a private investor living in Michigan; and Jim Quimby (real name withheld because of regulatory issues; interviewed January 23, 1014)), a senior vice president at a major international investment banking firm who is from Chicago. All participants were posed the same questions.

Q: *Describe what you do.*

Nick: I raise capital for companies that are interested in obtaining capital through the issuing of securities. We then buy and sell these securities once they are listed on an exchange.

Zach: I am a private investor and business owner.

Jim: I act as the CFO for a small group of high net worth families located in the U.S., managing their investment portfolios.

Q: *How long have you been investing?*

Nick: I have been investing personally since 1980 and professionally selling, marketing, and trading securities since 1990.

Zach: I have been investing since 1980.

Jim: I have been investing professionally for 29 years and personally for 34 years.

Q: *What has been your average return?*

Nick: Since I started, my returns have been above market rates. I do not invest money for clients.

Zach: Since 1990, after ten years of investing, when I started tracking my compound annual return, it has been 17.5%. I do not invest money for clients.

Jim: It really depends on what return and risk that my clients would like to have. My personal returns have been at or above broad market indexes.

Q: *What is the most important lesson that people should know about investing?*

Nick: The most important lesson that people should know about investing is to buy low and be patient.

Zach: The most important lesson that people should know about investing is the importance of diversification within your financial means.

Jim: The most important lesson is for people to consider time. If you are short-time trader, you will lose money as a nonprofessional. The wealthiest families invest for the long term and are not concerned about daily market fluctuations.

Q: *How would you describe your investing strategy or methodology?*

Nick: My investing strategy is what is called value investing. I like to buy equities or other investment vehicles that are out of favor and hold them until everyone loves them again.

Zach: I am a contrarian investor. I look for investment opportunities that have been ignored or oversold by the markets.

Jim: My philosophy, in the most general terms, is goal-oriented investing. You begin with goals and then work your way back to find the most appropriate mix of investments that match the person's goals. So, my strategy will differ for each client because each client has different goals. People should be investing toward a goal and then base their investment on this. People should work their way back, beginning with a goal or objective, and then find the appropriate investments to reach those goals.

Q: *What do you think about diversification?*

Nick: I think that diversification is good. No one is that smart to be able to narrow an investment picked down to one sector without incurring any risk. Each sector reacts differently to any economic event. So it is good to be invested in different sectors. You do not know what will happen, since there is a lot of uncertainty. The average person cannot follow the markets that closely. If there is any scandal or economic event, whatever gains one has made may be gone.

Zach: Diversification is the number one factor. Diversification can be useful, up to the point where you do not want to take significant risk with your savings that may affect your life. My philosophy was to insure that originally I had one year of my expenses saved in the form of cash. I increased that number to three years after my kids were born. Then I began to work with this cash and diversified it with equities like manufacturing companies, utilities, industrial companies, among many other types of equity investments.

Jim: I think diversification is very important for investors. We may achieve that by having a portfolio consisting of some large cap investments, small cap investments, depending on the client's goals. Bonds are more of a holding tank for cash to be used for other investment opportunities that may come about.

Q: *What do you think about technical analysis?*

Nick: I like using some technical analysis, along with fundamental analysis, because it tells you a lot about what the market thinks about the stock itself.

Zach: I have never believed that technical analysis is how someone should analyze investments. People who think technical analysis is useful in investing are really gamblers, not investors.

Jim: The lines have blurred between technical and fundamental analysis. You cannot look at any security without considering both methods unless you are investing with a 30-year time horizon. You need to be cognizant of some technical analysis. But it is more of a trading instrument for day trading equities.

Q: *What about fundamentals?*

Nick: Fundamental analysis is very important, especially historical earnings growth, the price of the investment, and the specific sector.

Zach: Fundamental analysis of investments is the basis of all of my investing.

Jim: Fundamental analysis is the only thing that is important, when analyzing a potential equity investment. When management sucks, management sucks. You may have a great product or service, but if the management of the company is not good, it is very hard to realize value.

Q: *How do you pick stocks or other investments?*

Nick: I pick stocks after doing lots of reading, find something that is interesting, or something that is recommended by someone that I follow and trust, and then I will try to do my own research on it.

Zach: I look for something that is of value ... by analyzing the target company's cash flow, growth, or asset growth. I also seek companies with a strong management team that has proven performance.

Jim: How I choose individual stocks or other investments really depends on the clients and their goals.

Q: *Do you like to invest in bonds or other debt securities?*

Nick: I do like to invest in bonds, as I think that there is a place for them in a portfolio, especially as you get closer to retirement age. In your forties, you begin to add bonds to your portfolio. Then as you get closer to retirement, you add more.

Zach: I like bonds as an investment only if they are tax-free. I have never invested in a corporate bond unless it is convertible to equity.

Jim: I have only bought two bonds in my life, personally. So it is not an investment class that I use a lot.

Q: *What exotic or unusual investments do you like?*

Nick: As for exotic, or more unusual investments, I like real estate property ownership. I have also liked to invest in currencies, but they are a younger person's game, especially for people living abroad who are being paid in a local currency. But investing in currencies is one of the most difficult forms of investing out there. And emerging market bonds are also quite complex, but have very good returns, if you can tolerate the risk.

Zach: I do not normally invest in exotic or unusual investments. I have only bought one call [Ed note: a call is an agreement that gives an investor the optional right to buy something at a specific price and within a specified time] in my life, and only because I had a lot of a particular stock in my portfolio. I bought the call because I thought the price was going up, so my 50 cents per call option turned into $7.00. I have never liked exotic investing because I have worked too hard for my money and exotic investing can have many risks associated with it.

Jim: I am not a fan of any investment structure that charges huge up-front fees like a hedge fund, as an example of an exotic investment. Hedge funds occupy a space that has been overcrowded lately, and they have underperformed. Many big pensions and retirement plans have invested in hedge funds and have had some problems. These exotic investments use the same leverage that created crashes in 2008 and 2009.

Q: *Is private equity investing a good idea?*

Nick: Private equity investing is really the domain of a wealthier investor.

Zach: Yes, private equity investing is a good idea. It represents half of my net worth today.

Jim: I used to do it, but I do not do this any longer. In private equity investing, of all types, the management is always the key to the success or failure of the investment.

Q: *What types or sizes of private companies have you invested in?*

Nick: I do not invest in private equity.

Zach: The size of your target company depends on your personal skill base as an investor. Some people like to invest in companies that need them to run them. Other people like to invest in companies that are much larger and have other people run them. I like to invest in private companies that need operating improvements, including those companies where sales have stalled, profitability is not being maximized, or the company needs operating capital to grow at a faster rate.

Jim: I do not invest in private equity.

346   **Q:** *What about franchises?*

Nick: I have never invested in franchises.

Zach: Franchises are good investments if we invest at an early stage of the business. Choosing how to invest in a franchise is always driven more by the fundamentals of the business that you are evaluating, than the legal structure of the business.

Jim: I have never looked at franchises.

Q: *What about micro cap stocks or mutual funds? Are they good investments?*

Nick: I like micro-capitalization mutual funds. But it is important to note that any micro capitalization mutual fund manager will know a lot about the performance of the stocks that comprise the portfolio. Usually, the smaller the company, the less information about the company is available.

Zach: I have never invested in either micro-cap stocks or micro-cap mutual funds.

Jim: Having micro-cap stocks or mutual funds like a venture fund has its place in a growth portfolio, and this makes sense. But not as a standalone investment strategy.

Q: *What about investing in currency?*

Nick: Currency investments are one of the most difficult ways to make money. But doing it as a hedge against the liability that is inherent in the currency that you may be earning, if you are working abroad, is not a bad idea.

Zach: There is simply too much political risk to invest in any currency.

Jim: I have used some currency investments if I have exposure through some international portfolios, but I use currency investments only to offset any risks in a domestic portfolio.

Q: *What newsletters do you read and why are they helpful?*

Nick: Blogs, blogs, and more blogs are really insightful. I also like to read *Kiplinger* magazine. I like to read interviews of money managers, and I also like to evaluate their character. Some of the best sources of financial information include *Mish* (for macroeconomics) , *The Big Picture* blog (general investing ideas), and someone who writes every day, Marc Faber (global market and economics analysis).

Zach: I do not read any newsletters on a regular basis.

Jim: I like the chartist.com because it provides some insight as to what is happening in the markets. I like to also follow Richard Bernstein, who was the former chief investment strategist at Merrill Lynch, in his newsletter.

Q: *What news and in what format are you plugged into?*

Nick: I am using probably 90% electronic information for my own research and analysis. I really like to use Bloomberg [http://www.bloomberg.com/], which has their own content and aggregates content from many sources, so you can search for specific stories on many topics.

Zach: I mainly follow the *Wall Street Journa* online and company press releases that are available on the site PR Newswire [www.prnewswire.com]. I also read the *New York Times* online for a political perspective.

Jim: My interest in different forms of news has changed over the years. So now, I like to read *Barron's, Forbes* and the *Wall Street Journal* online. I do not regularly read any print magazines or newspapers. I like to read such periodicals as *Scientific American, Discover Magazine,* and *National Geographic.* Occasionally, sources like *National Geographic* will cover a story that may indicate trends that happen many years ahead of the investing community. There are two articles that I can remember that were great; an article on gold, way before gold took off, that described what was happening with gold and how gold is used globally; and another on water resources and rights, and the huge economic impact that this will have. So, if you look at many issues currently coming up, water resources is a big one today. I think some of these issues may be investable concepts down the road. I like to watch TED speeches [www.ted.com], because I find them to be fascinating, with cool ideas that makes me think.

Q: *What are the best books on investing?*

Nick: Some of the best books on investing include Peter Lynch's book *One Up on Wall Street,* Mark Schwager's *Market Wizards,* and an obscure book called *The Little Book That Beats the Market.*

Zach: Peter Lynch's book *One Up on Wall Street* was really good when I first began to invest.

Jim: Aside from yours, I really liked *A Random Walk Down Wall Street,* written by Burton Gordon Malkiel. Additionally, when we think about investing, you also have to look at the psychology of the participants. One notable book is a book called *Abundance* (Diamandis and Kotler). A lot of the books on investing are kind of random. Most are useless in terms of understanding the principles of long-term investing. So, in addition to reading books on investing, you need to do your homework in order to understand what the business is and how does it make money. If you cannot answer this, you shouldn't buy the investment. Most people didn't understand what Amazon did, or what their business model was, yet Amazon changed retailing forever.

Q: *What types of government reports—like unemployment rate, interest rate changes, treasuries sales, housing starts—do you follow and why?*

Nick: I follow unemployment and payrolls. It is interesting to see how many jobs were added, or not, because it is a good gauge. I also keep current on interest rates and housing starts because they are both such a huge component of the economy. I occasionally follow auto sales because it is also such a big component in the economy. For example, housing demand affects refrigerator and big appliance sales. These statistics are applicable anywhere, but in order to understand the dynamics of countries that export a lot, it is important to look at their industrial output, exports and imports, fiscal deficits, and/or surpluses.

Zach: I look at the Federal Reserve Bank of Chicago, which is covering data from Chicago and Detroit, and overall U.S. data coming from the Federal Open Market Committee. I also like to follow the federal funds rate and yield curve data on U.S. Treasuries, which tells me, even if I do not invest in bonds, what is happening with capital flows, and whether or not money is growing or money is shrinking in our economy.

Jim: I follow all of them, but there are limitations. We have a tendency to want to see a trend within any single report that is published, but it hurts you if you are short term in thinking. For example, the report on new housing starts will change each month. Someone will write an article about how that indicates something. But we have to understand that people are paid to write these articles. Who cares what happens this month? We are destroying houses, and building new ones, everywhere. The monthly data is always meaningless in the short term.

Q: *How do you invest in a down market?*

Nick: Hopefully, when the market is down, and if you have cash available, you buy more of what you like because it is on sale. You can use the cash component of your portfolio.

Zach: In March of 2009, when the market bottomed out, it was the first time in my life that I bought many of the stocks that comprise the Dow Jones Industrial Average because they were cheap. I bought equities in about ten different companies.

Jim: During down markets, I buy.

Q: *How do you invest in an up market?*

Nick: During an up market, you have a certain allocation of investments in your portfolio that may require a degree of rebalance and reallocation, perhaps to a less favorable sector, as compared with the up market in a particular sector of equities.

Zach: You invest in bull markets very carefully, only because stocks have a tendency to be overvalued in a bull market and you may have to hold them for a very long time in order to realize gains.

Jim: During up markets, I buy.

Q: *Why does our age matter when it comes to investing?*

Nick: Our age really does matter when it comes to investing because your family's spending habits increase as you get older. You have less room to take big losses as you get older. You have to become more conservative in your investment choices, because there is less room for error.

Zach: Our age matters when it comes to investing because if you invest in equities and they have a significant drop, it may take ten years before you realize any significant gains. If you are 70 when you make these investments, you may be dead before you get to see the fruits of these investments. If you are 24, you can make a long-term investment without having to worry about making a return on the investment. Over a

349

longer period time, the stock market has averaged about 6.5 % gains over U.S. Treasuries, so you want to invest with a mindset looking at 15 to 20 years out. I have never invested in corporate bonds, but at some point in the next ten years I will have to look at bond investments instead of equity investments, given my age.

Jim: Our age only matters psychologically because the older that we get, the more worried we become about running out of money. But people who have generational wealth, who are investing for their great-grand children, think about money differently.

Q: *What influences the stock market prices the most?*

Nick: This is a difficult question to answer because it depends on what kind of market you are in, and in what stage. For example, in an advanced stage of the market, like in U.S. equities today in 2013–2014, factors like investor expectations, the Federal Reserve pulling away from liquidity, earnings and earnings growth affect the stock market prices the most.

Zach: The variables that affect the stock market the most are capital flows and liquidity, especially the overall liquidity of the marketplace. For example, a few years ago, when people could not borrow money, they started selling stocks. I am not a market timer, so I do not change my portfolio very much as the overall markets change. However, I could be 70% invested in equities or 95% invested in equities, depending on if the market is up or down.

Jim: Probably perceptions influence the stock market prices the most, since perceptions of booms or crashes become reality. So it is very important to know how to gauge perceptions. For many people, as they get older, the fear of losing the money outweighs fear of growing it. Because of this, even if you have a ten-year window before you retire and you act very conservatively, your money ultimately may be worth less than if you had a more aggressive stance. I think that the perception for many people is based upon what they read, hear, or see on the news, and it colors what people do. If the market goes down by 300 points, as it just did, it does not matter. You cannot be so concerned about day-to-day movements of markets if you are a long-term investor.

Q: *Can an individual investor outperform an index alone or only with help from a professional?*

Nick: An individual investor can outperform an index on their own. This is because an individual investor might just have some very good companies that they are familiar with, and very good information about these companies. The individual investor may also know a specific sector very well.

Zach: An individual investor definitely can outperform an index without the help of a professional, but it really depends on what time period that you are considering. Over a five-year period, the individual investor can absolutely outperform an index. However, without fundamental knowledge of the intricacies of how companies work, an individual would be lucky to outperform the market or an index without the assistance of a professional.

Jim: With or without an investment professional, you have to focus on what your goals are and what you want your returns to be, but not on the performance of any individual index. Besides, the term "outperformance" means different things to different people.

Q: *How much time should individual investors spend managing, researching, and following their portfolios?*

Nick: An individual investor should spend about five hours per week managing, researching, and following their portfolios.

Zach: An individual investor should spend as much time managing, researching, and following their portfolios as they enjoy doing it, whether it is a few hours per day or week.

Jim: Most of my highest net worth clients never look at their portfolios during the week. That being said, average individual investors assisted by a professional should review their statements and holdings at least quarterly. Still others should review their portfolios more frequently. But always review with an eye toward meeting your goals and not just moving assets around.

Q: *Can we individual investors compete and win or match the returns of big computer-assisted trades/program trading?*

Nick: Individual investors can compete and win or match the returns of big computer assisted trades/program trading if they are patient and have a long-term view because program trading is quite short term in nature.

Zach: Yes, individual investors can compete and win or match the returns of program trading, and even exceed the returns.

Jim: Big funds that use computer assisted trading or program trading do not make as much money as they used to. This is really characterized as trading, but not investing. If you are day trading, you will lose money to these systems. But if you are investing, you will win.

Q: *What about the movement of crowds and the panic buying and selling of investments of all types?*

Nick: The movement of crowds and panic buying and selling creates opportunities. As an example, panic buying of equities in 2000 or the panic selling of real estate in 2007 created many opportunities for sellers and buyers.

Zach: Panic buying and selling always creates buying opportunities, so it does not bother me.

351

Jim: I love panic because it always creates great opportunities. When people are scared, the herd mentality kicks in. For example, there may be a report about the country of Turkey defaulting on some loans or changing its interest rate, so people sell. But the real question is, if you are worried about the country of Turkey defaulting on loans or changing its interest rate, causing you to sell, what news or event will make you come back into the market? *Besides, how does that news impact your long term investment goals?*

Q: *What about our current economic policy? Does it help or hurt the individual investor?*

Nick: Low interest rates hurt savers in a big way, although some jobs are being created, but it is never enough. It is a good time for first time home buyers. The current Federal Reserve policy of printing money is making the markets reliant upon this money, rather than having the markets dependent upon fundamental analysis. With the increase in cheap money that is out there today, as well as the reliance upon government policy to increase share prices, it is not a good thing.

Zach: The transparency of the current economic policy of our government is helpful to the investing community. However, the current economic policy of deficit spending may hurt the investing community, as well.

Jim: The savings rate is perhaps one of the biggest issues affecting individual investors because the current economic policy doesn't benefit individual savers. The average individual investor has a hard time being able to save, with the tax code the way that it is.

Q: *Are mutual funds good investment choices, rather than buying individual stocks?*

Nick: Yes, mutual funds are good investment choices, if you find a good manager who you stick with. But you do need to be selective on choosing the right manager with a good track record—with five or more years of experience, ideally a ten-year track record—someone who has weathered several bear markets and bull markets.

Zach: Yes, the right mutual funds may make good investment choices, rather than buying individual stocks, in order to obtain some degree of diversification and having the ability to invest without having a lot of money.

Jim: I think it really depends on such factors as the size of the portfolio, whether or not it is a before-or-after-tax account. Certainly, larger portfolios require other types of investments.

Q: *Do you have different weights assigned to retirement portfolios versus after-tax portfolios?*

Nick: No, I do not have different weights assigned to my retirement portfolios versus my after tax portfolios at this time.

Zach: No, I do not have different weights assigned to my retirement portfolios versus my after tax portfolios at this time.

Jim: In terms of weighting before or after tax portfolios, people should look at their goals. It is really about their goals.

Q: *What attributes do you look at before you invest in an individual stock?*

Nick: Before I invest in an individual stock, I like to consider the target company's earnings growth. Ideally, I like to understand something about the business, whether or not it is cheap in price, and if there is a professional recommending it. If you look at the last five- or three year-periods of the stock price of the target company and find that it has been down by 30%, but during the most recent year, it is back up, and there is still room to grow, then I am interested. If the stock has had three bad years, but one recent year of increase, then it is an interesting stock. A good target company has to have strong cash flows. Poor cash management is a warning sign, especially if you have a company with increasing sales. Other warning signs are companies that are increasing debt.

Zach: Before I invest in any individual stock, I like to consider the target company's asset value compared with the cost to buy the share. I also like to analyze the target company's cash flow opportunity per share compared with the cost to buy the stock and the total debt outstanding as a multiple of the target company's cash flow.

Jim: Before investing in any one individual stock, it is very important to look at such things as the management of the company, understand how does the company make money, the market or markets that they are addressing, and whether or not the management team is properly addressing those markets. Then, it is good to use some form of fundamental analysis.

Q: *What attributes do you look at before you invest in a mutual fund?*

Nick: Before investing in a mutual fund, I like to find a manager with a long track record, especially through downturns in the markets. I also like to read reports of the manager to see if what he/she writes agrees with my views in general. It is also important to look at Sharpe ratios [Ed note: named after William Forsyth Sharpe, the ratio measures risk by figuring the risk premium (excess risk) per unit of deviation in an investment asset or trading strategy], as well as returns taking volatility into account, because you need high returns with low volatility.

Zach: I do not invest in mutual funds. I would have when I began investing in order to get that type of diversification that mutual funds may provide, but we did not have as many choices of mutual funds that we now have.

Jim: Before investing in a specific mutual fund, it is always important to look at how long the management team has been in place. This is primarily because if you are looking at the performance of the fund, you want to be sure that it is the same management team that created the track record that you are investing in today.

Q: *Is real estate a good investment?*

Nick: If the real estate investment is cheap, then yes.

353

Zach: Yes, owning a home is a good investment because our government subsidizes homeownership through the deductibility of mortgage interest.

Jim: Real estate is a good investment at different times. Recently, real estate has been a good investment because it is being supported by the Federal Reserve's fiscal policies of loose money, making loans available to consumers at low prices.

Q: *What types of real estate are good investments?*

Nick: I prefer to invest in residential real estate for leasing purposes because I don't know much about commercial or real estate investment trusts.

Zach: I do not have any real estate investments beyond my principal residence.

Jim: It is important to note that all real estate is at different states of the cycle and different types can be a positive adjunct to a portfolio. Many people, the last time around, before the real estate crash some years back, thought that house values would go up forever. So, they were leveraging their retirement portfolios to speculate on the purchases of real estate, which is not recommended. But having a piece of a portfolio that helps offset inflation through appreciation is a good idea.

Q: *Are metals good investments?*

Nick: Investments in metals may be good investments, especially if you are worried about inflation and if real interest rates are negative. I have preferred to buy gold or metal stocks, as well as physical metal.

Zach: Metals could be good investments, depending on the timing of when you actually buy. Many metals have recently had significant price fluctuations, both up and down, because of program trading and the stockpiling of certain metals by countries, among many other reasons. Copper is a good example of an investment in metals, with many price fluctuations

Jim: Do you mean industrial metals or all metals? Industrial metals, or metals used to make things may be good investments. But metals like gold, I have never understood why people buy gold, except for jewelry. Some buy gold because they think it will be used as some form of currency, which will never happen in our lifetime. I think that there are fewer needs for gold. When you add gold to a portfolio, it may hurt your portfolio returns, according to some studies.

Q: *Is cash ever a good investment?*

Nick: Yes, cash is a good investment, because you should always have cash on hand when opportunities arrive.

Zach: Yes, cash is a good investment, especially when you need the cash to make other investments.

Jim: When interest rates are rising, it is a great investment. Keeping a certain percentage of our portfolios in the form of cash makes a lot of sense because it allows the investor to take advantage of buying opportunities later on.

Q: *What types of cash investments are wise choices?*

Nick: When it comes to cash investments, I like to invest in Treasury bills only because money market funds might invest in other things that are more volatile. One tip is to make sure that you pick a money fund that invests only in treasury bills.

Zach: When I need to hold cash, I like to invest it in money market funds of varying types.

Jim: Putting away cash into savings accounts, at least [for] several months of living expenses, is a great idea, or using money market funds to store three months of expenses at a minimum and having this available should an opportunity present itself.

Q: *How do you make money in periods of near zero interest rates?*

Nick: You can make money in periods of near zero interest rates by investing in stocks that benefit from low rates, or by investing in companies that have good pricing power when higher interest rates kick in. I also look at growth companies that borrow a lot because they would benefit from the lower rates. Some other investments that may do well during periods of lower interest rates include property, as well.

Zach: Investors can make money in periods of near zero interest rates by looking for high growth businesses that may have components requiring a high use of cash because the cost of this cash is lower, so it may help their profits over time.

Jim: An investor can make money when interest rates are approaching zero percent by buying stocks when the market is down, or by investing in dividend-paying stocks and mutual funds, or by investing in ETF's. The object of having cash is not to make a return, but really for a security function. So, if you are sick or laid off from work, you have resources that may help you through it. But cash savings is really not investing. It is just asset allocation to cover our living expenses and to use if other opportunities come about.

Q: *How important are price earnings ratios when it comes to investing in individual stocks? If not P/E's, what fundamentals are key to analyzing a stock as a potential investment?*

Nick: When it comes to selecting individual stocks, price earnings ratios are important, but analyzing earnings growth and cash flow are also very important factors, as well.

Zach: Fundamentals are very important when it comes to evaluating potential stocks in which to invest, especially the price earnings ratios and the price earnings growth ratios, especially relative to the total market size available to the company where it is competing.

Jim: Using price earnings ratios makes sense, but if you are a value investor, using only price earnings ratios may not be correct. It is important to know that you cannot look at any one number as a gauge to invest in anything. The same is true if you only use price earnings growth ratios (peg ratios). But I do like to look at the rate of change in the growth of a company's earnings. It is a key factor, but you have to do your homework to see if this rate of growth is sustainable. If an investor does not understand a company's balance sheet, investing in things like exchange traded funds may be a better choice.

Q: *What about stock tips, either in the media or from individuals? Is it ever a good idea?*

Nick: Stock tips from the media in general or from individuals can be good for investors, as long as the tips are filtered by our own beliefs and ideas about the markets.

Zach: Stock tips in the media or advice from others is helpful only after research into the fundamentals of the company that is suggested. Without doing research and really looking at the fundamentals, I have lost money eight out of ten times when I did not do the research.

Jim: Without doing research, acting on any stock tips does not make sense. We have to always remember that acting on inside information is against the law. And we have to question from where did the person get the tip. More money has been lost than made using tips from sources. Remember, the guys appearing on financial shows on television are pushing their own bets.

Q: *Can an individual, nonprofessional compete with a professional and beat the market over the short, medium, or long term?*

Nick: Individual, non-professional investors can compete with professionals better over the long term, than the short term. Especially, if they know that particular sector that they are investing in, or if they know the company very well, they can do very well.

Zach: An individual, non-professional can compete with a professional and beat the market over both the short term and medium term. However, over the long term, without fundamental knowledge, the individual cannot compete with a professional.

Jim: With luck, anything can happen, in any term. But an individual investor competing against the huge research teams of investment houses will have a hard time.

Q: *How do you know when a boom or a crash is imminent?*

Nick: In order to see if a crash or boom is imminent, I like to look at sentiment. If everyone likes something, and if the stock price has been up a lot but continues to grow at an accelerating rate, and everyone suddenly jumps in, it's a signal. And the opposite is also true. When analysts stop covering an investment, you are probably getting near a bottom. After a massive run up in price, then the stock price tanks.

Zach: You do not know when a crash or boom is imminent. One indicator is when you first see that economic decline is on the horizon, and price earnings of companies are not adjusting to reflect this, it indicates that a correction may be imminent.

Jim: A market crash or boom will always happen when you are not expecting it. Crashes often happen when there is euphoria in the markets. Conversely, the markets nearly always go up when it seems that the times are the darkest. I like panic because investors are getting out and selling at the worst time, since they are so emotionally charged, and then the herd mentality kicks in, which always creates great buying opportunities.

Q: *What about trading rules? What are yours?*

Nick: Many people have specific price targets for an investment, so that if something comes along that is relatively better, and you have already made what you wanted to make from the investment idea, you can sell the initial investment in favor of the new one. But if you still believe in the company, you keep it. In general, you sell when you find something that is better, with less risk.

Zach: I have never had any trading rules. Why sell a great investment if it is still performing well? The only trading rule that I have added recently is if I buy a stock and make four times my money, I am willing to sell half of my position rather than 100% and redirect this into some other investment. When I follow trading rules, it is gambling, not investing.

Jim: I have had to use certain trading rules, mostly on the sell side. For example, if we are down by 30%, I sell if we don't buy more of the shares at a lower price. If you cannot make a good case to purchase the stock at any price, I am not going to keep owning the company.

Index

Note: (ill.) indicates photos and illustrations.

A

accountants, 311
accumulating wealth and savings, 9
actively managed mutual funds, 132, 303
actual cash value, 257
adjustable-rate mortgage (ARM), 40
AIG, 5
Alcoa, 5
Alexander Fund, 120
allocation, 8
all-or-none order, 80–81
allowances, 301–2
Altria Group, 5
antiques, 234
appraisal, 171
appraise out, 171
art investments, 231–34
assessment, 250
asset allocation strategy, 21
asset income multiple, 268
assets, 84
auto industry, 226

B

Babylon, 1
back-end ratio, 31
Bank of America, 5
bankruptcy, 46–47, 117
banks. *See also* credit unions
    Americans without bank accounts, 153
    definition, 152
    Federal Deposit Insurance Corporation (FDIC), 154–55
    fees and interest rates vs. credit unions, 155–56
    mutual funds, 153
    online, 161–63
    overdraft, 157–58
    people who do not use, 153
    reasons to use, 153
    selling stocks and mutual funds, 153
    services provided by, 152–53
bear market, 16–17
behavioral economics, 75
benchmarks, 306
beta, 60–61
blended funds, 125, 134
blogs, 10
blue chip stock, 3, 5
Bogle, Jack, 55, 289, 298, 300
bond funds, 133–34
bonds
    amount of withdrawals in 2013, 110
    bond ratings organizations, 118
    commission, 106–7
    corporate, 110–12
    coupon payment, 108
    defaults, 115–17
    definition, 105
    factors influencing price of, 105–6
    Federal Reserve, 89
    government, 112
    high yields for short-term maturities, 109
    how to buy, 107
    inflation, 88
    interest rates, 93, 108
    IOU, 106
    laddering, 109–10
    municipal, 114–16
    mutual funds, 106
    prevailing interest rates, 109
    price determination, 108
    principal, 107
    prospectus, 106
    reasons for investing in, 107
    relationship to health of economic system, 109
    risk, 109, 118
    safety of, 106
    savings, 113–14
    secured, 117–18
    Series EE Savings Bonds, 113–14
    Series I Savings Bonds, 113–14
    speculative, 118
    stocks vs., 105, 106
    tax-free/exempt, 107
    term, 109
    term/maturity categories, 108
    Treasury bills, 112, 113
    Treasury bonds, 112
    Treasury notes, 112
    treasurydirect.gov account, 114
    types of, 105
    unsecured, 118
    U.S. Savings Bonds, 113–14
    yield curve, 107
    zero coupon, 108
books, 10, 302
borrowing and declining interest rates, 93
Boston Personal Property Trust, 120
brokerage account, 82
brokers
    accreditation, 308–9
    certificates of deposit (CDs), 160
    choosing, 78, 308
    compensation, 308
    exotic investments, 307, 308
    as fiduciaries, 309
    financial planners vs., 311
    knowledge of investments sold, 307–8
    obligation to monitor performance of investments, 307
    online, 102–3
    referrals, 308
    types of, 308
budgeting
    categories, 49
    expense budget, 48
    "living beneath your means," 48
    "living within your means," 48
    steps in, 49
    zero-based, 49
Buffett, Warren, 225, 294

359

bull market, 17–18, 77
Bureau of Labor Statistics, 96
business insurance, 260–62
buy and hold, 21
buy low, sell high, 24 (ill.), 24–25
buybacks, 79
buy-stop order, 80

C

C corporations, 197, 202–3, 204
Calahan, Edward, 2
calculations
    cash flows, 100–101
    debt-to-equity ratio, 99–100
    Earnings Before Interest, Taxes, Depreciation and Amortization (EBITDA), 99
    Earnings Before Interest and Taxes (EBIT), 98–99
    goodwill, 100
    multiple, 101
    price/earnings ratio, 98
    price/earnings to growth ratio, 101
    price-to-book ratio, 99
campus-based aid, 284
cancelled order, 80
cap rate, 192
capital asset, 237
capital gains, 238, 240, 241
capital gains tax, 208, 238, 240–41
capital loss, 239–40, 240, 241
capital markets, 304
capitalization-weighted index, 129
cash, 28–29
cash account, 104
cash cushion, 28
cash flows, 100–101, 181
cash inflows, 182
cash investing, 151–52. *See also* certificates of deposit; money market funds; treasury bills
cash outflows, 182
cash-on-cash return, 191
certificates of deposit (CDs)
    broker, 160
    definition, 159
    disclosure statement, 160
    interest, 160
    risk, 160
    safety, 160
    terms and rules for, 160
certifications, 310, 311–12
Certified Financial Planner (CFP), 310, 312
Certified Fund Specialist (CFS), 312
Chartered Financial Analyst (CFA), 312

Chartered Financial Consultant (ChFC), 312
Chartered Investment Counselor (CIC), 312
children
    allowances, 301–2
    Bogle, Jack, 298
    Buffett, Warren, 294
    compounding interest, 298
    custodial account, 294
    delaying immediate gratification, 298
    earliest age to introduce financial concepts to, 291
    financial books, 302
    financial goals, 293–94
    financial hands-on training, 294
    financial literacy, 289–90, 300–301, 302
    financial rewards, 292
    financial websites, 302
    importance of investing as subject, 300
    importance of teaching finance when young, 300
    interest rates, 293
    investing concepts, 299
    irrevocable custodial account, 295
    matching allowances by parents, 301–2
    matching deposit from parent, 293
    minimum age for opening bank account, 294
    money games, 299
    parents discussing financial matters with, 290–91
    publicly traded companies, 297
    risk/reward, 293, 296
    savings goals, 293
    shared parental voice about money, 291
    short-term goals, 299–300
    small-step approach to investing, 298
    stocks, 296–97, 298
    tax-free gifts, 295–96
    Uniform Transfers to Minors Act (UTMA), 295
    value of delaying purchase, 292–93
    value of money, 291
    Wall Street Journal advice, 296
circuit breaker rules, 76
Cisco Systems, 4
Citigroup, 5
closed mutual fund, 126
closed-ended mutual fund, 126, 138–40
clutter, 174

Code of Hammurabi, 1
coins, 224–25
collective investment fund vehicle, 133
college rental housing, 187
college savings plan, 287, 288–89
commercial properties, 179, 192
commercial real estate
    cash flow, 181
    cash inflows, 182
    cash outflows, 182
    downsides to investing in, 184
    failures, 184
    good time for investing in, 181
    parking lots, 183–84
    questions to ask before investing in, 181–82
    real estate development, 179
    risk, 183
    sub-categories, 180
    time-intensive, 181
    types of, 181
    understanding and evaluating success of, 180
commission, 106–7
commission-based financial planners, 313, 315
commissions for executed trades, 237
commodities, 226, 230–31
commodity future, 227
Commodity Futures Trading Commission (CFTC), 228, 229–30
commodity trading, 229
comparables (comps), 172–73
compounding interest, 298
concentration, 8
condo insurance, 257
Conference Board, 90, 91
conflict of interest, 313
Consumer Price Index, 96
contents insurance, 261
control of finances, 24
corporate bonds, 110–12
corporate governance, 145–46
corporation, 202
correction, 77
correlation, 7–8
cost basis, 241
coupon payment, 108
Coverdell ESA, 271
Crash of 2008, 18
credit and declining interest rates, 93
credit card debt. *See also* debt
    average amount of, 35, 47
    average number of cards owned, 35
    best credit cards, 34
    credit history, 36
    credit rating, 36

debit card, 47–48
ease of credit cards, 35–36
eliminating, 35
fraud, 34
how much to afford, 34
ideal number of cards, 35
ideal percentage of, 33
minimizing, 33
number of credit cards in U.S., 35
number of households with credit cards, 47
older Americans, 33
paying balance in full each month, 36
paying off, 47
small businesses, 199
credit cards and small business, 199, 200
credit history, 36
credit rating, 36
credit unions. *See also* banks
amount of money in, 157
amount of money lent by, 157
definition, 155
fees and interest rates vs. banks, 155–56
joining, 156
number of, 157
number of users of, 157
origin of, 155
reasons for using, 155
safety in, 157
curb appeal, 173–74
custodial account, 294
cyclical investment, 8
cyclical stocks, 76–77

D

Dalian Commodity Exchange, 230
day order, 80
day trading, 102
debit card, 47–48
debt. *See also* credit card debt
average percentage of gross income used for, 30
back-end ratio, 31
consolidation, 31, 32
consolidator, 31–32
debt-to-income ratio, 31
front-end ration, 31
getting out of, 29
hidden cost of, 30
increasing, as good idea, 34
management, 30
paying down, 30
warning signs of problem, 30
debt consolidator, 31–32, 32
debt-to-income ratio, 31

deductible, 254
default, 25–26, 59, 115–17
deposit banks, 303
depressed real estate market, 175
derivative, 226
Direct Plus Loan, 286
Direct Stafford Loan, 285–86
directional, 144
disability insurance, 253, 262
disclosure statement, 160
discount brokers, 306
diversification, 6 (ill.), 6–7, 15, 58, 121, 138
dividends, 3, 79, 245
dollar cost averaging, 20–21
"Don't put all your eggs in one basket," 15
Dow, Charles, 4
Dow Diamonds, 141
Dow Jones Industrial Average, 3–5, 84
down payment, 40, 171
down real estate market, 175
Duffie, Darrell, 303, 304
dwelling coverage, 255

E

Earnings Before Interest, Taxes, Depreciation and Amortization (EBITDA), 99
Earnings Before Interest and Taxes (EBIT), 98–99
economic decline of 2008–2010, 18
Edison, Thomas, 2
education
campus-based aid, 284
children's investment funds, 289
college savings plan, 287, 288–89
cost of, 288
Direct Plus Loan, 286
Direct Stafford Loan, 285–86
federal assistance, 282
Federal Pell Grant, 284
Federal Perkins Loan, 285
Federal Supplemental Educational Opportunity Grant (FSEOG), 284
Federal Work-Study grant, 284
financial aid, 281, 282–83
529 Plan, 287–88
Free Application for Federal Student Aid (FAFSA), 282–83
grants, 283–84
increase in cost, 281
Pell grant, 284
PLUS Loan for Parents, 286
prepaid tuition, 288–89
Qualified Tuition Plan, 287

rapaying loans, 285
Stafford Loans, 285–86
stock market, 288
tax exemptions, 236–37
tuition increases, 288
work-study program, 284
education IRA, 271
educational grants, 283–84
effective tax rate, 196
emergency fund, 62
employment rate, 97
entrepreneurs, 200
equalized value, 250
equities, 22 (ill.), 22–23, 281
equity funds, 133–34
equity investments, 89
equity REITs, 194
errors and omissions insurance, 261
escrow account, 250
estate, 259–60
exchange traded funds (ETFs), 138–39, 140–41, 303, 304
executed trades, 237
exotic investments, 307, 308
expense budget, 48
expense ratios, 149–50

F

fear of investing, 14
Federal Deposit Insurance Corporation (FDIC), 154–55
federal filings, 203
Federal Funds Interest Rate, 92–93
Federal Housing Administration (FHA), 169
Federal Housing Administration (FHA) mortgage, 39
Federal Pell Grant, 284
Federal Perkins Loan, 285
Federal Regulatory Authority (FINRA), 308–10
Federal Reserve, 88 (ill.), 89, 92–93
Federal Supplemental Educational Opportunity Grant (FSEOG), 284
federal taxes, 245–47
Federal Work-Study grant, 284
fee-only financial planners, 314
fiduciaries, 309, 316
fill-or-kill order, 80
financial adviser, 10
financial aid, 281, 282–83
financial future, 228
financial markets
basis of, 87
Conference Board, 90, 91
full employment, 91
government shutdown, 92
importance of, 87
Index of Lagging Indicators, 91

key/leading economic indicator, 89–90
lagging indicators, 90–91
Leading Economic Index, 90
main, 87
needs-driven, 87
organizations that generate influential economic research, 91
Quit Rate, 90
financial planners
accountants vs., 311
aggressive/conservative approach, 314
boasting of huge returns, 315
certifications, 310, 311–12
Certified Financial Planner (CFP), 310, 312
Certified Fund Specialist (CFS), 312
Chartered Financial Analyst (CFA), 312
Chartered Financial Consultant (ChFC), 312
Chartered Investment Counselor (CIC), 312
commission-based, 313, 315
compensation, 314
conflict of interest, 313
criminal history, 315
cutting ties with, 316–17
disciplinary action, 313
discussion points, 316
experience, 311
fee-only, 314
fiduciary, 316
Form ADV, 315, 316
insurance brokers vs., 311
investment advisers vs., 310
litigation, 313
mistakes when using, 317
National Association of Personal Financial Planners (NAPFA), 313
need for, 316
number of, 310
partnerships, 314
questions to ask, 315
reasons for seeking advice of, 310–11
referral fee, 314
referrals, 315
responsibilities of, 310
services offered by, 313–14
similarities in clients, 312, 315
stockbrokers vs., 311
FINRA, 317, 318
first impressions, 174–75
Fitch Ratings, 118
529 Plan, 287–88
fixed income funds, 133–34

fixed-rate mortgage, 39
flat rate income taxes, 248
flexible spending account, 262
foreclosures, 42–43, 170
foreign financial assets, 238
Form ADV, 315, 316
Forum for Sustainable and Responsible Investment (US SIF), 147
401(k) plans
advantages of, 273
age differences in managing, 275
Americans who do not understand investment choices, 274
amount to save for, 273
borrowing, 276
choice-centered, 274
definition, 272–73
403(b) plan, 276
frequency of distributions, 276
knowledge of, 275
loans, 274
matching program, 275
maximum annual contribution, 276
mutual funds, 275
origin of, 273
participant-directed, 264
percentage who actively trade or manage, 274
percentage who do not invest in, 274
REITs, 193
risk in purchasing employer's stock, 274
taxes, 243, 245, 273
withdrawing money, 274
withdrawing money before retirement, 273
403(b) plan, 276
fraud
CFTC, 228–29
credit card, 34
investment, 20
mutual funds, 124
scams, 319
websites, 228
front-end ratio, 31
full employment, 91
fundamental analysis, 85, 86
fundamental investor review, 86–87
future of investing
actively managed funds, 303
benchmarks, 306
capital markets, 304
changing international landscape, 302
decrease in long-term investing, 304
deposit banks, 303
discount brokers, 306

ETFs, 303, 304
global stock exchange, 303
index funds, 303
investment advice, 305
investment banks, 303
limitation toward individual investors and investment products globally, 303
long-term capital, 304
mutual funds, 303, 304
passively managed funds, 303
short-term capital, 304
social networking, 306
socially responsible investing, 306
software, 304
sustainable investing, 305–6
futures exchange market, 227
futures price, 227
futures trading, 226, 228, 229

G

Gates, Bill, 62 (ill.)
gearing, 135
General Electric, 4, 4 (ill.)
general liability insurance, 261
General Motors, 5
global equities trading, 6
global macro, 144
global stock exchange, 303
Godfrey, Neale, 299
gold, 223–24, 225
Goldman Sachs, 4
goodwill, 100
government bonds, 112
government shutdown, 92
Graham, Ben, 55
Great Depression, 5
growth funds, 125
growth stocks, 76
"guaranteed returns," 319

H

Hammurabi, King, 1
Hammurabi Codes, 1
hardship distributions, 244
health insurance, 253, 262
health savings account, 262
hedge funds, 144–45
Hewlett-Packard, 5
high net worth individual, 9
high rates of returns, 20
hobby, 241–42
holding an investment, 13
home equity. See also mortgage; real estate
danger of, 44–45
definition, 43

desirability, 44
determining market price of house, 45
ease of securing, 45
home equity conversion mortgage, 45
home equity line of credit (HELOC), 44
reverse mortgage, 45–46
home equity conversion mortgage, 45
home equity line of credit (HELOC), 44
home office deduction, 216
home-based business, 260–62
home-based small businesses, 195, 213
homeowners' insurance, 38, 254–56
Honeywell, 5

I

"if it sounds too good to be true, it probably is," 319
immediate and heavy financial needs, 244
immediate order, 80
impact investing, 147–48
index funds
    actively managed mutual funds, 132
    attaction of, 129–30
    capitalization-weighted index, 129
    collective investment fund vehicle, 133
    definition, 126
    disadvantages of, 132
    future, 303
    importance of, 132
    management of, 130
    market indexes, 129, 130–31
    minimum investment requirement, 132
    mutual funds vs., 72–73
    number of, 129
    stocks vs., 72–73, 131–32
Index of Lagging Indicators, 91
indexes, life stage investing, 277
individual investor, 16
Individual Retirement Account (IRA), 264, 269–72
individual stocks. See stocks
industrial real estate, 180
inflation, 59, 87–88, 95, 97
information overload, 68
initial public offering (IPO), 70–71, 77
insider trading, 82–83
inspection, 172

institutional investor, 16
insurance
    actual cash value, 257
    business, 260–62
    condo, 257
    contents, 261
    deductible, 254, 256
    disability, 253, 262
    discounts, 256
    dwelling coverage, 255
    errors and omissions, 261
    estate, 259–60
    flexible spending account, 262
    general liability, 261
    health, 253, 262
    health savings account, 262
    home-based business, 260–62
    homeowners', 254–56
    legitimate company, 253
    life, 253, 254, 258–60
    medical exam, 260
    overinsuring, 256
    permanent life, 259
    premium, 254
    product liability, 261
    professional liability, 261
    renters', 254, 257
    replacement cost coverage, 257
    replacement value, 255
    sales commissions, 260
    tenants', 257
    term life, 258–59
insurance brokers, 311
intangible assets, 85
Intercontinental Exchange (ICE), 5, 6
interest income, 245
interest rates
    bonds, 93, 108
    declining, 93
    definition, 92
    Federal Funds Interest Rate, 92–93
    Federal Reserve, 92–93
    increasing, 95
    stock market, 93–95
    threshold, 94
    U.S. Treasury Bills, 93
interest-only loan, 39
Internal Revenue Service (IRS), 205, 245–46
international funds, 125
investing, 13
investment advisers, 124, 310
investment banks, 303
investment companies, 135–36
investment fraud, 317
investment property, 179
investment real estate, 179
investment types, 15
investor attitudes, 22, 23

investor mindset, 21–25
IOU, 106
irrevocable custodial account, 295

J

jewelry, 223, 224, 225

K

Ketchum, Richard, 309
Ketwich, Adriaan van, 120
key economic indicator, 89–90
Keynes, John Maynard, 91 (ill.)
KLD 400 Social Index, 147
Kraft Foods, 5

L

laddering, 109–10
lagging indicators, 90–91
land, 180
Leading Economic Index, 90
leading economic indicator, 89–90
level load, 127
leverage, 135
leveraged buyout, 221
life insurance, 253, 254, 258–60
life stage investing
    age of investor, 278
    changing income, 277
    definition, 277
    equities, 281
    factors to contemplate, 278
    indexes, 277
    investment behavior, 279–80
    limitations of, 278–79
    longevity, 281
    portfolio allocations, 279, 280
    purpose of, 277
    risk, 277
    risk profile changes, 278
    saving when young, 278
    types of funds used in, 277
limit order, 80
limited liability company (LLC), 204
Lipper, 143
Lipper Average, 143
liquidation, 117
liquidity, 165
"living beneath your means," 48
"living within your means," 48
loaded funds, 127
loan origination fees, 40
loan periods, 39
loans, 216
loan-to-value ratio, 39
local taxes, 249–51
location, 167–68, 186–87

long, 227
long position, 145
longevity, 281
longevity risk, 59
long-term capital, 304
long-term capital gain, 238, 239, 240
loss, 242

M

Madoff, Bernard, 318 (ill.)
margin, 228
margin account, 104
market correction, 23
market indexes, 129, 130–31
market order, 79
market risk, 58, 68
marking to market, 228
Masschusetts Investors' Trust, 120, 122
matching program, 275
median net worth, 9–10
medical exam, 260
medical insurance. See health insurance
Mei Moses Art Index, 233
MFS Investment Management, 120–21, 122
mill levy, 249
minimum investment requirement, 132
minority-owned small businesses, 196
miscellaneous property, 180
money market bank accounts, 159
money market funds
    attaction to, 152
    below net asset value of one dollar, 159
    definition, 158
    money market bank accounts, 159
    regulations, 158, 159
    safety of, 158
    tax situation, 159
    types of, 158
    uninsured by FDIC, 152
Moody's Investors Service, 118
Morningstar, 142–43
mortality risk, 59
mortgage. See also home equity; real estate
    adjustable-rate mortgage (ARM), 40
    average percentage of gross income used for, 30
    choosing a lender, 40–41
    definition, 36
    down payment, 40

    fewer potential buyers for houses, 36–37
    FHA, 39
    fixed-rate, 39
    foreclosure, 42–43
    fraud, 38
    homeowners' insurance, 38
    insurance, 39
    interest rates, 36
    interest-only loan, 39
    loan origination fees, 40
    loan periods, 39
    loan-to-value-ratio, 39
    mortgage insurance, 39
    obtaining, 38
    paying additional monthly amount, 42
    paying cash, 38
    paying down debts, 40
    points, 40
    preapproved loan, 41–42
    prequalification, 42
    selling existing house first, 41
    steps for getting, 40
    tax advantages, 37–38
    types of, 38–40
    underwater, 37
mortgage fraud, 38
mortgage insurance, 39
mortgage REITs, 194
multi-family apartments, 180, 189
multiple, 101
multiple listing service (MLS), 172
municipal bonds, 114–16
mutual funds. See also index funds; socially responsible investments (SRI)
    amount of money managed, 122
    art investing, 231
    average annual return of S&P 500, 124
    banks, 153
    beta, 60
    blended funds, 125, 134
    bond funds, 133–34
    bonds, 106
    cash investments, 151
    choosing, 123, 124
    closed, 126
    closed-ended, 126, 138–40
    definition, 119
    directional, 144
    diversification, 121, 138
    equity funds, 133–34
    exchange traded funds, 138–39, 140–41
    expense ratios, 149–50
    fees and costs, 149–50
    first in U.S., 120–21
    fixed income funds, 133–34
    401(k) plans, 275

    fraud, 124
    future, 303, 304
    gearing, 135
    global macro, 144
    gold, 225
    growth funds, 125
    hedge funds, 144–45
    how they make money, 121
    how they work, 121
    index fund or stock vs., 72–73
    index funds, 132
    international funds, 125
    investment company employees, 123
    investment types, 125
    level load, 127
    leverage, 135
    loaded, 127
    long position, 145
    main types of, 133–34
    median age of owner of, 122
    median number of owned, 123
    money invested in 2013, 119
    money market funds, 133–34
    no-load, 127–28
    number in existence, 125
    number of people owning, 122
    oldest, 122
    open-ended fund, 126, 142
    origins of, 119–20
    "past performance is no indication of future performance," 123–24
    percentage of American households with, 135
    percentage of household's financial assets, 123
    percentage typically invested in different categories, 137, 137 (ill.)
    performance, 137
    points to consider before investing in, 135–36
    pricing of, 121
    prospectus, 121
    regional funds, 125
    retirement, 268, 271
    retirement goals, 123
    risk-free, 121
    sales load, 127–28, 129
    sector/specialty funds, 125–26
    Securities and Exchange Commission, 124
    short position, 145
    simplification, 127-28
    size of companies in portfolio, 122
    stock funds, 133–34
    style box, 134
    success of high-performing, 119
    tax-cost ratio, 128

taxes, 243–44, 247
turnover rate, 122
types of, 125, 133–34
types of investors, 137
typical age range of investor of, 122
typical amount in account, 123
typical organization of, 134–35
Unit Investment Trusts, 141–42
value funds, 125
ways to buy, 123

N

NASDAQ, 9
NASDAQ Cubes, 141
NASDAQ 100 Index, 130–31
National Association of Personal Financial Planners (NAPFA), 313
National Association of Securities Dealers (NASD), 309
National Futures Association, 229
net investment income, 238
net investment income tax, 237
net worth, 9
neutral colors, 174
New York City rental properties, 188
New York Stock Exchange, 3, 5, 9, 66, 66 (ill.), 76
New York Stock Exchange Composite Index, 130
Nike, 4
no-load mutual fund, 127–28
NYSE Euronext, 5

O

office buildings, 180
older Americans, 200
online banking, 161–63
online calculator, 44, 191–92, 268, 293
online investing brokers, 102–3
online trading
    cash account, 104
    day trading, 102
    definition, 101–2
    features of, 104
    human broker vs. online broker, 103
    margin account, 104
    online investing brokers, 102–3
    opening an account, 104
    web sites, 102
open-ended fund, 126, 142
option, 227
options trading, 226, 228
overdraft, 157–58

P

palladium, 224, 226
parking lots, 183–84
partnership, 202
passively managed funds, 303
"past performance is no indication of future performance," 123–24
patience, 14
paying down debt, 30
paying self first, 28
Pell grant, 284
performance, 137
permanent life insurance, 259
personal art, 174
personal financial software, 50–51
personal investing basics
    accumulating wealth and savings, 9
    allocation, 8
    asset allocation strategy, 21
    bear market, 16–17
    beta, 60–61
    blogs on investing, 10
    bull market, 17–18
    buy and hold, 21
    buy low, sell high, 24 (ill.), 24–25
    concentration, 8
    control of finances, 24
    correction, 17
    correlation, 7–8
    Crash of 2008, 18
    cyclical investment, 8
    diversification, 6 (ill.), 6–7, 15
    dollar cost averaging, 20–21
    "Don't put all your eggs in one basket," 15
    Dow decline, 17
    economic decline of 2008–2010, 18
    equities, 22 (ill.), 22–23
    factors to consider before investing, 18
    fear of investing, 14
    financial adviser, 10
    financial products, 15
    fraudulent investment, 20
    high income, 24
    high net worth individual, 9
    high rates of return, 20
    holding an investment, 13
    increasing available funds, 33–34
    individual investor, 16
    institutional investor, 16
    investing, 13
    investment types, 15
    investor attitudes, 22, 23
    investor mindset, 21–25
    market correction, 23

median net worth, 9–10
    men vs. women, 75
    mistakes, 14–15
    most interesting books on, 10
    net worth, 9
    New York Stock Exchange, 9
    online information, 11 (ill.), 11–13
    patience, 14
    portfolio, 15
    present gratification vs. future gratification, 24
    protecting investments, 20
    Really Simple Syndication (RSS feeds), 12
    reasons for investing, 19
    rebalancing porfolio, 18
    research needed in, 308
    return on investment, 14
    risk, 25–26
    sources of information, 10–13, 11 (ill.)
    starting, 6
    stock exchanges, 8–9
    time, 20
    timing the market, 18
    total return, 13
personal investing goals
    conflicting, 51
    creating, 50
    designing steps, 51–52, 53, 54
    ease of, 53
    easily manageable, 51
    examples of, 51
    expense budget, 52
    investing regularly, 50
    long-term, 53
    near-term, 53
    personal financial software, 50–51
    preparation for, 53–54
    retirement, 54
    risk, 52–53
    short-term, 53
    speculation, 54–55
    steps to establishing, 50
personal investing history
    blue chip stock, 3, 5
    changing Dow companies, 4
    Code of Hammurabi, 1
    dividends, 3
    Dow, Charles, 4
    Dow Jones Industrial Average, 3–5
    General Electric, 4, 4 (ill.)
    global equities trading, 6
    Great Depression, 5
    Intercontinental Exchange (ICE), 6
    notable dates in NYSE history, 5
    removed Dow companies, 4–5

stock ticker machine, 2, 2 (ill.)
ticker symbol, 2, 3
Venice, 1
Wall Street Journal, 3, 4
photographs, 174
pitfalls of buying, 67
platinum, 224, 225
PLUS Loan for Parents, 286
points, 40
poker, 3
portfolio, 15
post-retirement benefits, 243
preapproved loan, 41–42
precious metals, 223–26
preferred stocks, 74
premium, 254
prepaid tuition, 288
prequalification, 42
present gratification vs. future gratification, 24
pre-tax dollars, 244
priced to sell, 175
Price/Earnings Ratio, 98
price/earnings to growth ratio, 101
Price-to-Book Ratio, 99
principal, 107
private capital, 220–21
private equity, 220–22
product liability insurance, 261
professional liability insurance, 261
property taxes, 170, 249–50
prospectus, 106, 121
Putnam Investments, 122

Q–R

Qualified Tuition Plan, 287
Quit Rate, 90
ratings companies
    information about, 142
    Lipper, 143
    Lipper Average, 143
    Morningstar, 142–43
    Standard & Poor's Indices Versus Active (SPIVA) Funds Scorecard, 143–44
real estate. *See also* commercial real estate; home equity; mortgage; real estate investment trusts (REITs); rental properties; renting; return on investment (ROI);
    second homes
        affordability, 166–67
        agents, 172
        appraisal, 171
        appraise out, 171
        attractive as investment, 179
        buying worst house on best block, 168
        capital gains tax, 240

clutter, 174
comparables (comps), 172–73
considerations before investing, 165
curb appeal, 173–74
depressed/down market, 175
down payment, 171
escrow account, 250
factors that affect house prices, 165
Federal Housing Administration (FHA), 169
first impressions, 174–75
foreclosures, 170
home mortgage debt rise, 169
house purchase costs, 178
inspection, 172
liquidity, 165
location, 167–68
metropolitan areas with greatest price growth, 186
moving out of house while trying to sell, 174
multiple listing service (MLS), 172
net worth, 176–77
neutral colors, 174
newly created subdivisions, 168
online information, 165, 168–69
percentage of households that own homes, 166, 166 (ill.)
personal art, 174
photographs, 174
price decline of 2006–2009, 168
priced to sell, 175
property taxes, 170, 250
reasons for buying house, 170
reducing price, 169
right agent, 175
shadow inventory, 166
speed of selling house, 169
staging, 174
up-and-coming locations, 168
walking away from deal before closing, 172
real estate agents, 172, 175
real estate investment trusts (REITs)
    classification as, 194
    commercial properties, 192
    definition, 192
    desirability of, 194
    equity REITs, 194
    401(k) plans, 193
    generating returns, 193
    mortgage REITs, 194
    number of, 193
    number of Americans investing in, 193
    origin of, 192
    profit from, 194

    real estate owned by, 193
rebalancing porfolio, 18
referral fee, 314
regional funds, 125
rental properties
    attracting tenants, 189
    college town, 187
    demand, 188
    location, 186–87
    multi-family apartments, 189
    New York City as most expensive, 188
    rental home vs. rental apartment complex, 188–89
    rent-to-income ratio, 188
    single-family house, 189
    U.S. Census data, 187
    vacancy rate, 187–88
    Wichita, Kansas, as least expensive, 188
renters' insurance, 254, 257
renting, 177–78
rent-to-income ratio, 188
replacement cost coverage, 257
replacement value, 255
retail/restaurant real estate, 180
retirement. *See also* 401(k) plans; life stage investing
    adjusting savings amount, 268
    age of, 266
    amount to save for, 267
    asset income multiple, 268
    calculator, 264
    common misperceptions about, 266
    Coverdell ESA, 271
    credit card debt, 33
    delaying, 269, 269 (ill.)
    education IRA, 271
    employment benefits, 265
    expense cushions, 263
    funding strategies, 267
    income needed for, 265
    Individual Retirement Account (IRA), 264, 269–72
    inflation, 95
    investment factors for enjoying, 265
    knowing how much money to save for, 264
    median retirement savings balance for people ten years from, 263
    mutual funds, 123, 268, 271
    new retirees, 266
    no money for, 264
    no savings, 263
    not having enough money set aside for, 268
    online calculator, 268
    personal investment goals, 54

portfolio, 264–65
reducing expenses, 268
Roth IRA, 270–71
SARSEP IRA, 270
SEP IRA, 270
Simple IRA, 270
starting to save at young age,
    267
strategies for reaching post-re-
    tirement income goals, 265
traditional IRA, 270
vesting, 272
working households with no
    money saved for, 263
retirement calculator, 264
retirement taxes, 242–44
return on investment (ROI)
    assumptions when using, 190
    calculating, 189
    cap rate, 192
    cash-on-cash return, 191
    cost method of calculating, 190
    costs included in, 190–91
    definition, 14
    limitations to using, 191
    online calculators, 191–92
    out-of-pocket method, 190
    small businesses, 217–20
reverse mortgage, 45–46
reverse stock split, 78
rewards, 60
risk
    beta, 60
    bonds, 109, 118
    certificates of deposit (CDs), 160
    commercial real estate, 183
    default, 25–26, 59
    definition, 25
    diversification, 58
    evaluating, 25
    examples, 25
    inflation, 59
    life stage investing, 277
    longevity, 59
    market, 58
    mortality, 59
    personal investment goals,
        52–53
    professional investors, 58
    progression, 56
    risk/return trade-off, 57–58
    risk/reward ratio, 55–56
    silent, 59–60
    small businesses, 208–9
    standard deviation, 58
    stocks, 67–68
    systematic, 57
    theoretical risk-free investment,
        56
    tolerance, 25, 26, 57
    types of, 58–60

unsystematic, 57, 58
risk/return trade-off, 57–58
Roosevelt, Franklin D., 155
Roth IRA, 270–71
Russell 200 Index, 130

S

S corporations, 197, 203–4
Salary Reduction Simplified Em-
    ployee Pension (SARSEP IRA),
    270
sales commissions, 260
sales load, 127–28, 129
sales tax, 249
saving
    cash as investment, 28–29
    cash cushion, 28
    definition, 27
    influences in, 27
    paying self first, 28
    reasons for, 27
    strategies for, 27–28
savings bonds, 113–14, 236–37
SBA CAPlines Program, 199
SBA loan, 198–99
scams
    FINRA recommendations to
        avoiding, 317, 318
    fraud, 319
    "guaranteed returns," 319
    "if it sounds too good to be
        true, it probably is," 319
    Internet, 317–18
    investment fraud, 317
    legitimacy of stock brokerage,
        319
    number of complaints, 318
    top complaints, 319
    unacceptable conduct examples,
        318
    ways to avoid, 318
Schedule A, 246, 247
Schedule B, 245
SEC website, 77
second homes
    as bad investment, 185
    cash outlays, 185
    gains on investment, 185
    hidden costs, 185
    investment property vs., 184–85
    reasons for owning, 186
    recent percentage of sales, 186
    S&P/Case-Shiller Home Price
        Index, 185–86
sector/specialty funds, 125–26
secured bonds, 117–18
Securities and Exchange Commis-
    sion, 124

Securities Investor Protection Cor-
    poration (SIPC), 309
self-employed business, 216
sell-stop order, 80
SEP IRA, 270
Series EE Savings Bonds, 113–14
shadow inventory, 166
short, 227
short position, 145
short-term capital, 304
short-term capital gain, 239, 240
silent partner, 211
silent risk, 59–60
silver, 225
Simple IRA, 270
simplification, 127-28
Simplified Employee Pension (SEP
    IRA), 270
Skilling, Jeffrey, 83 (ill.)
Small Business Administration
    loans, 217
small business taxes, 241–42
small businesses
    acquiring, 208
    acquisition risk, 208–9
    ages of people starting, 200
    biggest private equity lenders,
        221
    C corporations, 197, 202–3, 204
    capital gains tax, 208
    challenges, 215
    corporation, 202
    corrections, 214–15
    credit, 198
    credit card debt, 199
    credit cards, 199, 200
    debt investment, 209–10
    early steps before starting,
        204–5
    effective tax rate, 196
    entrepreneurs, 200
    equity position, 208
    ethnic, 200
    evaluating target company, 212
    exit strategy, 210–11
    failure of, 213–14
    federal filings, 203
    financial information needed,
        212
    financial management of,
        215–16
    financing, 197–200
    funding, 199
    home office deduction, 216
    home-based, 195, 213
    impact on U.S. economy, 195
    importance of, in U.S. economy,
        212
    income taxes, 216
    investing in, 206–12
    IRS guidelines, 205

leveraged buyout, 221
limited liability company (LLC), 204
loans, 197, 216
local investment, 211
managing, 212–17
metrics, 214–15
minority-owned, 196
monthly startups in U.S., 195, 200
most widely used legal form, 197
number employed by, 212
number of, 195, 212
older Americans, 200
partnership, 202
private capital, 220–21
private equity, 220–22
proper documentation, 211
return on investment (ROI), 217–20
S corporations, 197, 203–4
SBA CAPlines Program, 199
SBA loan, 198–99
self-employed business owners, 216
short-term loans, 199
silent partner, 211
Small Business Administration loans, 217
social media campaign, 219–20
sole proprietorships, 197, 201
"some of the best deals are those you walk away from," 207
starting, 200–206
startup money required, 197
success in creating jobs, 196
survival rate, 213
tax deductions, 206
techology-related, 200
transaction, 208
types of, 201–5
typical loan maturities for lines of credit, 199
unemployed starting, 196
valuation multiple, 222
women-owned, 196
social media campaign, 219–20
social networking, 306
Social Security System, 243
socially responsible investments (SRI)
affect on other areas of investing, 147
amount of money in, 146
appeal of, 147
conflicts, 148
corporate governance, 145–46
definition, 145

divestiture of companies doing business in apartheid-practicing South Africa, 146
ensuring that companies are acting socially responsible, 148–49
future, 306
growth of, 147
impact investing, 147–48
KLD 400 Social Index, 147
origin of, 146
US SIF (Forum for Sustainable and Responsible Investment), 147
sole proprietorships, 197, 201
"some of the best deals are those you walk away from," 207
S&P 500, 68–69
S&P/Case-Shiller Home Price Index, 185–86
SPDR Gold Shares ETF, 225
speculation, 54–55
Spiders, 141
spot market, 227
spot value, 228
Stafford Loans, 285–86
staging, 174
Standard & Poor's, 118
Standard & Poor's 500, 124
Standard & Poor's Indices Versus Active (SPIVA) Funds Scorecard, 143–44
standard deviation, 58
state taxes, 247–49
statutory amounts, 237–38
stock exchanges, 8–9, 84
stock funds, 133–34
stock market, 65–66, 66 (ill.)
education, 288
interest rates, 93, 94, 95
stock split, 78
stock ticker machine, 2, 2 (ill.)
stockbrokers. See brokers
stockout, 230–31
stocks
all-or-none order, 80–81
analysis, 74
assets, 84
behavioral economics, 75
beta, 60
bonds vs., 105, 106
broker choice, 78
brokerage account, 82
bull market, 77
buybacks, 79
buying, 73
buy-stop order, 80
children, 296–97, 298
correction, 77
cyclical, 76–77
day orders, 80

definition, 65
diversity, 69–70
dividends, 79
Dow Jones Industrial Average, 84
evaluating, 73–74
executing a trade, 81
fill-or-kill order, 80
fundamental analysis, 85, 86
fundamental investor review, 86–87
growth, 76
high-performing, 69, 69 (ill.)
historical performance, 70
immediate/cancelled order, 80
increasing interest rates, 95
index funds vs., 131–32
individual vs. index fund vs. mutual fund, 72–73
inflation, 88
information overload, 68
initial public offering (IPO), 70–71, 77
insider trading, 82–83
intangible assets, 85
limit order, 80
macroeconomic factors, 73
market forces, 74
market order, 79
market risk, 68
mistakes investors make, 68
myths involving earnings, 81
New York Stock Exchange circuit breaker rules, 76
overpaying, 70
pitfalls of buying, 67
preferred, 74
price, 70, 84
proceeds of stock issue, 65
purchasing directly from company rather than broker, 75–76
purchasing time lag, 79–80
reverse stock split, 78
risks, 67–68
SEC web site, 77
selecting, 71–72
sell-stop order, 80
sources of information, 83
S&P 500, 68–69
stock exchanges, 84
stock market, 65–66, 66 (ill.)
stock market indexes, 76
stock split, 78
stop order, 80
tangible assets, 84
technical analysis, 85
transaction after regular market hours, 81
volatility, 85
websites, 83–84

stop order, 80
style box, 134
subdivisions, 168
sustainable investing, 305–6
systematic risk, 57

T

tangible assets, 84
taxable investments, 235, 243
tax-cost ratio, 128
taxes
  assessment, 250
  capital asset, 237
  capital gains, 238, 240, 241, 247
  capital gains tax, 238, 240–41
  capital losses, 239–40, 241
  commissions for executed
    trades, 237
  cost basis, 241
  deductions, 237
  delinquency, 248
  dividends, 245
  earnings on investments, 246
  equalized value, 250
  estimated, 241, 242–43
  federal, 245–47
  filing, 248
  flat rate income, 248
  foreign financial assets, 238
  401(k) plan, 243, 245, 273
  hardship distributions, 244
  immediate and heavy financial
    needs, 244
  interest income, 245
  and investing, 235–38
  IRS forms, 245–46
  local, 249–51
  long-term capital gain, 238, 239,
    240
  loss, 242
  losses larger than gains, 241
  major cities with highest local
    taxes on capital gains, 251
  mill levy, 249
  mutual funds, 243–44, 247
  net investment income, 238
  net investment income tax, 237
  post-retirement benefits, 243
  pre-tax dollars, 244
  property, 249–50
  retirement, 242–44
  retirement plan, 245
  sales, 249
  savings bonds, 236–37
  Schedule A, 246, 247
  Schedule B, 245
  short-term capital gain, 239,
    240
  small business, 241–42

Social Security System, 243
state, 247–49
state income tax deductions,
  247
states that allow cities to impose
  income tax, 250–51
states that create most capital
  gains from residents' investments, 248
states with highest income tax
  rates, 248
states with no income tax or
  capital gains tax, 247
states with recent tax increases,
  248
states with unusual tax laws regarding gains on investments,
  248
statutory amounts, 237–38
tax exemptions for using savings
  bonds to fund education,
  236–37
taxable investments, 235, 243
tax-exempt investments, 235,
  243
withdrawal from retirement
  plan before age 59 1/2, 244
tax-exempt investments, 235, 243
tax-free gifts, 295–96
tax-free/exempt bonds, 107
technical analysis, 85
technology-related small businesses, 200
tenants' insurance, 257
term life insurance, 258–59
theoretical risk-free investment, 56
ticker symbols, 2, 3
time, 20
timing the market, 18
total return, 13
traditional IRA, 270
Treasury bills, 112, 113
Treasury bonds, 112
Treasury notes, 112
treasurydirect.gov account, 114
turnover rate, 122

U

Uniform Transfers to Minors Act
  (UTMA), 295
Unit Investment Trusts, 141–42
unsecured bonds, 118
unsystematic risk, 57, 58
U.S. Savings Bonds, 113–14
U.S. Treasury Bills, 93
U.S. Treasury Department, 94 (ill.)
US SIF (Forum for Sustainable and
  Responsible Investment), 147

V

valuation multiple, 222
value funds, 125
Venice, 1
vesting, 272
virtual banking, 161
Visa, 4
volatility, 85

W

Wall Street Journal, 3, 4
wealth
  amount to be considered
    wealthy, 61–62
  attracting, 62
  definition, 61
  emergency fund, 62
  importance of where one lives in
    influencing perception of, 62
  spending down savings, 63
  states with highest and lowest
    amount, 63
websites, 83–84, 102, 302
White, Harry Dexter, 91 (ill.)
Wichita, Kansas, rental properties,
  188
William I, King, 119, 120
Wilshire 5000 Total Market Index,
  130
women-owned small businesses,
  196
work-study program, 284

Y–Z

yield curve, 107
zero coupon bond, 108
zero-based budgeting, 49